CISI Chartered Wealth Manager Qualification

Unit 2 – Portfolio Construction Theory
Past Examinations

Summer 2015

BPP
LEARNING MEDIA

Published January 2015

ISBN   9781 4727 2486 1
e-ISBN 9781 4727 2489 2

British Library Cataloguing-in-Publication Data
A catalogue record for this book
is available from the British Library

Published by

BPP Learning Media Ltd
Aldine House, Aldine Place
London W12 8AA

www.bpp.com/learningmedia

Printed in the United Kingdom by Ricoh UK Limited
Unit 2, Wells Place
Merstham, RH1 3LG

Your learning materials, published by BPP Learning Media are
printed on paper obtained from traceable sustainable sources.

BPP
LEARNING MEDIA

Contents

BPP LEARNING MEDIA

Tax Rates and Allowances 2014/15

In answering questions, assume that tax rates and allowances for 2014/15 apply unless stated otherwise.

Personal allowance (born after 5 April 1948)	£10,000
Personal allowance income limit	£100,000
Personal allowance (born between 6 April 1938 and 5 April 1948)	£10,500
Personal allowance (born before 6 April 1938)	£10,660
Married couple's allowance (older spouse born before 6 April 1935)	£8,165
Age allowance income limit (born before 6 April 1948)	£27,000

Band	Taxable income	Earnings	Savings	Dividends
Starting rate	£0 – £2,880	20%	10%	10%
Basic rate	£2,881 – £31,865	20%	20%	10%
Higher rate	£31,866 – £150,000	40%	40%	32.5%
Additional rate	Over £150,000	45%	45%	37.5%

Capital Gains Tax

Annual exemption	£11,000
Standard rate	18%
Higher rate	28%

Inheritance Tax

Threshold	first	£325,000	Nil
	over	£325,000	Rate 40%

Companies – Financial year (from 1 April)

Main Corporation Tax Rate (if profits > £1,500,000)	21%
Small Profits Rate (if profits ≤ £300,000)	20%

June 2014 Examination

Part 1 – Portfolio Construction Theory

Section A (20 marks)

Answer ALL parts of the question in this section.

Tables of rates and allowances for 2013/14 are at the end of this paper.

Write the letter corresponding to your answer clearly in the answer book.

Question 1

(a) When market volatility is low the valuation of the stock market is often

  (a) low
  (b) rising
  (c) high
  (d) falling.   **(1 mark)**

(b) A client has inherited money and her circumstances have changed. You undertake a new fact-find and attitude to risk questionnaire. After explaining and advising on a new set of investment possibilities, your client asks, 'where do I sign?' What should be your next course of action?

  (a) Ask the client, in her own words, to describe the key features and risks of the proposed investment.

  (b) Hand her a contract and show her where to sign and date.

  (c) Inform her that she should pay for further advice from a different financial adviser to get a second opinion.

  (d) Instruct her that no client agreement document needs signing.   **(1 mark)**

(c) The table below is a correlation matrix of the returns of four stocks:

correlation matrix of the returns				
	Stock A	Stock B	Stock C	Stock D
Stock A	1	0.1	0.1	0.9
Stock B	0.1	1	0.3	0.4
Stock C	0.1	0.3	1	0.2
Stock D	0.9	0.4	0.2	1

If all four stocks are constituents in an equally weighted four stock portfolio which stock is the MOST diversifying?

  (a) Stock A
  (b) Stock B
  (c) Stock C
  (d) Stock D   **(1 mark)**

(d)   Which of the following is FALSE for a basic-rate taxpayer with a portfolio of equity and fixed-interest unit trusts and OEICs?

    (a)   Any losses from the portfolio are allowable for Capital Gains Tax calculations.

    (b)   All share buyback proceeds are subject to 10% tax credit.

    (c)   All dividends received are subject to 10% tax credit.

    (d)   The taxation of share buybacks on the OEICs held will be treated the same way as the unit trusts.   **(1 mark)**

(e)   Which of the following is LEAST useful as a value indicator?

    (a)   Price to share buyback.
    (b)   Price to cash flow.
    (c)   Price to earnings.
    (d)   Price to book value.   **(1 mark)**

(f)   A convertible bond issued by a company has a conversion ratio of 25 ordinary shares per £100 nominal. The market price of the convertible is £28. The ordinary shares are current trading at 64p. The conversion price and conversion premium are respectively closest to

    (a)   £1.12 and 75%
    (b)   89p and 40%
    (c)   £4.00 and 170%
    (d)   25p and 156%   **(1 mark)**

(g)   A Treasury bond due in 1 year has a yield of 2.2%; a Treasury bond due in 5 years has a yield of 2.8%. A bond issued by Wheels Motor Company due in 5 years has a yield of 4.5%. A bond issued by Slippery Oil Company due in 1 year has a yield of 4.1%. The default risk premiums on the bonds issued by Slippery and Wheels are respectively closest to

    (a)   2.3% and 1.9%
    (b)   2.3% and 1.3%
    (c)   1.9% and 1.7%
    (d)   1.3% and 1.7%   **(1 mark)**

(h)   The spot exchange rate between the British pound and the US dollar is 0.6£/US$. The spot exchange rate between the Canadian dollar and the British pound is 1.85 CAD$/£. What is the spot exchange rate between the US dollar and the Canadian dollar (US$/CAD$) closest to?

    (a)   0.32
    (b)   0.90
    (c)   1.10
    (d)   3.08   **(1 mark)**

(i)   Which is TRUE of the constant dividend growth model?

    (a)   The model assumes that dividends decrease at a constant rate.

    (b)   The model assumes that dividends increase at a constant rate.

    (c)   The model states that the market price of a stock is only affected by the amount of the dividend.

    (d)   The model states that the market price of a stock is only affected by the amount of the dividend and share buybacks.   **(1 mark)**

(j)   Which of the following BEST explains people's loss aversion?

    (a)   Myopic behaviour.
    (b)   Prospect theory.
    (c)   Inertia.
    (d)   Extreme Aversion.   **(1 mark)**

(k)   Which active management strategy does research suggest underperforms?

    (a)   A contrarian strategy.
    (b)   A continuation strategy based on investing in recent momentum.
    (c)   A continuation strategy based on investing in past winners.
    (d)   A strategy of small not big companies.   **(1 mark)**

(l)   Barber and Odean (2000) rank retail investors portfolios by turnover and report that the difference in return between the highest and lowest turnover portfolios is -7% per year. They attribute this to

    (a)   prospect theory
    (b)   unstable preferences
    (c)   extreme aversion
    (d)   overconfidence.   **(1 mark)**

(m)   You are helping design choice architecture for a defined contribution pension scheme. Five multi asset funds are to be made available for members. The trustees believe that one of the five is most appropriate for members' best financial interests and want to encourage members to select the fund but without recommending it formally. Where should this preferred fund be placed in the lineup of the five funds so that members are MOST likely to choose it?

    1   2   3   4   5

    (a)   At the start.
    (b)   Second or fourth.
    (c)   In the middle.
    (d)   At the end.   **(1 mark)**

(n)   When analysing the suitability of bonds for a portfolio you MOST likely to be highly interested in a bond's yield to call if

    (a)   the bond's yield to maturity is insufficient.
    (b)   the investor only plans to hold the bond until its first call date.
    (c)   interest rates are expected to rise.
    (d)   interest rates are expected to fall.   **(1 mark)**

(o)   UK Gilt Treasury 4.5% 2034 was priced at 127.33. What is the net income yield for a basic-rate taxpayer?

    (a)   2.47%
    (b)   2.83%
    (c)   3.18%
    (d)   3.53%   **(1 mark)**

(p)   A basic-rate taxpayer has a portfolio of several equity and fixed-interest unit trusts and Open Ended Investment Companies (OEICs). The taxation of dividends is

    (a)   positive and equal for both OEICs and unit trusts.
    (b)   lower for OEICs than unit trusts.
    (c)   higher for OEICs than unit trusts.
    (d)   nil for both OEICs and unit trusts.   **(1 mark)**

(q)   Which of the following is a characteristic of offshore 'reporting funds' (distributor) and offshore 'non-reporting funds' (non-distributor) held by a UK investor?

(a)   Reporting funds pay capital gains tax on disposals and income tax on reported income whereas non-reporting funds pay no capital gains tax but income tax on income distributed and gains on disposal.

(b)   Non-reporting funds pay capital gains tax on disposals and income tax on reported income whereas reporting funds pay no capital gains tax but income tax on income distributed and gains on disposal.

(c)   Reporting funds and non-reporting funds both pay capital gains tax but reporting funds pay income tax on reported income and non-reporting funds pay tax on income distributed.

(d)   Reporting funds and non-reporting funds both pay capital gains tax but non-reporting funds pay income tax on reported income and reporting funds pay tax on income distributed.

(1 mark)

(r)   If all the asset pairs in a portfolio have correlations of 0, the portfolio's return variance for all assets held is the

(a)   sum of the square of the fraction held in each asset times the asset's return variance.

(b)   sum of the fraction held in each asset times the asset's return variance.

(c)   square root of the sum of the square of the fraction held in each asset times the asset's return variance.

(d)   square root of the sum of the fraction held in each asset times the asset's return variance.

(1 mark)

(s)   A single man makes full use each year of his annual gift allowance. In addition, five years before death he made a potentially exempt transfer of £100,000. His estate is now valued at £500,000. The Inheritance Tax liability upon death in the 2014-2015 tax year is

(a)   £70,000.
(b)   £110,000.
(c)   £160,000.
(d)   £200,000.   **(1 mark)**

(t)   Which of the following is NOT consistent with regret aversion?

(a)   Selling winners too early.
(b)   Holding onto losers too long.
(c)   Mental accounting.
(d)   Inability to invest.   **(1 mark)**

Section B (40 marks)

These questions are compulsory.

2.67/

2. Your wealth management firm buys in 5-year forward-looking investment return forecasts for each of the major asset classes and uses these to create model portfolios for clients. The last set of investment return forecasts for the asset classes that your company purchased was March 2013 (assume this is exactly one year ago).

    One of the asset classes that is forecast 5 years ahead is nominal UK Medium term Government bonds. At March 2013, the average annual forecast for nominal UK Medium term Government bonds for the next 5 years was 1.3%. Your Chief Investment Officer (CIO) notes that for the 12 months between March 2013 and March 2014 the actual realised return was -4.0%. Assuming the 5 year return forecast struck in March 2013 remains unchanged, the 4% drop in Government bond returns over the past 12 months suggests a higher implied forward return over the next four years to March 2018. Your CIO asks you to calculate the new average annual forward return out to March 2018. Show all workings. You may wish to include a chart. **(5 marks)**

3. The earnings yield gap, presented in the chart below for the US market, sheds light on the relative valuation of bonds and equities for investment allocation purposes. The vertical axis is the earnings yield gap. The horizontal axis is time, starting 1979 and ending 2010

    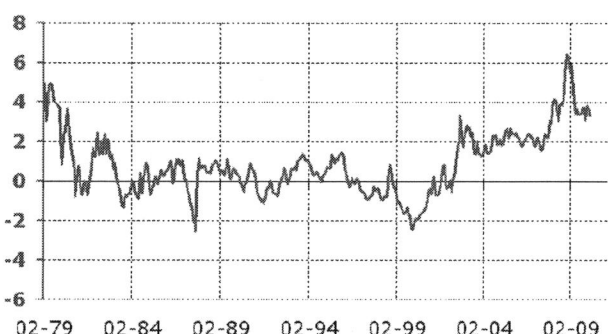

    (a) Explain the earnings yield gap model and how this works as an asset class valuation tool.
    (2 marks)

    (b) Do you think the best means of measuring the earnings yield gap is to use nominal or real values for the component data, and non-cyclically adjusted or cyclically adjusted. State why.
    (3 marks)

4. Your Chief Investment Officer (CIO) has handed you dividends, earnings and cash flow statement details for each of the 75 company constituents of a high dividend paying equity fund which your wealth management company runs inhouse for clients. The CIO asks you to sort the companies into three categories, or lists.

    List 1 comprises companies whose dividends can be expected to be unaffected by unexpected prolonged negative economic news. List 2 is the companies whose dividends are likely to be moderately affected in a downward direction by unexpected prolonged negative economic news. List 3 is made up of companies whose dividends are likely to be significantly affected in a downward direction. With the information handed to you, how would you go about the analysis in order to generate the three lists? **(5 marks)**

5. Given the following factor risk premiums and sensitivities, what is the expected return for a portfolio using a three-factor asset pricing model? Show all workings.

Factors	Risk premium to the factors	Portfolio sensitivity to the factors
1	1.2%	1.0
2	2.1%	2.0
3	2.0%	0.5

The risk-free rate is 1.5%. **(3 marks)**

6. Briefly discuss which companies are likely to issue convertible bonds, and why. **(4 marks)**

7. An analyst has collected the following data for two equities, A and B:

	A	B
Expected Return	5.5%	7.5%
Standard deviation of returns	12%	17%
Beta	0.8	1.4

The expected return on the equity market is 5% and on Treasury Bills 1.5%.

(a) Are equities A and B underpriced, overpriced or correctly priced according to the capital asset pricing model? Show all workings.

(b) On a chart with correctly annotated axes, show the location of both securities relative to the Security Market Line.

(4 marks)

8. You manage a £15m pension fund for a client and only use external managers. During a meeting with the client, you discuss the merits of structuring the external investment vehicles using pooled versus segregated investment mandates. Discuss the different VAT tax positions of pooled and segregated pension fund structures when outsourcing investment management to external fund managers. **(5 marks)**

9. Discuss how preference shares are classed for tax purposes. **(4 marks)**

10. The quarterly portfolio returns after deduction of fees for a fund manager and the returns on the appropriate benchmark are shown below. The annual tracking error based on the quarters below of 0.25%, -0.55%, 1.15% and 0.55%, is 1.41%.

	Return to the Manager before fees	Return to the Index	Tracking Error
Mar	-0.95%	-1.2%	0.25%
June	1.25%	1.8%	-0.55%
Sep	1.55%	0.4%	1.15%
Dec	2.05%	1.5%	0.55%

(a) Calculate the annual information ratio for the manager. Show all workings.
(b) Is the fund manager style active or passive? Explain.
(c) Briefly appraise the fund manager's performance relative to the benchmark.

(5 marks)

Part 2 – Taxation and Trusts

Section C (40 marks)

Answer ANY TWO of the THREE questions in this section. Each question carries 20 marks.

11. You are the Portfolio Manager of a UK based pension scheme. You have been asked to reconsider the current asset allocation and propose a more suitable new asset allocation:

   ▧ The scheme has a long-term stated investment time horizon of 20 years.

   ▧ Your principal investment target is to achieve an average annual return of inflation + 3%. Inflation is currently running at 2%.

   ▧ The ideal risk budget is to not exceed 15% volatility, expressed as standard deviation, but if good reasons are articulated this can change.

   ▧ Overall pension scheme costs are to be kept low.

   There are current risks and fears in the market:

   ▧ Market sentiment is that there is a strong likelihood the Eurozone will see a large listed corporate issuer default on a bond payment in the following weeks.

   ▧ The markets expects this to have a negative short-term impact on Eurozone corporate bonds lasting 6 months. There is a small possibility of contagion fear to corporate bond markets outside of the Eurozone.

   ▧ Relative to more normal times the current valuation of Eurozone corporate bonds look quite attractive.

   ▧ The market's current fears mean investors are holding back from allocating to riskier asset classes.

   ▧ Looking beyond the negative short-term sentiment and risk, once resolved your Chief Economist is projecting that the world economy will be coming out of a low point and on track to a healthy, prolonged, recovery.

   The current asset allocation is:

Cash	5%
UK Government Bonds	5%
Eurozone Government Bonds	15%
Developed Market Corporate Bonds	20%
Developed Market equities	50%
Emerging Market equities	3%
UK & Eurozone Direct property	2%

   The current portfolio has a volatility of 13%. You are asked to present a new asset allocation based on a reasoned interpretation of all of the factors above plus the table of forecast 5 year asset class returns and volatility below that have been provided by an actuarial company:

Asset	Cost	Expected Nominal Return	Volatility
Cash	0.04%	2%	2%
UK Government Bonds	0.08%	3%	5%
Eurozone Government Bonds	0.12%	3%	6%
Developed Market Corporate Bonds	0.20%	4%	7%
Developed Market equities	0.50%	5%	18%
Emerging Market equities	1.20%	8%	23%
UK & Eurozone Direct property	1.30%	8%	18%

Fully articulate your thinking process about how you would revise the portfolio if at all, taking into account all of the factors provided in the case and your knowledge and understanding. Include in your answer the revised expected portfolio return, volatility and costs. Ignore correlations as these are not provided. The volatility should not exceed the risk budget of 15% without strong reason.

(20 marks)

12. You are the manager of external fund selection at a defined contribution scheme. The scheme has a stated long investment time horizon. The members of the scheme have a low to moderate investment risk tolerance. You are currently procuring an emerging markets equity fund. After reviewing all the funds available, you have shortlisted the following five funds and fund managers:

Ruby 1 – primarily invests in large cap value companies. The fund has an excellent long term track record in outperforming the markets stretching back 15 years, however, it underperformed the market in the past 3 years.

Royal 2 –focuses on market timing and security mispricing. The fund invests in a broad range of industries and developing nations. The fund incorporates environmental, social and governance (ESG) factors in its investment process. The fund started 3 years ago and has been significantly outperforming its peers.

UB 3 – has consistently outperformed the market. The fund seeks to generate strong returns by investing in companies with sustainable earnings growth at attractive valuations. Since the fund manager's expertise is in retail companies, the asset allocation is heavily weighted towards retail companies.

HS 4 – is a low volatility, non-market capitalisation index fund. The stocks in the fund are weighted in inverse proportion to their volatility so that low volatility stocks are higher weighted. The fund focuses on investing in momentum as well as tracking the general emerging market index. Its performance has been stable in the past 15 years and in line with overall market performance.

SS 5 – considers ESG factors within the investment process. The fund has a buy and hold strategy. It is highly diversified and invests in more than 100 stocks in different industries and regions. So that the fund can react promptly to changing economic conditions, it has complete discretion to change its asset allocation between cash and stocks if needed.

Fund	Short term performance (3 years)	Long term performance (15 years)	Annual Management Charge
Ruby 1	9%	16%	0.15%
Royal 2	25%	N/A	0.20%
UB 3	16%	15%	0.25%
HS 4	10%	10%	0.10%
SS 5	18%	15%	0.50%

(a) Critically discuss which fund would you choose as the most suitable emerging market fund for the pension scheme, and why.

(b) Suggest FOUR other key manager metrics and measures that you would like to have to hand to help your decision, and how they would help your decision making.

(20 marks)

13. At a recent meeting with a long-term family client, your analyst presented three possible model portfolios to the family. These are model portfolios 1, 2 and 3 in the chart below. Rather than accepting one of these, a family member drew their ideal investment portfolio that combines low downside return and high upside return. This ideal portfolio has an asymmetrical spread of portfolio returns and is presented in the chart below:

Distribution of Expected Returns of 3 Model Portfolios and an Ideal Portfolio

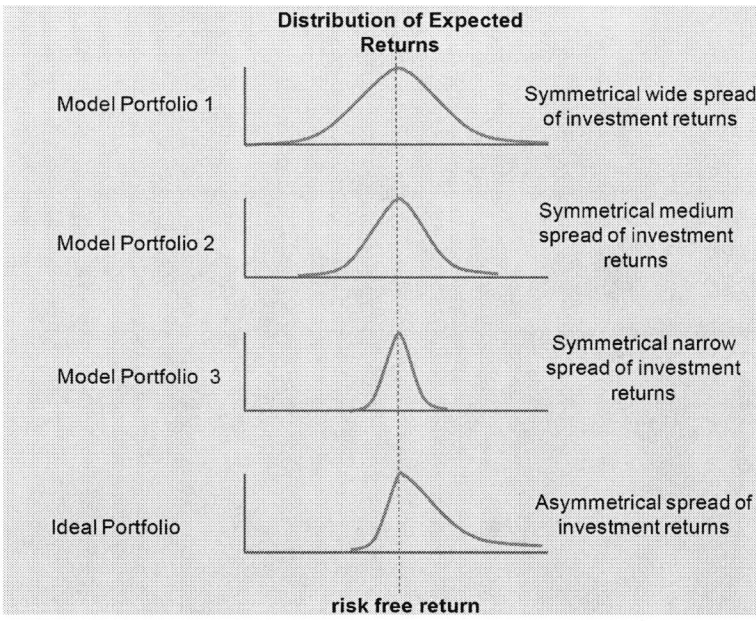

The family's investment time horizon is 20 years. The family asks you the different ways in which you could achieve a convex investment performance similar to their ideal portfolio over the investment time horizon and without incurring additional cost. Describe and appraise the different ways you could achieve the family's ideal portfolio over the long-term. **(20 marks)**

December 2013 Examination

Part 1 – Portfolio Construction Theory

Section A (40 marks)

Answer all parts of the question in this section

1. For parts (a) to (o) inclusive, write the letter corresponding to your answer.

    (a) The single-factor market model assumes there are how many sources of risk in asset returns?

    A   One
    B   Two
    C   Three
    D   Four   **(1 mark)**

    (b) The yield to maturity for a bond

    A   Is the geometric return on a bond held to maturity
    B   Is the average return on a bond held to maturity
    C   Is the rate of return over a particular investment period
    D   Depends on the unknown bond's price at the end of the holding period   **(1 mark)**

    (c) If a rating agency increases the probability of default on a bond by one grade, this can be expected to result in a promised yield to maturity

    A   Less than the expected yield
    B   Equal to zero
    C   Equal to the expected yield
    D   Greater than the expected yield   **(1 mark)**

    (d) For technical analysis trading to produce after cost returns that are consistently superior to a buy-and-hold strategy, the market would have to be

    A   Rising
    B   Falling
    C   Inefficient
    D   Undervalued   **(1 mark)**

    (e) What is a bond's coupon if it has a current (running) yield of 8% and a price of £1,250?

    A   8.0%
    B   10.0%
    C   11.0%
    D   8.5%   **(1 mark)**

    (f) The semivariance of an investment return series measures

    A   Two times all deviations from the mean
    B   The two closest quartile deviations to the mean
    C   The deviations below the mean
    D   The deviations above the mean   **(1 mark)**

(g)   Tactical asset allocation, or market timing, involves

    A   Deciding which assets are to be used to construct a portfolio

    B   Setting long-term weights for asset classes

    C   Intra-day trading that adjusts the portfolio to undervalued assets

    D   Short and medium-term changes to a core asset allocation via the study of economic data **(1 mark)**

(h)   A portfolio has an annual return of 3% (above the risk-free rate) and an annual standard deviation of 14%. What is the Sharpe Ratio?

    A   0.03 / 0.14
    B   0.14 / 0.03
    C   0.03 – 0.14
    D   0.14 – 0.03 **(1 mark)**

(i)   Two government bonds are sold at a par value of UK£1,000. Each pays interest of UK£90 annually. Bond A matures in 15 years; Bond B matures in 25 years. The yield to maturity on both bonds then rises to 10%. Both bonds will

    A   Increase in value, and B will increase more than A
    B   Increase in value, and A will increase more than B
    C   Decrease in value, and B will decrease more than A
    D   Decrease in value, and A will decrease more than B **(1 mark)**

(j)   An inflation linked bond is a bond

    A   That links to the rate of inflation but not deflation
    B   That links to the general level of prices up to a maximum of 10% change per annum
    C   With a coupon rate linked to the general level of prices
    D   With a par value linked to the general level of prices **(1 mark)**

(k)   Heidi sells a stock and then avoids following it in the media, afraid that it may then rise in price. What behavioural characteristic is this consistent with?

    A   Choice overload
    B   Inertia
    C   Fear of regret
    D   Mental accounting **(1 mark)**

(l)   According to behavioural economics, which of the following **least** counteracts people's tendency to overconfidence?

    A   Cooling-off periods
    B   Messages on scepticism
    C   Purchases that delay repayment
    D   Waiting periods **(1 mark)**

(m)   Which of the following **best** explains why people procrastinate over decisions?

    A   Regret aversion
    B   Choice overload
    C   Loss aversion
    D   Anchoring **(1 mark)**

(n)   A bank offers a UK Sterling (GBP) / US Dollar (USD) price of 1.5336/37. At what rate would a medium size UK Sterling-based wealth management company buy USD from the bank?

      A   As a price taker on the bid at 1.5336
      B   As a price maker on the bid at 1.5336
      C   As a price taker on the offer at 1.5337
      D   As a price maker on the offer at 1.5337   **(1 mark)**

(o)   A fund's annualised return and Sharpe ratio for two separate periods is reported below:

	1st 6 month period	2nd 6 month period
Annualised return	5.7%	5.7%
Sharpe ratio	0.35%	0.3%

Based on the information in the table, the

      A   Risk-free rate has declined
      B   Risk-free rate has increased
      C   Benchmark return has declined
      D   Benchmark return has increased   **(1 mark)**

(p)   The dividend payout ratio for the total market is 65%, the required rate of return is 13% and the expected growth rate of dividends is 8%. What is the current earnings multiple, or prospective P/E ratio? Show all workings.   **(2 marks)**

(q)   What is the total risk (standard deviation) of a portfolio if its systematic risk (standard deviation) is 17% and unsystematic risk (standard deviation) 8%? Show all workings.
      (3 marks)

(r)   An analyst has the following information:

      ▪   The standard deviation of the market returns is 16%.
      ▪   The standard deviation of Stock A's returns is 45%.
      ▪   The correlation coefficient between the returns on Stock A and the market is 40%.

What is the beta of Stock A? Show all workings.   **(2 marks)**

(s)   What are the main differences between warrants and convertible securities?   **(4 marks)**

(t)   A convertible bond issued by a company is trading at US$120. It offers the holder the option of converting US$100 nominal into 25 ordinary shares of the company. The ordinary shares are currently trading at US$3.80. What is the premium as a % of the conversion value?   **(2 marks)**

(u)   You advise a medium size company pension scheme. The scheme assets are UK£1bn. The trustees of the scheme ask you to show them how the portfolio value and weights of an equity and Treasury bill portfolio would change according to a long-term asset allocation process. So that you can perform the calculation, the trustees provide you with the following information.

Period 1 returns: equity –10%, Treasury Bill 0%.
Period 2 returns: equity –20%, Treasury Bill 0%.
Period 3 returns: equity +10%, Treasury Bill 0%.

The long-term asset allocation is 60% equity and 40% Treasury Bill. Rebalancing is at the end of each period.

     (i)   Calculate the portfolio value at the start and for the end of each of the three periods. Show all workings.

     (ii)   Calculate the portfolio weights for the end of each period prior to rebalancing. Show all workings.   **(4 marks)**

(v)   The following table reports index values and returns on a UK large company equity index. The standard deviation of the monthly returns is 0.044. The risk-free rate for the period of time is 1%.

Year	Month	Index (end month closing values)	Returns
	Dec	100	
2008	Jan	89	−0.110
	Feb	93	0.045
	Mar	91	−0.022
	Apr	103	0.132
	May	108	0.049
	Jun	104	−0.037
	Jul	103	−0.010
	Aug	105	0.019
	Sep	108	0.029
	Oct	109	0.009
	Nov	110	0.009
2009	Dec	114	0.036
	Jan	117	0.026
	Feb	115	−0.017
	Mar	116	0.009
	Apr	113	−0.026
	May	114	0.009
	Jun	116	0.018
	Jul	119	0.026
	Aug	120	0.008
	Sep	121	0.008

Standard deviation of monthly returns = 0.044, or 4.4%

(i)   Calculate the annualised return on the index. Show all workings.

(ii)   Calculate the annualised standard deviation of returns. Show all workings.

(iii) Calculate the Sharpe ratio. Show all workings.   **(4 marks)**

(w)   You are the chief investment officer for a fund management firm. You are helping two separate clients with an appropriate long-term asset allocation. You have established that Ms A has a risk tolerance factor of 3 and that Mr B has a risk tolerance factor of 9 (smaller number = less risk tolerance). The characteristics for four possible portfolios are as follows.

Portfolio	Asset Mix Stock	Asset Mix Bond	Expected return on portfolio	Risk (Standard deviation) of portfolio	Risk tolerance Ms A 3	Risk tolerance Mr B 9
1	5.0%	95.0%	5.0%	5.0%		
2	25.0%	75.0%	6.0%	9.0%		
3	70.0%	30.0%	7.3%	12.0%		
4	90.0%	10.0%	7.9%	25.0%		

(i)   Calculate the expected utility of each of the four portfolios for Ms A and Mr B.

(ii)   Which portfolio represents the optimal asset allocation for Ms A? Which portfolio is optimal asset allocation for Mr B?

(iii) Explain why there is a difference in these two outcomes.   **(4 marks)**

Section B (20 marks)

This question is compulsory

2. **Correlation Structure of Gold, Platinum, Silver, S&P500 and EAFE Returns**

	Gold	Platinum	Silver	S&P500	EAFE
A. Full sample period 1976 – 2004					
Gold	1.00	0.58	0.55	−0.03	0.14
Platinum		1.00	0.50	0.01	0.14
Silver			1.00	−0.02	0.11
S&P500				1.00	0.23
EAFE					1.00
B. 1976 – 1984					
Gold	1.00	0.67	0.61	0.06	0.29
Platinum		1.00	0.55	0.05	0.27
Silver			1.00	0.01	0.25
S&P500				1.00	0.14
EAFE					1.00
C. 1985 – 1994					
Gold	1.00	0.62	0.52	−0.12	0.07
Platinum		1.00	0.54	−0.03	0.13
Silver			1.00	−0.04	0.05
S&P500				1.00	0.17
EAFE					1.00
D. 1995 – 2004					
Gold	1.00	0.26	0.31	−0.09	0.04
Platinum		1.00	0.29	0.01	0.03
Silver			1.00	−0.05	0.03
S&P500				1.00	0.34
EAFE					1.00

. Gold is measured as US$/Troy ounce, Platinum is measured as US$/Troy ounce, Silver is measured as US$/Kilogram. S&P500 index is the proxy for stock market returns from a US investor's perspective. EAFE is MSCI Europe, Australasia, and Far East, in US$ and designed to measure the overall condition of overseas markets from a US investor's perspective. Sample period is 1 January 1976 to 1 April 2004.

(a) Looking at the table, appraise the correlation properties of precious metals and stock market returns in terms of the potential of gold, platinum, and silver to play a diversifying role in broad-based investment portfolios. **(10 marks)**

(b) The following information reports the annualised return and risk for the S&P500 and an equal weighted precious metals portfolio.

S&P500 risk and return

S&P 500 annualised return = 13%. S&P 500 annualised volatility = 12.0%

	Weight	Return	Weight × Return
Gold	33.3%	4%	1.33%
Platinum	33.3%	9%	3.00%
Silver	33.3%	6%	2.00%

Equal-weighted precious metal basket annualised return = 6.3%
Equal-weighted precious metal basket annualised volatility = 20%

(i)   On a chart with annualised risk measured on the x-axis and annualized return measured on the y-axis, plot the S&P500 and a precious metals basket portfolio. Given the correlations in part (a) above, draw the line that you believe would approximately represent the different asset mixes that link 100% S&P 500 to the 100% precious metals portfolio.

(ii)   Explain what the line tells us as investors.

(iii)   If the risk-free rate is 2%, draw the capital market line on the chart. Describe the portfolio combination you would select as the market portfolio. Justify your answer.

(iv)   Describe how you might best gain specific exposure to precious metals within a broad-based portfolio.   **(10 marks)**

Section C (10 marks)

Answer any two questions in this section. Each question carries 5 marks

3.   A client shows you the following chart and asks whether based on the evidence in the chart her equity portfolio should be structured to invest more in high score environment, social and governance stocks and less in those with low score environment, social and governance stocks. Consider the information reported below and critically appraise the client's question.   **(5 marks)**

Volatility of portfolio deciles by environment, social and governance (ESG) scores

FTSE Developed Index

In the following table, Risk % is annualized standard deviation. VaR% is 95% daily value at risk, Beta is the slope of daily stock returns regressed on the Developed or regional index. All stocks are first sorted from lowest to highest based on their environment score within their resident country. Having sorted by environment score into deciles, global deciles are assembled by pulling together all decile 1 stocks per country, all decile 2 stocks and so on through to all decile 10 stocks. Moving from decile to decile, changes in volatility are the impact of ESG not country. All stocks within each decile are US$ market capitalization weighted. The process is repeated for the social score, governance score and ESG combined score to provide four sets of decile sorts.

Decile	1	2	3	4	5	6	7	8	9	10
ESG Combined										
Risk %	29.0	24.5	25.1	22.8	23.0	23.1	22.5	23.2	21.6	21.4
VaR %	−2.73	−2.46	−2.31	−2.19	−2.18	−2.19	−2.27	−2.21	−2.11	−1.98
Beta	1.23	1.07	0.99	0.98	1.00	1.05	0.98	1.02	0.92	0.95
Environment										
Risk %	24.1	25.4	27.2	23.3	23.8	25.0	21.1	23.9	22.8	21.0
VaR %	−2.36	−2.51	−2.49	−2.25	−2.29	−2.39	−2.00	−2.35	−2.09	−2.07
Beta	1.05	1.14	1.21	1.01	0.94	1.06	0.93	1.05	1.02	0.90
Social										
Risk %	26.6	22.2	22.8	23.2	23.3	24.6	22.4	25.4	23.3	21.3
VaR %	−2.47	−2.07	−2.21	−2.35	−2.27	−2.38	−2.16	−2.47	−2.26	−2.07
Beta	1.16	0.89	1.00	0.97	1.01	1.06	0.94	1.14	1.04	0.93
Governance										
Risk %	25.0	23.6	23.3	24.8	21.7	21.3	22.6	24.0	24.9	21.8
VaR %	−2.38	−2.32	−2.27	−2.51	−2.03	−2.01	−2.19	−2.42	−2.35	−2.14
Beta	1.00	1.03	0.93	1.09	0.98	0.95	0.95	1.06	1.10	0.95

4. A high net worth client has a significant allocation of wealth in an unhedged FTSE Developed Index, comprising about 2,000 large and mid-capitalisation companies located in 24 developed countries. During a recent meeting, the client asks you about the merits of fully hedging the expected future foreign currency receipts. The client's portfolio is currently measured in UK£. Explain the factors to consider in evaluating a decision to hedge or leave unhedged the portfolio. **(5 marks)**

5. A client is interested in using 'smart beta' (ie, non-market capitalisation index techniques) emerging market equity funds to gain exposure to emerging market equities. Discuss the merits and drawbacks of 'smart beta', or non-market capitalisation index approaches for this asset class. **(5 marks)**

Part 2 – Taxation and Trusts

Section D (20 marks)

Answer all parts of the question in this section

6. Frank and Nora are new clients. They are thinking about setting up a new publishing business in the UK. They have a disabled daughter and want to provide some financial security for her future. Nora has income in 2014/15 of £90,000. They have come to you for some tax advice.

    (a) Frank asks you for some advice on the establishment of a trust for his disabled daughter. Advise him on

        (i) The types of trust available

        (ii) The tax treatment of each type of trust   **(4 marks)**

    (b) In June 2014, Frank disposed of one of his vintage cars for the sum of £20,000, with his three remaining classic cars being valued at £45,000. The four cars were originally purchased together in June 2007 for £20,000.

        Calculate the capital gains tax on the disposal.   **(4 marks)**

    (c) Frank receives some income from royalties on his new book in the sum of £25,000 in March 2015. He has no other income and is 69 years of age in January 2015. Calculate the income tax payable on the royalty income.   **(4 marks)**

    (d) Calculate Nora's income tax liability for 2014/15. Nora is aged 55.   **(4 marks)**

    (e) Give Nora some tax planning advice on the establishment of her new business.   **(4 marks)**

Section E (10 marks)

Answer any two questions in this section. Each question carries 5 marks

7. David is making a will and seeks your advice because his wife is domiciled outside the UK. A friend has told him that the normal Inheritance Tax exemption for gifts between spouses will not apply. Advise him what limits may apply.   **(5 marks)**

8. Explain how shares are valued for inheritance tax purposes.   **(5 marks)**

9. Explain the difference between residence and domicile for UK tax purposes.   **(5 marks)**

June 2013 Examination

Part 1 – Portfolio Construction Theory

Section A (40 marks)

Answer all parts of the question in this section

1. For parts (a) to (m) inclusive, write the letter corresponding to your answer.

    (a) In the chart below, which 2 letter grade valuation signals indicate a very negative and a very positive outlook on the valuation cycle?

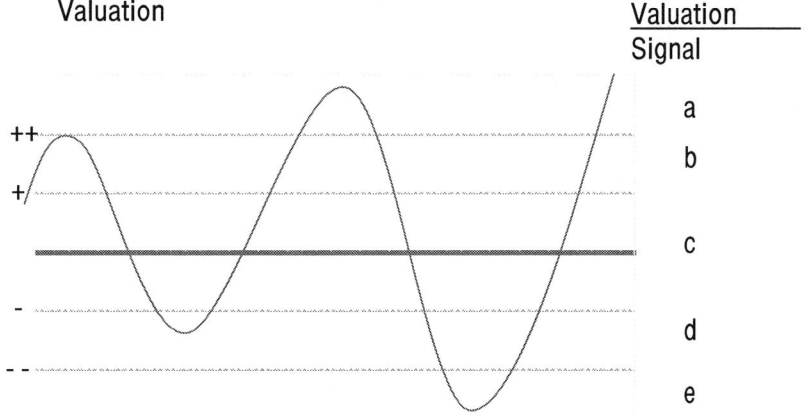

    A   e and a respectively
    B   d and b respectively
    C   b and d respectively
    D   a and e respectively   **(1 mark)**

    (b) Which is **not** true of covariance?

    A   The units are squared.
    B   The units of measurement are not standardised.
    C   A high negative figure may or may not indicate a weak relationship.
    D   A low negative figure may or may not indicate a strong relationship.   **(1 mark)**

    (c) Using the information below, what is the Treynor measure of portfolio performance?

Portfolio return	6%
Market return	5%
Beta of portfolio	0.95
Beta of market	1

Standard deviation of portfolio returns	5%
Standard deviation of market returns	7%
Risk-free rate	2%

    A   0.01
    B   0.04
    C   0.2
    D   0.8   **(1 mark)**

    (d) Which of the following is not true of a bond's yield to maturity?

    A   It is the average return if the bond is held to maturity.
    B   It depends on the bond's duration.
    C   It depends on the bond's coupon rate.
    D   It depends on the bond's maturity and par value.   **(1 mark)**

(e)   All of the following about the Information ratio for calculating a fund manager's performance are true **except**

    A   The Information ratio indicates the active return for the active risk taken.

    B   The Information ratio helps to indicate consistency of fund manager performance.

    C   The Information ratio indicates the percentage return above the risk-free rate for each unit of risk taken.

    D   The Information ratio indicates whether the extra charge for active management was worth it. **(1 mark)**

(f)   A fund's annualised return and Sharpe ratio for two separate periods is reported below:

	1st 6 month period	2nd 6 month period
Annualised return	5.7%	5.7%
Sharpe ratio	0.35%	0.3%

Based on the information in the table, the

    A   Risk-free rate has declined
    B   Risk-free rate has increased
    C   Benchmark return has declined
    D   Benchmark return has increased **(1 mark)**

(g)   Which of the following is **not** true of the holding period return on a bond?

    A   Holding period return is the rate of return over a particular investment period.

    B   Holding period return depends on the bond's price at the end of the holding period.

    C   Holding period return adds the value of the coupon payments to the change in the bond's price over a particular investment period.

    D   If the bond is held to maturity and there are no coupon payments, the holding period return will be known in advance. **(1 mark)**

(h)   Which of the following provides evidence against the stock market being semi-strong form efficient?

    A   Insiders earn abnormal trading profits.

    B   There is sizeable and persistent post-announcement drift in prices.

    C   Almost all the price response to significant company news tends to occur in the first ten minutes of the announcement.

    D   About 50% of pension funds outperform the market on average in any year. **(1 mark)**

(i)   Which of the following is **not** a factor in the multifactor CAPM asset pricing model?

    A   Leverage
    B   Momentum
    C   Size
    D   Beta **(1 mark)**

(j)   Which of the following would be wrong to argue if you wanted to cite support for the zero Beta version of the Capital Asset Pricing Model (CAPM)?

    A   If we assume no inflation a zero Beta asset is risk-free.

B The intercept of the Security Market Line is empirically higher than the CAPM risk-free rate.

C The Zero Beta CAPM can explain returns at least as well as the conventional CAPM.

D Empirically many investors hold money market funds rather than cash deposits or a risk-free Treasury. **(1 mark)**

(k) The spot exchange rate between the British pound and the US dollar is 0.7775 £/US$. The spot exchange rate between the Canadian dollar and the British pound is 1.8325 CAD$/£. Which is the US dollar/Canadian dollar spot cross exchange rate closest to?

A 0.7
B 1.2
C 1.4
D 1.8 **(1 mark)**

(l) Which is **true** of the constant dividend growth model?

A It assumes that dividends increase at a constant rate forever.

B It can be used to compute a stock price if it is correctly valued at any point in time.

C It states that the market price of a stock is only affected by the amount of the dividend.

D It considers capital gains, but ignores the dividend yield. **(1 mark)**

(m) Which is **not** a common relative valuation technique?

A Price-earnings ratio
B Price-cash flow ratio
C Price-book value ratio
D Price-cost of goods sold ratio **(1 mark)**

(n) Discuss whether it is easier to value publicly traded shares or publicly traded bonds.
  (3 marks)

(o) Define 'convexity' and 'modified duration'. Explain how together they are used to estimate a bond's percentage change in price in response to a change in interest rates. **(4 marks)**

(p) List **four** reasons why the tracking error of an index fund following a full duplication approach is unlikely to ever be zero. **(4 marks)**

(q) An analyst has the following information:

  ▪ The standard deviation of the market returns is 16%.
  ▪ The standard deviation of Stock A's returns is 45%.
  ▪ The correlation coefficient between the returns on Stock A and the market is 40%.

  What is the beta of Stock A? Show all workings. **(2 marks)**

(r) Given the following factor risk premiums and sensitivities, what is the expected return for a portfolio using a three-factor asset pricing model? Show all workings.

Factors	Risk premium to the factors	Portfolio sensitivity to the factors
1	1.5%	1.0
2	2.5%	2.0
3	6%	0.0

The risk-free rate is 2.0%. **(3 marks)**

(s) The following table reports the empirical distribution of US and UK equity market returns for 77 years as:

(i) The probability of encountering a loss, and

(ii) How much an investor might lose

Interpret these findings and critically discuss them.

Long Horizon US and UK Equity Market Risk and Return, 1920 – 1996						
	Probability of loss over time period			Value at risk (5% left tail)		
	1 Year	5 Year	10 Year	1 Year	5 Year	10 Year
US (Price change only)	37%	34%	34%	–28%	–46%	–51%
US (Total return)	31%	21%	16%	–25%	–34%	–22%
UK (Price change only)	40%	33%	45%	–25%	–55%	–51%
UK (Total return)	30%	22%	31%	–25%	–48%	–45%
Price change only excludes reinvestment of dividends. Total return includes reinvestment of dividends. Statistics are calculated from the empirical distribution of returns.						

(4 marks)

(t) Briefly describe and explain the key skills that a financial adviser needs in order to communicate effectively with all types of client. **(3 marks)**

(u) An analyst has collected the following data for two equities, A and B.

	A	B
Expected return	11.4%	5.2%
Standard deviation of returns	35%	17%
Beta	1.9	0.8

The expected return on the equity market is 6% and on Treasury Bills 2%.

(i) Are equities A and B underpriced, overpriced or correctly priced according to the capital asset pricing model? Show all workings.

(ii) On a chart with correctly annotated axes, show the location of both securities relative to the Security Market Line. **(4 marks)**

Section B (20 marks)

This question is compulsory

2. The following table reports investment statistics for seven types of collective investment fund. Assume each type of fund is pooled and open-ended.

Investment characteristics for seven fund categories			
	CAPM Beta	Expected return	Historic volatility
Balanced Managed	0.8	5%	10%
Equity Growth	1.2	7%	19%
Global Equity	0.95	6%	14%
Global High Yield	0.4	4%	8%
Direct Property Securities	0.7	6%	13%
Direct Property	0.5	7%	11%
Money Market	0.1	2%	4%
All figures are UK sterling based and total return. CAPM Beta compares the fund to a global market portfolio. Expected return is an average of historic returns and forward looking capital market assumptions. Historic volatility is the standard deviation of returns.			

(a) Define and describe each of the seven types of collective fund. **(7 marks)**

(b) A high net worth client is considering one of two courses of financial action. One course of action is to not require your portfolio management and to instead invest entirely in the Balanced Managed fund. The second course of action is to retain you to construct and manage a portfolio using some or all of the seven funds in the table. This will happen if the portfolio constructed has a high probability of outperforming the Balanced Managed fund after all costs and fees, and with a CAPM beta that is distinct from the Balanced Managed fund. The client has a moderate risk tolerance.

You commit to providing a written response concerning the second course of action. Set out the process you would use, including passive versus active mandates, selection of fund managers, and the blending process for the underlying funds in order to arrive at a portfolio that was constructed to outperform after costs and fees the Balanced Managed fund, that was within the client's risk tolerance, and delivered a dissimilar CAPM beta to that of the Balanced Managed fund. **(13 marks)**

Section C (10 marks)

Answer any two questions in this section. Each question carries 5 marks

3. In a meeting your colleague says 'immunization is a passive bond portfolio strategy'. Critically appraise this comment. **(5 marks)**

4. Explain the importance of setting an investment objective with a high net worth client. Include in your answer the principal types of investment objective and the considerations you would take into account when selecting and setting one. **(5 marks)**

5. Two assets A and B are available for investment:

	Asset A	Asset B
Expected return	4%	6%
Standard deviation	8%	15%
The correlation coefficient between A and B is 0.1		

The variance of a two asset portfolio is $\sigma_p^2 = w_1^2 \sigma_1^2 + w_2^2 \sigma_2^2 + 2w_1 w_2 \rho_{1,2} \sigma_1 \sigma_2$

(a) Calculate portfolio return and risk measured by standard deviation for portfolio 1 and portfolio 2 below:

	Asset A	Asset B
Portfolio 1	25%	75%
Portfolio 2	75%	25%

(b) Draw an approximate diagram showing the possible return and risk combinations of the two assets, including 100% Asset A and 100% Asset B.

(c) The risk-free rate is 2.5%. Knowing this, what conclusions can you now draw about the most efficient portfolio? **(5 marks)**

Part 2 – Taxation and Trusts

Section D (20 marks)

Answer all parts of the question in this section.

6. Mary is 86 and has asked you for some advice on the setting up of a trust for her grandchildren. Her husband Brian has recently passed away leaving an estate in excess of £2 million which together with her own available assets of £1 million makes a potential trust fund of approximately £3 million. Mary has four grandchildren: Tom, Dick, Harry and Sam. Tom, Dick and Harry are financially secure with good jobs and children of their own. Sam is disabled and in need of constant care and assistance from Mary's daughter, Tanya. Tanya owns a small house and is a teacher and is recently divorced.

   In addition to the above assets, Mary owns her own home which is currently valued at £380,000. She owns shares in Shell and Texaco worth £100,000 and a holiday home in Norway worth £60,000. Mary also has pensions with a total annual income of £51,000.

   (a)   Give Mary some advice on trusts available to her and explain how each is taxed in detail.

   (4 marks)

   (b)   What tax planning advice can you give Mary in relation to inheritance taxes?   **(4 marks)**

   (c)   Calculate how much income tax Mary should pay in 2014/15 given that she earns £51,000 from her pensions and £4,000 in dividend income.   **(4 marks)**

   (d)   Explain how Mary's Norwegian summer-house will be taxed if she sells it.   **(4 marks)**

   (e)   What other tax planning advice might you consider giving Mary in light of the above facts?

   (4 marks)

Section E (10 marks)

Answer any two questions in this section. Each question carries 5 marks

7. John is a French national. He has lived in the UK since July 2010 and paid his taxes in the UK on his employment since that date. In August 2010, he purchased 10,000 shares in Tesco at a cost of 300p each. Currently, these shares are worth 380p each. John is now leaving the UK for good and intends to sell his Tesco shares. Advise John on his tax situation.   **(5 marks)**

8. Jill is approaching retirement and interested in making a gift of her holiday home in Spain to her nephew, James. The holiday home was originally purchased in 2001 for £68,000 and is currently valued at £103,000. Advise Jill on the tax consequences of this transaction.   **(5 marks)**

9. James has purchased 50,000 shares in LVMH, a French company, on a number of separate occasions starting in 1972. He is now approaching retirement and is considering selling them in tranches of 10,000 shares. Advise James on the tax consequences, in particular the 'matching rules' operated by HMRC.   **(5 marks)**

December 2012

Part 1 – Portfolio Construction Theory

Section A (40 marks)

Answer all parts of the question in this section

1. For parts (a) to (k) inclusive, write the capital letter corresponding to your answer.

    (a) An analyst has collected the following data for an equity

	Equity
Expected return	4.7%
Beta	0.8

    The expected return on the equity market is 6% and on Treasury Bills 1.5%.

    Relative to the security market line, the equity is

    A   Overpriced
    B   Correctly priced
    C   Underpriced but not worth buying after trading costs
    D   Underpriced and worth buying after trading costs   **(1 mark)**

    (b) The table below shows different factors (betas), their risk premiums and sensitivities.

Factors	Risk premium to the factors	Portfolio sensitivity to the factor
Market	5%	1.0
Small company	7%	2.0
Company size	6%	0.5
Momentum	3%	0.5

    The risk-free rate is 3.0%. What is the expected return according to the traditional Capital Asset Pricing Model (CAPM)?

    A   8%
    B   11%
    C   25%
    D   26.5%   **(1 mark)**

    (c) In order to counteract the tendency toward indecisiveness when there is wide choice, which of the following would you least recommend?

    A   Reduced choice
    B   Use of defaults
    C   Use of opt-ins
    D   Use of opt-outs   **(1 mark)**

(d) A company has a current price of €20 a share, an expected growth rate in perpetuity of 6% and expected dividend per share next year (D1) of €1. You have a required rate of return of 10%. The expected return minus the required return is equal to

A   −0.83%
B   0.83%
C   1%
D   16%   **(1 mark)**

(e) According to behavioural economics which of these statements is correct?

A   The efficient market anomalies literature is consistent with investors' ability to process information correctly. Subsequent decisions are consistent and optimal.

B   The efficient market anomalies literature is consistent with investors' inability to process information correctly. Subsequent decisions are consistent and optimal.

C   The efficient market anomalies literature is consistent with investors' ability to process information correctly. Subsequent decisions are inconsistent and suboptimal.

D   The efficient market anomalies literature is consistent with investors' inability to process information correctly. Subsequent decisions are inconsistent and suboptimal.   **(1 mark)**

(f) Two government bonds are sold at a par value of £1,000. Each pays interest of £90 annually. Bond A matures in 15 years. Bond B matures in 25 years. The yield to maturity on both rises to 10%. Both bonds will

A   Decrease in value, and B will decrease more than A
B   Decrease in value, and A will decrease more than B
C   Increase in value, and B will increase more than A
D   Increase in value, and A will increase more than B   **(1 mark)**

(g) The value of a European call option on an asset with no cash flows is positively related to all of the following except

A   Volatility
B   Exercise price
C   Risk-free rate
D   Time to exercise   **(1 mark)**

(h) The single-factor market model assumes there are how many sources of risk in asset returns?

A   One
B   Two
C   Three
D   Four   **(1 mark)**

(i) For technical analysis trading to produce after-cost returns consistently superior to a buy-and-hold strategy, the market would have to be

A   Rising
B   Falling
C   Inefficient
D   Undervalued   **(1 mark)**

(j)   Which one of the following is not true of a Double Top price pattern?

A   The two market tops are at the same level
B   It marks the continuation of an uptrend
C   It indicates a significant level of resistance
D   It triggers the reversal of an uptrend   **(1 mark)**

(k)   Which one of the following situations is least likely to occur as a price reaches a resistance level?

A   A short-term reversal pattern develops
B   Selling pressure overwhelms buying pressure
C   Demand overcomes supply with more demand to spare
D   The price stops rising   **(1 mark)**

(l)   With reference to the chart below, describe and suggest the type of investment it portrays.

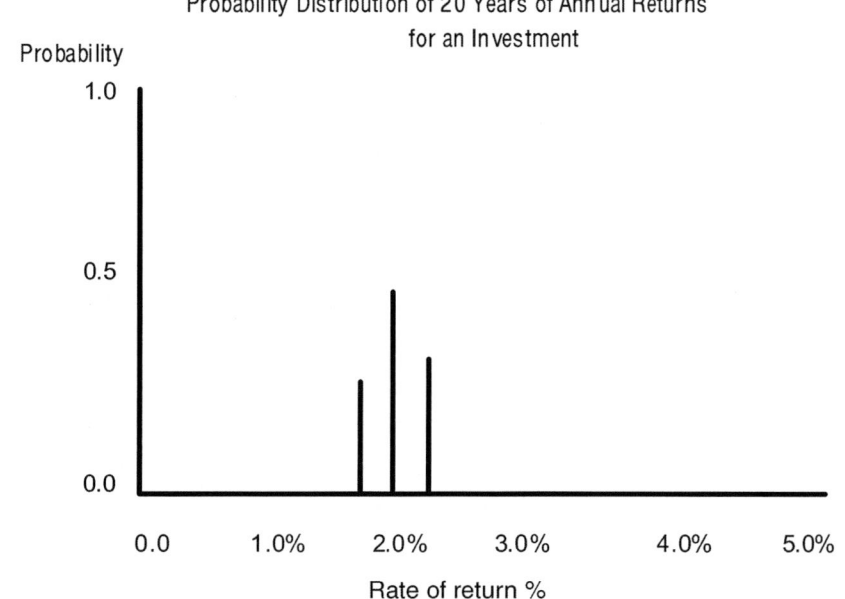

Probability Distribution of 20 Years of Annual Returns for an Investment

(3 marks)

(m)   Examine the chart below. Which portfolio is most efficient in a financial sense? Justify your answer. Show all workings.   **(4 marks)**

Investment characteristics for six portfolios holding risky assets			
Portfolio	Risk-free return %	Expected return %	Standard deviation %
1	4	5	5
2	4	7	7
3	4	9	10
4	4	11	15
5	4	13	21
6	4	15	28

(n)   List the data needed to calculate the equity risk premium.   **(1 mark)**

(o)   List the data needed to calculate the required rate of return on an equity.   **(2 marks)**

(p)   Discuss the components of the risk-free rate.   **(4 marks)**

(q)   For a long-term investor, why might a zero coupon five year bond make a more suitable risk free rate than a five year coupon paying bond?   **(2 marks)**

(r)   The dividend payout ratio for the total market is 65%, the required rate of return is 8% and the expected growth rate of dividends is 4%.

What is the current earnings multiple, or prospective P/E ratio? Show all workings.

(2 marks)

(s)   A pension fund manager of a growing pension fund is talking to a corporate governance manager.

Pension fund manager: 'I don't need or want dividends. As a long-term investor I want to capture as much of the illiquidity premium as I can. Dividends equate to liquidity and liquidity harms my desired rate of return.'

Corporate governance colleague: You do want dividends. They provide an important managerial discipline. Take them away and company boards become less accountable to shareholders. This increases the risk of business failure and that can really harm long-run returns.'

Critically appraise these two viewpoints and give an opinion.   **(4 marks)**

(t)   The table below reports the area under a normal distribution that will fall within a certain number of standard deviations.

Number of standard deviations	Proportion of values of a normal distribution that will fall within the standard deviations
1.0	0.68
1.282	0.80
1.645	0.90
1.960	0.95
2.326	0.98
2.576	0.99
2.807	0.995

The annual standard deviation of returns on a portfolio is 9.5%. Using the table above, what is the 95% Value at Risk? Show all workings.   **(3 marks)**

(u)   A risk manager has collected the following historic return observations that occurred within the worst 5% of occasions:

−3%, −3%, −3%, −8%, −11%, −16%, −28%

Calculate the Conditional Value at Risk and four further descriptive statistics of your choosing.   **(4 marks)**

Section B (20 marks)

This question is compulsory

2.   Three portfolio performance measures are listed below.

$$(r_p - r_f)/ \beta_p$$
$$(r_p - r_f)/ \sigma_p$$
$$(r_p - r_b)/ \sigma_{er}$$

Where:

r_p = return on the portfolio
r_b = return on the benchmark
r_f = risk-free rate
σ_p = standard deviation of portfolio returns
σ_{er} = standard deviation of excess returns $(r_p - r_b)$
β_p = beta of the portfolio

(a)   Calculate the Treynor measure for the portfolio and benchmark using the following values: Portfolio return 7%, UK equity market return 8%, portfolio beta 0.8, and risk-free rate 3%. Show all workings. **(2 marks)**

(b)   Calculate the Sharpe ratio measure for the portfolio and benchmark using the following values: Fund manager's return 7.5%, UK equity market return 7%, standard deviation of portfolio returns 15%, standard deviation of market returns 13%, and risk-free rate 2%. Show all workings. **(2 marks)**

(c)   Calculate the Information ratio measure for the portfolio using the following values, showing all workings:

Period	Portfolio return %	Benchmark return %
1	2.3	2.7
2	–3.6	–4.6
3	5.2	5.6
4	1.2	1.6
Compound return	4.99%	5.12%

(2 marks)

(d)   Discuss the Treynor, Sharpe ratio and Information ratio measures and appraise the advantages and disadvantages of each. **(14 marks)**

Section C (10 marks)

Answer any two questions in this section. Each question carries 5 marks.

3. An analyst has collected the following data for a portfolio comprising three asset classes.

Asset class	Portfolio data				Correlation matrix		
	Weight %	Return %	Standard deviation %		Equity	Real estate	Infrastructure
UK equity	70	12	21		1.0		
UK real estate	15	12	9		0.0	1.0	
Infrastructure	15	7	5		0.0	0.0	1.0

(a) Calculate the portfolio risk measured as standard deviation. Show all workings.

(b) Calculate the portfolio return. Show all workings.

(c) Your understanding of capital market theory causes you to doubt that the historic return and risk evidenced for UK real estate will be repeated in the future. Provide arguments to justify your scepticism. **(5 marks)**

4. Look at the three charts below.

Movement along Security Market Line

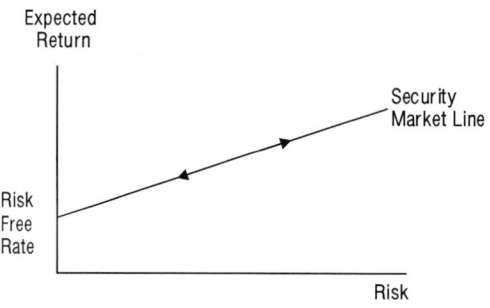

Change in Slope of Security Market Line

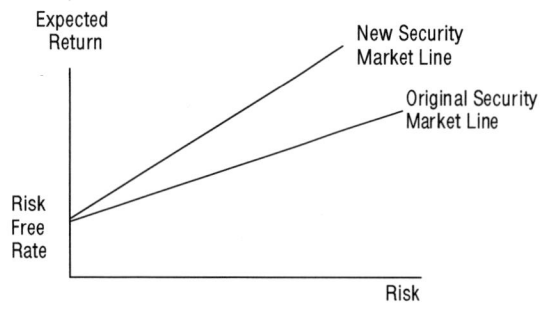

Shift in Security Market Line

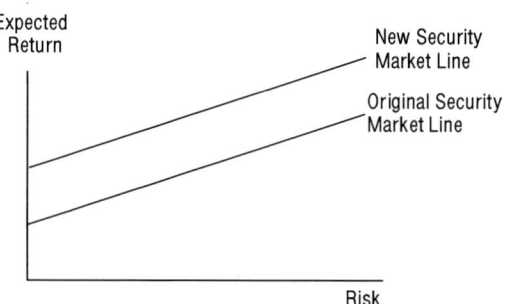

(a) What is the Security Market Line?

(b) Referring to the first chart, explain why an investment might experience a movement along the Security Market Line.

(c) Referring to the lower left chart, explain why the slope of the Security Market Line might change.

(d) Referring to the lower right chart, explain why a shift in the Security Market Line might occur. **(5 marks)**

5. A high net worth client wishes to switch his entire long-term portfolio towards an approach consistent with investing ethically without changing the current portfolio allocation. The current asset allocation of the portfolio is:

Asset class	Portfolio allocation
Cash	10%
Gilts	40%
Developed World equities	50%

The client asks you what the long-run average annual portfolio return might be:

▩ If the portfolio remains as it is
▩ If the portfolio adopts an ethical approach

For the long-run returns, you turn to a capital market assumptions provider.

You receive the following assumptions from them:

	Long-run expected average annual return	Volatility (annualised standard deviation)
Inflation	2.5%	
Nominal world equity return	5.5%	16%
Nominal gilt return	4.0%	7%
Nominal cash return	3.0%	0.2%

(a) Calculate the expected nominal long-run annual return if the portfolio remains as it is. Show all workings.

(b) Provide a critical account of any adjustments you would make to the long-run expected annual return and risk if the portfolio adopts an ethical approach. Your answer should include the adjustments you would make to each asset class. **(5 marks)**

Part 2 – Taxation and Trusts

Section D (20 marks)

Answer all parts of the question in this section.

6. Dick, the managing director of Carpali Limited, a UK resident company, has asked you for some financial advice in relation to some tricky tax questions which have arisen in discussions with Her Majesty's Revenue & Customs (HMRC). You have been asked to draft a Memorandum outlining your tax advice for each of the following situations:

    (a) Dick is living in the United Kingdom since July 2013 with substantial income from his UK company. He is a US national married to a UK national, Debbie. The US Revenue authorities insist that he submits an income tax return to them annually, even though he is resident in the UK.

    Now, HMRC want to tax him also on his UK income. He earns in excess of £100,000 each year. He seeks your advice on any possible solutions to this double taxation problem and on how best to save tax. **(4 marks)**

    (b) Dick asks you for some inheritance tax planning advice in relation to some gifts that he wishes to make to his family members, namely, his wife Mary and his two daughters, Sophie and Natalie. Natalie will get married in 2015. **(4 marks)**

    (c) Dick wishes to establish a trust fund for the benefit of one of his children who is visually impaired. He would like some advice on the options available and on the best way of saving tax in the process. **(4 marks)**

    (d) Dick has shares in a number of blue-chip companies in the USA and has decided to sell some to provide the capital for his daughter's trust fund. He wants to know how these share sales will be taxed in the UK given that he has acquired the shares in a variety of companies at different times over the last 40 years. **(4 marks)**

    (e) Dick receives substantial dividend income from a number of US companies and seeks your advice on how best to save tax on this income. **(4 marks)**

Section E (10 marks)

Answer any two questions in this section. Each question carries 5 marks.

7. John is single and has gross interest income of £12,000 per annum; dividend income of £42,000 and a pension of £28,000 per annum. Calculate his total UK tax liability for 2014/15. **(5 marks)**

8. Mike owns an antique table. He purchased it in 2006 for £6,000. On 1 July 2014, he sold the table for £19,400. Calculate his total UK Capital Gains Tax liability. **(5 marks)**

9. Jane died in August 2014. At the date of her death, she owned a house valued at £480,000. During her lifetime she made a number of gifts:

Date	Recipient	Value of the assets transferred at the date of the transfer (£)
July 2007	Matthew	100,000
August 2008	Mark	140,000
September 2009	Luke	260,000
October 2010	John	130,000

Calculate how much inheritance tax is payable, and by whom, on the death of Jane. **(5 marks)**

June 2012 Examination

Part 1 – Portfolio Construction Theory

Section A (40 marks)

Answer all parts of the question in this section

1. For parts (a) to (k) inclusive, write the capital letter corresponding to your answer.

    (a) Value at Risk at the 95% level of loss is

    A   1.45 × the standard deviation
    B   1.65 × the standard deviation
    C   1.95 × the standard deviation
    D   2.1 × the standard deviation   **(1 mark)**

    (b) A portfolio has an annual return of 3% (above the risk-free rate) and an annual standard deviation of 14%. What is the Sharpe Ratio?

    A   0.03 / 0.14
    B   0.14 / 0.03
    C   0.03 – 0.14
    D   0.14 – 0.03   **(1 mark)**

    (c) The spot Australian Dollar (AUD) / Japanese Yen (JPY) rate is quoted at 81.52 Yen. If the 1-year Australian interest rate is 4.75% and the 1-year Japanese interest rate 0.1%, will the price of the 1-year Forward Rate for Yen be

    A   The same as the spot rate?
    B   Higher than the spot rate?
    C   Lower than the spot rate?
    D   Unable to be determined until contract maturity?   **(1 mark)**

    (d) Which of the following provides evidence against the stock market being semi-strong form efficient?

    A   Insiders earn abnormal trading profits

    B   A sizeable and persistent post announcement drift in prices

    C   Almost all the price response to significant company news occurs in the first 10 minutes of announcement

    D   50% of pension funds outperform the market on average in any year   **(1 mark)**

    (e) Which of the following is not consistent with regret aversion?

    A   Selling winners too early
    B   Holding onto losers too long
    C   Preferences for the middle option when choosing
    D   Inability to invest   **(1 mark)**

    (f) Can the market beta be a number other than 1?

    A   Yes, any number
    B   Yes, between 0.5 and 1.5
    C   Yes, but it is 1 most of the time
    D   No   **(1 mark)**

(g)   A bank offers a UK Sterling (GBP) / US Dollar (USD) price of 1.5336/37. At what rate would a medium size UK Sterling based wealth management company buy USD from the bank?

    A   As a price taker on the bid at 1.5336
    B   As a price maker on the bid at 1.5336
    C   As a price taker on the offer at 1.5337
    D   As a price maker on the offer at 1.5337   **(1 mark)**

(h)   An inflation linked bond is a bond

    A   That links to the rate of inflation but not deflation
    B   That links to the general level of prices up to a maximum of 10% change per annum
    C   With a par value linked to the general level of prices
    D   With a coupon rate linked to the general level of prices   **(1 mark)**

(i)   Heidi sells a stock and then avoids following it in the media, afraid that it may subsequently rise in price. What behavioural characteristic is this consistent with?

    A   Choice overload
    B   Inertia
    C   Fear of regret
    D   Mental accounting   **(1 mark)**

(j)   Which of the following do technical analysts believe?

    A   Price movements are best explained by asset pricing models
    B   Prices are determined by investor psychology and supply and demand
    C   Prices are determined by fundamentals
    D   Price are determined randomly   **(1 mark)**

(k)   The slope of the regression of a security's investment returns against the market's returns is equal to

    A   Idiosyncratic risk
    B   The standard deviation
    C   Beta
    D   The risk premium   **(1 mark)**

(l)   When Company A received a US$3.5 billion settlement from Company B following a patent-infringement lawsuit, Company A's stock price fell, and Company B's rose. Why do you think this may have happened?   **(2 marks)**

(m)   List three reasons why an investor might prefer a fundamental index to a market capitalisation index.   **(3 marks)**

(n)   List three reasons why the tracking error of an index fund following a full replication approach is unlikely ever to be zero.   **(3 marks)**

(o)   What differences are there between futures and forward contracts? Explain your answer.   **(4 marks)**

(p)   The following table presents the share prices on two days for all the constituents of a price-weighted index:

Constituent stocks and their prices		
	A	B	C
Day 1	10	20	30
Day 2	12	22	32

Assuming that none of the stocks has engaged in a stock split, what is the percentage change in the index? Show all workings. **(4 marks)**

(q) A wealth manager requests a trading price for a security in a client's portfolio from a broker. Describe the different factors which might affect the width of the bid-ask spread that the wealth manager is given. **(3 marks)**

(r) Illustrate the following technical chart features by sketching a separate diagram for each feature. Label your diagram clearly to show the feature you are trying to illustrate.

    (i)   Support level
    (ii)   Resistance level
    (iii)   Uptrend line
    (iv)   Uptrend channel   **(4 marks)**

(s) Given the following factors (betas), their risk premiums and sensitivities, what is the expected return for a portfolio using a three-factor asset pricing model? The risk-free rate is 3.0 percent. Show all workings. **(3 marks)**

Factors	Risk premium to the factors	Portfolio sensitivity to the factors
1	10%	1.0
2	7%	2.0
3	6%	0.0

(t) A convertible bond issued by a company is trading at US$110. It offers the holder the option of converting US$100 nominal into 20 ordinary shares of the company. The ordinary shares are currently trading at US$4.50. What is the premium as a percentage of the conversion value? Show all workings. **(3 marks)**

Section B (20 Marks)

This question is compulsory

2. Critically discuss active and passive (ie index and immunisation) fixed income portfolio management strategies. **(20 marks)**

Section C (10 Marks)

Answer any two questions in this section. Each question carries 5 marks

3. A portfolio is invested unequally in just two risky securities, X and Y. The portfolio weight of X is 0.6 and of Y 0.4. The variance of X is 0.04 and of Y 0.09. The correlation coefficient between X and Y is 0.3.

    (a)   What is the portfolio risk, measured as variance? Show all workings.
    (b)   What is the portfolio risk, measured as standard deviation? Show all workings.
    (c)   How might you reduce risk further?   **(5 marks)**

4. An analyst has collected the following data for two equities, A and B.

	A	B
Expected return	11.4%	5.2%
Standard deviation of returns	35%	17%
Beta	1.9	0.8

The expected return on the equity market is 6% and on Treasury Bills 2%.

    (a)   Are equities A and B underpriced, overpriced or correctly priced according to the capital asset pricing model? Show all workings.

(b)   Draw a chart and on it show the location of both securities relative to the Security Market Line.

(c)   Annotate the chart axes.   **(5 marks)**

5.   Explain each of the following.

(a)   Duration

(b)   Convexity   **(5 marks)**

Part 2 – Taxation and Trusts

Section D (20 marks)

Answer all parts of the question in this section

6. James and John are UK residents. They have a software business which has an annual turnover of £250,000. They each own their own home in the UK and each has a small apartment in Spain.

    Each has a portfolio of FTSE 100 shares. James is mainly invested in Tesco plc and has 25,000 shares acquired in different amounts over a number of years since the 1970s. John is mainly invested in J Sainsbury plc and has around 200,000 shares acquired over a number of years since the 1970s. James is married to Nora and they have three teenage children. James would like the children to attend university and wants to put aside some money to cover their university fees and future weddings.

    John is divorced but has to pay monthly maintenance to his ex-wife of £300 and £200 maintenance for his two teenage daughters, one of whom has a visual impairment. John would like to create a trust fund for the future benefit of his daughter with the visual impairment. He would also like to give each of his daughters some money to travel around the world when they are 18.

    At the moment James and John operate as a partnership and each receives a salary of £75,000 a year before tax. They share any left-over profit after business overheads on a 50/50 basis. The business is doing well and is likely to expand in the coming years since they have recently been granted a Government contract to supply bespoke software products to the tax authorities. James and John envisage that turnover will treble as a result and that their salaries will also treble.

    James and John have asked for your advice on a number of issues. They need to set up a pension of some kind and recognise that they will have to take on staff and maybe a book-keeper.

    (a) What general advice can you give James and John to mitigate their current and future tax liabilities in the UK? What about tax planning for the future expenses in relation to university fees and weddings? How will future staff be taxed by them under the PAYE system?

    (4 marks)

    (b) What advice can you give John on setting up a trust fund for the future benefit of his visually impaired daughter? What are the tax advantages of doing this? Is there any alternative approach that you would suggest? **(4 marks)**

    (c) James is thinking about selling his Tesco shares and investing in Sainsbury. Explain the UK's 'matching rules' in relation to the capital gains taxation of share sales. What advice can you give him to minimise his UK capital gains taxation on those share sales? **(4 marks)**

    (d) James and John both receive significant dividend income each year from their share portfolios. What advice can you give them to minimise their liability to UK taxation on this income? If they give some shares to their children as gifts each year how will such gifts be taxed? If they give them some dividend income instead and retain the shares does that give a better result for tax? Are there any other approaches that they could consider that might save some tax and transfer some income to their children? **(4 marks)**

    (e) James is thinking about working from his apartment in Spain each winter. He estimates that he will spend October to March there but may spend Christmas in the UK. He wants to know whether there are any tax advantages in doing this. He also asks whether he will no longer be considered a resident of the UK. Both James and John are Spanish citizens and have lived in the UK since 1969. James is also worried about paying tax in the UK and in Spain on the same income and asks how he can prevent such double taxation. **(4 marks)**

Section E (10 Marks)

Answer any TWO questions in this section. Each question carries 5 marks

7.   Discuss how the UK taxes resident individuals and individuals who are not resident in the UK.

(5 marks)

8.   For inheritance tax purposes, how are lifetime transfers of assets taxed?   **(5 marks)**

9.   Give four examples of non-dividend savings income. How is such income taxed in the UK in relation to a UK resident individual that receives such income?   **(5 marks)**

BPP
LEARNING MEDIA

December 2011 Examination

Part 1 – Portfolio Construction Theory

Section A (40 marks)

Answer all parts of the question in this section

1. For parts (a) to (j) inclusive, write the capital letter corresponding to your answer.

    (a) What is the distinction between desired return and required return for an investor?

    A   In equilibrium there is no distinction.

    B   The desired return is the amount of return the investor needs to achieve in order to invest. The required return is the amount of return the investor expects based on the risk of the investment.

    C   The desired return is the amount of return the investor wants. The required return is the amount of return the investor needs to achieve in order to invest.

    D   The desired return is the amount of return the investor expects based on an asset pricing model. The required return is the amount of return the investor expects based on what investors received last year. **(1 mark)**

    (b) The rise in international investment has increased exposure to the performance obtained from the market globally and decreased the relevance of

    A   Investment volatility
    B   Alpha
    C   Beta
    D   Portfolio theory **(1 mark)**

    (c) An open-end mutual fund or unit trust is best described as

    A   A public limited company that invests in a variety of securities and companies

    B   An institutional investor that pools the money of individuals and invests in a range of securities

    C   An institutional investor that invests exclusively in primary market securities

    D   An institutional investor that invests exclusively in foreign capital markets

    E   A trust or company whose shares do not trade at net asset value **(1 mark)**

    (d) A strategic asset class is characterised by all of the following **except**

    A   Assets within the class should be defined by a simple description

    B   Assets within the class should all be statistically dissimilar

    C   Correlations between each asset class should be low enough to provide diversification

    D   All investable assets within a class should be classified in only one class **(1 mark)**

    (e) Which of the following is not a global systematic risk factor?

    A   Fraud by one or more corporate directors
    B   Wheat price
    C   Atmospheric carbon dioxide level
    D   Oil price **(1 mark)**

(f)   Tactical asset allocation (TAA) is carried out through

    A   Technical analysis of asset classes
    B   Movement of the strategic asset allocation on a forward-looking basis
    C   A belief in efficient markets
    D   Active short- and medium-term variations around the strategic asset allocation

(1 mark)

(g)   An inflation linked bond is

    A   A bond that links to the rate of inflation but not deflation

    B   A bond that links to the general level of prices up to a maximum of 10% change per annum

    C   A bond with a par value linked to the general level of prices

    D   A bond with a coupon rate linked to the general level of prices   **(1 mark)**

(h)   Bonds are known as fixed-income securities because they

    A   Set aside a fixed amount of capital to meet all coupon payments

    B   Were first issued to help older people to live on a fixed income in retirement

    C   Pay a fixed yield

    D   Promise a stream of income that is either fixed or determined by a set formula

(1 mark)

(i)   Two government bonds are sold at a par value of UK£1,000. Each pays interest of K£90 annually. Bond A matures in 15 years. Bond B matures in 25 years. The yield to maturity on both bonds then rises to 10%. Both bonds will

    A   Decrease in value, and B will decrease more than A
    B   Decrease in value, and A will decrease more than B
    C   Increase in value, and B will increase more than A
    D   Increase in value, and A will increase more than B   **(1 mark)**

(j)   What is the distinction between the expected return and an investor's realised return?

    A   Expected return is an equilibrium condition and realised return is a is equilibrium condition.

    B   The expected return is calculated net of the risk-free rate and the realised return s calculated gross of the risk-free rate.

    C   The expected return is the amount of return estimated by an asset pricing model and the realised return is the amount of return the investor receives.

    D   The expected return is the amount of return the investor expects and the realised return is the amount of return estimated by an asset pricing model.   **(1 mark)**

(k)   From 1 January 2003 to end 31 December 2014 a client's portfolio increased in value by 97.5%. What is the annualised portfolio return? Show all workings.   **(3 marks)**

(l)   A convertible bond has a par value of €1,000 and a current market price of €850. The current price of the issuing company's stock is €29 and the conversion ratio is 30 shares. What is the bond's market conversion value? Show all workings.   **(3 marks)**

(m) The table below shows asset class weights and returns for a portfolio.

Asset	Weight in Portfolio	Asset Class Return
Commodities	7%	-3.0%
Property	7%	11.0%
Cash	6%	1.0%
Bonds	30%	3.0%
Equities	50%	3.0%

What is the portfolio return? Show all workings. **(3 marks)**

(n) A portfolio of €10 billion has the following portfolio weights:

Asset	Weight in Portfolio
Bonds	40%
Equities	60%

Presuming no rebalancing of the portfolio, what is the portfolio value and new portfolio weights if the investment return on bonds is 0.0% and on equities −16.66%? Show all workings. **(3 marks)**

(o) A UK government bond due in one year has a yield of 5.7% and a second due in five years has a yield of 6.2%. A bond issued by a FTSE 100 company due in one year has a yield of 6.5% and a bond issued by a FTSE 250 PLC due in five years has a yield of 7.5%. What is the default risk premium on each corporate bond? Show all workings. **(3 marks)**

(p) A company has a current price of €40 a share, an expected growth rate in perpetuity of 11% and expected dividend per share next year (D1) of €2. You have a required rate of return of 12%. What investment return do you expect, and do you invest? Show all workings.

(3 marks)

(q) An analyst has collected the following data for two equities, A and B:

	A	B
Expected return	9%	8%
Standard deviation of returns	15%	10%
Beta	1.7	0.9

The expected return on the equity market is 7% and on Treasury Bills 3%. Are equities A and B underpriced, overpriced or correctly priced according to the capital asset pricing model? Show all workings. **(4 marks)**

(r) The following chart shows a phenomenon known as investment home bias. The chart reveals that UK defined benefit (DB) pension schemes allocate far more to UK equities than suggested by the UK's weight in a world equity index. What arguments are put forward by proponents to justify this allocation?

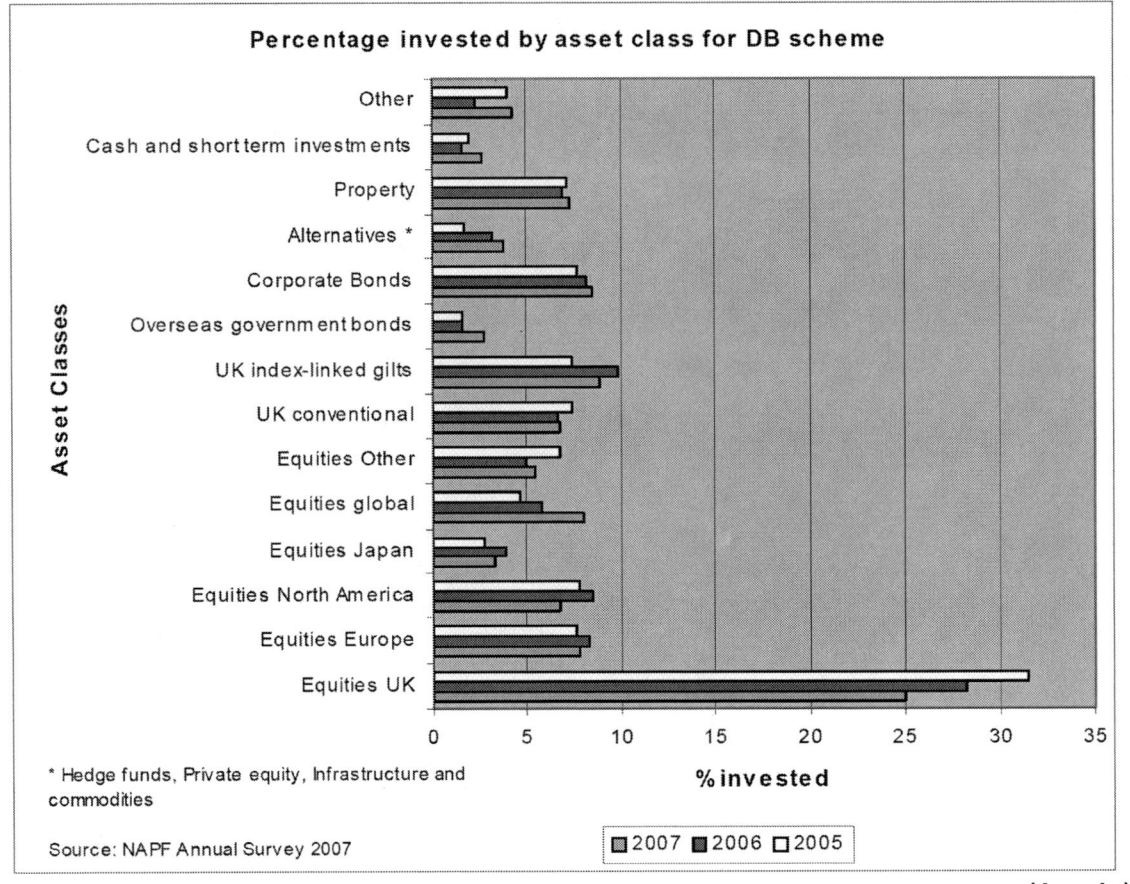

(4 marks)

(s)   What do you think is the best risk-free or safe asset for a long-term investor? Explain your answer.   **(4 marks)**

Section B (20 marks)

This question is compulsory

2.   (a)   What is the typical procedure for setting the strategic asset allocation for a large investor?

     (b)   Discuss when and how the following active strategies might be used to deliver an improvement in the strategic asset allocation process for the investor.

         (i)   Dynamic Asset Allocation
         (ii)   Liability Driven Asset Allocation
         (iii)   Risk Budgeting   **(20 marks)**

Section C (10 marks)

Answer any two questions in this section. Each question carries 5 marks

3.   What is the default spread and what does it indicate?   **(5 marks)**

4.   The table below reports the average annual nominal return on UK notice savings accounts and average annual UK inflation each year for five years.

Date	Nominal Return on Notice Savings Accounts	UK Inflation
2006	2.99%	4.43%
2007	3.81%	4.05%
2008	2.99%	0.95%
2009	0.39%	2.4%
2010	1.02%	4.77%

(a)   What is the compound five year nominal and real return on Notice savings accounts? Show all workings.

(b)   A client asks: 'Can an investor keep up with inflation whilst keeping risk free?' How would you answer this?   **(5 marks)**

5.   Explain each of the following.

(a)   Standard deviation
(b)   Value at risk (VaR)
(c)   Conditional value at risk (CVaR)   **(5 marks)**

Part 2 – Taxation and Trusts

Section D (20 marks)

Answer all parts of the question in this section

Victor has come to you for some investment and tax planning advice.

6. (a) Victor has been appointed a trustee of a UK trust and needs some advice on the powers granted to him and his fellow trustees under the Trustee Act 2000. **(4 marks)**

   (b) Victor has made some investments in his role as trustee in a number of international and European companies. He receives dividends from these companies and sometimes pays tax on these dividends in the foreign country as well as in the UK. He asks for your advice on how to reduce his tax liability in relation to such dividends. **(4 marks)**

   (c) Victor's wife is a housewife with no employment income. Victor and his wife are considering buying a three-bedroomed property to rent out. They plan to sell the property in a few years' time when the market improves. Victor asks you for some tax advice in relation to this proposed transaction. **(4 marks)**

   (d) Victor and his wife wish to make a joint-will and would like some advice from you on minimising future inheritance tax liabilities. They have two sons and two daughters. Their two daughters each have one child. In particular, Victor would like to create a trust for his grandchildren. **(4 marks)**

   (e) Victor's wife has shares in her own name in a large plc, purchased by her in 1978, 1989, 1996 and 2007. She is unclear as to how such shares will be taxed if they are sold in December 2014. Explain how the shares are taxed if all are disposed of in December 2014. **(4 marks)**

Section E (10 marks)

Answer any two questions in this section. Each question carries 5 marks.

7. For capital gains tax purposes, explain when a chargeable disposal occurs. Give an example. **(5 marks)**

8. Explain how trusts are taxed by the UK. **(5 marks)**

9. In relation to the taxation of off-shore funds, discuss

   (a) The taxation of such funds by the UK
   (b) The taxation of the individual investors in such funds by the UK **(5 marks)**

June 2011 Examination

Part 1 – Portfolio Construction Theory

Section A (40 marks)

Answer all parts of the question in this section

1.   For parts (a) to (j) inclusive, write the capital letter corresponding to your answer.

   (a)   For technical analysis trading to produce after-cost returns that are consistently superior to a buy-and-hold strategy, the market would have to be

   A   Rising
   B   Falling
   C   Inefficient
   D   Undervalued   **(1 mark)**

   (b)   What is a bond's coupon if it has a current (running) yield of 8% and a price of £1,250?

   A   8.0%
   B   10.0%
   C   11.0%
   D   8.5%   **(1 mark)**

   (c)   What is the investment phase called when people are in their early-to-mid earning careers and regularly putting aside amounts to meet expenditure needs later in life?

   A   Consolidation phase
   B   Foundation phase
   C   Drawdown phase
   D   Accumulation phase   **(1 mark)**

   (d)   Which is not a common relative valuation technique?

   A   Price-earnings ratio
   B   Price-cash flow ratio
   C   Price-book value ratio
   D   Price-cost of goods sold ratio   **(1 mark)**

   (e)   A Eurobond is

   A   Sold by an issuer in the currency of the issuer's own country and internationally tradeable
   B   Denominated in a currency not native to where it is issued
   C   Also known as a Yankee Bond
   D   Sold only to European investors   **(1 mark)**

   (f)   The semi-variance of an investment return series measures

   A   Two times all deviations from the mean
   B   The deviations above the mean
   C   The deviations below the mean
   D   The two closest quartile deviations to the mean   **(1 mark)**

(g)   The rate of growth of equity earnings is equal to retention rate

    A   Plus the return on equity
    B   Minus the return on equity
    C   Divided by the return on equity
    D   Times the return on equity   **(1 mark)**

(h)   Which of the following would not be a factor within the Arbitrage Pricing Theory (APT)?

    A   Fraud by one or more corporate directors
    B   Interest rates
    C   Gross Domestic Product
    D   Oil price   **(1 mark)**

(i)   Which type of stock has a high probability of a low or negative return and a low probability of a high return?

    A   Defensive
    B   Cyclical
    C   Speculative
    D   Value   **(1 mark)**

(j)   A portfolio has an annual return of 3% (above the risk-free rate) and an annual standard deviation of 14%. What is the Sharpe Ratio?

    A   0.03 / 0.14
    B   0.14 / 0.03
    C   0.03 − 0.14
    D   0.14 − 0.03   **(1 mark)**

(k)   A company has a current share price of $40, an expected growth rate in perpetuity of 4%, and expected dividend per share next year (D1) of $1. What is the expected rate of return? Show all workings.   **(3 marks)**

(l)   List four similarities between the Capital Asset Pricing Model (CAPM) and the Arbitrage Pricing Theory (APT).   **(4 marks)**

(m)   List four assumptions of the Capital Asset Pricing Model (CAPM).   **(4 marks)**

(n)   What is the expected return for a stock with a beta of 1.2, if the risk-free rate is 6% and the expected return on the market is 12%? Show all workings.   **(3 marks)**

(o)   A Eurozone investor has investment exposure in two currencies: the Euro and the US dollar. The Eurozone risk-free rate is 4%. The US risk-free rate is 3%. The expected appreciation of the US dollar is 2%. What is the foreign currency return?   **(3 marks)**

(p)   A Eurozone investor has investment exposure to two currencies: the Euro and the US dollar. The Eurozone risk-free rate is 2%. The world portfolio risk premium is 4%. The US dollar currency return is forecast at 1%. The factor exposures to world beta and currency denominated in Euro returns for three portfolios; A, B and C, are as follows:

Factor exposures			
	A	**B**	**C**
World beta exposure	1.2	1.4	0.8
Currency exposure	1.5	0.8	2.0

What is the expected return of each portfolio to the Eurozone investor? Show all workings.

    (4 marks)

(q)   What is the total risk (standard deviation) of a portfolio if its systematic risk (standard deviation) is 19% and unsystematic risk (standard deviation) 6%? Show all workings.

(3 marks)

(r)   Why might the earnings yield spread be a useful indicator for asset allocation?   **(3 marks)**

(s)   If the yield curve has humps and dips in it, but you expect these to disappear, what bond investment strategy are you most likely to consider?   **(3 marks)**

Section B (20 marks)

This question is compulsory

2.   (a)   Are governance issues worse or better if investing as a limited partner in private equity as opposed to investing directly in listed equities?

(b)   Which approaches and strategies for private equity might combine best with listed equity within a diversified portfolio?   **(20 marks)**

Section C (10 marks)

Answer any two questions in this section. Each question carries 5 marks

3.   As part of your monitoring activity as a wealth manager, you review the corporate governance of UK banks held in your discretionary client account equity portfolios. You see that one large UK-listed commercial bank has three board committees; nominations, remuneration and audit. Your firm has signed up to the UK Stewardship Code. In order to meet good standards of corporate governance and investor stewardship what steps would you now follow?   **(5 marks)**

4.   The table below reports the index, monthly returns and annual standard deviation of returns for an actively managed diversified portfolio and the relevant market portfolio. The actively managed portfolio beta is 1.05.

	Portfolio		Market	
Feb 13	100.0		100	
Mar 13	101.1	1.1%	100.4	0.4%
Apr 13	102.8	1.7%	101.2	0.8%
May 13	102.7	−0.1%	101.0	−0.2%
Jun 13	103.5	0.8%	102.1	1.1%
Jul 13	105.0	1.4%	103.1	1.0%
Aug 13	105.1	0.1%	103.5	0.4%
Sep 13	105.3	0.2%	103.4	−0.1%
Oct 13	104.1	−1.1%	102.9	−0.5%
Nov 13	104.7	0.5%	103.7	0.8%
Dec 13	104.4	−0.3%	103.1	−0.6%
Jan 14	105.4	1.0%	104.0	0.8%
Feb 14	107.9	2.4%	105.9	1.9%
Standard deviation		3.32%		2.54%
The risk-free is 2.5%				
Portfolio returns are presented net of fees				

(a)   Calculate the Treynor measures for both the actively managed portfolio and the market portfolio. Show all workings.

(b)   Annual fees of 1.0% are taken pro-rata from the fund at each calendar quarter end. Describe how you would recalculate portfolio performance gross of fees. Discuss whether the

appropriate performance comparison should be presented net of fees, gross of fees, or both. **(5 marks)**

5. From your client fact find, you have ascertained that a particular client's investment horizon is 20 years. Recent investment research you have read suggests it takes 30-40 years for a change in carbon dioxide emissions to lead a change in climate in the atmosphere and so to economics and society. Is this too far ahead to be of concern to the financial interests of your clients' investments? Briefly discuss. **(5 marks)**

Part 2 – Taxation and Trusts

Section D (20 marks)

Answer all parts of the question in this section

6. Frank and Nora are new clients. They are thinking about setting up a new publishing business in the UK. They have a disabled daughter and want to provide some financial security for her future. Nora has income in 2014/15 of £64,000. They have come to you for some tax advice.

    (a) Frank asks you for some advice on the establishment of a trust for his disabled daughter. Advise him on

        (i)   The types of trust available
        (ii) The tax treatment of each type of trust   **(4 marks)**

    (b) In June 2014, Frank disposed of one of his Chinese vases for the sum of £20,000, with the remaining three vases being valued at £45,000. The set of four vases were originally purchased in June 2012 for £10,000.

        Calculate the capital gains tax on the disposal.   **(4 marks)**

    (c) Frank receives some income from royalties on his new book in the sum of £17,500 in March 2015. He has no other income and reaches 69 years of age in January 2015. Calculate the income tax payable on the royalty income.   **(4 marks)**

    (d) Calculate Nora's income tax liability for 2014/15. Nora is aged 55.   **(4 marks)**

    (e) Give Nora some tax planning advice on the establishment of her new business. **(4 marks)**

Section E (10 marks)

Answer any two questions in this section. Each question carries 5 marks

7. What transfers of property are exempt from inheritance tax?   **(5 marks)**

8. When does a chargeable disposal arise for capital gains tax purposes?   **(5 marks)**

9. Explain the difference between residence and domicile for UK tax purposes.   **(5 marks)**

December 2010 Examination

Part 1 – Portfolio Construction Theory

Section A (40 marks)

Answer all parts of the question in this section

1. For parts (a) to (h), write the capital letter corresponding to your answer.

    (a) A bond is more volatile when it has

    A   A high coupon and a long maturity
    B   A low coupon and a short maturity
    C   A low coupon and a long maturity
    D   A deferred call feature and a sinking fund   **(1 mark)**

    (b) Which securities can be valued by dividing the annual dividend by the required rate of return?

    A   Corporate bonds
    B   Preferred stocks
    C   Common stocks
    D   Constant growth common stocks   **(1 mark)**

    (c) The convexity of a bond is influenced

    A   Positively by yield and positively by coupon
    B   Inversely by maturity and positively by coupon
    C   Positively by maturity and inversely by coupon
    D   Positively by coupon and positively by its bond rating   **(1 mark)**

    (d) The value of a European call option on an asset with no cash flows is positively related to all of the following except

    A   Volatility
    B   Exercise price
    C   Risk-free rate
    D   Time to exercise   **(1 mark)**

    (e) In a situation of corporate financial distress, which is most likely?

    A   Bondholders wish the company to take additional risk

    B   Equity holders wish the company to cut the dividend to conserve cash

    C   Equity holders wish the company to take additional risk

    D   Bondholders wish the company to sell part of the business and pay an extraordinary dividend   **(1 mark)**

(f) Beta is

    A   The covariance of a security's returns with the market portfolio divided by the variance of the market portfolio

    B   The correlation of a security's returns with the market portfolio divided by the variance of the market portfolio

    C   The variance of the market portfolio divided by the covariance of a security's returns with the market portfolio

    D   The variance of the market portfolio divided by the correlation of a security's returns with the market portfolio   **(1 mark)**

(g) A high probability of default on a bond can be expected to result in a promised yield to maturity

    A   Equal to the expected yield
    B   Greater than the expected yield
    C   Less than the expected yield
    D   Equal to zero   **(1 mark)**

(h) A factor portfolio is a portfolio with

    A   Factor sensitivities of zero to all factors

    B   A factor sensitivity of zero to a particular factor and one to all other factors

    C   A factor sensitivity of one to a particular factor and zero to all other factors

    D   A specific set of factor sensitivities designed to replicate the factor exposures of a benchmark index   **(1 mark)**

(i) List three techniques for constructing an index portfolio.   **(3 marks)**

(j) A company paid dividends per share of US$1.20 at the end of 2004. At the end of 2014 it paid dividends per share of US$3.50. What is the compound annual growth rate in dividends? Show all workings.   **(2 marks)**

(k) A company had a dividend payout ratio of 63% in 2014. What was the retention rate in 2014? Show all workings.   **(2 marks)**

(l) A portfolio is invested unequally in just two securities, X and Y. The portfolio weight of X is 0.6 and of Y 0.4. The variance of X is 0.04 and of Y 0.09. The correlation coefficient between X and Y is 0.3.

    (i)   What is the portfolio risk, measured as variance? Show all workings.

    (ii)   What is the portfolio risk, measured as standard deviation? Show all workings.

    (4 marks)

(m)   The table below shows the values, returns and standard deviation of returns on an index.

Year	Date	Index (closing values)	Returns
	Dec – 31	100	
2012	Mar – 31	89	–0.110
	Jun – 30	93	0.045
	Sep – 30	91	–0.022
	Dec – 31	103	0.132
2013	Mar – 31	108	0.049
	Jun – 30	104	–0.037
	Sep – 30	103	–0.010
	Dec – 31	105	0.019
2014	Mar – 31	108	0.029
	Jun – 30	109	0.009
	Sep – 30	110	0.009

Standard deviation of returns = 0.05998

(i)   Calculate the annualised standard deviation from the standard deviation of returns. Show all workings. **(2 marks)**

(ii)   Calculate the annualised return on the index. Show all workings. **(2 marks)**

(iii)   Describe one major merit and one major drawback of the presentation of annualised performance numbers. **(3 marks)**

(iv)   Suppose that the index values and returns in the table above relate to an overseas market and are expressed in nominal terms. Suppose also that the overseas marketplace is different to the jurisdiction in which the client resides.

What are the arguments for deflating the nominal performance numbers by the local country (overseas market) inflation rate when presenting performance to the client? What arguments are there for not doing so and instead staying with nominal performance numbers when presenting to the client? **(4 marks)**

(n)   An analyst has collected the following data for two equities, A and B:

	A	B
Expected return	11.4%	5.2%
Standard deviation of returns	35%	17%
Beta	1.9	0.8%

The expected return on the equity market is 6% and on Treasury Bills 2%. Are equities A and B underpriced, overpriced or correctly priced, according to the capital asset pricing model?

On a chart, show the location of both securities relative to the Security Market Line. Annotate the chart axes and show all workings. **(4 marks)**

(o)   A convertible bond issued by a company is trading at US$120. It offers the holder the option of converting US$100 nominal into 25 ordinary shares of the company. The ordinary shares are currently trading at US$3.80.

(i)   What is the premium as a percentage of the conversion value? **(3 marks)**

(ii)   Why are convertible bonds expected to trade at a premium, and what information does the premium provide the potential investor? **(3 marks)**

Section B (20 marks)

This question is compulsory

2. Conventional wisdom concerning the lifecycle approach to investing is that a person's labour income (their human capital) is bond-like. In contrast to this traditional expectation, recent research finds that labour income and corporate profits are co-integrated. This latter evidence suggests that labour income is more equity-like.

   Referring to the paragraph above, which hypothesis do you believe is more correct today, and why? In light of the argument you present, discuss whether portfolio exposure to equities should be negative, positive, hump-shaped or U-shaped relative to working age over the lifecycle? How does your argument and discussion above speak to the importance of understanding clients?

   (20 marks)

Section C (10 marks)

Answer any two questions in this section. Each question carries 5 marks

3. (a) Describe the major differences between commodity forward and futures contracts.

   (b) How is an understanding of such contracts important when appraising the suitability of common shares that offer exposure to commodities, eg mining companies? **(5 marks)**

4. The term structure of interest rates is expected to be upward sloping. What are the main reasons for this expectation? **(5 marks)**

5. Describe value, growth and momentum investing, and highlight similarities and differences. **(5 marks)**

Part 2 – Taxation and Trusts

Section D (20 Marks)

Answer all parts of the question in this section

6.   James has a small company with a turnover of £95,000 in the last tax year. He is resident in the UK. The company is resident in the UK.

Advise James on the tax implications in the following personal and company matters.

(a)   James purchased a house in 2010 for £190,000. He is thinking of selling the house in 2015.

(4 marks)

(b)   James purchased 5,000 CRH shares in July 2011 for £5,000. On 12 October 2014, the shares are valued at £1.25 each. He is considering selling some of these shares in 2015.

(4 marks)

(c)   James rented out his summer-house in Spain and received some rental income amounting to £12,500 in the last year. Spain imposed some taxation on that income.   **(4 marks)**

(d)   James receives a salary from his company in the sum of £15,000. The company has other business-related expenses amounting to £50,000 leaving it profits of £30,000.   **(4 marks)**

(e)   In 2015, the company will make a rights issue and issue some bonus shares.   **(4 marks)**

Section E (10 Marks)

Answer any two questions in this section. Each question carries 5 marks

7.   Larry is a single person and has a salary of £85,000 and received gross non-dividend savings income of £5,000 in the tax year 2014/15. Calculate his income tax liability for that year.   **(5 marks)**

8.   What are the purposes and benefits of creating a trust? Give three examples of different types of trust and explain the relevance of each for tax purposes.   **(5 marks)**

9.   Explain how shares are valued for inheritance tax purposes.   **(5 marks)**

June 2010 Examination

Part 1 – Portfolio Construction Theory

Section A (40 marks)

Answer all parts of the question in the section

1   For parts (a) to (f) inclusive, write the capital letter corresponding to your answer.

(a)   The capital asset pricing model (CAPM) suggests that

A   All investors will hold some combination of a broadly based market index and the risk-free asset

B   Less risk-averse investors will overweight high-beta stocks relative to the market portfolio

C   More risk-averse investors will underweight high-beta stocks relative to the market portfolio

D   Less risk-averse investors will hold less of a broadly based index and more of the risk-free asset   **(1 mark)**

(b)   Which of the following statements about modern portfolio theory is **false**?

A   All portfolios on the capital allocation line are perfectly negatively correlated

B   The capital market line is developed under the assumption that investors can borrow or lend at the risk-free rate

C   Risky assets have uncertain future returns, and uncertainty is measured by the variance or standard deviation of returns

D   For a portfolio made up of the risk-free asset and a risky asset, the standard deviation is the weighted proportion of the standard deviation of the risky asset   **(1 mark)**

(c)   The single-factor market model assumes there are how many sources of risk in asset returns?

A   One
B   Two
C   Three
D   Four   **(1 mark)**

(d)   The international capital asset pricing model assumes that

A   The risk-free rate is the investor's domestic risk-free rate, and the market portfolio is the market capitalisation weighted portfolio of all risky assets in the world

B   The risk-free rate is the investor's domestic risk-free rate, and the market portfolio is the market capitalisation weighted portfolio of all risky assets in the domestic market

C   The risk-free rate is the London Interbank Offered Rate (LIBOR), and the market portfolio is the market capitalisation weighted portfolio of all risky assets in the world

D   The risk-free rate is the London Interbank Offered Rate (LIBOR), and the market portfolio is the market capitalisation weighted portfolio of all risky assets in the domestic market.   **(1 mark)**

(e)   The slope of the regression of a stock's returns against the market's returns is equal to

    A   Idiosyncratic risk

    B   The standard deviation

    C   Beta

    D   The risk premium   **(1 mark)**

(f)   An investment objective of 7% annual return averaged over each four year period is

    A   A benchmark-driven objective

    B   An absolute return objective

    C   A best efforts objective

    D   A relative return objective   **(1 mark)**

(g)   Given the following factors (betas), their risk premiums and sensitivities, what is the expected return for a portfolio using a three-factor arbitrage pricing theory model? Show all workings.

Factors	Risk premium to the factors	Portfolio sensitivity to the factors
1	10%	1.0
2	7%	2.0
3	6%	0.0

The risk-free rate is 3.0%   **(3 marks)**

(h)   The spot exchange rate between the British pound and the US dollar is 0.7775 £/US$. The spot exchange rate between the Canadian dollar and the British pound is 1.8325 CAD$/£, what is the US dollar/Canadian dollar spot cross exchange rate? Show all workings.

                                                (3 marks)

(i)   The standard deviation of the returns of the market is 0.05. The covariance of the returns of the market with a stock is 0.005. What is the stock's beta? Show all workings.   **(3 marks)**

(j)   What is the total risk (standard deviation) of a portfolio if its systematic risk (standard deviation) is 17% and unsystematic risk (standard deviation) 8%? Show all workings.

                                                (3 marks)

(k)   Relative to the Capital Market Line, security A is underpriced by 8.0% and security B underpriced by 5.0%. Security A is issued by firm X and security B is issued by firm Y. Firms X and Y are both London Stock Exchange quoted companies of similar size and with similar quality of financial statements. They have similar capitalisations and each has a free float of 1. Why might an investor rationally decide to purchase security B rather than security A for the portfolio?   **(4 marks)**

(l)   An analyst has collected the following data for two equities, A and B.

	A	B
Expected return	9%	8%
Standard deviation of returns	15%	10%
Beta	1.7	0.9

The expected return on the equity market is 7% and on Treasury Bills 3%. Are equities A and B underpriced, overpriced or correctly priced, according to the capital asset pricing model? Show all workings.   **(4 marks)**

(m) Why do shares with superior voting rights usually command a price premium relative to shares with fewer or no voting rights, given the same set of cash flows and valuation technique? **(4 marks)**

(n) According to empirical research, how quickly does portfolio risk fall as the number of securities in a portfolio is increased, and is there a point when portfolio risk stops falling? **(3 marks)**

(o) What is meant by the global level of systematic risk, and what factors might it include? **(4 marks)**

(p) Which of the formulae below is most appropriate for calculating the portfolio risk of a two-stock portfolio if the correlation between the two securities is 0.4? Explain your answer.

(i) $\sigma_{a+b} = \sqrt{p_a^2\sigma_a^2 + p_b^2\sigma_b^2 + 2p_ap_bCov_{ab}}$

(ii) $\sigma_{a+b} = \sqrt{p_a^2\sigma_a^2 + p_b^2\sigma_b^2 Cov_{ab}}$

(iii) $\sigma_{a+b} = p_a\sigma_a + p_b\sigma_b$

(iv) $\sigma_{a+b} = \sqrt{p_a^2\sigma_a^2 + p_b^2\sigma_b^2}$

Where p = weight of security and σ = standard deviation. **(3 marks)**

Section B (20 marks)

This question is compulsory

2. How can a wealth manager use insight and evidence from behavioural finance to improve the design and management of funds and services to clients? **(20 marks)**

Section C (10 marks)

Answer any two questions in this section. Each question carries 5 marks

3. (a) A person earning low income and with low financial wealth wants to put aside a small amount each month continuously for 15 years in order to purchase a physical asset in 15 years' time. Would you propose a high or a low risk asset allocation at the outset, and how would you intend to vary risk exposure over the 15 year investment?

   (b) Empirical research finds that a significant minority of people with low income and low financial wealth have a low capacity for risk taking yet a high risk tolerance. Why might this be?

   (5 marks)

4. The following statistics describe the returns to Market A and Market B.

Market characteristic	Market A	Market B
Standard Deviation	11.0	17.0
Mean	1.2	1.5
Median	1.4	2.0
Skewness[1]	−3.0	−5.5
Excess Kurtosis[2]	4.0	−2.0

[1] a perfectly normal distribution has 0 skewness
[2] a perfectly normal distribution has 0 excess kurtosis

Based on the characteristics in the above, carefully describe Market A and B and what you expect an investor's experience to be in each market? **(5 marks)**

5. A high net worth individual personally manages her investments. She has a relatively high risk tolerance but she is also loss averse. As a result of high risk tolerance she has 60% of her portfolio in equities. As a result of loss aversion she has in place a loss aversion strategy in which for each 8% fall in a European equity benchmark she sells 25% of her total equity allocation. Once sold, the proceeds are held in cash.

   (a) Critically appraise this loss aversion strategy.

   (b) Would her system have worked in major financial crises of the past?

   (c) Are there obvious other low cost alternatives for a high net worth individual with high risk tolerance and loss aversion? **(5 marks)**

Part 2 – Taxation and Trusts

Section D (20 marks)

Answer all parts of the question in this section

6. Albert is a UK citizen residing in the UK, having recently returned to the UK on 31 December 2014 after working in Dubai for seven years. Albert has carried out a number of recent transactions and seeks some tax advice from you.

    Explain to Albert the tax implications of the following actions.

    (a) In December 2013, Albert purchased 1000 shares in an Australian mining company for the equivalent of £1.80 per share. He sells these shares on 1 January 2015, the day after he arrived back in the UK, for £3.00 per share. Albert mentioned that the shares were non-UK shares and that he gave the instructions to his broker to sell the shares prior to leaving Dubai. Owing to problems with the computer system at the brokers' office in Dubai, the transaction did not take place until 1 January. **(4 marks)**

    (b) In January 2015, Albert sells his house in the UK which he purchased for £200,000 in December 2005. Albert rented the house to some work colleagues while he was working in Dubai. The sale price is £340,000. In December 2014, Albert moved into a brand new bungalow, when he returned from Dubai. **(4 marks)**

    (c) Albert owns a two-bedroom apartment in Dubai which he has rented out to work colleagues from 31 December 2014 for the equivalent of £500 per week. The apartment is mortgage-free. Albert purchased the apartment in 2006 using his savings. The rent is paid into Albert's bank account with ABC Bank, Luxembourg. Albert intends to allow the rental income to accumulate 'offshore'. **(4 marks)**

    (d) Albert has interest income from a UK bank account amounting to £3,000. He also has interest income from a savings account in Dubai amounting to £6,000. Both relate to the tax year ending on the 5 April 2015. Albert's employment income in the UK is £100,000 per annum. **(4 marks)**

    (e) In January 2015, Albert makes a gift of £10,000 to his niece Mary for her marriage to Anthony. He makes a gift of £5,000 to his nephew Malcolm in February 2015. Albert also makes two gifts to UK charities amounting to £3,000 in March 2015. **(4 marks)**

Section E (10 marks)

Answer any two questions in this section. Each question carries 5 marks

7. Alexander owns an antique table and six chairs which he purchased as a set in 2003 for £90,000. He sells four chairs in May 2014 for £90,000. The value of the table and remaining two chairs in April 2014 is £80,000. Calculate the gain on the chairs that have been sold.

    (5 marks)

8. James dies in December 2014, leaving shares worth £400,000. In March 2015, the executors sell shares in M plc for £100,000 which were valued at £130,000 for probate purposes. They also sold shares in P plc for £25,000 which were valued at £35,000 for probate value purposes. The executors paid £1,250 in commission and fees to the stockbrokers who handled the transactions. Calculate the revised probate value of the shares. **(5 marks)**

9.   Explain the following terms.

    (a)   Bare trust
    (b)   Interest in possession trust
    (c)   Discretionary trust
    (d)   Accumulation and maintenance trust
    (e)   Charitable trust   **(5 marks)**

December 2009 Examination

Part 1 – Portfolio Construction Theory

Section A (40 marks)

Answer all parts of the question in this section

1. For parts (a), (b) and (c), write the capital letter corresponding to your answer clearly.

    (a) If a portfolio is managed so that it grows through a combination of income and capital gain, its investment objective can be best described as:

    A   Capital preservation
    B   Long/short
    C   Total return
    D   Liability-driven   **(1 mark)**

    (b) The inability to sell an asset quickly at a fair price is associated with

    A   Trade failure risk
    B   Liquidity risk
    C   Exchange rate risk
    D   Financial risk   **(1 mark)**

    (c) The equity risk premium is equal to:

    A   The return on a stock minus the risk-free rate
    B   The return on the market minus the risk-free rate
    C   The stock beta times the market risk premium
    D   The stock beta times the risk-free rate   **(1 mark)**

    (d) What is the distinction between an investor's desired return and required return?

                                                                  (3 marks)

    (e) An analyst has collected the following data for two equities, A and B.

	A	B
Expected return	12%	11%
Standard deviation of returns	8%	10%
Beta	1.5	1.0

    The expected return on the equity market is 10% and the risk-free rate for the coming 12 months is 4%.

    Are equities A and B underpriced, overpriced or correctly priced according to the Capital Asset Pricing Model? Show all workings.   **(4 marks)**

    (f) A UK investor is considering the investment suitability of a Yen-denominated Japanese bond. The current exchange rate is 150 Yen to 1 Pound Sterling. Inflation in Japan is 0% and interest rates are 2%. Inflation in the UK is 3% and interest rates are 5%. The investor expects that over the next 12 months interest rates and inflation will not change from the rates above and that whilst the nominal exchange rate will change, the real exchange rate will remain constant. What UK Sterling return will the investor obtain if the Japanese bond is purchased and sold 12 months later? Show all workings.

                                                                  (3 marks)

(g)   One of your fund management clients is a Eurozone-domiciled individual that only wishes to invest in Eurozone-domiciled securities. Based on this client's circumstances you have constructed a portfolio that is 60% Eurozone equities and 40% Eurozone corporate bonds. The Eurozone portfolio equity beta is 1.2. The Eurozone risk-free interest rate is 4%. The Eurozone equity risk premium is 3%. The Eurozone corporate bond risk premium is 1% and the corporate bond illiquidity premium is 0.5%.

What is the expected annual return on the total portfolio for your client? Show all workings.

(4 marks)

(h)   The investment return generating process of commodities is different to that of private equity, real estate and infrastructure projects. Comment and give your opinion.   **(4 marks)**

(i)   Can the market beta be a number other than 1? If so, why; if not, why not?   **(3 marks)**

(j)   The dividend payout ratio for the total market is 65%, the required rate of return is 13% and the expected growth rate of dividends is 8%. What is the current earnings multiple, or prospective P/E ratio? Show all workings.   **(3 marks)**

(k)   An analyst has the following information.

  ▪   The standard deviation of the market's returns is 16%.
  ▪   The standard deviation of Stock A's returns is 30%.
  ▪   The correlation coefficient between the returns on Stock A and the market is 70%.

What is the beta of Stock A? Show all workings.   **(3 marks)**

(l)   What is the current price of a zero coupon bond with a 20 year maturity, a nominal value of £1,000, and a 7% yield to maturity? Show all workings.   **(3 marks)**

(m)   A bond has a current yield of 8% and a price of £1,250. What is the bond's coupon? Show all workings.   **(3 marks)**

(n)   Which investment vehicles are able to use gearing and what are the merits and drawbacks of doing so?   **(4 marks)**

Section B (20 marks)

This question is compulsory

2.   The head of institutional business at your fund management company asks you to design a default fund for a workplace defined contribution pension scheme. The following facts are given.

The investment horizon is long-term.

The average annual return objective over the economic cycle is the UK Consumer Price Index (CPI) plus 2%.

Both traditional and alternative asset classes are permitted.

Fund management charges must be less than or equal to 25 basis points per annum (0.25%).

There needs to be low overall portfolio transaction costs.

Explain the reason behind the selection for each of the asset classes you propose for the default fund. How is each asset class, both of itself and in terms of its marginal contribution to the overall default fund, consistent with the objectives and constraints above? What style of investment have you selected for each asset class, and why?   **(20 marks)**

Section C (10 marks)

Answer any two questions in this section. Each question carries 5 marks

3. A prospective high net worth client telephones you and says she would like you to manage her investment portfolio. You agree and following legal due diligence the account is set up. The client transfers the portfolio from her previous fund manager (an in specie transfer). You do not have the opportunity to meet the client and ascertain her circumstances prior to her travelling on business. She will be out of contact for three weeks. You review her portfolio and discover that 50% of the total portfolio is invested in conventional bonds that will mature within the next three days.

    (a) What investment action would you take for the client, and why?

    (b) Ordinarily, what would have been your preferred course of action when taking on a new client?

    (5 marks)

4. Consider the chart below:

Correlation of selected stock markets with the US equity market (5-year periods from 1971, US$)			
	Correlation with US		
5-year period	Japan	Europe	Europe, Africa, Far East (EAFE)
1971–1975	0.40	0.61	0.59
1976–1980	0.12	0.28	0.36
1981–1985	0.32	0.49	0.46
1986–1990	0.25	0.64	0.44
1991–1995	0.22	0.65	0.47
1996–2000	0.48	0.62	0.66

Source: Solnik B, and McLeavey D (2003), International Investments, Pearson Addison Wesley.

    (a) What are the maximum and minimum values to a correlation coefficient, and why?

    (b) Explain the pattern of correlations in the chart above and the meaning that this has for realised, or actual, portfolio diversification.

    (5 marks)

5. You manage portfolios with a placement value of £250,000 to £500,000 for wealthy individuals.

    (a) What are the advantages and disadvantages of passive or active managed funds rather than individual securities for these clients?

    (b) What are the key investment suitability criteria that you will be looking for when choosing actively managed funds?

    (c) What particular aspects do you need to be mindful of in the construction of the portfolio?

    (5 marks)

Part 2 – Taxation and Trusts

Section D (20 marks)

Answer all parts of the question in this section

6. Charles, a UK-resident individual, is considering leaving the UK for a few years. He comes to you for some advice on 1 April 2015. He intends to sell his dwelling which is located in London, some shares, some 'classic' cars and his collection of UK stamps.

    Charles is planning to move to France.

    Charles wishes to mitigate his tax liabilities and has asked your advice on the following:

    (a) Charles bought his dwelling in March 2009 for £280,000. On 1 April 2015 it is valued at £350,000. He has found a buyer at this price.

    (b) Charles bought 5000 Marks & Spencer shares in June 2005. At the time the shares were valued at £30,000 (or £6 each). He now wishes to sell 2000 of those Marks & Spencer shares for £8,000 (or £4 each).

    (c) Charles has four classic cars – a Jaguar, a Maserati, a Mercedes and an MG Midget.

         He bought the Jaguar in July 1979 for £2,000. It is now valued at £12,000.

         He bought the Maserati in January 1984 for £1,000. It is now valued at £6,000.

         He bought the Mercedes in February 1987 for £1,000. It is now valued at £7,000.

         He bought the MG Midget in December 1990 for £2,500. It is now valued at £1,500.

         Charles has found buyers for each of the cars at these prices.

    (d) Charles has a unique collection of UK stamps covering a variety of subjects accumulated over many years. On 1 April 2015, the stamps are valued at £20,000. The 'flowers' part of the collection was purchased separately on 1 April 2015 for £7,000. The value of the remaining collection on that date was £15,000. Charles is considering selling the whole collection.

         (a) to (d): You are required to write a memorandum to Charles outlining your tax advice in relation to each of these transactions. **(4 marks each)**

    (e) You are also required to give Charles some general tax planning advice in relation to his UK capital gains tax liabilities given that he is leaving the UK and may be returning in a few years. **(4 marks)**

    (Total 20 marks)

Section E (10 marks)

Answer any two questions in this section. Each question carries 5 marks.

7. Explain the relevance of each of these terms for UK taxation purposes:

    (a) Residence
    (b) Domicile
    (c) Fiscal year (give an example)
    (d) Exempt income (give examples)

    (5 marks)

8. Mike and Michele had the following capital gains and losses in 2014/15.

	Mike	Michele
	£	£
Capital gains	10,250	7,500
Capital losses	4,750	9,000

Calculate the amounts chargeable to capital gains tax (if any), and the amount of losses that can be carried forward. **(5 marks)**

9. Explain the uses of offshore funds and discuss how they are treated under the UK's tax system.
(5 marks)

June 2009 Examination

Part 1 – Portfolio Construction Theory

Section A (40 marks)

Answer all parts of the question in this section

1. For parts a, b, and c, write the capital letter corresponding to your answer.

    (a) A bond will have greater volatility when it has a

    A   High coupon and a short maturity
    B   High coupon and a long maturity
    C   Low coupon and a short maturity
    D   Low coupon and a long maturity   **(1 mark)**

    (b) Empirical examination of the relationship between change in stock prices and change in the economy has shown that the relationship is

    A   Weak, and that stock prices turn after the economy does
    B   Weak, and that stock prices turn before the economy does
    C   Strong, and that stock prices turn after the economy does
    D   Strong, and that stock prices turn before the economy does   **(1 mark)**

    (c) The annual interest paid on a bond relative to its prevailing market price is called the

    A   Yield to maturity
    B   Coupon rate
    C   Effective yield
    D   Current yield   **(1 mark)**

    (d) An analyst has calculated the yield to maturity for a coupon paying bond that matures in ten years' time. Is reinvestment risk relevant to the yield the analyst has obtained, and if so why?   **(3 marks)**

    (e) In your opinion, is a risk premium earned by holding foreign currency?   **(3 marks)**

    (f) What is the duration of a zero coupon bond that will mature in five years' time? Explain your answer.   **(3 marks)**

    (g) For a long-term investor, which one of the following do you think will be the very lowest risk asset class?

    ■   Property
    ■   Commodities
    ■   Ten year government bonds
    ■   Ten year inflation-linked government bonds

    Explain your answer.   **(3 marks)**

    (h) If the exchange rate for US dollars in Australia is 0.7927, what is the equivalent quote in the United States for Australian dollars?   **(2 marks)**

    (i) Why do corporate governance experts suggest that large institutional shareholders are partly to blame for the current financial crisis?   **(4 marks)**

    (j) Why are equities a high risk asset class?   **(4 marks)**

(k)   An analyst has the following information.

- The standard deviation of the market returns is 16%.
- The standard deviation of Stock A's returns is 45%.
- The correlation coefficient between the returns on Stock A and the market is 40%.

What is the beta of Stock A? Show all workings.   **(3 marks)**

(l)   Why are equities said to be growth assets?   **(3 marks)**

(m)   Why are equities said to be earnings-linked assets?   **(3 marks)**

(n)   Given the following factor risk premiums and sensitivities, what is the expected return for a portfolio using a three-factor arbitrage pricing theory (APT) model? Show all workings.

Factors	Risk premium to the factors	Portfolio sensitivity to the factors
1	1.5%	1.0
2	3.5%	2.0
3	6%	0.0

The risk free rate is 2.0%.   **(3 marks)**

(o)   £100 is invested in an asset which is expected to generate a return of 7% per annum for ten years. Returns are taxed each year at a rate of 25%. What is the expected after-tax accumulation? Show all workings.   **(3 marks)**

Section B (20 marks)

This question is compulsory

2.   (a)   On a chart with risk measured on the x-axis and return measured on the y-axis, plot the line that shows the different possible combinations of two risky securities when the correlation between the two securities is:

  (i)   Positive 1.0
  (ii)   Negative 1.0
  (iii)   Zero

Explain the effect that these three correlation possibilities will have on the nature of portfolio diversification and risk.

(b)   What is the opportunity set of possible risky portfolios, and how is the efficient frontier of securities derived from this? Annotate your answer using one or more charts.

(c)   How does the shape of the efficient frontier change once a risk-free asset is introduced? Annotate your answer using one or more charts. Would you specify a nominal or real risk-free rate, and would you select a risk-free rate based on a one-week, one-month, several months, one year or several years holding period? Explain your answer.

(d)   How is the efficient frontier constructed and what does it reveal to an investor?

(e)   Would you expect to pay active or passive (index) fund management fees to access the risk and return combinations on the efficient frontier?

(20 marks)

Section C (10 marks)

Answer any two questions in this section. Each question carries 5 marks

3. An analyst has collected the following data for three possible investments.

Stock	Price today	Forecast price one year from today	Dividend	Beta
A	25	31	2	1.6
B	105	110	1	1.2
C	10	10.80	0	0.5

The expected return on the market is 12% and the risk-free rate for the coming 12 months is 4%. The standard deviation of the market portfolio is 40%.

(a) What is the forecasted 12 month total return for Stock A? Show all workings.

(b) What is the covariance of Stock B with the market portfolio? Show all workings.

(c) Using the securities market line, is stock C overvalued, undervalued, or correctly priced? Show all workings. **(5 marks)**

4. A large investor has sought to diversify its portfolio by investing across equity and fixed income assets. The investor has asked one of its risk managers to perform an analysis of the factor risk premiums that explain the additional yield on corporate bonds over government bonds. The risk manager has determined that corporate illiquidity and credit risk factors have similar premiums, but that there are marked differences in the correlation of the credit risk of each bond to the common shares of the corporate issuer.

Company	Corporate bond	Illiquidity factor (%)	Credit risk factor (%)	Correlation of credit risk to underlying common shares
1	A	25	65	10%
2	B	28	62	85%

(a) (i)   What is meant by a risk premium to illiquidity for a corporate bond?
      (ii) What is meant by a risk premium to credit risk for a corporate bond?

(b) What factors might credit risk and equity risk have in common?

(c) If the investor decides to sell one of the bonds, A or B, which is it most likely to sell and why? **(5 marks)**

5. Mumbojumbo plc has issued preference shares at £10 par value. The shares pay a 9% annual dividend. Fefafufi plc has issued preference shares at £10 par value. The shares pay a 10% annual dividend.

(a) Angelica would like to sell her preference shares in Fefafufi plc. Similar preference shares available on the stock exchange are currently yielding a 7% dividend. What is each preference share in Fefafufi plc worth?

(b) Recent deterioration in the performance of the economy and in Mumbojumbo means that investors now require a 10% return. What price would you be willing to pay for one preference share if you receive your first dividend one year from now?

(c) Why might a risk-averse investor want to hold preference shares rather than ordinary shares? **(5 marks)**

Part 2 – Taxation and Trusts

Section D (20 marks)

Answer all parts of the question in this section

6. Tommy is an Italian national but is now resident in the UK and is a high net worth individual. He is 62 years of age and plans to retire when he is 70.

    Tommy has a number of properties in European countries but none in the UK. Their value is in excess of £10,000,000. He regularly receives dividends from shares in excess of £200,000 per annum from a varied portfolio of shares in UK and international companies. He also maintains over £4,000,000 in cash deposits in banks around the world in a variety of currencies. He earns interest annually on these accounts.

    Tommy seeks your advice on establishing a new business in the UK. The new business will provide services to website designers in the UK and around the world. He has some initial questions for you concerning the taxation of this new business and his future exit strategy.

    (a) What business format should Tommy choose and what are the tax implications of the various choices? **(5 marks)**

    (b) What ongoing UK tax considerations must Tommy consider? **(5 marks)**

    (c) What UK inheritance tax planning should Tommy consider? **(5 marks)**

    (d) What UK capital gains tax planning should Tommy consider? **(5 marks)**

Section E (10 marks)

Answer any two questions in this section. Each question carries 5 marks

7. For the Trustee Act 2000:

    (a) Explain why it was introduced.
    (b) What major changes did it bring about?
    (c) What special obligations did it impose on trustees?
    (d) Explain the powers of delegation and insurance granted to trustees.
    (e) Explain the duty of care imposed on trustees.

    (5 marks)

8. James Wilkinson died in July 2014. Prior to his death, James set up a discretionary trust (in March 2009), transferring £500,000 into the trust. There were no other lifetime transfers.

    Calculate any inheritance tax payable as a result of the transfer. **(5 marks)**

9. Explain the following capital gains tax reliefs:

    (a) Holdover relief
    (b) Principal Private Residence relief
    (c) Exempt gifts
    (d) Enterprise Investment Scheme relief
    (e) Taper relief

    (5 marks)

December 2008 Examination

Part 1 – Portfolio Construction Theory

Section A (40 marks)

Answer all parts of the question in this section

1. The chart below illustrates the relationship between portfolio risk and diversification.

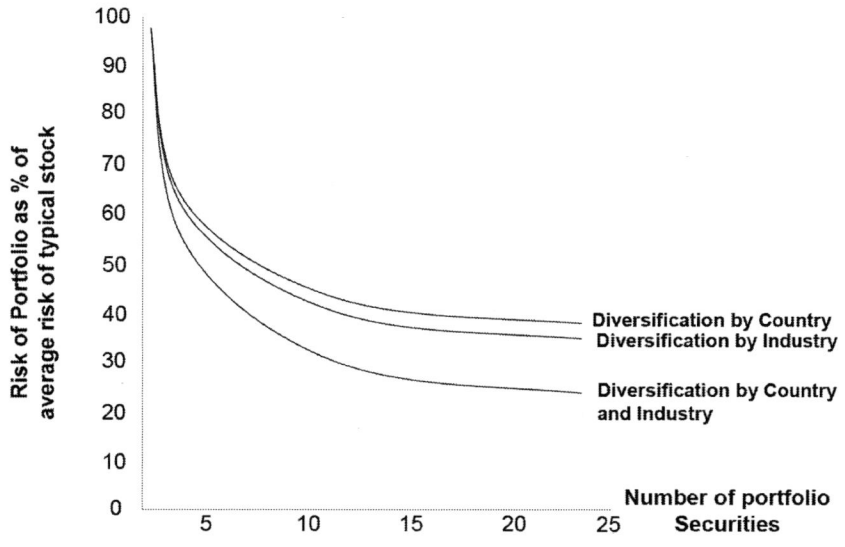

Source: Cavaglia, S; Brightman, C; and Aked, M (2000). Financial Analysts Journal, September-October p41-54

(a) What principal outcomes about risk and diversification can be observed from the chart?

(3 marks)

(b) List three reasons for a positive relationship between the value of portfolio costs and the number of portfolio securities. **(3 marks)**

(c) If the correlation coefficient for two securities A and B is 0.27, which of the following four portfolio risk formulae is most correct and why?

   (i) $\sigma_{a+b} = \sqrt{p_a{}^2\sigma_a{}^2 + p_b{}^2\sigma_b{}^2 + 2p_a p_b Cov_{ab}}$

   (ii) $\sigma_{a+b} = \sqrt{p_a{}^2\sigma_a{}^2 + p_b{}^2\sigma_b{}^2}\ Cov_{ab}$

   (iii) $\sigma_{a+b} = p_a\sigma_a + p_b\sigma_b$

   (iv) $\sigma_{a+b} = \sqrt{p_a{}^2\sigma_a{}^2 + p_b{}^2\sigma_b{}^2}$

   Where p = weight of security and σ = standard deviation **(3 marks)**

(d) The following chart illustrates the annual risk and return for two securities, A and B, and their correlation coefficient.

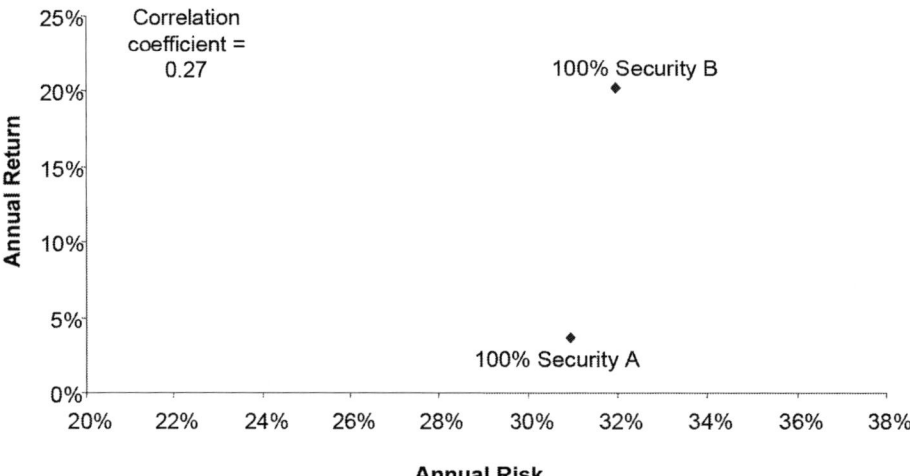

Efficient Frontier for Two Securities, A and B

Draw a rough copy of the chart in your exam answer book. Draw the locus of points that you would expect the efficient frontier to comprise for combinations of the two securities. Justify the shape of the efficient frontier you have drawn. **(4 marks)**

(e) In the example above, (d), suppose there exists a third security, C, which is a risk-free asset with an annualised return of 2.5%. Suppose also that Securities A, B and C are the only assets in the market and that investors can borrow without limit at the risk-free rate. On the same chart used to answer (d) above:

(i) Draw the capital market line.

(ii) In words, justify the shape of the capital market line you have drawn.

(iii) Annotate on the chart and explain where you would expect to find investors located and not located. **(4 marks)**

(f) If the risk of security A is 31%, the risk of security B 32%, and the correlation between securities A and B is 0.27, what is their covariance? Assume that risk is measured as standard deviation. **(3 marks)**

(g) What are the principal reasons why an investor might select a portfolio from the opportunity set that does not reside on the efficient frontier? **(4 marks)**

Parts (h) to (j) refer to the paragraph below:

Peter Shrew owns a small engineering company. He is setting up a trust based defined contribution occupational pension scheme for his employees. He has selected you as fund manager for the pension scheme's assets. Prior to his first meeting with you, Peter performs an Internet search on the legislative background surrounding corporate governance and responsible investment. Peter takes the results of three Internet searches to his meeting with you in order to receive comment on them.

(h) The result of the first search is:

Statutory Instrument 1999 No. 1849

Trustees of occupational pension schemes are to disclose in the Statement of Investment Principles:

'The extent (if at all) to which social, environmental and ethical considerations are taken into account in the selection, retention and realisation of investments'

Advise Peter whether this is legislative or voluntary, and what investment action the pension scheme needs to take. **(4 marks)**

(i) The result of the second search is:

The UK Corporate Governance Code

Section E.1 of the Corporate Governance Code states that:

'There should be a dialogue with shareholders based on the mutual understanding of objectives. The board as a whole has responsibility for ensuring that a satisfactory dialogue with shareholders takes place.'

Advise Peter whether this is legislative or voluntary, and what the Institutional Shareholder Committee Principles require fund managers to do. **(4 marks)**

(j) The result of the third search is:

The 2007 Institutional Shareholders' Committee's "The Responsibilities of Institutional Shareholders and Agents – Statement of Principles"

On voting, The Principles state that:

'Institutional shareholders and/or agents should vote all shares held directly or on behalf of clients wherever practicable to do so.'

Advise Peter whether this is legislative or voluntary, and in what instances shares might not be practicable to vote? **(4 marks)**

(k) Describe the principal agent relationship that motivates the initiatives associated with the role of institutional shareholders in the corporate governance process. **(4 marks)**

Section B (20 marks)

This question is compulsory

2. Describe the efficient market hypothesis and the classic forms it takes. For each of the classic forms of market efficiency, which investment styles listed in a) and b) below are most appropriate and why?

(a) Active investment styles:

    (i)   Growth
    (ii)   Value based on informational inefficiency
    (iii) Value based on corporate inefficiency
    (iv) Small capitalisation securities
    (v)   Large capitalisation securities

(b) Passive index investment style **(20 marks)**

Section C (10 marks)

Answer any two questions in this section. Each question carries 5 marks

3. A UK investor is considering the investment suitability of a Yen-denominated Japanese bond. The current exchange rate is 150 Yen to 1 Pound Sterling. Inflation in Japan is 0% and interest rates are 2%. Inflation in the UK is 3% and interest rates are 5%. The investor expects that over the next 12 months interest rates and inflation will not change from the rates above and that whilst the nominal exchange rate will change, the real exchange rate will remain constant. Assume no coupon payment.

    (a) Will the Yen appreciate or depreciate and by what percentage over the next 12 months?

    (b) What is the local currency Yen return on the Japanese bond?

    (c) What is the UK Pound Sterling return to the investor from purchasing and holding the Japanese bond? **(5 marks)**

4. Sheila Timsbury-Higgins plans to retire in ten years' time. Her retirement income will be the annuity she purchases with the proceeds of her personal pension after she has taken the 25% cash allowance. Her personal pension is currently 100% invested in equities. She asks for your advice about an appropriate path for the asset allocation (sometimes referred to a 'flight path' or 'glide path') of her pension given her annuity and cash allowance aspirations.

    (a) Copy the table below in your exam answer book. Propose and input a percentage allocation to the various assets as retirement approaches. For example, you could choose a stable equal weighted allocation and input 33.33% in each cell. Each row should sum to 100%.

Asset Allocation for Sheila Timsbury-Higgins			
Years to Retirement	Equities	Bonds	Cash
10			
8			
6			
4			
2			
0			

    (b) Explain the principal motivations for the asset allocation path you have selected for Sheila. **(5 marks)**

5. (a) What is the beta of a stock if the covariance of the stock with the market portfolio is 0.25, and the standard deviation of the market returns is 0.3? Show all workings.

    (b) What is the total risk (standard deviation) of a portfolio if its systematic risk (standard deviation) is 19% and unsystematic risk (standard deviation) 6%? Show all workings.

    (c) The recent financial crisis emphasises that many single stock and market return distributions tend to exhibit leptokurtosis and negative skewness. How does this empirical finding caution against the reliance of standard deviation as a measure of the dispersion of stock returns? **(5 marks)**

Part 2 – Taxation and Trusts

Section D (20 marks)

Answer all parts of the question in this section

6.   Gerry is a self-employed musician and received income from working in an orchestra in the year of £50,000. In addition he received overseas income from two sources. He received £5,000 from a concert he played in Germany; this was after tax deductions of £5,000. He received £2,000 from a Mozart concert he played in Austria; this was after tax deductions of £200. Gerry is single and has two sisters, Kate and Amanda. Gerry wants you to calculate his UK tax liability for the year.

Gerry has also come to you for some inheritance tax advice and is keen to purchase a 100-acre farm in Shropshire. He would also like to make maximum use of his inheritance tax exemptions and reliefs and to receive some basic inheritance tax planning advice. He has heard of the terms 'potentially exempt transfers' and 'exempt lifetime transfers' and enquires about their meaning. Gerry' sisters are his only relatives.

(a)   Calculate Gerry's UK income tax liability for the year (2014/15).   **(4 marks)**

(b)   Explain self-assessment and payments on account to Gerry.   **(4 marks)**

(c)   Explain the terms 'potentially exempt transfer' and 'exempt lifetime transfers', giving examples.   **(4 marks)**

(d)   List the main inheritance tax exemptions and reliefs that may be of interest to Gerry.   **(4 marks)**

(e)   Give Gerry some basic inheritance tax planning ideas, given that his sisters are his only relatives.   **(4 marks)**

Section E (10 marks)

Answer any two questions in this section. Each question carries 5 marks

7.   James is single and has a salary of £20,000 in 2014/15. He also receives gross interest income of £7,000 and dividends with a gross value of £33,000.

Calculate his total tax liability.   **(5 marks)**

8.   Catherine bought 2,500 shares in the Harvis company for £25,000 in November 1990. In April 1992, there was a 1 for 5 rights issue at a subscription price of £8 per share. Catherine subscribed for the 500 shares to which she was entitled. Subsequently, Catherine sold 2,000 shares for £30,000 in May 2014.

Calculate the gain on the disposal of the shares (assuming they are non-business assets).   **(5 marks)**

9.   Explain the concepts of 'residence' and 'domicile' and their relevance for UK tax purposes to individuals.   **(5 marks)**

June 2008 Examination

Part 1 – Portfolio Construction Theory

Section A (40 marks)

Answer all parts of the question in this section

1. Investment management firm Tip Top manages an active and passive Europe, Africa and Far East (EAFE) equity portfolio for a large US pension scheme. The active portfolio's benchmark employs free float adjusted market capitalisation weights. Pinnacle's policy is to not allow the active portfolio weights to deviate by more than 15% from the benchmark weights. An internal review meeting is held to discuss performance to date and future strategy for the EAFE portfolios. Attendees at the meeting include the Chief Investment Officer, the fund managers and an in-house statistician. The Chief Investment Officer is presented with Tables 1 and 2 below.

Table 1

Descriptive statistics for the actively managed EAFE portfolio		
Market	*Market weights*	*36-month return performance*
Europe	0.7	15.30%
Far East	0.2	21.20%
Africa	0.1	11.10%

Table 2

Performance statistics for the active EAFE portfolio, passive EAFE portfolio and EAFE benchmark			
	Active portfolio	*Passive portfolio*	*Benchmark*
36 month return performance		17.10%	17.40%
Monthly standard deviation of returns	3.90%	3.65%	3.60%
Correlation of monthly returns relative to benchmark	0.82	0.99	1

The portfolio information contained in Tables 1 and 2 are total returns (ie dividends reinvested), net of fees and costs, US dollar denominated, and for a full 36 months. The benchmark has no fees or costs. At the meeting the statistician presents the output of an unconstrained optimisation for an Active EAFE portfolio. The optimiser software recommends the following market weights.

Far East: 0.4
Africa: 0.4
Europe: 0.2

(a) What is the 36–month return for the active portfolio? **(2 marks)**

(b) What is the annualised standard deviation of returns for the active portfolio, passive portfolio and benchmark? (Show all workings) **(3 marks)**

(c) What is the annualised return for the active portfolio, passive portfolio and benchmark? (Show all workings) **(3 marks)**

(d)   One of the fund managers would like the active portfolio to have a growth bias. What is the investment philosophy behind growth investing and how does it relate to thematic investing? **(4 marks)**

(e)   One of the fund managers would like the active portfolio to have a value bias. What is the investment philosophy behind value investing and what is the difference between a value strategy based on informational inefficiency and a value strategy based on economic inefficiency? **(4 marks)**

(f)   Why might an unconstrained optimisation on the EAFE benchmark suggest a fundamentally different allocation to the current active portfolio? **(5 marks)**

(g)   What percentage of the active portfolio's total risk is company-specific? **(3 marks)**

(h)   Write a short paragraph on each of the three indexation techniques that Tip Top might employ to construct its passive portfolio. **(7 marks)**

(i)   What is a tracking error, and why would the US pension scheme client become more concerned as the tracking error on the passive fund moves further away from zero? **(5 marks)**

(j)   Why will the standard deviation and the return of the passive portfolio not equal those of the benchmark, unless by chance? **(4 marks)**

Section B (20 marks)

This question is compulsory

2.   Using the terms in (a) to (f) below, describe the effects of adding alternative asset classes to a conventional portfolio of equities and fixed income. Illustrate your answer with examples from private equity, infrastructure funds, commodities, and hedge funds.

   (a)   Expected return
   (b)   Diversification
   (c)   Risk
   (d)   Liquidity
   (e)   Divisibility
   (f)   Transaction costs (including fees)

(20 marks)

Section C (10 marks)

Answer any two questions in this section. Each question carries 5 marks.

3. Mary Jeane, a professional portfolio manager, is about to meet David Tate, a new client who currently has a UK £700,000 portfolio. List as a series of points the investment planning process that Mary Jeane should undertake in order to construct a suitable investment portfolio for David Tate. **(5 marks)**

4. Assume you have the following information.

	Stock A	Stock B
Estimated return	12%	11%
Standard deviation of returns	8%	10%
Beta	1.5	1.0

    Also assume that you expect the market and Treasury bills to return 10% and 4% respectively. Are stocks A and B underpriced or overpriced according to the Capital Asset Pricing Model (CAPM)? Show all workings. **(5 marks)**

5. (a) What are the principal financial risks to a long-term holder of gilt edged securities and a long-term holder of UK corporate bonds of equal value and maturity?

    (b) What are the principal financial risks to a holder of shares and bonds in the same company in which the interest rate risk of the bonds has been fully hedged?

    Explain your answers. **(5 marks)**

Part 2 – Taxation and Trusts

Section D (20 marks)

Answer all parts of the question in this section.

6. John has a wife, Mary, and three children, Andy, Billy and Cathy. Andy has a wife, Susie, and three children, Xavier, Yvonne and Zena. Billy and Cathy are both unmarried and have no children. All reside in the UK.

    John, now aged 65, is a high net worth individual and has been a client of LMN Advisers for many years. He has recently made an appointment to discuss his retirement plans and to obtain some initial tax planning advice on his wealth portfolio.

    John has been diagnosed with cancer and, although the disease has been caught at its early stages, he is fearful that it may shorten his life and that he needs to organise his affairs and prepare for the worst case scenario.

    John's assets include:

    - Family home worth around £2m. This is jointly owned by John and Mary.

    - Country Cottage in Spain worth around £750,000.

    - Marks and Spencer shares purchased on the following dates.

        - 17 January 1988 at 85p per share 5000 shares

        - 22 February 1991 at 118p per share 3000 shares

        - 14 October 1995 at 212p per share 1000 shares

        - 26 September 2003 at 422p per share 1000 shares

    - Cash in bank £1,350,000 earning interest at 5%.

    - Pension £100,000 a year payable from age 65.

    In September 2014, John has sent a list of questions in advance of the meeting and asks your advice concerning a number of tax matters.

    (a) How will sales of Marks and Spencer shares be taxed in the UK if John sells them in tranches of 2,000 shares? **(4 marks)**

    (b) What general inheritance tax planning advice can you give John relating to his asset portfolio? **(4 marks)**

    (c) In relation to John's annual pension of £100,000, is there any income tax saving advice that you can give him? **(4 marks)**

    (d) In relation to John's children and grandchildren, John is keen to establish a trust fund of £1,000,000 to cover any education, emergency financial and healthcare needs of his children and grandchildren, and any future grandchildren. What advice on establishing a trust can you give him and what are the long-term tax advantages of using such a trust? **(4 marks)**

    (e) What tax implications are there for John if he sells the Spanish cottage? **(4 marks)**

Section E (10 marks)

Answer any two questions in this section. Each question carries 5 marks.

7.   Mr T is a teacher and he received income from this profession in the year 2014/15 of £50,000. In addition, he received overseas income from two sources. He received £7,000 from the first source, after tax deductions of £3,000 in the overseas country. He received £13,000 from the second source, after tax deductions of £4,500 overseas. Mr T is single.

Calculate Mr T's UK tax liability for the year.   **(5 marks)**

8.   A non-business asset acquired in May 1988, at a cost of £38,000, is disposed of in June 2014 for £92,000.

Calculate the gain or loss.   **(5 marks)**

9.   Mrs B dies on 1 December 2014, leaving shares worth £500,000. The executor sold for £27,000 some of these shares in XYZ plc, which were valued at £60,000 for probate purposes. Subsequently, some additional shares in ABC plc with a probate value of £38,000 were sold for £49,000. The commission and other dealing costs on the sales came to £800.

Calculate the revised probate value of the shares.   **(5 marks)**

Answers

June 2014 Examination Answers

Examiner's comments

The task of this exam is to assess knowledge and understanding of portfolio construction within wealth management against the unit syllabus. Occasionally the exam may draw on a small number of low mark questions from the Financial Markets syllabus or the level assumed to enter for the Chartered qualification. The exam does not test the Applied Wealth Management syllabus.

On successful completion of this exam candidates will have demonstrated strong conceptual and applied knowledge and understanding of the principal analytical tools of portfolio construction, familiarity and comfort with the application of quantitative and qualitative problems in portfolio construction, and an ability to rigorously analyse problems in portfolio construction. Up-to-date knowledge and understanding of significant financial events and developments may be examined.

Questions on taxation will tend to comprise 10% to 30% of the exam, either stand-alone or integrated within another question. For the first time, the Summer 2014 exam incorporated questions on taxation. Questions will continue on tax issues relevant to major asset classes, securities, funds and strategies. The focus is taxation of the portfolio / fund / strategy rather than taxation of the individual. There may occasionally be a question concerning CGT or IHT. Where there are, a low number of marks is likely to be allocated and this is more likely to appear as an MCQ. Questions on tax in the exam focused on VAT of segregated v. pooled funds, taxation of preference shares, Gilts, OEICs, reporting funds, and IHT, for a total of 14 marks. Numerical questions will tend to comprise 20% to 50% of the exam. Questions that examine charts and tables will tend to comprise 5% to 20% of the exam. Interpretative questions will tend to comprise 20% to 50% of the exam.

Part 1 – Portfolio Construction Theory

Section A

1. **Multiple choice questions**

   (a) **C** A steadily rising market leads to lower volatility.

   (b) **A** This option (A) allows you to check whether the client understands the features and risks of the proposed investment.

   (c) **C** Of all the stocks, Stock C has the lowest correlation with the other stocks.

   (d) **B** There is no 10% tax credit on share buyback proceeds.

   (e) **A** Share buyback is not a significant indicator of value.

   (f) **A** The question concerned the conversion value of a convertible bond that has a par value of £100, a current market price of £28, a current price of the issuing company's stock of 64p and a conversion ratio of 25 shares.

   Conversion price = £28 / 25 = £1.15

   £1.15 / 64p = 1.75

   Thus, the share price must rise by 75% to reach the conversion price.

   (g) **C** Slippery 1-year bonds: 4.1% – 2.2% = 1.9%. Wheels 5-year bonds: 4.5% – 2.8% = 1.7%.

   (h) **B** £/US\$ × CAD/£ = CAD/\$US.

   Thus, CAD/\$US = 0.6 × 1.85 = 1.11

   Therefore, \$US/CAD = 1/1.11 = 0.90

   (i) **B** The answer follows from the name 'constant dividend growth model'.

   (j) **B** Loss aversion was first proposed to explain the endowment effect – the effect of people placing a higher value on a good that they own than on an identical good that they do not own. According to prospect theory, losses have a greater emotional impact than an equivalent amount of gains.

   (k) **C** A continuation strategy is an approach to active management that tries to exploit a positive serial correlation in asset prices.

   (l) **D** Barber and Odean wrote a paper on this topic entitled '*Boys will be boys: gender, overconfidence, and common stock investment*'. Theoretical models predict that overconfident investors trade excessively. Psychological research demonstrates that, in areas such as finance, men are more overconfident than women. Barber and Odean found that trading reduces men's net returns by 2.65 percentage points a year, as compared with 1.72 percentage points for women.

   (m) **C** Choice architecture 'nudges' the consumer to make or to become aware of particular choices.

   (n) **D** If interest rates are expected to fall, the firm is more likely to call the issue and to re-finance at lower rates.

   (o) **B** 4.50 × 0.8 / 127.33 = 2.83%

   (p) **A** The tax treatment is the same for the two types of fund.

BPP LEARNING MEDIA

(q)   **A**   Reporting funds pay CGT on disposals and income tax on reported income. Non-reporting funds pay no CGT, but they pay income tax on income distributed and gains on disposal.

(r)   **A**   In the special case of uncorrelated assets (Correlation = 0), the variance of the return on the portfolio is the sum of the squares of the fractions held in each asset multiplied by the variance of the return on the asset: to combine the risks of completely independent (uncorrelated) returns/securities, we must combine the variances appropriately weighted.

(s)   **B**   The PET uses £100,000 of the nil rate band. £225,000 of the nil rate band remains, and so £275,000 of the estate remains to be taxed, at 40% = £110,000.

(t)   **C**   Mental accounting is the name given to the propensity of individuals to organise their world into separate 'mental accounts'. Investors tend to treat each element of their investment portfolio separately. This can lead to inefficient decision-making.

Section B

2. **Investment return forecasts**

   Examiner's comment. This question asked for candidates' understanding and application of compounding and annualised numbers, an area that is regularly tested.

   The average annual forecast for nominal UK medium term Government bonds for the next five years was 1.3%. However, the actual performance in year 1 = − 4%. Presuming that the forecast for the five years remains unchanged, the new revised forward return must look like the chart below.

   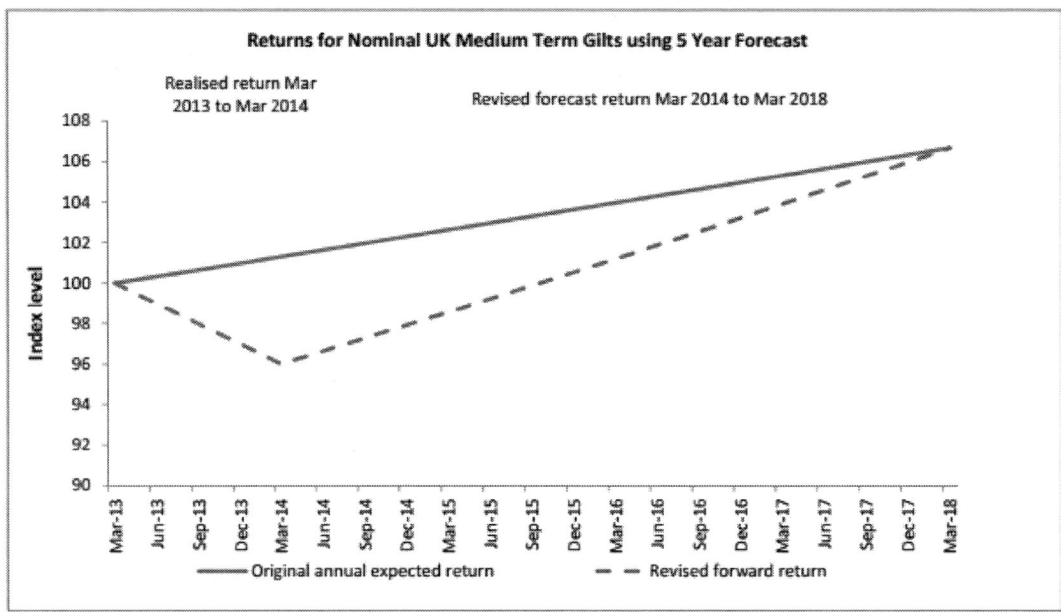

   The original expected total return over the five years is 6.67%. [(1.013%)^5 = 1.0667]. Starting at an index value of 100, the index will be 106.67

   But the market fell 4% in Year 1. Starting at an index value of 100, the index at the end of Year 1 will be 96.

   The new expected total return over next four years is (106.67 / 96)$^{0.25}$ −1 = 2.67%.

   An alternative answer, for which good marks were given, was 6.67% − 4% = 10.67%.

   (1+ 10.67%)$^{0.25}$ − 1 = 2.57%.

   (For this basic but extremely real-life manipulation of expected v. actual performance, five marks were awarded.)

3. **Earnings yield gap**

   Examiner's comment. The question was generally well answered. The question concerned the Fed model as a valuation tool for switching into and out of equities.

   (a)   There is no perfect way of measuring the value of an asset class, but a popular metric for measuring that of bonds and equities is the earnings yield gap, or the so-called Fed model. This compares the forward equity earnings yield, or the inverse of the price/earnings ratio, to the bond yield (a risk-free asset). The measure has historically been good, but not without problems. While often technically correct, the magnitude of the signal has at times been weak and at times strong. For example, the model correctly predicted each 4 major market turning points since 1995, but the magnitude of the signal was strong for 2 and weak for 2, so investors are likely to have missed these without other intelligence. For a given equity yield, the earnings yield gap can be used to identify zones of under and overvaluation and to forecast possible forthcoming market adjustments. A yield outside of + 4 to − 2 is often taken as a signal of major pending market adjustment.

The earnings yield gap is easy to understand, apply, and consistent with discounted cash flow models that show an inverse relationship between value and the discount rate − with the earnings yield being adjusted by a risk-free government interest rate as a proxy for a discount factor of future earnings. The model assumes the partial predictability of stock returns, which many empirical studies confirm.

(b)   *Cyclically adjusting*

Earnings should arguably be smoothed over something like a 10-year horizon just like the Shiller PE. This measures the average of the past 10 years real company profits to the current market price. The idea of cyclically adjusting is to smooth out highs and lows by looking across the economic cycle. This avoids the standard P/E problem of shares looking expensive when profits collapse in a recession, and cheap when profits are at their peak − usually the opposite of the truth. Ten years is an arbitrary period, and there are of course objections.

Inflation adjusting

To address the criticism that bond yields are nominal while profits have some inflation link, a specification of the equity earnings yield should arguably be employed that controls for inflation. The numerator and denominator of each component of the equity earnings yield is often adjusted for inflation.

4.   **Dividends**

Examiner's comment. Some scripts sorted companies by market capitalisation, sector or valuation. Weaker scripts focused only on market beta.

In order to determine the quality and sustainability of dividends, we should focus on the cash flow coverage of dividends paid on common stock. This provides key information about the capacity to maintain dividend if growth slows. Cash flow coverage of the dividend paid is important to focus on for it is a predictor of future dividend and payout. Information on cash flow coverage is found in the cash flow statement.

Three sources of cash flow are key:

▪   Operating activities: the cash effects of transactions that go to determine net income

▪   Investing activities: buying (and selling) property, plant, and equipment; acquiring and disposing of securities of other entities

▪   Financing activities: issuance and reacquisition of a firm's debt and capital stock

Assuming that cash dividends are paid only after net debt repayments, the task is to assess whether dividends are being paid from operating, investing and issuance cash flows or whether the beginning cash balance is needed to make the payment.

No dividend effect companies may be companies whose dividends are fully covered from operating and investing cash flow net of any cash outflow from debt repayments and net of a decrease in bank deposits. Company growth rate may also be relevant − a dividend paying company with slow grow this less likely to be affected by significantly lower growth forecasts.

Moderate dividend effect companies may be those whose dividends are not fully covered from operating and investing cash flow and that are likely to require additional net cash inflow from issuance. A dividend paying company with moderate growth is likely to be affected by sudden and significant lower growth forecasts.

High dividend effect companies may be those whose dividends are not fully covered from operating, investing and issuance cash flows and for whom the beginning cash balance is used to fund the dividend. This last category is most at risk of a dividend cut, though companies that have a large cash balance could continue to pay dividends even with a 'low quality' dividend profile. A dividend paying company with high growth is likely to be most affected by sudden and significant lower growth forecasts.

5. **Asset pricing model**

Expected return = 1.5% + 1.2% × 1.0 + 2.1% × 2.0 + 2.0% × 0.5 = 7.9%

6. **Reasons for issuing convertible debt**

Examiner's comment. In order to understand the degree of diversification of a convertible bond portfolio, we need to know how similar the companies that issue them are. Good answers started with a short description of convertible bonds and their characteristics. This was followed by a discussion about which companies have a higher propensity to issue.

Companies in the following circumstances are likely to issue convertible debt.

- Companies that believe they can benefit from lower debt capital financing costs because their future equity is attractive. Management try to signal that the company's future prospects are more positive than the market believes.

- Companies with shareholders who do not want immediate earnings dilution. If the equity price does rise above conversion, then earnings are likely to have risen substantially, which is more palatable to dilution averse shareholders. If stock is from Treasury then no dilution, plus debt is extinguished so the balance sheet is altered.

- Companies with directors and/or owners who wish to keep control of the company while small and rapidly growing but who are happy to give this up in the future.

- A company with a low credit rating that believes it has high growth prospects. If growth prospects are fulfilled, the debt will not need to be paid back.

- A company with a lack of fixed assets as security for the debt. The conversion rights help the company to issue unsecured debt without prohibitive coupon and servicing costs.

- A company that wishes greater alignment of interests between bondholders and shareholders concerning the risk-taking of the company.

7. **Capital asset pricing model**

(a) Required return for Stock A = 1.5% + 0.8 × (5.0% − 1.5%) = 4.3%. The expected return for Stock A is 5.5%. Stock A is undervalued. This is above the SML.

Required return for Stock B = 1.5% + 1.4 × (5.0% − 1.5%) = 6.4%. The expected return for Stock B is 7.5%. Stock B is undervalued. This is above the SML.

(b) Security Market Line (SML): X-axis is beta; Y-axis is the expected/required return.

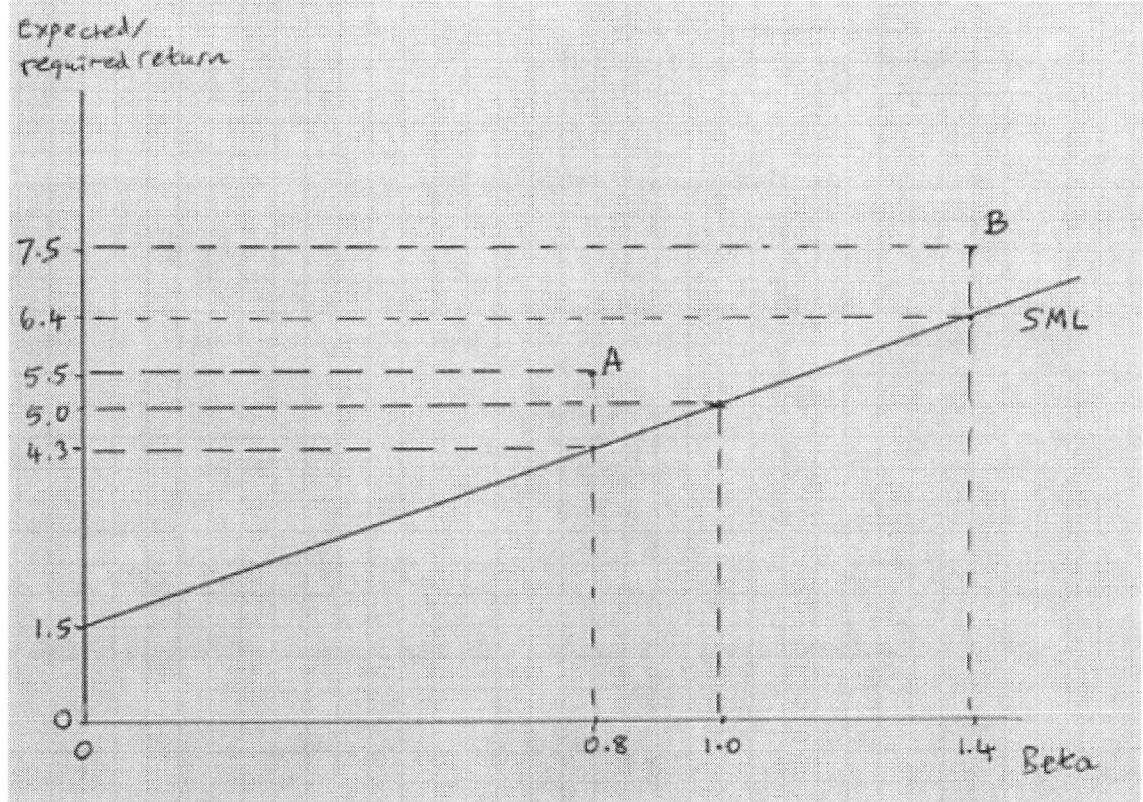

8. **Fund managers and VAT**

    VAT at the standard rate of 20% is paid on top of the relevant transaction value of certain goods and services.

    Investment management services provided through pooled funds and insurance wrappers are VAT-exempt, including OEICs, authorised unit trusts, and closed-end investment funds such as investment trust companies (ITCs). Due to their use of pooled funds, defined contribution pension schemes will not usually pay VAT on investment management services.

    Discretionary, segregated investment management services such as segregated investment mandates managed through external asset managers are not exempt from VAT on the annual management charge (AMC).

    Where the AMC and transaction costs are periodically billed together, the European Court of Justice (ECJ) recently confirmed an earlier opinion of the Advocate General that the management of a discretionary portfolio service and the buying and selling of securities within that service consists of two elements that are so closely linked that they form a single economic supply. This means that the AMC and transaction costs should be billed together and VAT added to the total amount.

    Where the segregated arrangement accrues separately per transaction for dealing and the separate transaction costs can be identified, then no VAT is payable on the transaction costs. VAT is then payable only on the AMC. Most investment managers who used to invoice by the former method have now changed to separate invoicing.

9. **Preference shares and tax**

    Preference shares are a return of profit, as dividends in the hands of the shareholder. Under IFRS, they will be shown as equity and will sit above the line in the accounts. This means that the usual dividend 10% notional tax credit is attached. The 10% tax credit is non-reclaimable. The dividend tax treatment is the same as other shares.

The capital tax treatment is also the same as other shares, ie. Gains are subject to capital gains tax. Preference shares can be held in tax wrappers, such as a stocks and shares ISA or a self-invested personal pension (SIPP). As with ordinary shares, buyers of UK-listed preference shares pay 0.5% stamp duty.

Zero coupon preference shares may be interesting to additional-rate income tax clients, for there is then a significant tax difference between the additional-rate income tax rate (45%) and the higher CGT rate (28%).

The tax position means preference shares are more like equity than bonds.

10. **Fund performance**

(a)   Information ratio = Active return / Tracking error

Where:

Active return is (Fund – Benchmark)

Tracking error is the Standard deviation of the active return.

The annual tracking error of 1.41% is provided in the question. We then need to calculate the annual fund return and the annual benchmark return. One way is to create an index of returns, as follows.

	Return to manager	Return to index	Fund	Index
			100.00	100.00
Mar	−0.95%	−0.012	99.05	98.80
Jun	1.25%	0.018	100.29	100.58
Sep	1.55%	0.004	101.84	100.98
Dec	2.05%	0.015	103.93	102.50

Information ratio = 3.93% − 2.50% / 1.41% = 1.014

(b)   The information ratio (IR) measures a portfolio manager's ability to generate excess returns relative to a benchmark by looking at the active bets taken. It attempts to identify consistency of fund manager performance. The ratio identifies if a manager has beaten the benchmark by a lot in a few months or a little every month (because this will be reflected in the standard deviation of the return difference). The higher the IR, the more consistent is a manager.

The IR can be used as an indicator of active or passive (index) management style.

An index fund would have an IR close to 0 because there is little or no active return. Many 'closet' active managers have an average IR of + or − 0.2.

Rarely is the number + or − 0.5 or more. In this case, there is a high information ratio of 1.01, and so the style is certainly active.

(c)   The active bets from the benchmark have been well executed in general, because in only one quarter (Quarter 2) is the active return negative. The consistent out-performance is a good sign.

Part 2 – Taxation and Trusts

Section C

11. **Pension scheme asset allocation**

    Examiner's comment. Candidates scoring high marks set out the policy, process, and justifications, before delivering a solution. Those who simply produced a new allocation with little explanation as to why tended not to score high marks.

    The current allocation is 40% bond assets, 55% growth assets and 5% cash. An initial question concerns whether this allocation is right or wrong, given the objectives and constraints of the fund and, if so, how and why? Of the bond assets, half is in Government bonds and half in corporate bonds. Of the growth assets (equities), the bulk is in developed markets equities. Government bonds and developed market equities have relatively low volatility, thus helping to ensure the fund's objective of volatility not exceeding 15%. Additionally, Government bonds and developed market equities have relatively low costs within their respective categories.

    (One set of candidates successfully argued the current allocation was right and scored well for doing so. A second set of candidates argued that the allocation to bonds and growth-seeking assets was about right but that some recycling was needed within the bond weighting and within the growth asset weighting. We then need to explain the motivation behind the recycling, which few candidates did well.

    There are some issues to consider if the asset allocation is modified.

    Does recycling involve a change to long-term asset allocation or is this tactical asset allocation?

    Is the recycling contrarian or pro-cyclical, ie: Is the recycling designed to up-risk the portfolio because the pension fund is a long-term investor, a patient form of capital, and because risky asset classes appear overlooked right now? Or is the aim a risk-off strategy to recycle away from corporate bonds towards UK Government bonds?

    Market timing right can be very difficult to get right, so are you confident that you can make the switch out of safer assets and into risky assets in time?

    (These are some of the points that the examiner was hoping to see explained.)

    It is possible to argue for a change in the allocation between cash, bonds, and growth assets. (A third set of candidates did this.) The changed allocation could involve increasing cash, emerging market equities and property, while reducing developed market equities and bonds. It needs to be made clear whether the proposal is a new long-term asset allocation or a tactical asset allocation.

    If a move to higher cash levels is proposed, then this should be justified.

    Why should members of a pension scheme pay annual management charges (AMCs) and other charges to invest in cash? Why is the liquidity needed, given that the funds are locked away in a pension scheme?

    A further point is: If the long-term investment objective is inflation + 3%, does a high weight to emerging markets and property increase the risk of failing to achieving this?

12. **Pension scheme asset allocation**

    Examiner's comment.. All funds were recommended in answers to part (a). The key to good marks lay in the policy to be adopted and the decision making process. Some candidates addressed the question through a process of elimination ruling out those they would not choose. The three most popular choices were Ruby 1, HS 4, and SS 5. For (b), high scoring scripts described the metric and how it is calculated.

(a)   The investment mandate is long-term with a likely low to moderate overall risk tolerance. Emerging markets (EM) are an inherently risky asset class which suggests that a fund with concentration risk is likely not to be appropriate. An assumption needs to be made concerning whether the allocation to EM is part of permanent/core long-term strategic allocation or a tactical allocation. If the former, a diversified mixed fund would be appropriate whereas, if the latter, a more concentrated and style based fund may be appropriate.

Let us assume that the purpose is long-term strategic allocation to EM. The scenario depicted by the five funds from a buyer's point of view is very realistic in that no fund is head and shoulders better than others. There are a mix of positives and negatives associated with each. As is often the case, there is no clear first best, but there are a number of second bests.

A positive of Ruby 1 is a focus on large-cap value companies, but a concern is that the fund has under-performed for three years. We should consider: Is this important to a long-term investor? The under-performance of the last three years could be due to a change in fund manager key personnel, or out could be due, for example, to lower performance by large-cap stocks over the period.

Royal 2 positives are: a good short-term track record, and incorporating ESG factors within security selection. In EM markets, ESG factors remain a matter of concern because of less developed governance and regulatory structures in such markets, as well as the prevalence of corruption and irregularities in many such markets. A concern is the short-term track record of Royal 2 and the likely concentrated nature of a fund that is focused on market timing and mis-pricing.

A positive of UB 3 is a Growth At Reasonable Price (GARP) style, but the sector concentration is a concern. The heavy concentration in retail companies exposes the funds to consumer downturns.

A positive of HS 4 is the low volatility approach, but a concern is the momentum style, which suggests a more tactical approach to EM. This might not good for a long-term strategic allocation.

A positive of SS 5 is the passive buy and hold approach which suggests high diversification, but a concern is the top-down discretion around risk-on to risk-off. An external manager moving into cash could influence the overall pension scheme's beta.

(b)   **Other metrics and measures** [four required]

Quantitative measures

- ▨ **TER**: this is the total expense ratio, enabling the costs of different funds to be compared

- ▨ **Reduction in yield** indicates the amount by which the investment yield is reduced, in percentage terms, by charges

- ▨ **VaR (Value at Risk)** is the amount by which the value of an investment or portfolio may fall over a given period of time at a given level of probability. The idea behind the calculation is to discover how much value could be lost within a given period, ie what is the probable worst case loss over that time?

    For example, if VaR is £1m at a probability level of 5% for one week, this indicates that there is a 5% probability that the value of a portfolio will fall by more than £1m over the next week. It therefore gives investors an idea of the amount of potential loss and the probability of that loss arising.

The parametric method of calculating VaR assumes that the distribution of investment returns is normal, meaning that it can be described by the returns and risks of the investments concerned. It estimates the standard deviations of investments and their correlations with other investments, using historical data or future estimates. Given this information, it is possible to calculate the return and standard deviation of the overall portfolio.

- **Conditional value at risk (CVaR)** measures 'tail loss'. It asks: If we do end up in the tail of say, the 5% of worst outcomes, what is the average loss we will incur? If we added up all the possible losses in the bottom 5% and took the average, this is CVaR.

- **Treynor measure**: the higher the measure, the better the performance of the fund when we take account of risk. The measure is calculated as [Portfolio return – Risk-free return]/[Portfolio beta]

- **Jensen alpha**: this measure shows whether a manager has out-performed another manager, based on the systematic risk. The alpha value is defined relative to the security market line.

- **Sharpe ratio**: this uses the total portfolio risk or standard deviation as its indication of risk. It is calculated as: [Portfolio return – Risk-free return]/[Portfolio risk]

- **Appraisal ratio**: this enables evaluation of active management by reference to a passive tracker fund. The ratio assesses th abnormal return (alpha) by reference to the related unsystematic risk. Appraisal ratio = [Portfolio abnormal return] / [Portfolio unsystematic risk]

- **Information ratio**: this may be used for a similar purpose to the appraisal ratio in that it considers, in comparison to the benchmark, the excess return of the portfolio against the excess risk. This can be compared to the Sharpe measure for the benchmark in order to determine the impact of active performance.

  Information ratio = [Portfolio return – Benchmark return] / Standard deviation of excess returns of portfolio over benchmark]

Qualitative measures

- Meeting the team face-to-face at their offices for half or whole day

- Tenure and experience of team working together

- Commitment of organisation to the asset class

- Previous reports that explain performance, the judgements taken and whether performance is justified by these

13. **Investment strategies**

You cannot expect to achieve returns above the risk-free rate unless you take risk, and taking risk implies the potential for loss.

In other words, reduction and/or elimination of the risk of loss can only be achieved by the reduction and/or elimination of the potential for returns.

Thus, there are inherent challenges to asymmetric return profiles. A guarantee or promise is more expensive the longer term this is, because it requires more capital reserves, locked-in for longer, and it carries systemic risk.

Is the family prepared to pay this for the sake of downside protection?

Seeking a guaranteed product is one option. When buying a guaranteed product, the investor transfers control of the asset allocation. The guarantor will from then on manage the asset allocation in order to eliminate his risk, which results in the elimination of the risk premium.

Is the family prepared to relinquish control of the asset allocation to an insurer?

Guaranteed products typically aim to eliminate the risk of nominal loss.

Is the family prepared to have inflation gradually erode their capital?

Some candidates discussed using a combination of protective puts and call options. These however do require constant rolling over and cost.

Candidates discussed the following investment solutions in which asset allocation and investment discretion is retained.

- **Constant proportion portfolio insurance (CPPI)**. Portfolio insurance is a technique for limiting the potential loss on a portfolio, at the expense of giving up some of the potential profits. The approach is based on options theory, where the holder of a call option has unlimited exposure to any potential profits, but limited exposure to losses. CPPI comprises two categories of asset: the underlying fund of risky assets, and the reverse account, which comprises risk-free assets – usually cash, which may be consumed over the life cycle of the insurance, which is typically five or six years. The underlying principle of CPPI is that the total asset value must never fall below the floor– the present value of the protected amount paid back on the maturity. In managing the assets, the proportion of risky assets is increased when the portfolio value moves away from the floor, and reduced when it moves towards the floor.

- An **asset liability model** where there is a hedge portfolio, and a performance portfolio that uses leverage.

- **Risk budgeting techniques**. Risk budgeting allocates risk rather than money to asset classes. At the outset, a maximum portfolio risk is specified. The contribution to portfolio risk of the different asset classes is monitored. Assets weights are altered to maintain the desired level of portfolio risk, eg if equities become more volatile, their exposure may need to fall to actively maintain the desired level of portfolio risk. The proceeds from the sale of equities are recycled to lower-risk assets. In this manner, aggregate risk of a portfolio is decomposed into its constituents. The aim is to actively set and allocate risk to enhance the returns available from risk premiums without over-paying for them relative to their risk.

- **Investment based on low valuation**, involving buying only when assets are inexpensive on valuation cycle, and then buy and hold

- **Investment based on market timing** by using economic, sentiment, behavioural, financial, and political indicators

December 2013 Examination Answers

Part 1 – Portfolio Construction Theory

Section A

1. (a) **B** The single factor model (CAPM) assumes that each security contains:

      ▓ Systematic risk

      ▓ Unsystematic risk

    (b) **B** The yield to maturity of a bond is the internal rate of return earned by the buyer of the bond today at the market price, assuming that the bond will be held until maturity, and that all coupon and principal payments will be made on time.

    (c) **D** The expected yield will be lower than the promised yield, because the expected yield factors in the probability of default.

    (d) **C** To be successful, technical analysis needs to be able to exploit market inefficiency.

    (e) **B** Assume the par value of the bond is £1,000. The calculation can be performed in two ways.

      1. Current yield = Coupon/Bond price per £1.

        8% = Coupon/(£1,250/£1,000)

        Therefore:

        Coupon = 8% × 1.25 = 10%, or £100 (ie 10.0% of £1,000 par)

      2. Coupon ÷ £1,250 = Current yield = 0.08.

        Therefore, Coupon = £100 (ie 10.0% of £1,000 par)

    (f) **C** The semi-variance measures variation below the mean only.

    (g) **D** Market timing is a type of tactical asset allocation.

    (h) **A** Sharpe ratio = (Portfolio return – Risk-free rate)/Standard deviation of portfolio returns = 0.03/0.14.

    (i) **C** The higher yield means that both will decrease in value. The present value of the redemption proceeds is a greater part of the value of Bond A than that of Bond B and the change in yield will affect Bond B more than Bond A.

    (j) **D** An index-linked bond pays a par value that adjusts according to the general level of prices. This changes coupon payments, but not the coupon rate.

    (k) **C** Regret aversion leads people to regret a poor decision more than they take satisfaction from a good decision.

    (l) **C** You might have reached the correct answer by a process of elimination.

    (m) **B** Choice overload is alternatively called 'overchoice'. Faced with too many choices, consumers have trouble making optimal choices, and may as a result procrastinate and possibly refrain from making a choice at all.

    (n) **A** A medium-sized wealth management company is not a large enough player to move prices, and so will be a price 'taker'. £1 will buy the slightly lower amount of $1.5336. If the company were instead buying £1, it would have to pay the slightly higher amount of 1.5337.

(o) **B** Sharpe ratio = (Portfolio return − Risk-free return)/Portfolio risk

The Sharpe ratio uses the standard deviation of portfolio returns as a measure of portfolio risk. The fund return has not changed, and so the portfolio risk has also not changed. Since the Sharpe ratio has fallen, the remaining term (the risk-free rate, which is negative in the ratio) must have increased.

(p) Payout ratio = D/Earnings

According to the dividend growth model:

Price = $D_1 \times 1/(r_e - g)$

Price/Earnings (P/E) ratio = Payout ratio/(Required rate of return − Expected growth rate of dividends)

P/E = Payout ratio/$(r_e - g)$

= 0.65/(0.13 − 0.08) = **13**

(q) **Total risk**

$\sigma_i^2 = \sigma_s^2 + \sigma_u^2 = 17^2 + 8^2 = 353$

$\sigma_i = 18.788\%$

(r) Let Stock A be represented by 'a'.

The market is represented by 'm'.

Beta = Covariance of the investment and the market / Variance of market

Beta = $cov_{a,m} / var_m = \sigma_a \sigma_m Cor_{a,m} / var_m$ = 0.45 × 0.16 × 0.4 / 0.16² = 0.0288 / 0.0256 = 1.125

(s) A warrant gives the holder the opportunity to purchase a pre-determined number of shares at a pre-determined price at some point in the future. Warrants are usually, but not always, issued by investment trusts. They are often issued as a sweetener, or inducement to invest, because investment trusts tend to trade at a discount. They may also be used by IPO companies where the share price after IPO may be expected to fall below the IPO price. Capital gains tax is payable on disposal of an exercised warrant. The exercise of a warrant requires a firm to issue a new share of stock (the total number of shares outstanding increases). This makes warrants dilutive. Warrants also result in cash flow to the firm when the warrant holder pays the exercise price.

A covered equity warrant is a little different, and is really a long-dated call option over shares. It is issued by a third party with a holding of the shares of the company in question, so that when an investor exercises the warrant, he or she will receive shares that already exist.

As with convertible debt, warrant terms may be tailored to meet the needs of the firm. Warrants are protected − like convertible debt − against stock splits and dividends in that the exercise price. The number of warrants held is adjusted to offset the effects of the split.

Convertible securities link to two different assets whereas warrants link to just one. A convertible security gives its holder the right to exchange bonds or preferred stock for a fixed number of shares of common stock regardless of the market price of the securities at the time. Conversion is available at certain times during the convertible security's life, usually at the discretion of the bondholder. The convertible will have value even if the bond remains unconverted. The issuer sets a conversion ratio so that conversion will not be profitable unless there is a substantial increase in stock prices and/or a decrease in bond prices. In other words, convertible bonds are usually issued deep out of the money. Convertible bonds rank higher in the list of creditors than common shares that warrants usually link to.

(t)   Conversion value for US$100 nominal is: 25 × 3.80 = US$95.00

The bond is trading at US$120, and so the premium is currently:

US$120.00 – US$95.00 = US$25.00

The premium as a percentage of the conversion value is therefore: 25/95 = 26.3%

(u)

Long-term asset allocation weight and returns									
	Equity Return	T Bill Return	Equity	T Bill	Equity value	Bond value	Portfolio value	end eq weight	end bd weight
Initial period 1			60%	40%	600	400	1000	0.60	0.40
Period 1	–10%	0%			540	400	940	**0.57**	**0.43**
Initial Period 2			60%	40%	564	376	940	0.60	0.40
Period 2	–20%	0%			451.2	376	827.2	**0.55**	**0.45**
Initial Period 3			60%	40%	496.3	330.9	827.2	0.60	0.40
Period 3	10%	0%			546.0	330.9	876.83	**0.62**	**0.38**

(v)   (i)   Annualised return is $121/100^{12/21} – 1$ = 11.5%

(ii)   Annualised standard deviation is 0.044 x $\sqrt{12}$ = 15.2%. When annualising a standard deviation, take the square root of the number of observations per year – in this case 12, because the returns are monthly.

(iii)   Calculated as: (11.5% – 1%) / 15.2% = 0.691

Or: annualise risk-free as: $(11.5\% – ((1+0.01)^{12/21} – 1)) / 15.2\%$

(Either calculation is acceptable.)

(w)   We need to match each client to the most appropriate portfolio and this can only be achieved by incorporating the numerical risk tolerance score within the overall calculation. This is calculated as: Expected return – Risk of portfolio

Risk of portfolio to client is calculated as standard deviation / risk tolerance factor. This gives an investment suitability, and client utility, per portfolio.

Portfolio	Stock	Bond	Expected return on portfolio	Risk (Std Dev) of portfolio	Risk tolerance Ms A 3	Risk tolerance Mr B 9
1	5.0%	95.0%	5.0%	3.0%	**4.0%**	4.7%
2	25.0%	75.0%	6.0%	9.0%	3.0%	5.0%
3	70.0%	30.0%	7.3%	12.0%	3.3%	**6.0%**
4	90.0%	10.0%	7.9%	25.0%	– 0.4%	5.1%

The highest level of utility, ie the largest value of the three potential allocations, is the optimal asset mix for Ms A = Portfolio 1, and for Mr B = Portfolio 3.

Ms A is less risk tolerant. This means she prefers a lower risk portfolio, other things equal. Mr B is more risk tolerant. This means he prefers a higher risk portfolio, other things equal.

In the formula, the expected portfolio return to different asset mixes is reduced by the formula: risk of portfolio / risk tolerance factor. This formula acts as a risk penalty. The risk tolerance is the denominator so, the smaller it is, the greater is the risk penalty that reduces expected return. This will generally lead to a less risk tolerant investor being matched to an

asset mix with lower risk and a more risk tolerant investor being matched to an asset mix with higher risk.

Section B

2.   **Examiner's comment.** Section B of the paper asked a question about the diversification qualities of precious metals and portfolio construction using them. The mean, median and modal mark was 14, 14, and 13 out of 20 respectively. The maximum mark was 19 and the minimum 2.

(a)   The correlations of precious metal returns with each other and with equity returns were all reported in the Table. In Panel A of the Table for the full sample period, the following three features are important.

(i)   The returns for all three precious metals have zero correlations with the S&P 500 return. This result indicates that the responsiveness of the precious metal market to the US stock market is close to zero.

(ii)   The correlations between EAFE and precious metal returns, although low, are positive at around 0.14. This no doubt reflects the considerable role and influence that gold/gold mining has in the non-US markets, in contrast to its role in the US economy.

(iii)   The correlations between the precious metal returns are high (0.5 to 0.6), but not so high that any of the three metals is redundant from an investment perspective.

Panels B, C, and D in the Table present correlations for various sub-periods. Through all sub-periods, the correlations between the S&P 500 return and the precious metal returns remain close to zero. This includes through the lingering high energy prices and high inflation of the 1970s in panel A, and the stock market rise and fall of the late 1990s and early 2000s in panel C.

Interestingly, a downward trend over time is visible in the correlation between returns to EAFE and returns to the precious metals. In addition, although the precious metal correlations remain high throughout all the sub-periods, they tend to display a similar downward trend.

During periods of high market risk, precious metals appear no more correlated with stock market returns. The fact that this finding is robust to use of EAFE as a substitute market benchmark for the S&P 500 should allay any concerns that the negative effect is peculiar to the United States.

This result suggests that, from an overall perspective, all three precious metals are potentially valuable diversifying assets as part of an investment portfolio. However, the economic impact is unclear from looking at correlations alone.

In summary, the Table suggests that some diversifying benefits are provided by precious metals, particularly with reference to the S&P 500.

(b)   **Examiner's comment.** This part was not answered well. This more technical part to the question required candidates to apply portfolio theory by finding an optimal portfolio including precious metals.

(i)

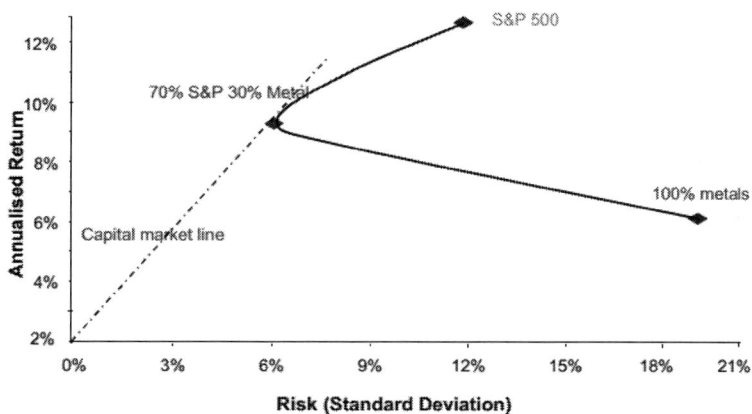

Portfolio Risk and Return: S&P 500 and Precious Metals Portfolio

Approximately, this allocation would lead to a portfolio with weights at 70% of a basket tracking the S&P500, and 30% of an equal-weighted basket of precious metals.

(ii)   The line joining the point of minimum risk to the portfolio at the highest upper-left point, the S&P500 shows the set of asset mixes that is expected to offer the maximum return for any given level of risk. This is an efficient frontier of possible portfolios.

(iii)   See the capital market line on the diagram above. An investor should choose a portfolio depending on their level of risk tolerance. This is reflected in indifference curves which could be depicted on the diagram. The portfolios on the capital market line comprise the market portfolio and risk-free stock. The investor would choose the portfolio corresponding to where the highest indifference curve just touches the capital market line.

(iv)   An investor could gain specific exposure to precious metals within a broad-based portfolio through investing in exchange traded funds (ETFs), gold bullion shares, derivatives such as futures contracts, and exchange traded commodities (ETCs).

Section C

3.   **Examiner's comment**. The question tested candidates' ability to appraise how integrating environmental, social and governance factors within portfolio selection may influence the volatility of a globally diversified equity portfolio. Answers were generally not of a high standard, with a mean, median and modal mark of 3, 3 and 2 respectively. The maximum mark was 4 and the minimum 1. Some candidates did not understand how to interpret decile portfolio data.

The FTSE Developed Index comprises 24 developed countries and about 2,000 constituent stocks. This means there are approximately 200 stocks in each decile. The footnote explains that the deciles are country neutral, so each portfolio decile has the same country weights. This equates to each portfolio decile having fewer than 10 companies per country. This is likely to mean some exposure to idiosyncratic risk in each portfolio decile. We do not know the time period or the base currency. Higher deciles hold higher environment score, social score and governance score stocks.

Moving from left to right and from low to high deciles, volatility falls gradually. The progression to lower volatility is smoothest and strongest for the environment, social and governance (ESG) combined sort. For all four sorts, the change in volatility is most evident within the tails – deciles 1 and 10. Volatility in the lower deciles is higher than the volatility of the Developed index and

volatility in the highest decile is lower. This result indicates that a managed fund or index that is overweight in high ESG score stocks will produce lower volatility than the comparator benchmark. While the reduction in volatility is clearly economically important from low to high deciles, the relationship for the middle deciles is mixed.

Turning to the betas, these decline from the lowest to the highest decile, but even for the highest deciles the betas remain close to 1 at between 0.9 and 0.95. The relationship between volatility and beta across the deciles is not strong. The fact that lower volatility is robust to analysis of betas should allay concerns that higher ESG score stocks are simply lower beta stocks. Value at Risk is lower among higher ESG deciles, suggesting less volatility for at least 95 per cent of days.

The findings appear to ignore company size and it may be that a positive association between company size and ESG score dominates the results.

The results are potentially interesting. If the client wishes to be overweight in high ESG performance investments, then this may be a potentially profitable way of doing so, but we need to know more. There appears to be a benefit in underweighting decile 1 and overweighting decile 10, provided that this achieves sufficient diversification. Returns are not mentioned here: this analysis is restricted to risk.

4. **Examiner's comment**. The question asked candidates to explain the merits of hedging the FTSE Developed Index. The question was not well answered. The mean, median and modal mark was 3 out of 5. The maximum mark was 5 and the minimum 0.

A significant proportion of wealth invested leads to a conversation with the client about whether the risk is appropriate given the client's risk tolerance. At the same time, developed market benchmarks are quite different to emerging market benchmarks, in which devaluation risk is presented.

The merits of hedging currencies lies in the correlations between returns on domestic and foreign developed stock markets and their correlation with the return on the spot currencies.

An unhedged position adds extra risk in the form of the variance of the spot FX rates. Often exchange rate volatility can be quite substantial, sometimes even exceeding the volatility of the stock market. However, the correlations between the spot FX rates and the domestic and foreign stock markets may offset the impact of high variance of the spot FX rates, and so an unhedged portfolio may have low volatility.

There may even be additional diversification benefits from holding all the currencies, so we would want to know the correlation structure of the currencies to be hedge, to consider expected returns as well as risk, and to provide a measure of net portfolio performance.

Other factors to consider include the following.

- Results of hedging are not invariant to the choice of home currency in which returns are measures or the time horizon. A strong and relatively appreciating home currency may merit an unhedged position: the opposite of a relatively depreciating currency. So, we need to consider the strength of the home currency.

- Many large companies already invested in will earn revenue internationally in a variety of currencies and will themselves be hedged. Additional hedging could lead to low additional benefit for the costs of hedging.

- Further factors to weigh together are the costs of hedging, the time period, the expected depreciation, the strength of the home currency, the correlation structure, expense and the ability to roll over currency contracts (as will usually involve buying futures or forwards, which are sold in contracts).

5.   **Examiner's comment**. The question asked candidates for the merits and drawbacks of non-market capitalisation techniques to gain exposure to emerging market equity funds. By and large the question was well answered. The mean, median and modal mark was 3, 3, and 4 out of 5. The maximum mark was 5 and the minimum was 0.

Merits

Emerging equity markets are generally considered less efficient than developed markets (shares are more likely to be mis-priced), which means that active investment management approaches have potentially greater opportunities to succeed.

We should be wary of market capitalisation index approaches in emerging market equities because emerging equity markets are more concentrated. The top 25 stocks in the FTSE EM index account for 25% of the index, whereas in FTSE World they account for just 15%. There is also greater sector concentration in emerging equity markets, with 54% of the index in the top 3 sectors as opposed to 45% in developed markets.

Without active management, this can mean greater concentration and less diversification in an index tracking portfolio. In times of high capital inflow, money gets sucked into large over-valued stocks and sectors and a more concentrated market can exacerbate this problem.

Portfolio investment flows in and out of emerging market countries can produce spikes in correlations that significantly reduce the diversification properties within emerging markets, and between emerging markets and developed markets. With many emerging market economies also being highly dollar-based, when there is a turbulent period in one or more of these economies, many or all can be affected.

Both of these conditions contribute to a correlation/covariance matrix of stock returns in emerging markets that is far less stable than that of developed economies. Active management provides more opportunity to respond and adjust.

The development of alternative indices or 'smart beta' has potential to provide low-cost non-market capitalisation weights. They re-weight the constituents or subset of constituents of a market cap index in order to improve on the portfolio construction in some way (eg, focus on value stocks, or reduce the portfolio volatility). Alternative beta indices look different to market cap indices. This is not 'enhanced indexation': it is a different way of constructing an equity portfolio. Investors need first to understand what they are buying and why.

Active management in emerging markets tends to be expensive and the best managers are generally at or close to capacity, so alternative indexation may be able to deliver value for money.

Drawbacks

Many of the smart beta indices are by design underweight in the largest stocks of the market capitalisation universe. When markets are rising in the biggest stocks, alternative indices will lag.

Liquidity is more of a concern for alternative indices than for market cap indices. While some are liquid, some are not, and there is no incentive to manage overall assets in any particular strategy because compensation for managers is in the form of management fees and not performance fees.

Many alternative indices are based on historic norms, eg reversion to mean, historic valuation, historic correlations. As with any quantitative process, they will not pick up market developments, eg tapering of quantitative easing, and the knock-on effect on emerging market flows and currencies. The screening process can amount to little more than data mining. These simulated data sometimes do not factor in turnover and costs.

Part 2 – Taxation and Trusts

Section D

6. **Examiner's comment**. This was a question about trusts, capital gains tax and income tax. The mean, median and modal mark was 13, 13, and 12 out of 20 respectively. The maximum mark was 19 and the minimum 5.

(a) **Types of trust**

(i) A trust is an arrangement under which a person, the 'settlor', transfers property to another person, the 'trustee' or trustees, who is required to deal with the trust property on behalf of certain specified persons, the 'beneficiaries'.

A trust may be:

▪ An interest in possession (IIP) trust, where the beneficiaries are automatically entitled to receive all of the income of the trust as it arises, or

▪ A discretionary trust, where the trustees can determine which beneficiaries to make payments to and how much they will receive.

A trust with a disabled beneficiary has some tax advantages – for example, a higher CGT annual exemption than that of other trusts (see part (ii)). Additionally, lifetime gifts to such trusts are not chargeable to inheritance tax (IHT), in the case of discretionary and interest in possession (IIP) trusts.

Frank and Nora might set up a bare trust, as a relatively simple option, provided that they are happy with their daughter having access to the trust property when she comes of age.

In a bare trust, also known as a simple trust, there is a sole beneficiary. The trustee has no discretion over payment of income or capital to the beneficiary, who has an immediate and absolute right to both capital and income at age 18 (in England and Wales). The basic purpose of a bare trust is to restrict benefits going to children before they reach 18 and to try and avoid paying tax on the saving. On coming of age, the beneficiary of the trust can instruct the trustee how to manage the trust property, and then has the right to take actual possession of the trust property at any time.

(ii) The income tax treatment is different for each type of trust.

IIP trustees' tax position

▪ Interest income is taxed at 20%
▪ Dividends are taxed at 10%

Interest is usually received net of a 20% tax credit by the trust (as it is by an individual). Dividends are received with a 10% notional tax credit. As both of these tax credits satisfy the trustees' liability for these types of income, no further tax is due from the trustees.

The IIP beneficiary (sometimes called the 'life tenant') is entitled to receive the trust income once the trustees have paid the tax due.

The beneficiary will receive a statement of income from the trust showing the amounts they are entitled to receive along with the associated tax credit (ie, the tax paid by the trustees). They will then include these amounts in their own tax calculation.

The income paid to the beneficiary retains its nature so, if it is interest income in the trustees' hands, it will be taxed as interest income on the beneficiary and so on.

Discretionary trusts have a standard, or basic rate, band of £1,000. The first £1,000 of income is taxed at the basic rates, ie at 10% (dividends), and 20% (interest income). As for individuals, the basic rate band is applied first to non-savings income, then savings income and finally dividends. Many smaller trusts will have no further tax to pay.

Any remaining income is taxed at the rates that apply to additional rate taxpaying individuals (2014/15):

- Interest income is taxed at 45% (the trust rate)
- Dividends are taxed at 37.5% (the dividend trust rate)

Beneficiaries of discretionary trusts are only taxed if they receive income payments from the trust.

Any payments of income to beneficiaries are made net of tax at 50% and are taxed on them at the rates that apply to earnings income. The trustees will again provide a statement of income to the beneficiaries showing the relevant figures.

For CGT purposes, there is no need to distinguish between the type of trust. 'Settled property' is any property held in a trust, other than a trust where the beneficiary is absolutely entitled to trust property (a 'bare trust'). In a bare trust, gains are treated as made by the beneficiary not the trustee.

If a settlor puts an asset into any type of trust, he makes a disposal for CGT purposes. It will be deemed to take place at market value.

Where a trust has a disabled beneficiary, the annual exempt amount for CGT purposes is raised to £11,000 (2014/15).

For trusts for the disabled, the rule that makes lifetime gifts to trusts chargeable to IHT does not apply. However, IHT may still be due when the transferor dies within seven years of the transfer.

(b) Cars, including vintage cars, are deemed to be a wasting asset, and so no capital gains tax is payable by Frank on their disposal.

(c) Frank qualifies for the age allowance of £10,500 rather than the ordinary allowance of £10,000 because he was born between 6 April 1938 and 6 April 1948 and his income is less than £27,000 in 2014/15.

Taxable income: £25,000 − £10,500 = £14,500

Income tax payable: £14,500 × 20% = £2,900

(d) Nora's 2014/15 income = £90,000

Taxable income: £90,000 − £10,000 = £80,000

Income tax payable:

£31,865 × 20% = £6,373

£48,135 × 40% = £19,254

Total income tax liability = £25,627

(e) The new business might be set up as a self-employed venture (sole proprietorship), as a partnership, or as a private limited company.

A limited company is a separate legal entity from its owners: the company's liabilities are the responsibility of the company, not of its directors or shareholders. However, directors of small businesses are commonly required by a lender to provide personal guarantees, and then they become liable to repay the debt if the company cannot.

A company pays corporation tax on its profits and can only distribute the remaining retained profits to directors and shareholders. This can result in tax being paid by both the company and by the directors or shareholders when they extract money from the company. However, there are also National Insurance implications. The company structure provides some flexibility in determining the proportions of salary and dividends, compared with a sole trader. Dividends are not subject to national insurance.

As a self-employed business, the sole trader is responsible for paying tax and national insurance contributions (NICs), through a self-assessment tax return. Class 2 NICs must normally be paid (unless profits fall below the small earnings exception), and also Class 4 if profits are above a specified level. HMRC should be notified when the business starts trading.

The couple should keep a careful note of expenses so that all business expenses can be claimed against tax. Businesses run by sole traders or partnerships have an annual investment allowance (AIA) for 100% of the first £250,000 of their expenditure on most plant and machinery. (This rate, increased from £25,000 previously with the aim of stimulating economic growth, applies for a temporary period of two years from 1 January 2013.) Companies are also able to claim capital allowances.

Depending on the level of turnover, the business may need to be registered for VAT.

Frank is a basic rate taxpayer while Nora is a higher rate taxpayer. For tax years in which this applies, tax planning could include ensuring that Frank is paid income to use up this allowance, if income is available from the business. However, for personal reasons, spouses may not wish their individual financial circumstances to be dictated too closely by tax planning. This will depend on the individuals' own preferences.

In the UK, IR35 seeks to counter tax avoidance by what are called 'personal service companies'. IR35 seeks to prevent workers from setting up limited companies via which they would work as employees to take advantage of a more favourable remuneration structure. A business could be caught by these rules if the end client exercises a degree of control over the work.

Section E

7. IHT charges are based on domicile status. Individuals domiciled in the UK are liable to tax on their worldwide assets, while individuals whose domicile lies outside the UK are only liable to IHT on assets situated in the UK.

Irrespective of their actual domicile, an individual whose domicile is other than in the UK is treated as being domiciled in the UK for IHT purposes if they are:

- UK-domiciled within the three years preceding a relevant transfer, or
- UK resident for 17 out of 20 years ending with the year of assessment in which the transfer occurs

Transfers between UK-domiciled spouses – and civil partners – are completely exempt from IHT.

However, the IHT-exempt amount that a UK-domiciled individual can transfer to a non-UK domiciled spouse or civil partner has historically been set at £55,000. This has now been increased to the level of the nil rate band applying at the time of the transfer, ie £325,000 for transfers taking place on or after 6 April 2013.

Additionally, under a new election regime, individuals domiciled other than in the UK and who are married or in a civil partnership can elect to be treated as UK-domiciled for IHT purposes.

Where an individual chooses not to elect for UK-domiciled treatment, their overseas assets would, as now, be exempt from IHT but any transfers from their spouse or partner would be subject to the increased cap of £325,000. Individuals who choose to make an election would benefit from uncapped IHT-exempt transfers from their spouse or civil partner, but subsequent disposals by them would be liable to IHT (subject to their own nil-rate band), whatever the location of the assets.

8. Quoted shares are valued at the lower of:

- The quoted bid price plus one quarter of the difference between the bid and offer prices, and
- The average of the lowest and highest recorded bargains on the day

Prices are taken from the Stock Exchange Daily Official List (SEDOL).

Where the share is being quoted ex-dividend, the net amount of the next dividend should be added to the value.

Where quoted investments are sold by an executor at a loss in the twelve-month period after death, the loss on sale is deducted from the value of the investments before inheritance tax is charged. This prevents there being a loss due to the forced sale of shares to meet inheritance tax liabilities.

The following conditions must be met.

- The seller of the shares must be the person liable to pay tax on them
- The investments must be listed
- The sale must take place within twelve months of death

The value of the chargeable estate is reduced by the loss on sale, which is calculated as the difference between the sale proceeds (or market value of the shares, if significantly higher) and the value of the shares in the estate. This may then result in a repayment of inheritance tax.

Where part of the proceeds is reinvested in other investments within two months of the last relevant sale in the twelve-month period, the relief is restricted by the following fraction.

Restriction = Loss × [Purchase price of new investments]/[Gross proceeds from investments sold]

Valuations in unquoted securities are more difficult to decide, as there is no active market in the shares.

Under the self-assessment procedures, taxpayers are responsible for either calculating the appropriate amount of tax due or, in the case of individuals, for providing the appropriate figures to enable HMRC to calculate it on their behalf. If a valuation is not provided on the correct basis, a taxpayer's tax return may be challenged by HMRC.

The correct basis of valuation for tax purposes is the 'market value' as defined in S160 Inheritance Tax Act 1984, that is: 'The price which the property might reasonably be expected to fetch if sold in the open market at that time, but that price shall not be assumed to be reduced on the grounds that the whole property is to be placed on the market at one and the same time.'

Appropriate valuation methods the taxpayer may use include earnings, assets, dividend yield or an industry-specific valuation method. The taxpayer should consider the company's performance and financial status as shown by, say, three years' accounts up to the valuation date, any information normally available to shareholders, the size of the shareholding and shareholders' rights, the company's dividend policy, yields and price earnings ratios of comparable companies or sectors and the commercial and economic background at the valuation date.

There may be ongoing negotiations with HMRC's Shares and Assets Valuation (SAV) in order to establish an accepted valuation.

9.   From 6 April 2013, a new statutory residence test was established, and the concept of 'ordinary' residence was abolished for tax purposes.

If an individual satisfies any of the following automatic overseas tests, then he is non-resident.

Automatic overseas tests

(a)   Was resident in the UK for one or more of the three previous tax years and spends fewer than 16 days in the UK in the current tax year

(b)   Was not resident in the UK for any of the previous three tax years and spends fewer than 46 days in the UK in the current tax year

(c)   Leaves the UK to carry out full-time work overseas, or

(d)   Dies in the current tax year, subject to conditions which include spending fewer than 46 days in the UK

If the individual does not satisfy any of the automatic overseas tests, the individual will be automatically UK-resident if he meets any of the following automatic UK tests.

Automatic UK tests

(a)   He spends 183 days or more (ie more than six months) in the UK during the tax year

(b)   There is a period of more than 90 days, part of which falls within the tax year, when he has a home in the UK and no home overseas (disregarding any home at which he is present for fewer than 30 days in the tax year)

(c)   He dies in the current year, subject to conditions which include having been UK-resident in the previous three tax years, or

(d)   He meets a full-time UK work test, as set out in the taxation rules

If the individual meets none of the automatic overseas tests and none of the automatic UK tests, he must look at the 'sufficient ties' test, which compares the number of days spent in the UK against the number of 'connection factors' that apply, such as whether he has a UK-resident family, or accommodation in the UK.

A person is **domiciled** in the country in which he has his permanent home. A person may be resident in more than one country, but he can be domiciled in only one country at a time.

Where the individual was born determines his or her domicile of origin. A person retains this domicile until he acquires a different domicile of dependency (if, while he is under 16, his father's domicile changes) or domicile of choice if he permanently settles in another country.

A resident and domiciled individual is taxed on his general earnings on a receipts basis.

A non-resident is taxed on his general earnings in respect of UK duties on the receipts basis but there is no UK income tax on foreign earnings (those in respect of non-UK duties).

A UK resident who is not UK-domiciled ('non-doms')may claim the remittance basis for a particular tax year, so that he is only liable to UK income tax on overseas income to the extent that it is brought (remitted) to the UK. Such an individual is liable to the remittance basis charge if he claims the remittance basis for a tax year, subject to the following residence rule.

■   If the individual has been UK-resident for at least 7 of the 9 tax years preceding that tax year, the remittance basis charge payable is £30,000 annually.

■   If the individual has been UK-resident for at least 12 of the 14 tax years preceding that tax year, the remittance basis charge payable is £50,000 annually.

Resident 'non-doms' who have been resident in the UK for less than 7 years can still elect for the remittance basis of tax, but there is no annual charge.

June 2013 Examination Answers

Part 1 – Portfolio Construction Theory

Section A

1. **Multiple choice and short answer questions**

    (a)   The correct answer is D.

    Valuation signal 'a' indicates over-valuation, while 'e' indicates under-valuation.

    (b)   The correct answer is A.

    Units are not squared when calculating the covariance.

    (c)   The correct answer is B.

    Treynor measure = (Portfolio return – Risk-free return)/Portfolio beta = (6 – 2)/0.95 = 4.2%, or 0.04.

    (d)   The correct answer is B.

    The duration of a bond is the weighted average of the times until cash flows will be received.

    (e)   The correct answer is C.

    The information ratio can indicate the additional return achieved by a fund for the additional risk undertaken, in comparison to a benchmark.

    (f)   The correct answer is B.

    Sharpe ratio = (Portfolio return – Risk-free return)/Portfolio risk

    The Sharpe ratio uses the standard deviation of portfolio returns as a measure of portfolio risk. The fund return has not changed, and so the portfolio risk has also not changed. Since the Sharpe ratio has fallen, the remaining term (the risk-free rate, which is negative in the ratio) must have increased.

    (g)   The correct answer is C.

    The holding period return is, put simply, the percentage (ie, rate of) return during the period held. Adding coupon payments to the change in price of a bond does not give a *rate* of return.

    (h)   The correct answer is B.

    With semi-strong form efficiency, we would expect the price response to company news to be immediate, and not to be subject to 'drift'. The semi-strong form hypothesis allows for insiders to have a superior level of knowledge and hence, to have a trading advantage.

    (i)   The correct answer is A.

    The multi-factor CAPM considers systemic risks.

    (j)   The correct answer is A.

    An appropriate safe asset to a diversified investor might be one with zero covariance to beta but this may not be an asset totally free of risk. Several types of securities have zero beta but are not risk-free. A zero-beta asset is safe in the sense that it has zero covariance to beta. Its standard deviation of returns will not be zero.

Answers B, C and D each lend empirical support and are used as evidence of a zero-beta CAPM being a better specification than the risk-free CAPM. Answer A is not necessarily true, and an assumption of no inflation is not relevant.

(k) The correct answer is A.

1 / 0.7775 = US$ 1.286 / £1

1.286 / 1.8325 = 0.702 US$ / C$

The US$/C$ cross rate is 0.702.

(l) The correct answer is A.

The constant dividend growth model assumes that dividends grow at a constant rate in the future.

(m) The correct answer is D.

Price:Cost of goods sold is not commonly calculated. The gross profit margin is calculated as [Sales revenue – Cost of goods sold]/Sales revenue.

(n) **Examiner's comment**. Answers were of a good standard.

The answer is: Bonds.

Bonds have a final maturity date and promised payments at fixed periods of time whereas shares do not. Bonds need fewer input assumptions. All information required to find yield and appropriate discount rate for bonds is normally publicly available – for example, coupon, maturity, duration, credit rating. This makes bonds more straightforward to value (though not necessarily more accurately).

There are different valuation techniques to measure the value of equities, any or all of which can be used. For example, the dividend growth model requires estimation of dividend growth rate and cost of capital, which are notoriously hard to determine.

(o) To deal with the ambiguity of the 'maturity' of a bond making many payments, we measure the average maturity of the bond's promised cash flows. Frederick Macaulay (1938) termed the effective maturity concept the duration of the bond. Macaulay's duration equals the weighted average of the times until each payment is received, with the weights proportional to the present value of the payment. Duration is shorter than maturity for all bonds except zero coupon bonds. Duration is equal to maturity for zero coupon bonds. Modified duration uses Macaulay's duration to calculate the per cent change in a bond's price to a per cent change in its yield.

Modified duration is a linear approximation of the price – yield relationship that is in reality actually a curve. The curvature means that the duration rule for bond price change, which is based only on the slope of the curve at the original yield, is an approximation.

Convexity captures this and measures the curvature of the bond's price-yield curve. Adding a term to account for the convexity of the bond increases the accuracy of the approximation.

(p) **Examiner's comment**. This question was answered well.

Tracking error is unlikely to be zero due to the following [four required].

(i) Transaction costs that occur when constructing an index tracking portfolio or when occasional rebalancing occurs due to change in the composition of the index, contributions, withdrawals/dividend received.

(ii) Timing of buying / selling stocks when they leave or enter the index.

(iii) Round-lot purchases – stocks may only be able to be bought in 100s which means that there may be a slight mismatch in the weight that a stock has in the index and the weight actually allocated in the tracking portfolio.

(iv) Possible restrictions on foreign ownership, if index has not only domestic constituents.

(v) Change in price due to entering or leaving index. The fund may trade after constituents enter or leave the index.

(vi) Index, if total return, normally assumes ex-dividend date is payment date. Payment date may be 6 weeks following ex-dividend date.

(vii) Dividend reinvested may be performed gross when in the fund it is reinvested net. Some dividend payments may be too small to be amenable to reinvestment.

(q) **Examiner's comment**. Answers were generally of a poor standard.

Beta = $0.40 \times 0.45 / 0.16 = 1.125$

(r) **Examiner's comment**. Answers were of a high standard.

Expected return = $2\% + (1.5\% \times 1.0) + (2.5\% \times 2.0) + (6.0\% \times 0.0) = 8.5\%$

(s) **Examiner's comment**. This question was poorly answered. The question required interpretation of data. Some candidates seemed to believe that the question concerned kurtosis and skewness but this is not the case. Top marks would have been awarded for the following.

US: When price change only is used, the investment period is almost irrelevant to the probability of encountering a loss. When total return is used, the probability of a loss falls as the investment period lengthens. This shows the importance of dividends to equity returns.

UK: When total return is used, the probability of encountering a loss is lower than when capital return is used. When looking at total return and capital return separately, the probability of encountering a loss does not fall as the investment period lengthens.

The probability of loss statistics demonstrate that the common concept in the media that equities are less risky the longer you hold them for is only partially correct – correct if we look at total returns but not capital only returns. Equities are no less risky the longer you hold them.

The probability of loss takes no account of how much you might lose if you do incur a loss. A low probability of loss but with the loss you may lose all your wealth puts a different picture on risk. VaR is the maximum percent loss in the value of your wealth that would be expected to occur with a probability of 95%. If the 1 year VaR for the UK is 25% there is a probability of 95% that you will lose less than this and a 5% probability of this loss or worse.

The table shows that the maximum percentage of your wealth that you might lose with a 95% probability tends to increase over the holding period.

Under this definition of risk, shares appear more risky the longer you hold them, contrary to what we often hear from the media and financial advisers.

The 5- and 10-year VaRs are not so different from one another. This might be due to economic cycle effects.

(t) **Examiner's comment**. This question specifically asked about communication skills rather than other types of skills.

To achieve a meeting that is most likely to lead to good outcomes and to communicate effectively, the adviser needs to build trust. Then, clients will open up and tell about their circumstances.

Personal skills. Be sensitive when questioning, and empathic.

Organisational skills – diary management, paperwork – need to keep notes. Before you meet, agree an agenda. Explain what you hope to achieve, what the meeting will do, and why. Let the client know if they will have an opportunity to ask questions.

Ability to compromise. Be willing to meet the client half-way. This makes the client feel more sure, safe, and in control – that they and their circumstances are the focus. You may believe that one product is best, they another: Is there a middle ground?

Good communication skills. Clear, succinct and plain English communication helps the client to understand the advice you are giving. Open-ended questions are preferable to closed-ended questions. Ask questions that are neutral. The adviser needs to elicit correct responses, and to assess them properly in the meeting.

Patience. Give the client time to consider and respond.

Technical competence. You need to be technically able – to have passed exams, to have kept your knowledge up-to-date.

Integrity – high personal and ethical standards. Be honest, and dependable.

(u) **Examiner's comment**. Answers were of a very good standard.

(i) Required return for Stock A = 2% + 1.9 × (6% − 2%) = 9.6%. The expected return for Stock A is 11.4%. Stock A is undervalued. This is above the SML.

Required return for Stock B = 2% + 0.8 × (6% − 2%) = 5.2%. The expected return for Stock B is 5.2%. Stock B is correctly priced. This is on the SML.

(ii) Security Market Line (SML): X-axis is beta; Y-axis is the expected/required return.

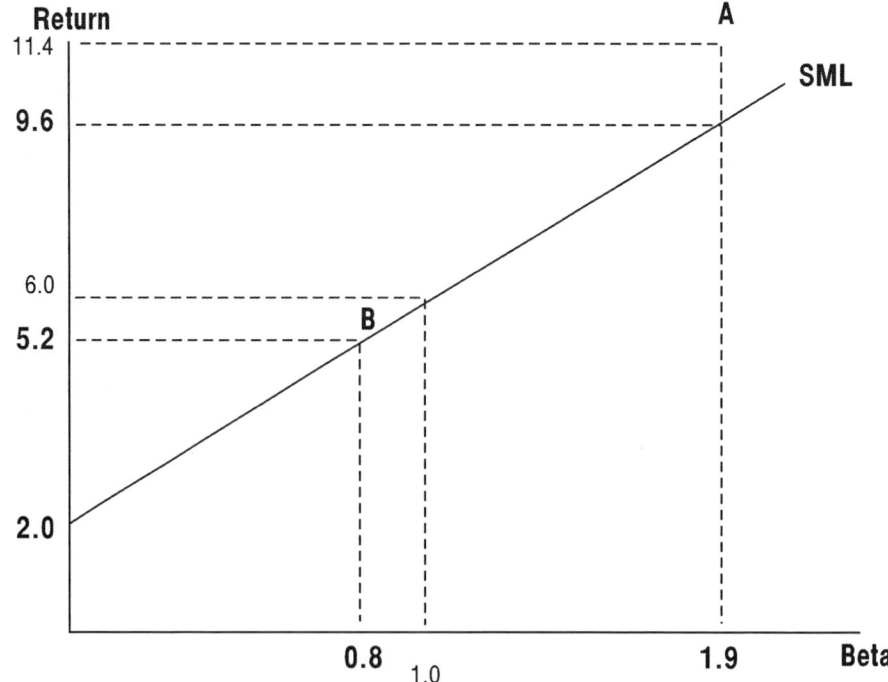

Section B

2. **Collective funds**

    (a) The Investment Management Association (IMA) and the Association of British Insurers (ABI) publish sector definitions for funds.

    Balanced managed fund. Funds in this sector have a range of different investments. However, there is scope for funds to have a high proportion in company shares (equities). This type of mixed investment fund is normally based on between 40 and 85% equity exposure (including convertibles). There is no minimum fixed income or cash requirement. There is a minimum 50% investment in established market currencies (US Dollar, Sterling & Euro) of which 25% must be Sterling. The Sterling requirement includes assets hedged back to Sterling.

    Equity growth fund. A growth fund mainly targets capital growth or total return and are distinguished from those that are designed for capital protection. The fund may target a particular geographical area or sector (such as smaller companies). Such funds are likely to target equities that are expected to experience acceleration in growth of earnings per share. In more aggressive funds, the investments are often in smaller and micro-cap stocks which are expected to experience rapid growth, although they may include sector specialist funds such as technology, banking, or biotechnology.

    Global equity fund. These are funds which invest at least 80% of their assets globally in equities. The main focus of funds which elect to be classified to the IMA 'Global' sector should be geographic diversification. Funds are diversified within the relevant country or region, or globally. Global funds which focus solely on a single industry sector may also elect to be classified to the Global sector, subject to maintaining geographic diversification – for example, all types of Global Commodity funds (Agriculture/ Resources/Gold), Global Financials, and Global Pharmaceuticals funds

    Global high yield fund. According to the ABI definition, this category comprises funds which invest at least 80% of their assets in non-UK fixed interest securities, and funds which invest at least 50% of their assets in sub-investment grade and/or emerging market fixed interest securities, without geographical restriction. Fixed interest securities are defined as Government sovereign bonds, local authority bonds, supranational bonds and corporate bonds, convertibles, preference shares, and permanent interest bearing shares.

    Direct property securities fund. In line with the ABI definition, these are funds that invest at least 80% of their assets in property securities quoted on the UK stock market and direct property located in the UK. Property securities include real estate investment trusts, shares issued by companies that own, develop or manage direct property and Property Index Certificates.

    Direct property fund. These funds normally invest at least 80% of their assets in UK property. Managers may occasionally use Property Index Certificates or other property instruments for up to 20% of the property investment.

    Money market fund. These are funds which invest their assets in short-term money market instruments, as defined in the COLL regulatory Handbook.

    (b) **Examiner's comment**. No candidates suggested that the Balanced Managed fund might actually be appropriate. This was a possible answer, and presumably a candidate would recommend a further client meeting to establish this to be the case. Candidates instead suggested an alternative course of action. Some did not have the conviction to propose an asset allocation which was central to the second part of the question. The question was interpretive, there is no one correct answer. The best scripts told a clear, concise and

consistent story. The key was to suggest a portfolio that would be risk-diversified, liquid, avoid unnecessary costs and charges, and have a beta different to that of the Balanced Managed fund. Candidates scoring lower marks failed to achieve these good practice techniques within their asset allocation.

One reasonable approach to the question, but by no means the only one, is as follows.

	CAPM Beta	Expected return	Historic volatility	Suggested weight
Balanced Managed	0.8	5%	10%	50%
Equity Growth	1.2	7%	19%	–
Global Equity	0.95	6%	14%	–
Global High Yield	0.4	4%	8%	25%
Direct Property Securities	0.7	6%	13%	10%
Direct Property	0.5	7%	11%	10%
Money Market	0.1	2%	4%	5%

As an approximation, the weighted average of the historic volatility figures gives volatility for the portfolio of 9.5%.

The weighted average of the expected returns produces an expected return for the portfolio of 5%.

The weighted average of the betas produces a beta for the portfolio of 6.2%.

The adviser might tell the client: 'I have produced an alternative asset allocation the stated purpose of which is to deliver a similar expected return but with lower volatility and Beta.

'This is a quite different portfolio to the Balanced Managed fund. The alternative asset allocation is more diversified, combining the large equity and government bond allocation found in the Balanced Managed fund with high yield debt and property.

'If markets conditions remain benign, both the Balanced Managed fund and my alternative suggestion are likely to perform similarly. If the economic environment deteriorates I would suggest that the alternative asset allocation will deliver far more stability.'

The adviser would offer reasons why this is likely to be the case, citing a more diversified beta and different sources of risk premia. The adviser would then set out whether active or passive (indexed) funds would be suggested, and why, along with likely costs and fees relative to the Balanced Managed fund.

Section C

3. **Immunisation**

Examiner's comment. The question tested candidates' understanding of whether immunisation is a passive bond portfolio strategy. Answers were of a good standard.

Passive managers take bond prices as fairly set, and seek to control only the risk of their fixed-income portfolio.

Arguments for passive strategy

Immunisation does not involve attempts to identify mispriced securities. Immunisation strategies seek to establish a virtually zero-risk profile, in which interest rate movements have no impact on the value of the portfolio or fund. A pension fund may try to insulate its portfolios from interest rate risk altogether. The pension fund wishes to protect the future value of the portfolio.

An immunised portfolio is performed by matching the interest rate exposure of assets and liabilities, ie matching the duration of the assets and liabilities. Price risk and reinvestment rate risk exactly cancel out. The result is that the value of assets will track the value of liabilities whether rates rise or fall.

For example, an increase in interest rates will cause a capital loss but at the same time this will increase the rate at which reinvested income will grow. This occurs because bond investors face two offsetting types of interest rate risk: price risk and reinvestment rate risk. If the portfolio duration is chosen appropriately, these two effects will cancel out exactly.

When the portfolio duration is set equal to the investor's horizon date, the accumulated value of the investment fund at the horizon date will be unaffected by interest rate fluctuations. For a horizon equal to the portfolio's duration, price risk and reinvestment risk exactly cancel out.

Arguments for active strategy

As interest rates and asset durations change, a manager must rebalance the portfolio of fixed-income assets continually to realign its duration with the duration of the obligation.

Even if interest rates do not change, asset durations will change because of the passage of time. So even if an obligation is immunised at the outset, the durations of the asset and liability will fall at different rates with time. Without portfolio rebalancing, durations will become unmatched.

Conclusion

Immunisation is a passive strategy only in the sense that it does not involve attempts to identify undervalued securities. Immunisation managers still actively update and monitor their positions.

4. **High net worth client objectives**

Examiner's comment. The question was not especially well answered, with some answers lacking succinctness and directness in answering the question.

An investment objective is set to help achieve the overall objectives of the client.

The following are examples.

1. Maximise the probability of obtaining an average annualised net return over any 3 year period greater than x, with volatility no greater than y.

2. To achieve with 99% probability that the fund covers 100% of a specified liability within acceptable risk.

Principal types of investment objective

- Target replacement income
- Benchmark driven
- Best efforts
- Liability or lump-sum driven

(Candidates were expected to be able to define or provide an example of each.)

Some fundamentals of setting an investment objective

- Real or Nominal?
- One or more, eg one for growth, one for consolidation, one for drawdown?
- Achievable by risk premiums (beta) alone, or achievable only with alpha?
- What is the client risk tolerance? What is the return objective? How achievable are these?

The asset allocation chosen will be determined by the need to meet the investment objective. The type of asset allocation, eg long-term strategic, CPPI, asset-liability, risk parity, will also be determined by the need to meet the investment objective.

(Candidates were expected to be able to succinctly discuss these and similar considerations around setting an investment objective.)

5. **Two-asset portfolio**

    Examiner's comment. The question asked candidates to produce an efficient frontier and introduce a risk-free rate to determine an approximate market portfolio. By and large, the question was well answered.

    (a)

Portfolio	Variance	Covariance	Sum	Std. dev.	Return
1	0.013	0.00135	0.0144	11.6%	5.5%
2	0.005	0.00135	0.0064	7.4%	4.5%

    (b)

Asset A	Asset B	Portfolio risk	Portfolio return
100	0	8.0%	4.0%
75	25	7.4%	4.5%
25	50	11.6%	5.5%
0	100	15.0%	6.0%

    With this information, we can draw an approximate efficient frontier. We add the risk-free rate of 2.5%, as shown in the diagram.

    (c) Minimum variance will be around 80% asset A and 20% asset B. Most efficient is around 70% asset A and 30% asset B. The most efficient portfolio is now not the minimum risk portfolio. To the left is lending, to the right is borrowing.

Return

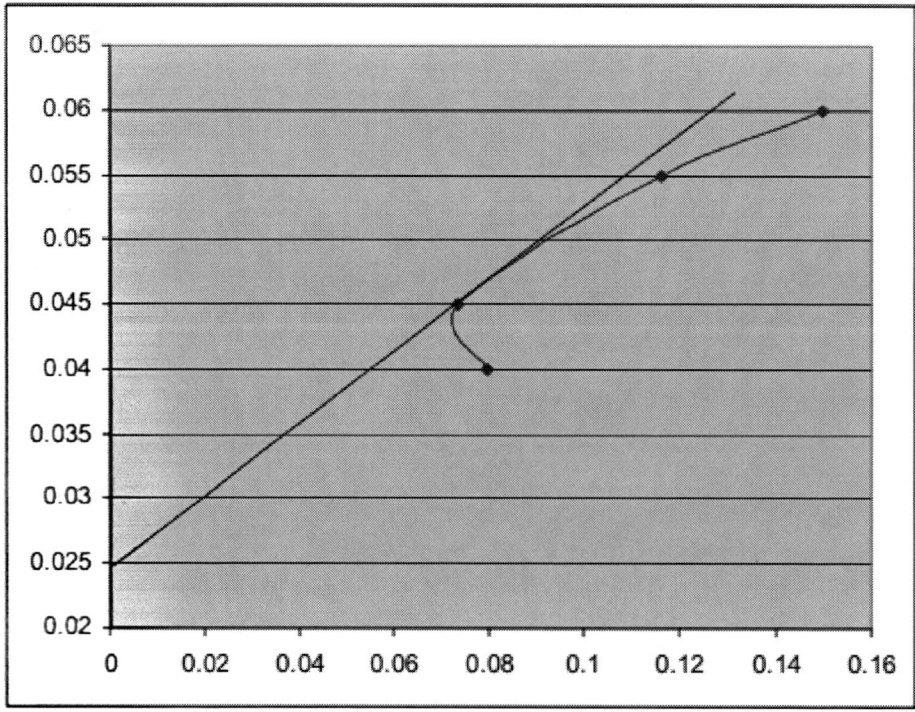

Risk

Part 2 – Taxation and Trusts

Section D

6. **Tax planning**

   (a) A trust is an arrangement under which a person, the 'settlor', transfers property to another person, the 'trustee' or trustees, who is required to deal with the trust property on behalf of certain specified persons, the 'beneficiaries'.

   In a bare trust, also known as a simple trust, there is a sole beneficiary. The trustee has no discretion over payment of income or capital to the beneficiary, who has an immediate and absolute right to both capital and income at age 18 (in England and Wales). The basic purpose of a bare trust is to restrict benefits going to children before they reach 18 and to try and avoid paying tax on the saving. On coming of age, the beneficiary of the trust can instruct the trustee how to manage the trust property, and then has the right to take actual possession of the trust property at any time.

   Two other types of trust with differing tax treatments are:

   - An interest in possession (IIP) trust, where the beneficiaries are automatically entitled to receive all of the income of the trust as it arises, and

   - A discretionary trust, where the trustees can determine which beneficiaries to make payments to and how much they will receive.

   How can a suitable trust be established?

   A discretionary trust may be set up by will. The discretionary trust allows the transferee flexibility about who is to benefit from the trust and to what extent. This can be useful if there are beneficiaries of differing ages and whose financial circumstances may differ.

   Although gifts to trusts during lifetime can lead to an IHT charge, as a chargeable lifetime transfer (CLT), there can be tax benefits from setting up trusts during the settlor's lifetime.

   If a discretionary trust is used, the settlor can preserve the maximum flexibility in the class of beneficiaries and how income and capital should be dealt with.

   If the settlor is included as a beneficiary of the trust, the gift will be treated as a gift with reservation.

   What are the long-term tax advantages of a trust?

   The rate of inheritance tax on principal charges and exit charges within a discretionary trust set up by will depend on the settlor's cumulative transfers in the seven years before his death and the value of the trust property.

   A CLT takes place when a discretionary trust is set up. The trust suffers the IHT principal charge once every ten years and the exit charge when property leaves the trust.

   With regard to lifetime trusts, as long as the cumulative total of CLTs in any seven-year period does not exceed the nil rate band, there will be no lifetime IHT to pay on creation of the trust. The trust will be subject to IHT at 0% on the ten-year anniversary and later advances, unless the value of the trust property grows faster than the nil rate band.

   IIP trustees' tax position is that interest income is taxed at 20% and dividends are taxed at 10%. As the usual tax credits generally satisfy the liability, no further tax is due from the trustees. The IIP beneficiary (or 'life tenant') is entitled to receive the trust income once the trustees have paid the tax due. The income paid to the beneficiary retains its nature so, if it

is interest income in the trustees' hands, it will be taxed as interest income on the beneficiary, and so on.

Discretionary trusts have a standard, or basic rate, band of £1,000. The first £1,000 of income is taxed at the basic rates, ie at 10% (dividends), and 20% (interest income). As for individuals, the basic rate band is applied first to non-savings income, then savings income and finally dividends. Many smaller trusts will have no further tax to pay. Any remaining income is taxed at the rates that apply to additional rate taxpaying individuals (2014/15):

- Interest income is taxed at 45% (the trust rate)
- Dividends are taxed at 37.5% (the dividend trust rate)

Beneficiaries of discretionary trusts are only taxed if they receive income payments from the trust. Any payments of income to beneficiaries will be made net of tax at 45% and are taxed on them at the rates that apply to earnings income.

For CGT purposes, there is no need to distinguish the type of trust. 'Settled property' is any property held in a trust, other than a trust where the beneficiary is absolutely entitled to trust property (a bare trust). In a bare trust, gains are treated as made by the beneficiary not the trustee.

If a settlor puts an asset into any type of trust, he makes a disposal for CGT purposes. It will be deemed to take place at market value.

We note that Mary's grandson Sam is disabled. Where a trust has a disabled beneficiary, the annual exempt amount for CGT purposes is raised to £11,000 (2014/15).

For trusts for the disabled, the rule that makes lifetime gifts to trusts chargeable to inheritance tax does not apply. However, inheritance tax may still be due when the transferor dies within seven years of the transfer.

(b) Worldwide assets of individuals domiciled in the UK are liable to inheritance tax (IHT). The chargeable estate comprises all assets less all liabilities at death, less exempt legacies, transfers and other allowances.

Inheritance tax (IHT) will be chargeable at 40% on the total value of Mary's chargeable estate on death that exceeds £325,000 (2014/15). A reduced rate of 36% applies where 10% or more of the net estate on death is left to charity.

If Mary makes any lifetime transfers and survives seven years after giving them, the transfers will be free of IHT.

Gifts made during are chargeable to IHT if the donor dies within seven years of making the gift. Gifts given in the last seven years of life are treated as Potentially Exempt Transfers (PETs) and the recipient may be liable for IHT, subject to taper relief according to the time that elapses between the gift and the death of the donor.

There is a small gifts exemption covering £250 per recipient, and an additional annual exemption for gifts up to £3,000 per fiscal year.

There are exemptions from IHT for types of 'excluded property', and certain other types of gift.

Mary cannot give away the family home (eg to her grandchildren) and continue to live in it, and gain any tax advantage. The gift would be treated as a 'gift with reservation'.

(c)   We are not given of information on any additional income from Mary's capital of approximately £3 million. (Does it comprise non-dividend paying investments?)

Mary's income tax liability 2014/15

Pension income: £51,000.

Dividend income: £4,000.

Taxable income: £55,000 – £10,000 = £45,000.

Income tax on non-savings income:

£31,865 × 20% = £6,373

£9,135 × 40% = £3,654

Income tax on dividend income:

£4,000 × 32.5% = £1,300

Mary's total income tax liability = £11,327

To know how much Mary must pay, we would deduct tax suffered on the dividends.

Gross dividends are £4,000 × 100/90 = £4,444. Tax suffered = £444.

We would also deduct the tax paid on Mary's pension income through PAYE, but this information is not given in the question.

(d)   We shall assume that Mary's has elected for her principal private residence exemption to apply to her UK home, since it is of substantially higher value than the home in Norway.

Assuming that Mary is a UK resident, sale of the holiday home (as with other assets, wherever in the world they are situated) will give rise to a taxable capital gain or loss, as applicable, in the UK. This is calculated by deducting the base cost from the arm's-length disposal proceeds.

If the cottage was bought before 31 March 1982, the base cost will be the 31 March 1982 value. If it was bought after this date, the base cost is the actual cost.

Where an asset is bought or sold in overseas currency, it must be translated into sterling using the rate applicable at the time of purchase or sale. The gain or loss is calculated using sterling figures.

If Mary has capital losses brought forward, she can set these off against a gain. Any loss which cannot be set off is carried forward to set against future chargeable gains.

Taxable gains less the annual exemption of £11,000 (2014/15) are added to the individual's income to determine in which tax band the gains fall: As Mary is a higher or additional rate taxpayer, the higher capital gains tax rate of 28% applies (2014/15).

There may be a liability to tax in Norway. In accordance with the relevant double taxation treaty (between the UK and Norway), double taxation relief is available to offset any double taxation suffered on assets disposed of abroad.

(e)   Mary could consider investing in the Enterprise Investment Scheme (EIS), if she is prepared accept the high risks associated with these investments. The EIS is a scheme designed to promote enterprise and investment by helping high-risk, unlisted trading companies raise finance by the issue of ordinary shares to individual investors who are unconnected with that company.

In outline, an EIS-qualifying company is a smaller unquoted (or AIM) trading company which exists wholly to carry on a qualifying business activity for a minimum of three years. Most trades are qualifying activities, but some – including banking, dealing in commodities and property development, for example – are excluded. The company must meet various size criteria to be small enough to qualify for the EIS.

Individuals who subscribe for EIS shares are entitled to income tax relief. Individuals can claim a tax 'reducer' of the lower of 30% of the amount subscribed for qualifying investments and the individual's tax liability for the year after deducting VCT relief. The maximum qualifying investment is £1,000,000.

Unused EIS relief cannot be carried forward to be used in later years. A taxpayer can claim to carry back all or part of the investment to the previous year, using any unused part of that year's limit.

The relief may be withdrawn if certain events, such as the sale of the shares, occur within three years.

Where EIS income tax relief is available, there are also capital gains tax reliefs. Where EIS shares are disposed of after the three-year period any gain is exempt from CGT. If the shares are sold within three years any gain is computed in the normal way. If EIS shares are sold at a loss at any time, the loss is allowable but the acquisition cost of the shares is reduced by the amount of EIS relief attributable to the shares. The loss is eligible for share loss relief against general income.

EIS reinvestment, or deferral, relief may be available to defer chargeable gains if an individual invests in EIS shares in the period commencing one year before and ending three years after the disposal of the asset.

The Seed Enterprise Investment Scheme (SEIS) is a tax-advantaged venture capital scheme similar to the EIS. The SEIS is focused on smaller, early stage companies carrying on, or preparing to carry on, a new business in a qualifying trade. The scheme makes available tax relief to investors who subscribe for shares and have a stake of less than 30 per cent in the company.

Venture capital trusts (VCTs) are listed companies which invest in unquoted trading companies and meet certain conditions. There is some similarity with the EIS rules, for example to ensure that only smaller companies qualify. The VCT scheme differs from EIS in that the individual investor may spread his risk over a number of individually higher-risk, unquoted companies.

Mary could use VCTs to save income tax on dividends, but again only if she wishes to invest in risky ventures. There is also no capital gains tax to pay on VCT investments, whatever the length of the holding period.

An individual investing in a VCT obtains tax benefits on a maximum qualifying investment of £200,000 in the tax year. There is a tax reduction of 30% of the amount invested. There is a withdrawal of relief if the shares are disposed of within five years or if the VCT ceases to qualify. Dividends received are tax-free income. Capital gains on the sale of shares in the VCT are exempt from CGT (and losses are not allowable).   In addition, capital gains which the VCT itself makes on its investments are not chargeable gains, and so are not subject to corporation tax. There is no minimum holding period requirement for the benefits of tax-free dividends and the CGT exemption.

Mary could make full use of her ISA allowance of £15,000 (2014/15 maximum, from 1 July 2014), to shelter dividends on stocks and shares investments from the higher rates of income tax. Disposal of investments within ISAs are also free from capital gains tax.

Section E

7. **French national**

We are asked to advise John on his tax situation. Based on the information given, this has two aspects: John's residence in and departure from the UK, and the sale of his Tesco shares.

Residence in and departure from the UK

Before coming to the UK, John would most probably be treated as having French domicile. To acquire a domicile of choice, a person must sever his ties with the country of his former domicile and settle in another country with the clear intention of making his permanent home there. It appears that John's period of living in the UK was probably not intended to be permanent, and John would then be treated as having retained his French domicile.

A resident but non-domiciled individual will normally be taxed on all general earnings on the receipts basis, wherever the duties of his employment are carried out. This is how John has been taxed on his UK employment. As a UK resident, John is entitled to the income tax personal allowance (£10,000 for 2014/15). The remittance basis, if claimed or if automatic, applies to non-UK earnings of such persons.

After John leaves the UK during a tax year, by claiming extra-statutory concession A11, he will only pay UK tax on income for that part of the year that he was in the UK.

Sale of Tesco shares

A person who is resident but non-domiciled in the UK can choose one of two ways of having their capital gains taxed:

(a)   The arising basis, in which case the person is liable to pay UK tax when they dispose of an asset in the UK or abroad

(b)   The remittance basis, in which case the person is liable to pay UK tax on gains that arise in the UK and foreign gains that are remitted to the UK

John could choose the remittance basis, and he has not lived in the UK long enough to incur the remittance basis charge. If he sells his Tesco shares while living in the UK, he would be subject to tax on the basis that the gain arises in the UK. However, as a non-domiciled individual who has claimed the remittance basis, John would not receive the annual capital gains tax exemption (£11,000 for 2014/15).

Assuming that John does not claim the remittance basis, then if he sells the Tesco shares while still living in the UK, he will be able to claim the annual exempt amount. Since this allowance exceeds the gain of £8,000 on the shares, there would be no capital gains tax to pay.

What if John sells the shares after leaving the UK? Extra-statutory concession D2 ensures that, if John leaves the UK during the tax year, he will not normally pay capital gains tax for the portion of a tax year that he is not resident in the UK. In the tax years after John leaves the UK, he is non-resident and, again, no capital gains tax liability arises.

The double tax treaty between the UK and France will normally ensure that John does not pay tax twice on the same income or gains.

8. **Holiday home**

We shall assume that Jill and James are UK residents.

If Jill owns a main residence in the UK which she treats as her principal private residence (PPR), and she does not let the holiday home as a trade, then a chargeable capital gain will be deemed to arise on the gift, as explained below.

If Jill uses the home to live in during some of the year, and she does not have another residence that she wishes to treat as her PPR, then she may have nominated the home in Spain as her PPR. In that case, no capital gains tax arises on the sale.

You can nominate which residence is to be treated as your PPR for any period. Your nomination must be made within two years of the date you first have a particular combination of residences. If there is a change in your combination of residences, a new two-year period begins.

The final 36 months of the period of ownership always qualify for relief, regardless of how the owner uses the property in that time, as long as the dwelling house has been their only or main residence at some point.

According to rules applying from 2012/13 onwards, if the holiday home is a furnished holiday letting (FHL), which is available to let for not less than 210 days per fiscal year, is let to the public for at least 105 days per fiscal year, and is not let for periods of longer-term occupation for more than 155 days during the year, then the FHL may be treated as a trade. These revised rules are being phased in by 2014/15 for FHLs that met the old rules in 2011/12. These rules provide capital gains tax reliefs for traders, including hold-over relief for gifts of business assets.

In the absence of any hold-over reliefs, the gift of the holiday home to James is treated as if Jill had disposed of the property at its market value of £103,000. A chargeable gain of £103,000 – £68,000 = £35,000 arises. After deducting the annual capital gains tax exemption of £11,000 (2014/15), CGT would be payable at 18%, or at 28% to the extent that income plus gains are within the higher or additional rate band, on £24,000.

Where an asset is bought or sold in overseas currency, it must be translated into sterling using the rate applicable at the time of purchase or sale. The gain or loss is calculated using sterling figures.

Business hold-over relief, if applicable, would enable the chargeable gain to be postponed, usually until the transferee disposes of the asset. A claim must be made for the relief. This would restrict James' ability to claim the property as his PPR.

Entrepreneurs' relief is available to reduce the gains on a material disposal of business assets, including FHLs. There is a lifetime limit of £10 million of gains on which entrepreneurs' relief can be claimed. Gains qualifying for entrepreneur's relief up to the lifetime limit are subject to a reduced rate of CGT of 10%.

If the home is a buy-to-let property, the disposal is liable to capital gains tax. The straightforward letting of property is not a trade.

If Jill dies within seven years of making the gift, there are potential inheritance tax (IHT) implications. The market value of the gift (£103,000) is a potentially exempt transfer (PET).

The first £325,000 of gifts in the seven-year period will not be chargeable to IHT, since they will fall within the exempt band (2014/15). However, these lifetime transfers will use up the exempt band, making more of the estate on death fully chargeable (at 40%). An annual gifts exemption of £3,000 applies, and can be carried forward to the next year, potentially making £6,000 available if no other gifts were made. Taper relief will apply to any IHT due on the PETs. If the donor died within three years of making the gift then IHT will be due at the full 40% rate. For gifts made 3-4 years before death, there is taper relief at 20%, 4-5 years at 40%, 5-6 years at 60%, and 6-7 years at 80%.

IHT due as a result of such a gift will usually be payable by the recipient of the gift. Alternatively, HMRC may seek payment from the deceased person's estate.

If the gift had been subject to a hold-over relief claim, the donee's base cost for capital gains tax will be increased by any IHT payable.

9.   **Matching rules**

If James is a UK resident, a disposal of shares will give rise to a taxable capital gain or loss as applicable, which is calculated by deducting the cost from the arm's-length disposal proceeds. Matching rules determine how share disposals are dealt with for tax purposes (see below).

If James has capital losses brought forward, he can set these off against a gain. Any loss which cannot be set off is carried forward to set against future chargeable gains.

Taxable gains less the annual exemption of £11,000 are added to the individual's income to determine in which tax band the gains fall: The following rates apply (2014/15):

■   18% – for taxable gains falling within the individual's basic rate tax band

■   28% – for taxable gains above the individual's basic rate band

For individuals, share disposals are matched for CGT purposes with acquisitions, in the following order.

(a)   Same day acquisitions

(b)   Acquisitions within the following 30 days ('bed and breakfast' rule): if more than one acquisition, it is dealt with on a 'first in, first out' (FIFO) basis

(c)   Any shares in the share pool

Any shares purchased before 31 March 1982 are brought into the share pool at their 31 March 1982 value.

For the share pool, the numbers and costs of shares are tracked. In the case of a disposal, the cost attributable to the shares sold is deducted from the amounts within the share pool.

The proportion of the cost to take out of the pool should be computed using the $A/(A + B)$ fraction that is used for any other part disposal.

To minimise CGT liabilities, James might consider transferring shares to his spouse (or civil partner before disposal, so as to take advantage of their annual exemption and the possibility that they are not a higher rate taxpayer. Disposals between spouses/civil partners who are living together give rise to no gain and no loss, whatever actual price (if any) was charged by the person transferring the asset to their spouse/civil partner. This means that there is no chargeable gain or allowance loss and the transferee takes over the transferor's cost.

James might also consider phasing the sales over different tax years, to take advantage of the CGT annual exemptions available in each year. However, caution should be exercised before making decisions about disposals mainly for tax reasons, as the investment logic needs to be considered.

December 2012 Examination Answers

Part 1 – Portfolio Construction Theory

Section A

1. **Multiple choice and short answer questions**

    (a) The correct answer is A.

    Expected return = Risk-free return + Beta × Market risk premium

    Expected return = 1.5% + 0.8 × (6% − 1.5%) = 1.5% + 3.6% = 5.1%.

    This is higher than the 4.7% return available at the current price, and so the equity is overpriced.

    (b) The correct answer is A.

    Expected return = Risk-free return + Beta × Market risk premium

    Expected return = 3% + 1 × 5% = 8%.

    (c) The correct answer is C.

    'Opt-ins' imply that people have to actively decide on an action or a preference. This is problematic because wide choice increases the probability of not making any choice.

    (d) The correct answer is C.

    Expected return = Dividend yield + Growth = 1/20 + 6% = 5% + 6% = 11%

    Expected return − Required return = 11% − 10% = 1%

    (e) The correct answer is D.

    The efficient market hypothesis implies that investors process information correctly. Anomalies suggest that this is incorrect, and that subsequent decisions may be inconsistent and suboptimal.

    (f) The correct answer is A.

    Bond B, having a longer duration than A, will be more sensitive to the rise in the yield to maturity (redemption yield).

    (g) The correct answer is B.

    A call option is an option to buy an asset. A higher exercise price is less attractive to the option holder, and so the value of the call option is negatively correlated to the exercise price.

    (h) The correct answer is B.

    The Capital Asset Pricing Model is a single factor model, and allows the decomposition of risk into two sources: market and firm-specific components.

    (i) The correct answer is C.

    Technical analysis seeks to take advantage of market inefficiency because it assumes that market participants' decisions are based on past price action of securities.

    (j) The correct answer is B.

    If a security price shows the pattern of a double top, this will be a break in an upward trend, and not a continuation of it.

(k)   The correct answer is C.

In technical analysis, a resistance level is said to be reached when a price is rising. (This is the opposite of a support level, which may be encountered when prices are falling.) Demand 'overcoming' supply, and there being 'spare' demand is thus not consistent with reaching a resistance level, at which demand is likely to weaken, according to the analysis.

(l)   The chart shows an investment with very little uncertainty, regardless of economic conditions that will have varied over 20 years. This suggests the investment is likely to be something like a cash, money market, Treasury or other similar short-term instrument or product. No investment provides perfect certainty but the investment represented in the chart has provided relatively safe returns. The chart does not indicate whether the returns are nominal or real.

(m)   Sharpe ratio = (Portfolio return – Risk-free return)/Standard deviation of portfolio return

We can calculate Sharpe ratios for each portfolio as follows.

Portfolio 1: (5 – 4)/5 = 0.20

Portfolio 2: (7 – 4)/7 = 0.43

Portfolio 3: (9 – 4)/10 = 0.50

Portfolio 4: (11 – 4)/15 = 0.47

Portfolio 5: (13 – 4)/21 = 0.43

Portfolio 6: (15 – 4)/28 = 0.39

The Sharpe ratio calculates portfolio return per unit of risk. The portfolio with the highest Sharpe ratio delivers most return per unit of risk. On this basis, Portfolio 3 is the most efficient. Portfolio theory would recommend investing in some combination of Portfolio 3 and the risk-free rate, depending on the investor's risk profile.

(n)   Required rates of return on other investment types will vary from the risk-free rate, The equity risk premium is required by equity investors who are taking a risk on the outcome of the investment. The premium is the additional return that equity investors require over and above the risk-free rate.

Accordingly, the data we need to calculate the risk premium comprises the risk-free rate and the return on the equities market.

(o)   **Examiner's comment.** Good answers mentioned the risk-free rate, return on the market and beta. Some candidates gave an answer using dividend discount model components.

List the data needed to calculate the required rate of return on an equity.

Using the Capital Asset Pricing Model, we can calculate the required return on an equity investment from the formula:

Required return = Risk-free rate of return + Beta factor × [Return on market – Risk-free rate of return]

The beta factor of a security is a measure of how its returns move with the market.

The data needed to calculate the required rate of return on an equity therefore comprises: the risk-free rate; the return on the market; and the beta factor.

(p)   The risk-free rate is fundamental to portfolio theory. Portfolio theory highlights that investors need to know the return to bearing no or little risk. The risk-free rate typically assumes no default risk and returns that are uncorrelated with idiosyncratic and systematic risk.

One component is a return for bearing illiquidity even if, for the lender, this means forgoing alternative uses of funds for a very short amount of time.

A second component is expected inflation. Investors will require a return equal to expected inflation in order not to erode the purchasing power of money lent. This means that a change in the expected rate of inflation will feed through to a change in the nominal risk-free rate. With perfect certainty, the risk-free rate will always represent a positive real return but, when expected and actual returns depart from each other, this may not be the case.

A third component is the influence of the central bank and commercial banks via the ease, or conversely the tightness, of money. Central bank policy may be influenced by real economic growth.

(q) A zero coupon bond has only one cash flow. The bond is purchased at a discount, with the pr ice rising to par at redemption. This equates to no re-investment risk.

A conventional five-year bond will not yield a risk-free return over five years, even if it is issued by a default-free entity, because the typically semi-annual coupons will have to be reinvested at future rates that are not known.

(r) P/E ratio = Payout/(k − g)

where k = Required rate of return, and g = Growth rate of dividends.

P/E ratio = 0.65/(0.08 − 0.04) = 0.65/0.04 = 16.25

(s) **Pension fund manager viewpoint**. It is possible for cash dividends to be a drag on investment performance by lowering a fund's intended beta and expected return, through the portfolio cash level being unintentionally high.

It is possible that companies with high expenditures on R&D, innovation, patenting and discovery will have a balance sheet that is less cash-generative and therefore more illiquid. This could equate to low dividend payments, but also to higher expected returns.

A pension fund is typically investing for around 30 years into the future and, if it is a growing scheme, it may have low need for liquidity. This points to investments in infrastructure, private equity, real estate, and tomorrow's companies.

Corporate governance manager viewpoint. Dividend payments are a valued and relied on source of income for some shareholders. Dividend payments are also a source of financial discipline for corporate boards. In many markets, there is a separate general meeting resolution to approve the final dividend, so this discipline is real.

Companies which have not identified and justified reinvestment opportunities and which also have low payout ratios are a cause of investor concern. Low or no dividends might be because of a high bonus pool, poor cash flow generation, raising doubts over the ongoing continuation of the company. A fund manager would then wish to oppose unjustifiably low dividend payouts.

(t) Value at Risk ranks all returns in descending order and asks how bad will be the return 95% of the way down the rank.

The worst 5% of returns is the 90% level under the 2-tail normal distribution, split 5% worst, 5% best. We take the reading at the 90% level.

Thus, the answer is: 1.645 × SD of 9.5% = 15.63% below the mean.

(u) Conditional Value at Risk (CVaR) is the average, or mean, loss of the 5% of worst outcomes.

The data presented already are the worst 5% of outcomes and their mean is −10.29%.

Descriptive statistics chosen could have included the maximum, minimum, mode, median, range, and inter-quartile range.

Maximum = –3%

Minimum = –28%

Mode = –3%

Median = –8%

Range = –25%

Inter-quartile range = –13.5% – (–2%) = –10.5%

Section B

2. **Portfolio performance measures**

(a) *Treynor measure*

Treynor measure = (Portfolio return – Risk-free return)/Portfolio beta

Portfolio: (0.07 – 0.03)/0.8 = 0.05

Benchmark: (0.08 – 0.03)/1.0 = 0.05

(b) *Sharpe ratio*

Sharpe ratio = (Portfolio return – Risk-free return)/Standard deviation of portfolio return

Portfolio: (0.075 – 0.02)/0.15 = 0.37

Benchmark: (0.07 – 0.02)/0.13 = 0.38

(c) *Information ratio*

Compound portfolio return:

Period 1: 100 × 1.023 = 102.3
Period 2: 102.3 × 0.964 = 98.62
Period 3: 98.62 × 1.052 = 103.75
Period 4: 103.75 × 1.012 = 105.00

Compound portfolio return = 5.0%

Compound benchmark return:

Period 1: 100 × 1.027 = 102.7
Period 2: 102.7 × 0.954 = 97.98
Period 3: 97.98 × 1.056 = 103.47
Period 4: 103.47 × 1.016 = 105.13

Compound benchmark return = 5.13%

Returns have been sampled four times. Therefore:

Standard deviation of excess returns = $\sqrt{[\ ¼ × \{(−0.004)^2 + (+0.01)^2 + (−0.004)^2\ (−0.004)^2\}}$

$= \sqrt{[0.000148/4]} = 0.006$

Information ratio =

(Compound portfolio return – Compound benchmark return)/Standard deviation of excess returns

$= (0.05 - 0.0513)/0.006 = -0.217$

(d)   A common performance test is whether actively departing from a benchmark leads to improved risk-adjusted performance. Treynor, Sharpe Ratio and Information Ratio measure this. They are different ways of measuring performance.

All measures are risk-adjusted, but the definition of risk varies. The **Treynor ratio** uses beta. The measure looks at the return to systematic risk. This is suitable for a diversified investor but can be hard for clients to understand. The Treynor measure is based on the Security Market Line. Treynor can be useful for measuring returns across different sectors and for any portfolio where a client holds a number of portfolios.

The **Sharpe ratio** is the 'excess' return of an asset over the return of a risk-free asset divided by the standard deviation of returns: ie, total risk, systematic and unsystematic. The Sharpe ratio is more intuitive to understand, and more applicable for clients who may not be fully diversified. The Sharpe Ratio is based on the Capital Market Line – appropriate for investors with one portfolio.

The **information ratio** is a measure of active return, the difference between the portfolio return and the return on the benchmark index, divided by the standard deviation of the active return, or tracking error. The information ratio measures a portfolio manager's ability to generate ex cess returns relative to a benchmark by looking at the active bets taken. The information ratio also attempts to identify consistency of fund manager performance. The ratio identifies if a manager has beaten the benchmark by a lot in a few months or a little every month (because this will be reflected in the standard deviation of the return difference). The higher the information ratio, the more consistent a manager. The information ratio can be used as an indicator of active or passive (index) management style. Like the Treynor measure, this can be hard for clients to understand.

Section C

3.   **Asset classes**

(a)(b)   Weighted returns:

UK equity: $0.70 \times 0.12 = 8.4\%$

UK real estate: $0.15 \times 0.12 = 1.8\%$

Infrastructure: $0.15 \times 0.07 = 1.05\%$

Portfolio return = $8.4 + 1.8 + 1.05 = 11.25\%$

Portfolio risk = $\sqrt{\sum[\text{Weight}^2 \times \text{Standard deviation}^2]}$

Calculate: $\text{Weight}^2 \times \text{Standard deviation}^2$

UK equity: $0.07^2 \times 0.21^2 = 0.49 \times 0.0441 = 0.021609$

UK real estate: $0.15^2 \times 0.09^2 = 0.0225 \times 0.0081 = 0.000182$

Infrastructure: $0.15^2 \times 0.05^2 = 0.0225 \times 0.0025 = 0.000056$

Portfolio risk = $\sqrt{[0.021609 + 0.000182 + 0.000056]} = \sqrt{0.021847} = 14.78\%$

(c) Looking ahead, the correlation of real estate to equity is likely to be greater than zero.

Real estate will provide less diversification than was historically the case. Why?

Wealth effects from real estate mean that real estate is likely to be more closely linked with the stock market going forward. Wealth within real estate can be accessed for current consumption, which changes economic expenditure and company earnings.

4. **Security market line (SML)**

(a) The SML is the line that reflects the relationship between systematic risk and return available for all risky assets in the capital market at a given time – ie, the return to systematic risk calculated by the Capital Asset Pricing Model. This will help investors to select investments that are consistent with their risk preferences. Some consider only low systematic risk and others consider higher systematic risk. The line shows the required rate of return for a given level of risk.

(b) A movement along the SML demonstrates a change in the risk characteristics for a specific investment, eg a change in its systematic risk, liquidity risk, or financial risk. A firm might increase its financial leverage, or its cash flow generation might fall. The security moves up the SML to reflect its higher risk and the commensurately higher required return of investors. The change affects only the individual investment.

(c) A change in slope of the SML occurs in response to new attitudes of investors toward risk, ie risk aversion. Investors now require a higher rate of return for the same level of risk. This is also a change in the market risk premium. A change in the market risk premium will affect all risky investments. In practice we find that the market risk premium is not constant, which suggests that the slope of the SML does change over time. This might be due to yield changes in other classes, eg credit risk premium or default risk premium. This will change other yields, including the equity market risk premium.

(d) A shift in the SML reflects a change in expected real growth, inflation, or the ease or tightness of money. This causes a change in the risk-free rate. A shift in the SML will affect all risky investments.

5. **Ethical investment**

(a) Calculate: Long-run forecast average annual return x Portfolio weighting

Equities: $5.5\% \times 50\% = 2.75\%$

Bonds: $4.0\% \times 40\% = 1.60\%$

Cash: $3.0\% \times 10\% = 0.30\%$

The portfolio return is the sum of the figures above.

Portfolio return = $2.75\% + 1.60\% + 0.30\% = 4.65\%$

(b) **Cash**. We need to ensure the cash is lent in ways that meet the ethical policy of the client. There may be a need to switch to a different cash manager/provider. This is expected to have a negligible impact on cash return as rates are so similar. We leave the capital market assumption unchanged, at +0.5% above inflation.

Bonds. Gilts pass ethical screens because the Government affords freedoms to people and has signed major international conventions and treaties. This means that the gilts part is unchanged. No switch is necessary. We leave the capital market assumption unchanged, at +1.5% above inflation.

Equities. Not all world equities are likely to meet the ethical policy of the client. This is likely to require switching the equity investments to ethical developed world equity. The FTSE 4

Good is one example of an ethical world equity index. Some industries are under-represented and some companies excluded. As the index is less representative of the total market, in theory this equates to higher risk and lower expected return. We should be mindful that the evidence for this remains inconclusive. This will depend year-to-year on the relative performance of over- and under-represented sectors.

Prudence might lead you to propose a slightly lower estimate for ethical equity return. Change capital market assumption to, for example, +5.3% nominal, an annual drop of 0.2%, and an increase in volatility to 17%.

We do not know the size of the long-run ethical equity risk premium. Making an estimate is problematic but the client is asking for one. Prudence may be a safer position to take, although the hazard here is that an unjustifiably lower estimate may deter the client from investing ethically at all.

Part 2 – Taxation and Trusts

Section D

6. **Tax advice memorandum**

    MEMORANDUM

    To: Client

    From: Adviser

    Date: XX December 2014

    (a)   You have asked for advice concerning your income tax liabilities and issues of double taxation.

    The residence and domicile status of an individual will determine which sources and how much of the person's worldwide income and gains is chargeable to UK tax.

    In the tax year 2014/15, you were resident in the UK. A person is domiciled in the country in which he has his permanent home. For your domicile to change, you would normally have severed ties with your country of former domicile and have settled in the new country with the clear intention of making it your permanent home.

    An annual remittance basis charge applies to non-domiciled individuals who have lived in the UK for more than seven years who choose the remittance basis. Resident 'non-doms' who have been resident in the UK for less than seven years can still elect for the remittance basis of tax, but there is no annual charge.

    The 'remittance basis' of taxation is where you pay UK tax on your UK income and capital gains, and also on any foreign income and capital gains that you bring (or 'remit') to the UK. The remittance basis contrasts with the 'arising' basis, whereby you pay UK tax on your UK income and capital gains plus all of your foreign income and capital gains. The remittance basis could be advantageous to you if you have unremitted income in the US or from elsewhere overseas that is taxed at lower rates in the foreign jurisdiction than it would be in the UK.

    For salary paid to you by Carpali Limited ('the company'), the company should normally have deducted income tax through the PAYE system. The statement that 'HMRC want to tax him' suggests that some separate contact has been made by HMRC, possibly as part of an investigation. The UK operates a self-assessment system for the taxation of individual and so it is a requirement that you account for any tax due through the self-assessment system.

    Income received from the company as dividends is deemed to carry a notional tax credit of 10%.

    Arranging for income received from the company to be paid as dividends rather than salary will create savings in national insurance contributions (NICs). No NICs are payable on dividends.

    If your spouse has not used her personal allowance and basic tax rate band with other income, to save tax, you may wish to consider dividends being received by her through a shareholding in the company.

    For 'US persons' – a category comprising US citizens and permanent residents – the rules for filing income, estate, and gift tax returns and paying estimated tax are generally the same whether the person is in the US or abroad. The person's worldwide income is subject to US income tax, regardless of where the person resides.

However, a double taxation treaty is in effect between the US and the UK, so that foreign taxes paid due be set against the US tax liability.

You should seek the advice of a tax professional with appropriate knowledge and experience of the US-UK double taxation treaty, and of preparing returns for the UK's HMRC and the US Internal Revenue Service (IRS).

(b)   You have asked about the inheritance tax (IHT) implications and IHT planning potential of gifts you may make to your wife and to your two daughters. As I am sure you can well appreciate, any tax advantage is only one of the factors you may wish to consider in making a gift.

IHT is generally charged at the rate of 40% on the total value of the chargeable estate that exceeds the 'nil rate band' of £325,000 (2014/15). You and your wife will each be entitled to a nil rate band on death.

Where a spouse or civil partner dies, any unused proportion of the nil rate band of the deceased spouse or civil partner can be claimed on the death of the surviving spouse or civil partner.

Gifts made by an individual during their lifetime to another individual will usually be exempt from IHT unless they are made in the last seven years of the individual's life, when they will be chargeable for IHT. A lifetime gift is therefore potentially exempt from IHT at the date of the gift. If the donor survives seven years thereafter, it becomes exempt.

IHT due as a result of such a gift will usually be payable by the recipient of the gift.

If the donor dies within three to seven years of the gift being made, then the rate of IHT is reduced by a percentage, depending on how long before death the transfer was made. This if the time between the gift being made and the date of death is 3 to 4; 4 to 5; 5 to 6; or 6 to 7 years, then the tax due is reduced by a taper relief of 20%; 40%; 60% or 80% respectively.

Some transfers will be automatically exempt from inheritance tax, even if they are made within seven years of death. Here we focus on exemptions that are relevant to your particular concern of making gifts to your family.

Gifts made during the donor's lifetime (but not on death) not exceeding £250 per recipient per fiscal year are exempt from IHT.

Gifts made during an individual's lifetime (but not on death) in consideration of marriage are exempt from IHT. The amount of the exemption depends on who is making the gift. Gifts by a parent of the bride or groom are exempt up to £5,000.

Over and above all the other exemptions, any gifts made by an individual during their lifetime (but not on death) are exempt from IHT up to £3,000 per fiscal year.

Should a particular gift be covered by another exemption (eg the small gifts exemption), then it does not use up the £3,000 annual exemption, which can be applied to other gifts. The annual exemption is applied chronologically, so that the first gift, not covered by other exemptions in the tax year, will receive the benefit.

The £3,000 annual exemption is available for carry forward, for one year only.

(c)   As you may well be aware, a trust is an arrangement under which a person, the 'settlor', transfers property to another person, the 'trustee' or trustees, who is required to deal with the trust property on behalf of certain specified persons, the 'beneficiaries'.

Two types of trust with differing tax treatments are:

▪   An interest in possession (IIP) trust, where the beneficiaries are automatically entitled to receive all of the income of the trust as it arises, and

▓   A discretionary trust, where the trustees can determine which beneficiaries to make payments to and how much they will receive.

IIP trustees' tax position is that interest income is taxed at 20% and dividends are taxed at 10%. As the usual tax credits generally satisfy the liability, no further tax is due from the trustees. The IIP beneficiary (or 'life tenant') is entitled to receive the trust income once the trustees have paid the tax due. The income paid to the beneficiary retains its nature so, if it is interest income in the trustees' hands, it will be taxed as interest income on the beneficiary, and so on.

Discretionary trusts have a standard, or basic rate, band of £1,000. The first £1,000 of income is taxed at the basic rates, ie at 10% (dividends), and 20% (interest income). As for individuals, the basic rate band is applied first to non-savings income, then savings income and finally dividends. Many smaller trusts will have no further tax to pay.

Any remaining income is taxed at the rates that apply to additional rate taxpaying individuals (2014/15):

▓   Interest income is taxed at 45% (the trust rate)
▓   Dividends are taxed at 37.5% (the dividend trust rate)

Beneficiaries of discretionary trusts are only taxed if they receive income payments from the trust. Any payments of income to beneficiaries will be made net of tax at 45% and are taxed on them at the rates that apply to earnings income.

For CGT purposes, there is no need to distinguish the type of trust. 'Settled property' is any property held in a trust, other than a trust where the beneficiary is absolutely entitled to trust property (a 'bare trust'). In a bare trust, gains are treated as made by the beneficiary not the trustee.

If a settlor puts an asset into any type of trust, he makes a disposal for CGT purposes. It will be deemed to take place at market value.

Where a trust has a disabled beneficiary, the annual exempt amount for CGT purposes is £11,000 (2014/15).

For trusts for the disabled, the rule that makes lifetime gifts to trusts chargeable to inheritance tax does not apply. However, inheritance tax may still be due when the transferor dies within seven years of the transfer.

(d)   In this section, we explain the taxation of shares that you may be selling to provide capital for a trust fund.

As a UK resident, you are liable to pay UK capital gains tax on any taxable gains on disposals of the foreign holdings. It should be possible to credit the UK liability against any US liability if any should arise, taking advantage of the double taxation treaty.

For UK capital gains tax (CGT) purposes, a chargeable gain is computed by taking the proceeds and deducting cost. A gain or loss is computed by taking the proceeds and deducting the cost, translated to sterling. Shares purchased before 31 March 1982 will be 're-based' to their 31 March 1982 value.

Incidental costs of acquisition and disposal can be set against any gain.

Allowable capital losses are deducted from chargeable gains in the tax year in which they arise. Any loss which cannot be set off is carried forward to set against future chargeable gains.

Capital gains are taxed at 18% to the extent that income and gains fall within the unutilised basic rate tax band, and the rest is taxed at 28%.

Gains can be set off against each individual's £11,000 annual CGT exemption (2014/15), in the year of disposal. You may wish to make disposals across more than one tax year, to take advantage of this annual exemption.

Assuming that you are living together with your wife in the tax year, in order to take advantage of any unutilised annual CGT allowance she may have, or to take advantage of the 18% rate if she is not within the higher rate tax band, you may consider making a gift of shares to your wife, enabling her to make the disposal.

Disposals are matched with acquisitions in the following sequence.

- On the same day
- In the next 30 days
- In the remaining share pool

On a part-disposal, a proportionate part of the original cost will be set against the proceeds to calculate the chargeable gain.

(e) Finally, we consider the issue of the taxation of your dividend income from US stocks.

For funds released by selling any of these stocks, you may consider you and possibly also your wife making use of Individual Savings Accounts. These allow an individual to invest £15,000 each (2014/15) per tax year in stocks within a tax wrapper that shelters these funds from further tax on dividends, and from capital gains tax. Alternatively, Venture Capital Trust investments offer tax reliefs on certain higher-risk investments.

You should however be aware that UK-based tax wrappers will not be recognised by the US Internal Revenue Service (IRS) – a relevant consideration, should you decide to move back to the US.

In circumstances of making disposals of shares, you may also wish to consider the use of trusts, on which we provided some key points earlier.

However, more specifically, you have asked about how to save tax on your substantial dividend income from a number of US companies, and so we assume that you wish to retain these investments in the US.

The UK tax liability on dividends is as follows.

- There is no further tax to pay for a basic rate taxpayer

- A higher rate taxpayer has a liability to pay 22.5% tax on the gross dividend in addition to the 10% tax credit

- An additional rate taxpayer has a liability to pay 27.5% tax on the gross dividend in addition to the 10% tax credit (2014/15 rates)

To ensure that you are not over-paying tax, you should ensure that you take advantage of the US/UK double taxation treaty to credit any US tax on the dividends against your UK liability.

We have explained earlier that a non-domiciled individual can elect to be taxed on a remittance basis. However, income that is not remitted is likely, in that case, to attract a US tax liability.

Section E

7. UK tax liability

	Non-savings income £	Savings income £	Dividend income £	Total £
Pension income	28,000			
Interest income		12,000		
Dividend income			42,000	
Total income	28,000	12,000	42,000	82,000
Less personal allowance (2014/15)	(10,000)			(10,000)
Taxable income	18,000	12,000	42,000	72,000

	£	£
Income tax on non-savings income		
£18,000 × 20%		3,600
Tax on savings income		
£12,000 × 20%		2,400
Tax on dividend income		
£1,865 × 10%		186
£40,135 × 32.5%		13,043
Total tax liability		19,229

We are not told John's age but, even if he was born before 6 April 1948, his income is too high to receive the additional age-related allowance.

The question asks for the total tax liability. Note that, to arrive at the tax payable, we would need to deduct tax suffered on the pension income and the interest income, as well as the 10% tax credit on dividends.

8. Capital gains tax

	£
Proceeds	19,400
Less: cost	(6,000)
Net gains	13,400
Less: annual exemption (2014/15)	(11,000)
Taxable gain	2,400

The above calculation assumes that Mike's only chargeable disposal was of the antique table.

The CGT liability will depend on whether the gains fall within the basic rate band, or above it, taking into account Mike's total income and gains. Within the basic rate band, the CGT payable will be £2,400 × 18% = £432. Above the basic rate band, the CGT payable will be £2,400 × 28% = £672.

9. **Inheritance tax**

    To establish who pays how much tax, we work through the lifetime transfers chronologically. The transfer to Matthew in July 2007 is exempt since it falls outside the seven-year period. The nil rate band is used up first by the gifts made furthest back in time.

	£
August 2008 transfer to Mark	
Inheritance tax on first £140,000 of estate	–
September 2009 transfer to Luke	
Inheritance tax on next £185,000 of estate	–
Inheritance tax on next £75,000 of estate at 40%	30,000
Less: Taper relief at 40% (4 to 5 years since gift)	(12,000)
Payable by Luke	18,000
October 2010 transfer to John	
Inheritance tax on next £130,000 of estate at 40%	52,000
Less: Taper relief at 20% (3 to 4 years since gift)	(10,400)
Payable by John	41,600
Property at death	
Inheritance tax on £480,000 at 40%: payable from the estate	192,000

June 2012 Examination Answers

Part 1 – Portfolio Construction Theory

Section A (40 marks)

1. **Multiple choice questions**

    (a)   **B**

    (b)   **A**

    (c)   **C**

    (d)   **B**

    (e)   **C**

    (f)   **D**

    (g)   **A**

    (h)   **C**

    (i)   **C**

    (j)   **B**

    (k)   **C**

    (l)   Most probably, the company's share price fell as the market was expecting a higher settlement. The company whose share price rose was seen to have to pay less than expected. The news was material and investors expected a higher settlement.

    Alternatively or additionally, other non-financial terms of the settlement may have been worse than expected. This could have been due to a ban on use of certain technology, or a ban from selling in certain markets.

    (m)   A fundamental index is constructed by taking into account more general economic movements that may reflect the broader economy and economic growth. Such indices may weight stocks by one or a combination of various economic factors, such as sales, earnings, cash flow and book value. The fundamental factors used are typically accounting figures used in corporate valuation, as fundamental index methodology treats these figures as more accurate indicators of a company's value than the listed market value (capitalisation).

    A fundamental index may favour stocks based on fundamental characteristics that can reveal stocks' ability to generate wealth. These fundamentals may be attractive because they are reflective of a client's own investment thesis. They are also potentially attractive to investors who reject the efficient market hypothesis.

    Other reasons for fundamental indices are based on criticisms of a market capitalisation approach. The latter assigns weights based on the market value of all of its stock ('market cap'). The main reason to move away from the market cap index is that the largest market cap stock may be the most overvalued. In some countries, a few large stocks tend to dominate the index, so what appears to be a market trend is actually driven by a small number of companies, perhaps in one or two sectors only.

(n)   Tracking error is not likely to be zero due to the following.

- ▨   Transaction costs that occur when constructing an index tracking portfolio or when occasional rebalancing occurs due to change in the composition of the index, contributions, withdrawals or dividend received.

- ▨   The timing of buying/selling stocks when they leave or enter the index.

- ▨   Round-lot purchases – it may only be possible to buy stocks in lots of 100, creating a slight mis-match between the weight that a stock has in the index and the weight actually allocated in the tracking portfolio.

- ▨   Possible restrictions on foreign ownership, if the index has not only domestic constituents.

- ▨   Changes in price due to entering or leaving index – the fund may trade after constituents enter or leave the index.

- ▨   The index, if a total return index, normally assuming ex-dividend date is payment date – in reality, the payment date may be up to six weeks following ex-dividend date.

- ▨   Some dividend payments may be too small to be amenable to reinvestment.

(o)   Futures contracts are standardised contracts in terms of size and delivery dates. They are contracts between a customer and a clearing house – often traded on an exchange. When traded is on-exchange, the instruments are regulated. As a result, futures contracts are more liquid than non-exchange contracts, and so are usually more suitable for portfolio investors. The contract specifies the quantity and quality of the underlying asset. Profits and losses on futures contracts are realised immediately, as they are marked to market. Margins must be maintained to reflect price movements. While losses and gains are potentially unlimited, if the price of the underlying does change, the holder of a futures contract can in principle sell.

Forward contracts are customised ('tailored') contracts in terms of size and delivery dates. With price agreed at the start of the contract, there are a finite number of outcomes. Forward contracts are private over-the-counter contracts between two parties, and may involve search costs. Such contracts allow for more precise hedging by companies because the contract is specifically tailored to the client need. Forwards contracts are not regulated. They are an obligation, and so are difficult to reverse. Profit or loss on a forward contract is realised on the delivery date. The price agreed is usually paid upon physical delivery. Delivery must be taken on the contract date. Margins are set once, on the day of the initial transaction.

(p)

	A	B	C
Day 1	10	20	30
Day 2	12	22	32
Return	0.20	0.10	0.067
Weight	0.17	0.33	0.50
Weighted return	0.033	0.033	0.033

A faster method also obtaining full marks is to take advantage of the index being price-weighted. With the prices being the weights, the index calculation can be shortened to:

Sum of Day 1 prices = 60

Sum of Day 2 prices = 66

Change = 10%

(q)   The tradability of the stock is a major determinant of the size of the bid-ask spread. This will depend on company size, liquidity, trading volume, and supply and demand for the stock.

Other factors include the following.

■   **Recent price volatility**. More volatility => wider spread

■   **Company or sector news flow**, eg profit warnings, which lead market makers and brokers to not want to hold inventory

■   **Size of the trade**. Extremely large size => wider spread

■   **Type of market place**. Institutional (inter-bank) and more professional => narrower spread. Retail => wider spread

■   **Creditworthiness of the client**. Better credit => narrower spread

■   Number of market makers and brokers quoting and willing to hold inventory. More competition => narrower spread

(r)   Note that the trendline joins a series of upper or lower inflexion points.

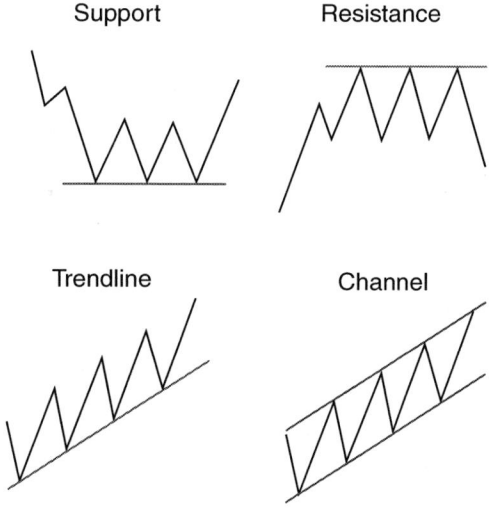

Support   Resistance

Trendline   Channel

(s)   Expected return = 3% + (10 % × 1.0) + (7% × 2.0) + (6.0% × 0.0) = 27.0%

(t)   Conversion value = Conversion ratio × Market price

20 shares × $4.50 = US$90.00

The bond is trading at US$110, so the premium is currently $110 – $90 = US$20

Premium as a percentage of the conversion value is $20/$90 = 22.2%

Section B

2.   **Fixed income portfolio management strategies**

Passive management

By and large, passive management applies to the whole bond portfolio, and not just sections of it. Passive managers take bond prices as fairly set and mostly seek to control only the risk of their portfolio.

Two passive bond portfolio strategies are indexation and immunisation. Both strategies view the determination of prices as efficient. The two strategies have different risk. A bond-index portfolio will have the same risk-reward profile as the bond market index to which it is tied. An immunisation strategy will seek to establish a virtually zero-risk profile, in which interest rate movements have no impact on the value of the firm.

Bond index fund

A bond index fund creates a portfolio that mirrors the composition of an index based on a broad market. Three major indexes of the broad bond market are the Barclays Capital (US) (formerly Lehman) Aggregate Bond Index, the Salomon Broad Investment Grade (BIG) Index, and the Merrill Lynch Domestic Master Index. The three indices are market-value weighted, total return. All three include a variety of issuers – government, corporate, mortgage-backed, and Yankee bonds.

Of the hundreds and sometimes thousands of issues, many are infrequently traded. It can be difficult to purchase each security in the index in proportion to its market value. Bond index funds also face rebalancing problems, with bonds continually dropped from the index as their maturities fall below one year. New bonds are added as they are issued. This results in turnover, and the manager makes corresponding portfolio changes to ensure a close match between the composition of the portfolio and the bonds included in the index. Due to this, a stratified sampling or similar approach is practised. The characteristics of the portfolio in terms of maturity, coupon rate, credit risk, industrial representation and so on match the characteristics of the index, and the performance of the portfolio likewise should match, with some limited departure.

Immunisation

With immunisation, the investor tries to insulate the portfolio from interest rate risk altogether. Many defined benefit pension funds are today concerned with protecting the future values of their portfolios. The ability to meet future obligations fluctuates with interest rates. This makes investors interested in interest rate risk, and they will seek to match the interest rate exposure of assets and liabilities. The value of assets will then track the value of liabilities whether rates rise or fall. This is performed by matching the duration of the assets and liabilities. If this is successful, bond price risk and reinvestment rate risk exactly cancel out.

Fixed income investors face two offsetting types of interest rate risk: price risk and reinvestment rate risk. Increases in interest rates cause capital losses but at the same time increase the rate at which reinvested income will grow. If interest rates were to fall, coupons can only be reinvested at a lower rate, but this is offset by the increase in the capital value of the bonds that were yielding a higher rate. If the portfolio duration is chosen appropriately, the two effects will cancel out exactly. When the portfolio duration is set equal to the investor's time horizon end date, the accumulated value of the investment fund at the horizon end date will be unaffected by interest rate fluctuations. For a horizon equal to the portfolio's duration, price risk and reinvestment risk exactly cancel out. The netting off guarantees the gross redemption yield and so helps match the liability.

As interest rates and asset durations change, a manager must rebalance the portfolio of fixed income assets to realign its duration with the duration of the obligation. Even if interest rates do not change, asset durations will change solely because of the passage of time. This means that if an obligation is immunised at the outset, as time passes the durations of the asset and liability will fall at different rates. Duration generally decreases less rapidly than does maturity. Without portfolio rebalancing, durations will become unmatched. This makes immunisation a passive strategy only in the sense that it does not involve attempts to identify undervalued securities.

Active management

Two sources of potential value here are:

■ Interest rate forecasting, which tries to anticipate movements across the entire spectrum of the fixed income market. If interest rate declines are anticipated, managers will increase portfolio duration (and vice versa).

■   Identification of relative mis-pricing within the fixed income market. An analyst, for example, might believe that the default premium on one particular bond is unnecessarily large and therefore that the bond is underpriced.

There are several active management techniques.

Anomaly switch or substitution swap

This involves swapping bonds that are similar – an exchange of one bond for a nearly identical substitute. The substituted bond is of essentially equal coupon, maturity, quality, call features, sinking fund provisions, and so on. This swap would be motivated by a belief that the market has temporarily mispriced the two bonds, and that the discrepancy between the prices of the bonds represents a profit opportunity. Example: Sale of a 20-year maturity, 8% coupon Toyota bond that is priced to provide a yield to maturity of 8.05%, coupled with a purchase of an 8% coupon Honda bond with the same time to maturity that yields 8.15%. A bridge swap falls under this category.

Policy switch or rate anticipation swap

This means swapping bonds that are dissimilar in anticipation of policy changes such as a change in central bank interest rate. If investors believe that rates will fall, they will swap into bonds of longer duration. Conversely, when rates are expected to rise, they will swap into shorter duration bonds. For example, the investor might sell a 5-year maturity Treasury bond, replacing it with a 25-year maturity Treasury bond. The new bond has the same lack of credit risk as the old one, but longer duration.

The inter-market spread may be used when an investor believes that the yield spread between two sectors of the bond market is temporarily out of line. For example, if the current spread between corporate and government bonds is considered too wide and is expected to narrow, the investor will shift from government bonds into corporate bonds.

Riding the yield curve or pure yield pickup swap

This is a means of increasing return by holding higher-yield bonds. When the yield curve is upward-sloping, the yield pickup swap entails moving into longer-term bonds. This is an attempt to earn an expected term premium in higher-yield bonds. The investor is willing to bear the interest rate risk that this strategy entails. If the yield curve is 'normal' and stays so, the investor who swaps the shorter-term bond for the longer one will, other things being equal, earn a higher rate of return.

Tax swap

The term 'tax swap' refers to a swap to exploit some tax advantage. For example, an investor may swap from one bond that has decreased in price to another if realisation of capital losses is advantageous for tax purposes.

Section C

3.   **Portfolio risk**

(a) $\sigma_{a+b} = \sqrt{p_a^2\sigma_a^2 + p_b^2\sigma_b^2 + 2p_ap_b\text{Cov}_{ab}}$

Where:

Cov_{ab} = Correlation$_{ab}$ × Standard deviation$_a$ × Standard deviation$_b$

Portfolio variance = $(0.6^2 \times 0.04) + (0.4^2 \times 0.09) + (2 \times 0.6 \times 0.4) \times 0.3 \times \sqrt{0.04} \times \sqrt{0.09}$

= 0.0144 + 0.0144 + 0.00864 = 0.0374

(b)   Portfolio standard deviation = $\sqrt{0.0374}$ = 0.194 or 19.4%

(c)   Risk can be further reduced by including more asset classes and by including a risk-free asset.

4.   Equity valuation

(a)   Required return for Stock A = 2% + 1.9 × (6% − 2%) = 9.6%

The expected return for Stock A is 11.4%. Stock A is undervalued. This is above the Securities Market Line.

Required return for Stock B = 2% + 0.8 × (6 % − 2%) = 5.2%

The expected return for Stock B is 5.2%. Stock B is correctly priced. This is on the Securities Market Line.

(b)/(c)

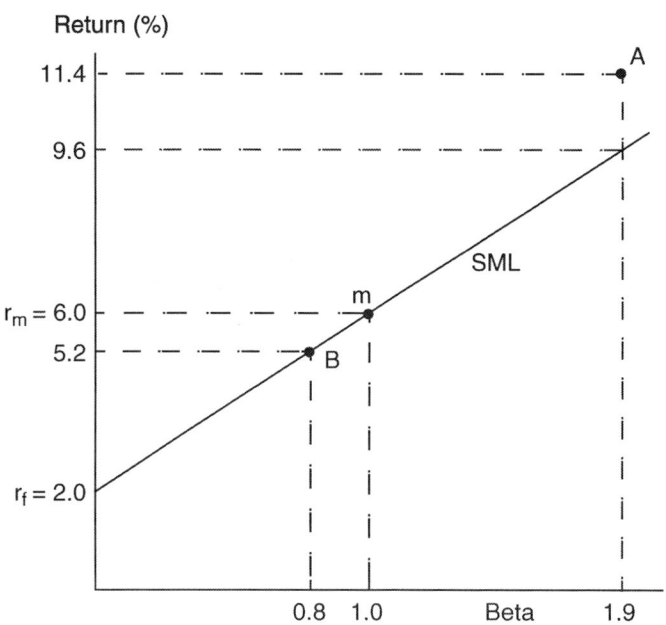

The x-axis of the chart is beta (ie, risk for a diversified investor). The y-axis is expected/required return.

5.   Explain terms

(a)   **Duration**

To deal with the ambiguity of the 'maturity' of a bond making many payments, we need a measure of the average maturity of the bond's promised cash flows. This is performed by taking the time-weighted present value of all future cash flows of a bond. In this way, duration measures the price sensitivity of a bond to changes in interest rates. It is the fulcrum in the length of time to receipt of all cash flows. This is analogous to volatility for equities.

Frederick Macaulay (1938) termed the effective maturity concept the duration of the bond. Macaulay's duration equals the weighted average of the times until each payment is received, with the weights proportional to the present value of the payment.

A high coupon, short duration bond will not vary in price as much as a low coupon high duration bond. Duration is shorter than maturity for all bonds except zero coupon bonds. Duration is equal to maturity for zero coupon bonds.

(b) **Convexity**

Duration and convexity are first and second derivatives that measure changes in price. The duration formula asserts that the percentage price change is directly and linearly proportional to the change in the bond's yield.

If this were exactly so, however, a graph of the percentage change in bond price as a function of the change in its yield would plot as a straight line, with slope equal to $-D$. The relationship between bond prices and yields is in fact not linear. This is because duration changes as the yield changes. Convexity measures this by making an adjustment to the Macaulay's duration to arrive at the new bond price. Bonds with greater convexity have more curvature in the price-yield relationship. Duration alone is a good approximation for only small changes in bond yields.

The duration approximation (a straight line) always understates the value of the bond; it underestimates the increase in bond price when the yield falls, and it overestimates the decline in price when the yield rises. This is due to the curvature of the true price-yield relationship. Curves with shapes such as that of the price-yield relationship are said to be convex, and the curvature of the price-yield curve is called the convexity of the bond.

Part 2 – Taxation and Trusts

Section D

6.   **Tax advice**

(a)   James and John might consider making gifts in advance to children for expenses such as university fees or weddings. Junior ISAs (£4,000 maximum per year (2014/15, from 1 July 2014)) can be set up for children who are not entitled to a child trust fund (CTF). (Children born between 1 September 2002 and 2 January 2011 are entitled to a CTF.) Income from other assets given to a child by parents will be taxable on the parent if it exceeds £100 gross per year. It should be noted that, in common law, children cannot be bound to a contract to buy shares and so they are usually precluded from owning shares directly before they are aged 18.

Gifts to children could help to mitigate future inheritance tax (IHT) liabilities, and maximum use could be made of exemptions and reliefs.

James and John can each shelter some assets from capital gains tax and tax on income by subscribing to ISAs which can hold equities and other investments (£15,000 maximum annual contribution (2014/15, from 1 July 2014)).

James and John might consider the conversion of the partnership into a limited company. Incorporation can offer advantages in that profits left in a company attract corporation tax at lower rates than the income tax that partners must pay on profits. However, a limited company will pay national insurance contributions (NICs) at a higher rate than members of a partnership and this can add significantly to the tax payable by both the company and individual.

The partnership will be required to deduct Pay As You Earn income tax and National Insurance Contributions from employees' pay. This will be payable by the partnership to HMRC, on the employees' behalf.

(b)   A trust with a disabled beneficiary has some tax advantages – for example, a CGT annual exemption of £11,000 (2014/15) – double that of other trusts. Additionally, lifetime gifts to such trusts are not chargeable to inheritance tax, in the case of discretionary and interest in possession (IIP) trusts.

John might set up a bare trust, as a relatively simple option, provided that John is happy with his daughter having access to the trust property when she comes of age.

In a bare trust, also known as a simple trust, there is a sole beneficiary. The trustee has no discretion over payment of income or capital to the beneficiary, who has an immediate and absolute right to both capital and income at age 18 (in England and Wales). The basic purpose of a bare trust is to restrict benefits going to children before they reach 18 and to try and avoid paying tax on the saving. On coming of age, the beneficiary of the trust can instruct the trustee how to manage the trust property, and then has the right to take actual possession of the trust property at any time.

Another possibility is for John to make a gift to his daughter but to utilise his ISA allowance first and then make the gift of that money to her.

Buying long-term care insurance is another possibility that John might consider.

(c)   For individuals, share disposals are matched for CGT purposes with acquisitions, in the following order.

(i)   Same day acquisitions

(ii)   Acquisitions within the following 30 days ('bed and breakfast' rule): if more than one acquisition, it is dealt with on a 'first in, first out' (FIFO) basis

(iii)   Any shares in the share pool

Any shares purchased before 31 March 1982 are brought into the share pool at their 31 March 1982 value.

For the share pool, the numbers and costs of shares are tracked. In the case of a disposal, the cost attributable to the shares sold is deducted from the amounts within the share pool. The proportion of the cost to take out of the pool should be computed using the A/(A + B) fraction that is used for any other part disposal.

To minimise CGT liabilities, James might transfer shares to his wife before disposal, so as to take advantage of Nora's annual exemption and the possibility that she not be a higher rate taxpayer. As a higher rate taxpayer, James will pay CGT at 28%, while a basic rate taxpayer will pay CGT at 18%. James might also consider phasing the sales over different tax years, to take advantage of the CGT annual exemptions available (£11,000 in 2014/15). If James wishes to become non-UK resident, delaying the disposals until he has lived abroad for three full tax years would remove the UK CGT liability, but there may still be a capital gains tax levied by the country to which he moved.

(d)   If James and John will make use of their ISA allowances in full, the dividends on shares in ISAs will be free of additional tax, although the notional tax credit on dividends cannot be reclaimed. Shares could be moved into ISAs through a 'Bed & ISA' transaction with a broker, when a chargeable disposal for CGT purposes is deemed to take place. Dividends on shares transferred to another person such as a spouse who is a basic rate taxpayer will avoid the tax that James and John must pay on dividends as higher rate taxpayers (32.5%), and as possible additional rate taxpayers (37.5%) in the future.

Income from investments given to a child by parents will be taxable on the parent if it exceeds £100 gross per year. However, as noted in the answer to part (a), children cannot generally hold shares directly, and many companies' articles require shareholders to be aged 18 or over. For children, shares would typically be held in a bare trust.

A child will be entitled to the individual income tax allowance, and they can take advantage of the lower or basic tax bands. Money paid into a Junior ISA or existing Child Trust Fund is excepted from this rule.

If James and John retain their shares, they will be taxed on the dividends, even if the dividends are then given to their children.

Contributions to any existing Child Trust Fund or to a Junior ISA will enable some transfer of assets which would then be sheltered from tax on income arising.

(e)   From 6 April 2013, a new statutory residence test was established, and the concept of 'ordinary' residence was abolished for tax purposes.

If an individual satisfies any of a number of 'automatic overseas tests', then he is non-resident.

A person is domiciled in the country in which he has his permanent home. A person may be resident in more than one country, but he can be domiciled in only one country at a time.

A resident and domiciled individual is taxed on his general earnings on a receipts basis.

A non-resident is taxed on his general earnings in respect of UK duties on the receipts basis but there is no UK income tax on foreign earnings (those in respect of non-UK duties).

Whether James remains UK-resident for tax purposes will depend partly on the length of stays in the UK. He would still be treated as UK-domiciled. If not UK-resident, James may be able to take advantage of tax rates in Spain, if lower than in the UK.

The provisions of the Spain-UK Double Tax Convention are likely to prevent potential double taxation in each jurisdiction.

Section E

7.   Residence and domicile

From 6 April 2013, a new statutory residence test was established, and the concept of 'ordinary' residence was abolished for tax purposes.

If an individual satisfies any of the following automatic overseas tests, then he is non-resident.

Automatic overseas tests

(a)   Was resident in the UK for one or more of the three previous tax years and spends fewer than 16 days in the UK in the current tax year

(b)   Was not resident in the UK for any of the previous three tax years and spends fewer than 46 days in the UK in the current tax year

(c)   Leaves the UK to carry out full-time work overseas, or

(d)   Dies in the current tax year, subject to conditions which include spending fewer than 46 days in the UK.

If the individual does not satisfy any of the automatic overseas tests, the individual will be automatically UK-resident if he meets any of the following automatic UK tests.

Automatic UK tests

(a)   He spends 183 days or more (ie more than six months) in the UK during the tax year

(b)   There is a period of more than 90 days, part of which falls within the tax year, when he has a home in the UK and no home overseas (disregarding any home at which he is present for fewer than 30 days in the tax year)

(c)   He dies in the current year, subject to conditions which include having been UK-resident in the previous three tax years, or

(d)   He meets a full-time UK work test, as set out in the taxation rules.

If the individual meets none of the automatic overseas tests and none of the automatic UK tests, he must look at the 'sufficient ties' test, which compares the number of days spent in the UK against the number of 'connection factors' that apply, such as whether he has a UK-resident family, or accommodation in the UK.

A person is **domiciled** in the country in which he has his permanent home. A person may be resident in more than one country, but he can be domiciled in only one country at a time.

Where the individual was born determines his or her domicile of origin. A person retains this domicile until he acquires a different domicile of dependency (if, while he is under 16, his father's domicile changes) or domicile of choice if he permanently settles in another country.

A resident and domiciled individual is taxed on his general earnings on a receipts basis.

A non-resident is taxed on his general earnings in respect of UK duties on the receipts basis but there is no UK income tax on foreign earnings (those in respect of non-UK duties).

A UK resident who is not UK domiciled may claim the remittance basis for a particular tax year, so that he is only liable to UK income tax on overseas income to the extent that it is brought (remitted) to the UK. Such an individual is liable to the remittance basis charge if he claims the remittance basis for a tax year, subject to the following residence rule.

- If the individual has been UK-resident for at least seven of the nine tax years preceding that tax year, the remittance basis charge payable is £30,000 annually.

- If the individual has been UK-resident for at least 12 of the 14 tax years preceding that tax year, the remittance basis charge payable is £50,000 annually.

Resident 'non-doms' who have been resident in the UK for less than seven years can still elect for the remittance basis of tax, but there is no annual charge.

Persons who are not resident in the UK are exempt persons for capital gains tax (CGT) purposes. As chargeable persons, UK-resident individuals are liable to CGT on their chargeable disposals of chargeable assets.

The liability to inheritance tax (IHT) is based on the chargeable estate of an individual who has died. All individuals who are domiciled in the UK will be liable to IHT on all their assets worldwide. Individuals not domiciled in the UK will be liable to IHT on their UK assets.

8. **Lifetime transfers**

    A lifetime transfer made seven years before death or earlier will usually be exempt from inheritance tax. The exception to this is the chargeable lifetime transfer (CLT).

    A gift to other individuals while retain a beneficial interest in the assets given away (gift with reservation) is not recognised for inheritance tax (IHT) purposes.

    The first £325,000 of gifts in the seven-year period will not be chargeable for inheritance tax, since they fall within the exempt band (2014/15). IHT due as a result of such a gift will usually be payable by the recipient of the gift. If the recipient does not pay, then HMRC can resort to the deceased person's estate for payment.

    If the donor died within three years of making the gift then IHT will be due at the full 40% rate. If the donor died within three to seven years of the gift being made, then the rate of IHT falls. The inheritance tax rate payable is reduced by a percentage depending on how long before death the transfer was made (3–4 yrs: 20%; 4–5 yrs: 40%; 5–6 yrs: 60%; 6–7 yrs: 80%).

    Certain lifetime transfers are chargeable to inheritance tax when they are made, a major example being a transfer into a discretionary trust. Such a transfer will suffer inheritance tax on transfer at half the death rate, ie 20%. Should the transferor die within seven years of the transfer, additional tax will be payable to bring the rate paid up to 40% (less any taper relief, if applicable). The inheritance tax due on the lifetime transfer is usually payable by the transferor.

9. **Non-dividend savings income**

    Most people have income which is made up of a mixture of 'earnings' (eg, salary or pensions) and 'savings income'.

    Non-dividend savings income includes: *[four examples required]*

    - Interest from a bank or building society

    - Interest from Government bonds (gilts)

    - Interest (coupon) from fixed interest securities such as corporate bonds

    - Interest from National Savings & Investments (NS&I)

    - The income part of a purchase life annuity

    - Chargeable gains on life policies

Some savings income, eg on gilts, corporate bonds and NS&I investments, is received gross. The gross figure will be included in the income tax computation.

Some other savings income, eg bank and building society interest, is taxed at source, and is received net of 20% tax. The amount received is grossed up by multiplying by 100/80 and is included gross in the income tax computation. The tax deducted at source is deducted in computing tax payable and may be repaid.

Although bank and building society interest paid to individuals is generally paid net of 20% tax, if a recipient is not liable to tax, he can recover the tax suffered, or he can certify in advance that he is a non-taxpayer and receive the interest gross.

The tax computation calculates taxable income first. Then, income tax is applied to non-savings income, at the relevant rate for the tax band, and then it is applied to the savings income.

A savings income starting rate of 10% applies only where savings income falls below the starting rate limit. As already mentioned, income tax is charged first on non-savings income. So, in most cases, an individual's non-savings income will exceed the starting rate limit and the savings income starting rate will not be available on savings income. However, if an individual's non-savings income is less than the starting rate limit, then savings income will be taxable at the 10% savings income starting rate up to the starting rate limit.

December 2011 Examination Answers

Part 1 – Portfolio Construction Theory

Section A

1. **Short questions**

    (a) **C** The answer can be understood from the common language meanings of the terms.

    (b) **B** Alpha represents the investment manager's skill.

    (c) **B** These are types of collective fund: being open-ended, the shares or units will trade close   to or be priced at the net asset value.

    (d) **B** Assets within an asset class should not be statistically dissimilar from one another. We want assets within each asset class to be relatively similar to one another but dissimilar between asset classes.

    (e) **A** The instance of fraud is not a global market factor.

    (f) **D** Market timing is a type of tactical asset allocation.

    (g) **C** An index-linked bond pays a par value that adjusts according to the general level of prices. This changes coupon payments, but not the coupon rate.

    (h) **D** The income stream may not be fixed in amount across different periods, but if so it will be determined by a set formula.

    (i) **A** The higher yield means that both will decrease in value. The present value of the redemption proceeds is a greater part of the value of Bond A than that of Bond B and the change in yield will affect Bond B more than Bond A.

    (j) **C** The expected return can be described as the amount of return estimated by an asset pricing model while the realised return is the amount of return actually received.

    (k) **Examiner's comment**. A common mistake was for candidates to incorrectly count the number of years. The number of full years is 12.

    Annualised return = $(1+0.975)^{1/12} - 1 = 5.8\%$

    (l) The question concerned the conversion value of a convertible bond that has a par value of €1,000, a current market price of €850, a current price of the issuing company's stock of €29 and a conversion ratio equal to 30 shares.

    Conversion value = Conversion ratio × Market price

    30 shares × €29 per share = €870

    A conversion to shares would currently yield €20 over the value of the convertible bond.

    (m) **Weighted portfolio return**

Asset	Weight in portfolio	Asset class return	Weight x Return
Commodities	7%	− 3.0%	− 0.2%
Property	7%	11.0%	0.8%
Cash	6%	1.0%	0.06%
Bonds	30%	3.0%	0.9%
Equities	50%	3.0%	1.5%

    Sum of Weight × Return = 3.0%

(n)   **Examiner's comment**. The question was very poorly answered, with many candidates scoring zero marks. The answer required calculating the portfolio value and new portfolio weights following an investment return on bonds of 0.0% and on equities −16.66%. Many candidates did not read the question properly and computed a +16.66% return for equities rather than −16.66% as in the question.

Initial portfolio value = €10bn

Allocation to equities = €6bn
Allocation to bonds = €4bn

Performance on equities = − 16.66%
Equities: (€6bn × (1 − 0.166)) = €5bn

Performance on bonds = 0%
Bonds = (€4bn × (1 − 0)) = €4bn

New portfolio value = €9bn

Portfolio weights are now:

■   55% (€5bn/€9bn) equities
■   45% (€4bn/€9bn) bonds

(o)   **FTSE 100 company bond**

FTSE 100 company bond due in one year has a yield of 6.5%
UK government bond due in one year has a yield of 5.7%

6.5% − 5.7% = 0.8%

FTSE 250 company bond

FTSE 250 company bond due in five years has a yield of 7.5%
A UK government bond due in five years has a yield of 6.2%

7.5% − 6.2% = 1.3%

(p)   The total return on a share in one year's time is capital appreciation plus dividends.

Current share price = €40 and is expected to grow 11% per annum

Dividend yield = (€2.00 /€40.00) × 100 = 5%

11% + 5% = 16% expected return

The required return is 12%. The expected return exceeds the required return by 4%. Yes, I would invest.

The formula used is the Gordon Growth Model.

Expected rate of return = (Dividend / price) + Growth rate

Expected rate of return = $D_i/P_0 + g$

= (€2.00/€40.00) × 100 + 11%

= 5% + 11% = 16%

(q)   Required return for Stock A = 3% + 1.7 × (7% − 3%) = 9.8%.

The expected return for Stock A is 9%. Stock A is overvalued.

Required return for Stock B = 3% + 0.9 × (7 % − 3%) = 6.6%.

The expected return for Stock B is 8%. Stock B is undervalued.

(r) **Examiner's comment**. This question asked candidates to provide arguments for investment home bias. Answers were of a good standard, with many scoring high marks.

- Overseas transaction costs may be greater than those at home, and custodian and tax charges too.

- Investing at home involves no explicit currency risk. This helps with the payment of £ sterling liabilities.

- UK equities are a good match for UK inflation. This helps because defined benefit pension scheme liabilities will be indexed to inflation/salary growth.

- Investors may be using a peer group benchmark rather than a market weight benchmark.

- A great amount of the earnings of large UK-listed companies come from overseas in any case.

- UK investors have familiarity and expertise about their own economy and public listed companies.

- Good corporate governance, regulation and disclosure standards provide a strong case for overweighting the UK relative to other markets.

- UK has a dividend paying culture. This helps meet cash flow demands.

(s) A long-term investor needs to consider inflation, especially in today's moderate inflation environment.

Cash deposit rates generally do not keep up with the cost of living. Cash is arguably the safest asset in the sense that there exists the safety net of the Financial Services Compensation Scheme. The FSCS means that deposit accounts are largely free of default risk, up to the compensation limit of £85,000 per person per claim. Larger sums can be split across different deposit takers. Cash deposits made in the home currency avoid currency risk.

In the long term, deposit rates are at risk from negative real yields. The future trajectory of inflation cannot be known with certainty. The economic history of conventional bond performance shows that some of the return to holding a government bond can be eroded by inflation. At times of unexpected inflation, there are negative returns. Conventional long maturity Government bonds may therefore not be lowest risk, though in times of deflation they provide safety.

A long-term bond is helpful because it reduces reinvestment risk.

The most likely security that fits the description is a long-term inflation linked government bond. This moves us away from nominal returns towards real returns. There always remains the risk of deflation, so even inflation-linked UK government bonds are not risk-free to a long-term investor. There is also the problem that demand is so high for some issues that the price makes the yield too expensive to be worth purchasing.

Ultimately, it is difficult to find a completely risk-free asset. Looking for safe assets is likely to be more productive. This brings about the concept of a zero-beta CAPM rather than a risk-free CAPM.

Section B

2.   **Asset allocation**

Examiner's comment. Candidates focused far too much on the client fact-find and setting benchmarks while omitting discussion about the determination of asset allocation. A wide-scale lack of engagement with asset allocation was evidenced.

(a)   We begin with a brief discussion of the client fact find: from this, set the objective. Before we set out on investment, we need to articulate where it is going, when, and how. An investment objective provides a clear rationale for investment decisions. Without one, there is no basis for what we are trying to achieve. This might be expressed as a return, a risk, and with a timescale. Determine what levels of risk and return are required to achieve the agreed investment objective. How are strategic weights then set?

First, we need to model asset classes. If we believe historic returns and the sequence or path to be important, we use actual historic data. If we believe historic returns to be important but the sequence unimportant, we might want to use boot-strap historic data. If we believe historic returns to be unimportant but the mean and standard deviation important, we can use sampling techniques with similar mean and standard deviation as past. Alternatively, we could use interpretive scenarios.

How we approach the above determines the asset class returns used in modelling and assessing an appropriate strategic asset allocation. The standard approach to determining the asset allocation is 'mean variance optimisation'. Mean variance optimisation involves identifying the different asset classes and their relative proportions that should deliver the required rate of return of the investment objective at an acceptable level of risk. Asset allocation is generally undertaken with a long-term investment horizon. This is strategic asset allocation (SAA) – one of the most important elements of portfolio construction.

SAA needs to be based on client circumstances. Strategic asset allocation combines capital market expectations (efficient frontier) and investor's risk tolerance and investment constraints. A broad asset mix is justified based on investment theory that you are only rewarded for non-diversifiable risk, that is, systematic risk (market risk). The asset mix is a key tool to manage the risk of any fund via diversification, ie risk reduction.

An SAA can be static or dynamic. A criticism of static SAA is that it is not sufficiently adaptive to changing real circumstances.

(b)   **Active strategies**

(i)   **Dynamic asset allocation** recognises that investment often takes place in the context of a value we wish to protect or even an actual liability. Dynamic asset allocation divides a portfolio into a risky asset sub-portfolio (or performance portfolio) and a safe asset sub-portfolio (or hedge portfolio). This can help if the need is for both protection and upside. The portfolio is re-balanced between the risky asset and the safe asset depending on performance of the risky asset. The aim is to preserve a defined amount of capital. A common technique is constant proportion portfolio insurance (CPPI). As a portfolio value falls, more and more is placed in the safe asset. It stops a loss, but it takes away some upside potential.

The 'hedge portfolio' will hold assets that meet some defined value or liability. Assets will be a good match for the liability, ie: nominal or real. The performance portfolio will hold the remainder of the assets. Now go for very risky sources of risk premium on the performance assets. This can include leverage but must not endanger payment of liabilities. Leave the hedge portfolio to meet the liabilities. The performance portfolio will be estimated to have a maximum loss. The amount remaining can be added to the value of the hedge sub-portfolio to cover the minimum defined value or liability.

(ii) **Liability-driven asset allocation**. Some investors have liabilities that they are obliged to meet and the investment manager's objective must take these into consideration.

For example, pension funds and life assurance companies will have statistical projections of their liabilities into the future and the fund must attempt to achieve these.

A further consideration is the exposure to currency risk. If the pension fund or other investor itself has liabilities in, say, US dollars, then buying US investments can better match their currency exposure.

A pension fund has an obligation to ensure that the present value of liabilities equals the present value of assets. The stream of future pension liabilities is reasonably predictable by actuaries. This suggests that it is desirable to ensure the future cash flows from assets required to meet those pension payments are also reasonably predictable. This, in turn, suggests that bonds (or similar nominal returning assets) should play a significant role in the portfolios of pension funds. Bonds will generate cash flows from interest and redemption proceeds, which will allow the liabilities to be met as they arise.

Discretionary customers may be seeking to match liabilities, for example, in school fee planning or mortgage repayment planning. The same broad principles apply to liability matching clients regardless of who they are.

If the return from bonds is insufficient to achieve this required return, then we must use other assets. The result of the use of other assets is that we may achieve the higher return required, however, the risk associated with the use of these other assets means that the liabilities may not be exactly met – there may be a mismatch.

The time horizons for the attainment of the return or the matching of the liabilities will clearly influence the types of investments that will be worthwhile for the fund.

A fund whose purpose is to meet some liabilities in, say, two years' time, may find that the investment vehicle is a two-year low-coupon gilt. This will especially be the case if the client is a higher-rate taxpayer as he will be able to benefit from a tax-free capital gain on these gilts at redemption.

(iii) **Risk budgeting**. What if you have no pre-defined liabilities or if you think that dynamic asset allocation does not give you sufficient upside after large drops? Risk budgeting allocates risk rather than money to asset classes.

At the outset, a maximum portfolio risk is specified. The contribution to portfolio risk of the different asset classes is monitored. Assets weights are altered to maintain the desired level of portfolio risk, eg if equities become more volatile, their exposure may need to fall to actively maintain the desired level of portfolio risk. The proceeds from the sale of equities are recycled to lower risk assets. In this manner, aggregate risk of a portfolio is decomposed into its constituents.

The aim is to actively set and allocate risk to enhance the returns available from risk premiums without overpaying for them relative to their risk.

Section C

3. Default spread

The default spread is the difference between the average yield on corporate bonds of a given credit rating and the average yield on gilts of the same maturity.

Mostly, the spread measures the risk premium given the greater likelihood of default on the corporate bond. This also provides an idea of the marginal cost of funds to issuers with a similar credit rating.

To the extent that the corporate bond is more illiquid than the gilt, the spread will also measure illiquidity risk. This makes it important to choose liquid issues in order to isolate the default risk.

The default spread can be used as an economic indicator. In a confident economy, default spreads tends to narrow. When there is widespread economic pessimism, the spread tends to widen. The spread may further widen when there is a crisis. The state of the spreads can therefore be used to predict the position in the economic cycle for market timing purposes.

4. Nominal and real returns

(a) **Examiner's comment.** Candidates were required to calculate the five-year nominal and real return on notice savings accounts. The large majority of candidates were unable to calculate the real return.

The calculation for a real return is:
Real return = (1+ nominal return)/(1 + inflation)

This calculation is performed cross-sectionally for each year. The correct calculation and set of returns is presented in the table below. Each return is first calculated cross-sectionally. Next, the annual real returns are computed as time-weighted returns.

Date	Return: Notice Savings Account	UK inflation	Nominal return: Notice Savings Account	Real return: Notice Savings Account
			100.00	100.00
2006	2.99%		102.99	98.62
2007	3.81%	4.05%	106.92	98.40
2008	2.99%	0.95%	110.12	100.39
2009	0.39%	2.40%	110.56	98.43
2010	1.02%	4.77%	111.69	94.90
			11.69%	− 5.10%

(b) **Examiner's comment.** Some candidates mentioned and justified interesting possibilities within a diversified approach, including timber and gold.

The short answer is that it does not seem possible to keep up with inflation while keeping risk-free, at least over long periods.

Often the first and most important objective for a savings/investment vehicle is to keep up with the change in the cost of goods and services, ie inflation.

To keep up with inflation during the past 20 years, it has not been possible to do so without taking at least some investment risk. Having determined that investment risk has to be taken, the question is: How much risk is it appropriate to take?

Also, how uneven are we prepared for this growth to be, relative to inflation? Holding a mix of investments, for example a fixed rate bond, index-linked government bonds, conventional government bonds and a broad equity index, may strike a sufficient balance between taking a small amount of diversified risk while potentially achieving inflation returns. In effect, this takes a diversified approach to keeping pace with inflation.

5. **Explain terms**

    (a) **Standard deviation** is the amount of variation a portfolio is subjected to 68% of the time, ie approximately two out of every three occasions. It measures the variation about the mean value.

    (b) **Value at risk (VaR)** is the variability of loss of a portfolio or asset at a specified probability. VaR takes a probabilistic approach to: How much may be lost on a bad day? VaR defines 'bad day' statistically, in terms of the percentage probability that losses will be greater than a given amount given distribution of returns over past period. Often, VaR is expressed as the maximum percentage loss in the value of a portfolio that occurs on 95% of loss occasions.

    (c) **Conditional value at risk (CVaR)** asks: If I do end up in the tail of say, the 5% of worst outcomes, what is the average loss I will incur? If we added up all the possible losses in the bottom 5% and took the average, this is CVaR. It is the expected outcome of a portfolio / asset should the value/probability fall below a certain level. CVaR is often expressed as the expected return on the portfolio in the worst 5% of the cases. It is a measure of 'tail loss'.

    Standard deviation, VaR and CVaR all give different readings.

Part 2 – Taxation and Trusts

Section D

6.   **Case study question**

(a)   The Trustee Act 2000 grants the following powers to trustees.

■   **Investment powers**. Trustees can make any investment of any kind that they could as if the funds were their own, except for investment in overseas land. Trustees are however subject to a fundamental duty to act in the best interests of all the beneficiaries.

■   **Power to delegate**. The Act allows trustees to delegate to agents any of their functions, including their powers of investment. This means that they can employ discretionary fund managers and delegate many other decision-making functions.

■   **Statutory duty of care**. The Act imposes a statutory duty of skill and care, which applies when trustees carry out certain functions such as exercising their powers of investment, employing agents, using nominees and custodians and insuring trust properties. This is a subjective test that takes into account the knowledge, experience and professional status of the trustee.

■   **Trustee remuneration**. Where there is more than one trustee, they have the power to authorise one or more of their number to charge for services to the trust if they are acting in a professional capacity.

■   **Authority to insure trust property**. The Act gives to trustees the power to insure in full any property that is subject to the trust against risk of loss or damage due to any event as if the property were their own.

(b)   **Examiner's comment**. The question encouraged a discussion and most candidates spotted that using Victor's spouse might save tax along with double tax relief (unilateral and treaty).

Some candidates who assumed 'his tax liability' referred to Victor acting as a trustee were not penalised.

A number of candidates mentioned domicile but failed to examine the issue (or even consider the issue in relation to Victor's spouse). From a UK adviser point of view, checking the domicile of Victor and his spouse is an important planning consideration.

Overseas governments may withhold tax. Under the OECD Model for double taxation agreements that apply between many countries, preferential rates of withholding tax are applied to, for example, payments of rent, interest and dividends. The usual rate is frequently replaced by 15% or less.

Double taxation relief is given to taxpayers in their country of residence by way of a credit for tax suffered in the country where income arises. This may be in the form of relief for withholding tax only or, given a holding of specified size in a foreign company, for the underlying tax on the profits out of which dividends are paid.

If no relief is available under a double taxation agreement, UK legislation provides for unilateral relief. However, unilateral relief is not available if relief is specifically excluded under the terms of a double tax agreement.

Under the rules for unilateral relief, the UK tax on the foreign income is the difference between the UK tax before DTR on all income including the foreign income, and the UK tax on all income except the foreign income.

(c)   **Examiner's comment**. Generally, answers were too brief with candidates losing easy marks.

Most candidates spotted the significance of the spouse's (unemployed) situation and suggested putting the property in her name.

Stronger candidates also suggested putting the property in joint names before the future sale and moving-in to establish a principal private residence exemption if only in part.

Other excellent candidates mentioned the inheritance tax risks and included references in their planning.

There was little discussion on whether the property should be purchased in the UK or abroad.

A few candidates mentioned REITs and holiday letting relief. There was no reference to rollover relief.

(d)   **Examiner's comment**. This question, which concerned inheritance tax planning and establishment of a trust for Victor's grandchildren, was generally well answered.

Some answers were too brief. For example, often, only a discretionary trust was mentioned and there was little discussion about the tax advantages and disadvantages of each type of trust.

Candidates who discussed a variety of inheritance tax planning ideas scored the top marks. A few candidates discussed making the joint will and what that entailed.

Worldwide assets of individuals domiciled in the UK are liable to inheritance tax (IHT). The chargeable estate comprises all assets less all liabilities at death, less exempt legacies, transfers and other allowances. IHT is paid on the chargeable estate above a nil rate.

Gifts made during are chargeable to IHT if the donor dies within seven years of making the gift. Gifts given in the last seven years of life are treated as Potentially Exempt Transfers (PETs) and the recipient may be liable for IHT. Exemptions include small gifts and an annual exemption.

There are exemptions from IHT for types of 'excluded property', gifts between spouses and civil partners, and certain other types of gift. Unless exempt, potentially exempt transfers (PETs) constitute a chargeable disposal for CGT purposes.

(e)   **Examiner's comment**. This question concerned the sale of Tesco shares acquired at different times for a portfolio.

Most candidates noted that the 1977 shares would need to be re-based to 1982 prices.

Indexation and taper relief were mentioned by some candidates, as were matching rules, share pooling and part disposals.

One candidate mentioned accounting for the gains in the self-assessment form.

Ascertaining the share pool caused problems for some candidates.

For capital gains tax (CGT) purposes, a chargeable gain is computed by taking the proceeds and deducting cost. A gain or loss is computed by taking the proceeds and deducting the cost. Incidental costs of acquisition and disposal are deducted.

Individuals pay CGT on their taxable gains. Gains are taxed at 18% (within the basic rate band) or 28% (above the basic rate band). Individuals are entitled to an annual exemption.

Allowable capital losses are deducted from chargeable gains in the tax year in which they arise. Any loss which cannot be set off is carried forward to set against future chargeable gains. Losses must be used as soon as. Allowable losses brought forward are only set off to

reduce current year chargeable gains less current year allowable losses to the annual exempt amount.

There are special rules for matching shares sold with shares purchased. Disposals are matched first with shares acquired on the same day, then within the following 30 days, and finally with the share pool.

Spouses/civil partners are treated as separate people for CGT purposes. Transfers of assets between spouses/civil partners give rise to neither a gain nor a loss.

Section E

7.   Chargeable disposals include the following, unless exempt.

- Sales of assets or parts of assets
- Gifts of assets or parts of assets
- Receipts of capital sums following the surrender of rights to assets
- The loss or destruction of assets
- The appropriation of assets as trading stock

Individuals, partnerships, companies and trustees are chargeable persons. Persons who are not resident in the UK are exempt persons.

An example of a chargeable disposal is the sale of some listed company shares by an individual, where the shares are not held in an ISA or Child Trust Fund.

Transfers of assets on death are exempt disposals.

All forms of property, wherever in the world they are situated, are chargeable assets unless they are specifically designated as exempt (examples of exempt assets are: gilts, qualifying corporate bonds, ISA investments, EIS and VCT investments, NS&I Savings Certificates, foreign currency for private use and private motor cars).

8.   There are two main types of trust for income tax purposes – trusts with an interest in possession, and non-interest in possession (ie, discretionary) trusts.

Trustee expenses are only deductible for the purposes of computing tax for discretionary trustees. Trust expenses are deducted first from dividend income.

Interest in possession beneficiaries are treated as entitled to trust income (net of expenses) as it arises. Income is taxed in the first instance on the trustees. The trustees do not have a personal allowance, nor is the trust income split into different bands of income as it is for an individual. Instead all trust income is taxed at the basic rate of tax applicable to the type of income.

Discretionary trust beneficiaries are only taxable on income paid to them or applied for their benefit.

Income used to pay trustees' expenses is taxed at the basic rate of tax, ie 10% where such expenses are paid out of dividend income, 20% when paid out of savings income or non-savings income. The amount of income so used is the amount of the expenses, grossed-up at 10% or 20% as appropriate. Dividend income is used to cover such expenses before savings income and then non-savings income is used.

Once expenses are deducted, discretionary trusts then have a standard, or basic rate, band of £1,000 (2014/15). The first £1,000 of taxable income is taxed at the basic rates, ie at 10% (dividends), 20% (savings and non-savings income). As for individuals, the basic rate band is applied first to non-savings income, then savings income and finally dividends. Many smaller trusts will have no further tax to pay and will not need to file a tax return.

If the settlor or his spouse can benefit from a settlement, the income of the trust will be taxed on the settlor.

Where a settlor has made more than one settlement, the £1,000 is divided by the number of settlements made by the same settlor, with a minimum amount of £200 for each trust. Any remaining income is taxed at one of two special trust tax rates. These are 45% (on non-dividend income) and 37.5% (on dividend income) (2014/15) − known as the 'trust rate' and the 'dividend trust rate' respectively.

For CGT purposes, there is a deemed disposal at market value for the settlor when a trust is set-up during lifetime. Gift relief is available as there is also a CLT for IHT purposes.

Trustees are normally entitled to half an individual's annual exemption.

Principal Private Residence (PPR) relief is available to trustees on the disposal of a trust property, if a beneficiary has lived in it as their main residence.

When assets leave a relevant property trust, there is a deemed disposal at market value. Gift relief is available as there is also an IHT exit charge.

When assets leave a qualifying interest in possession trust, there is usually no gain and the assets receive a tax-free uplift to market value. However, a CGT charge may arise when assets leave the trust on the life tenant's death if gift relief was claimed when the assets were originally put into the trust.

9. **Taxation and offshore funds**

(a) In general terms, there will be no tax paid by an offshore fund. However, there may be withholding tax which may not be reclaimable by the fund. In addition, a fund may be subject to a small amount of local tax.

Jersey funds are subject to a flat yearly corporation tax and Luxembourg funds to a tax on the asset value each year.

The expenses of an offshore fund cannot be offset against its income.

(b) The taxation of the individual investor in an offshore fund will depend on whether the fund has reporting or non-reporting status.

These rules came into force on 1 December 2009, with the Offshore Funds (Tax) Regulations 2009.

The relevance of reporting fund status for UK investors is that gains realised on disposals of investments in reporting funds will in most circumstances be subject to tax on chargeable gains.

Gains realised on disposals of investments in non-reporting funds ('offshore income gains' or OIGs) will be subject to less favourable treatment as they will generally be charged to tax on income on gains as they arise.

June 2011 Examination Answers

Part 1 – Portfolio Construction Theory

Section A

1. (a) **C** To be successful, technical analysis needs to be able to exploit market inefficiency.

    (b) **B** Coupon = £1,250 × 8%, ie £100, or 10%.

    (c) **D** The accumulation phase is when people are in their early-to-mid earning careers and regularly putting aside amounts to meet expenditure needs later in life.

    (d) **D** Common relative valuation techniques include price/earnings ratio, price/cash flow ratio, and price/book value ratio.

    (e) **B** A Eurobond is a bond denominated in a currency that is not native to its place of issue.

    (f) **C** The semi-variance measures variation below the mean only.

    (g) **D** The rate of growth of equity earnings is equal to retention rate multiplied by the return on equity.

    (h) **A** Interest rates, GDP and oil prices could all influence returns on a security in the APT model.

    (i) **C** A speculative stock has a high probability of a low or negative return and a low probability of a high return.

    (j) **A** Sharpe ratio = (Portfolio return – Risk-free rate)/Standard deviation of portfolio returns = 0.03/0.14.

    (k) Use the Gordon Growth Model.

    Either:

    Expected rate of return = (Dividend/Price) + Growth rate

    $1.00/$40.00 + 4.0% = 2.5% + 4% = 6.5%

    Or:

    Price = Dividend/(Expected return – Growth rate)

    $40 = $1/(Expected return – 4.0%)

    Expected return – 4.0% = 1/40

    Expected return = 4.0% + 2.5% = 6.5%

    (l) **Similarities between CAPM and APT**

    ▪ Both are equilibrium theories of expected return.

    ▪ Both use the risk free rate as their intercept.

    ▪ Beta in the CAPM is a composite factor which is equivalent to the weighted average of the betas of the relevant factors in the APT model.

    ▪ In equilibrium, there is no unsystematic or idiosyncratic return. All expected returns derive from systematic, or common, factor(s).

(m) **Assumptions of CAPM**

- Two statistics, mean and variance, are sufficient to describe investor preferences over the distribution of future returns in a portfolio.

- Investors prefer higher expected returns to lower expected returns for a given portfolio risk, and prefer lower volatility to higher volatility for a given portfolio expected return.

- All investors can borrow and lend at the risk-free rate.

- All investors have the same expectations about means, variances, and co-variances of security returns.

(n) $r = r_f + \beta(r_m - r_f)$

Expected return, $r = 6\% + 1.2 \times (12\% - 6\%) = 0.132$, ie 13.2%

(o) *Either:*

The domestic currency is EUR. The interest rate differential is 1% (Domestic – Foreign).

The expected appreciation of the US dollar is 2%.

Foreign currency return = Expected appreciation – Interest rate differential =

2% – 1% = 1%

Or:

Foreign currency return = Overseas interest rate + Expected appreciation – Domestic interest rate =

3% + 2% – 4% = 1%

Or:

A compound calculation:

Assume EUR 1 = USD 1.

€100 invested in the US money markets grows to $103 at end of period 1.

At end of period 1, EUR 0.98 = USD 1.

Foreign currency return = 103 / 0.98 = 1.05, ie 5% appreciation.

5% – 4% (domestic interest rate) = 1%.

(p) The question requires using a factor model such as APT to calculate the expected return for two portfolios.

Expected return (portfolio A) = 2% + (1.2 × 4%) + (1.5 × 1.0%) = 8.3%

Expected return (portfolio B) = 2% + (1.4 × 4%) + (0.8 × 1.0%) = 8.4%

Expected return (portfolio C) = 2% + (0.8 × 4%) + (2.0 × 1.0%) = 7.2%

(q) Systematic and unsystematic risk are combined by adding variances and then taking the square root to obtain the standard deviation.

$\sqrt{[0.19^2 + 0.06^2]} = \sqrt{[0.0361 + 0.0036]} = \sqrt{0.0397} = 0.1992$, ie 19.92%

(r) The earnings yield spread measures the total return from bonds – the total return on equities. The earnings yield spread is one of a number of measures, such as dividend yield spread, that assess prevailing relative returns on bonds and equities.

Since equities tend to have greater risk (and so greater expected return), the expectation for this measure is negative. Historically, the earnings yield spread has averaged between –3%

to −5%. We need to be mindful of inflation, which is lower today that historically, so the lower of this range is more probable.

With −3% representing a neutral setting, the current level relative to it gives information about the stage of the economic cycle. If zero or positive, bonds would represent a dominant asset class, offering higher returns at lower risk. This indicates lower exposure to shares. If the earnings yield spread is negative and widening (becoming more negative), this indicates increasing exposure to shares. In this way, the measure is used as an asset allocation indicator.

(s) The yield curve is typified by a smooth relationship between yield and maturity. On occasion, at various maturities, there may be humps and/or dips in the curve.

The strategy depends on which way investors feel the yield curve will go. If the humps or dips are expected to disappear, then the prices of the bonds on the hump can be expected to rise (and their yield fall), and the prices of the bonds in the dips can be expected to fall (and their yields rise).

A policy-switching strategy would involve switching between two types of bonds, purchasing the high-yield bond and selling the low-yield bond.

A bridge swap is a possibility. Bonds on either side of the bridge are correctly priced while a bond on the bridge has too high a yield. Selling the correctly priced bonds and purchasing the high yield bond means overall duration remains the same while expected return is increased. The strategy may involve switching between dissimilar bonds or similar bonds in maturity, credit rating and sector.

Section B

2. (a) Private equity is associated with greater expected return than listed equity due to greater expected return illiquidity, uncertainty, and low portability.

Private equity vehicles introduce an additional agent between firm and investors as limited partners. The additional agent is the general partner (GP).

The limited partners have no voting rights, cannot requisition a meeting, and cannot be sure that the GP has not held back the best investments for their own investment. It is also hard to develop an understanding as to whether the GP is taking excessive risk, or whether a GP's stated exit strategy is to maximise return or because cash is needed elsewhere in the GP's business. GP skill versus luck is not observable. How possible is it to distinguish a high-quality GP from a low-quality GP? These points suggest that governance is more opaque than listed equity and so worse.

An alternative perspective is that the GP screens the universe of investable opportunities for suitability. The GP monitors and influences decision making, gets involved in strategy and leadership, refreshment of the board and succession (often through having a board position), and is incentivised through investment in the firm.

Since private firms have lower levels of disclosure, less regulation and greater accounting discretion, the GP an essential conduit of investment return for the limited partners. The GP acts as the eyes and ears of the limited partners. The closer proximity of the GP to the economic heart of the investments, and alignment of their financial interests with those of the limited partners, suggests that governance is better.

(b) The private equity risk premium is based on broad exposure to the asset class, ie once idiosyncratic risk has been all but diversified away. The danger for the investor is that by targeting this risk premium on its own, it ends up looking and feeling similar to the listed equity risk premium plus an amount for illiquidity. This is because both capture growth in

GDP and similar changes in the economic cycle. The expected return to private equity, while higher than that for listed equity, may therefore offer limited diversification.

This reasoning suggests that an investor seeking diversification within a fund that contains listed equity may wish to consider certain types of private equity, for example:

■ Small firms at the start of rapid growth or research phase

■ Medium size firms seeking scale

■ Large companies, sometimes listed, that want to be private. This may include distressed companies and companies for which a listed company management structure is not most suitable

■ Infrastructure funds are sometimes also structured as private equity vehicles

According to the investor's holdings of listed equities, as well as the need for liquidity and portability, certain types above may be a better fit for the improvement of risk and expected return. The aim is to achieve real ex-post diversification.

Section C

3. As the firm is a signatory to the Stewardship Code, the following steps would be considered.

■ Check the bank annual report for the corporate governance statement. This should explain why there is not a risk committee, which is suggested in the 2009 Walker Report.

■ Check the audit committee report to establish if this committee has taken on some or all of the role of bank risk.

■ If the explanation is unsatisfactory, open dialogue with the bank to hear its point of view and establish facts.

■ If the reasoning remains unconvincing, encourage the company to fully comply or explain as required by the Code on Corporate Governance.

■ Voting rights can be used to put your position across more formally, along with your intention to vote a particular way and the reasons why.

■ Finally, consider coordinating actions with other significant shareholders, for example canvassing colleagues to establish their viewpoint on the matter and finding common ground with them for a way forward. This might include discussing a shareholder proposal or requisitioning a general meeting.

4. (a) Treynor measure = (Return − Risk-free rate)/Beta

Managed portfolio

$(7.9\% − 2.5\%)/1.05 = 5.1\%$

Market portfolio (Index)

$(5.9\% − 2.5\%)/1.0 = 3.4\%$

(b) Recalculating portfolio performance gross of fees requires the same class of calculation as dividend reinvestment. Reinvest the fees. This is performed by adding 0.25% to the month's return at the end of each quarter. The fees were deducted quarterly not monthly. The fees added back to the month's return at the end of each quarter then get reinvested and earn the portfolio return, ie they are compounded at the prevailing rate of return.

Gross of fees allows for more accurate presentation of active management and the skill of the manager. Gross of fees performance can be compared to an index or benchmark. Gross of fees performance includes trading costs but excludes fixed fees (eg fund manager, custody). Net of fees provides what the investor receives, and is best for peer group comparisons. Both are useful for different reasons.

5. **Reasons why the time horizon is relevant**

   (a) Securities are valued based on their net present value. An important question to feed the discussion is whether the market may discount this far ahead. If it does, emission information about the future, albeit seemingly distant, will move security prices today.

   (b) Even if the market does not discount this far ahead, regulation and legislation might change in the short term which alters prices. Also, taxes and subsidies might alter in the short term to encourage new markets and deter more CO_2 emitting markets.

   (c) Lastly, uncertainty about the science behind climate change and information disclosure can bring uncertainty into security prices, and therefore volatility.

   Reasons why the time horizon might not be relevant

   (a) The information is not precise, specific or reliable enough to act on.
   (b) The evidence on whether the market discounts this far ahead is inconclusive.

Part 2 – Taxation and Trusts

Section D

6.   (a)   (i)   A trust is an arrangement under which a person, the 'settlor', transfers property to another person, the 'trustee' or trustees, who is required to deal with the trust property on behalf of certain specified persons, the 'beneficiaries'.

A trust may be:

- An interest in possession (IIP) trust, where the beneficiaries are automatically entitled to receive all of the income of the trust as it arises, or

- A discretionary trust, where the trustees can determine which beneficiaries to make payments to and how much they will receive.

A trust with a disabled beneficiary has some tax advantages – for example, a higher CGT annual exemption than that of other trusts (see part (ii)). Additionally, lifetime gifts to such trusts are not chargeable to inheritance tax (IHT), in the case of discretionary and interest in possession (IIP) trusts.

Frank and Nora might set up a bare trust, as a relatively simple option, provided that they are happy with their daughter having access to the trust property when she comes of age.

In a bare trust, also known as a simple trust, there is a sole beneficiary. The trustee has no discretion over payment of income or capital to the beneficiary, who has an immediate and absolute right to both capital and income at age 18 (in England and Wales). The basic purpose of a bare trust is to restrict benefits going to children before they reach 18 and to try and avoid paying tax on the saving. On coming of age, the beneficiary of the trust can instruct the trustee how to manage the trust property, and then has the right to take actual possession of the trust property at any time.

(ii)   The income tax treatment is different for each type of trust.

IIP trustees' tax position

Interest income is taxed at 20%, and dividends are taxed at 10%.

Interest is usually received net of a 20% tax credit by the trust (as it is by an individual). Dividends are received with a 10% notional tax credit. As both of these tax credits satisfy the trustees' liability for these types of income, no further tax is due from the trustees.

The IIP beneficiary (sometimes called the 'life tenant') is entitled to receive the trust income once the trustees have paid the tax due.

The beneficiary will receive a statement of income from the trust showing the amounts they are entitled to receive along with the associated tax credit (ie, the tax paid by the trustees). They will then include these amounts in their own tax calculation.

The income paid to the beneficiary retains its nature so, if it is interest income in the trustees' hands, it will be taxed as interest income on the beneficiary and so on.

Discretionary trusts have a standard, or basic rate, band of £1,000. The first £1,000 of income is taxed at the basic rates, ie at 10% (dividends), and 20% (interest income). As for individuals, the basic rate band is applied first to non-savings income, then savings income and finally dividends. Many smaller trusts will have no further tax to pay.

Any remaining income is taxed at the rates that apply to additional rate taxpaying individuals (2014/15):

- Interest income is taxed at 45% (the trust rate)
- Dividends are taxed at 37.5% (the dividend trust rate)

Beneficiaries of discretionary trusts are only taxed if they receive income payments from the trust.

Any payments of income to beneficiaries are made net of tax at 50% and are taxed on them at the rates that apply to earnings income. The trustees will again provide a statement of income to the beneficiaries showing the relevant figures.

For CGT purposes, there is no need to distinguish between the type of trust. 'Settled property' is any property held in a trust, other than a trust where the beneficiary is absolutely entitled to trust property (a 'bare trust'). In a bare trust, gains are treated as made by the beneficiary not the trustee.

If a settlor puts an asset into any type of trust, he makes a disposal for CGT purposes. It will be deemed to take place at market value.

Where a trust has a disabled beneficiary, the annual exempt amount for CGT purposes is raised to £11,000 (2014/15).

For trusts for the disabled, the rule that makes lifetime gifts to trusts chargeable to inheritance tax does not apply. However, inheritance tax may still be due when the transferor dies within seven years of the transfer.

(b) Disposal proceeds: £20,000

Deemed cost = £10,000 × 20,000/£(20,000 + 45,000) = £3,077

Gain = £20,000 − £3,077 = £16,923

Assuming no other gains in 2014/15, deduct annual exemption:

£16,923 − £11,000 = £5,923

Capital gains tax payable (basic rate taxpayer) = £5,923 × 18% = £1,066

(c) Frank is within the income limit of £27,000 (born before 6 April 1948), and so his age allowance is £10,660 (2014/15).

Taxable income: £17,500 − £10,660 = £6,840.

Income tax payable: £6,840 × 20% = £1,368.

(d) Nora's 2014/15 income = £64,000.

Taxable income: £64,000 − £10,000 = £54,000.

Income tax payable:

£31,865 × 20% = £6,373

£22,135 × 40% = £8,854

Total income tax liability = £15,227.

(e) The new business might be set up as a self-employed venture (sole proprietorship), as a partnership, or as a private limited company.

A limited company is a separate legal entity from its owners: the company's liabilities are the responsibility of the company, not of its directors or shareholders. However, directors of

small businesses are commonly required by a lender to provide personal guarantees, and then they become liable to repay the debt if the company cannot.

A company pays corporation tax on its profits and can only distribute the remaining retained profits to directors and shareholders. This can result in tax being paid by both the company and by the directors or shareholders when they extract money from the company. However, there are also National Insurance implications. The company structure provides some flexibility in determining the proportions of salary and dividends, compared with a sole trader. Dividends are not subject to national insurance.

As a self-employed business, the sole trader is responsible for paying tax and national insurance contributions (NICs), through a self-assessment tax return. Class 2 NICs must normally be paid (unless profits fall below the small earnings exception), and also Class 4 if profits are above a specified level. HMRC should be notified when the business starts trading.

The couple should keep a careful note of expenses so that all business expenses can be claimed against tax. Businesses run by sole traders or partnerships have an annual investment allowance (AIA) for 100% of the first £250,000 of their expenditure on most plant and machinery. (This rate, increased from £25,000 previously with the aim of stimulating economic growth, applies for a temporary period of two years from 1 January 2013.) Companies are also able to claim capital allowances.

Depending on the level of turnover, the business may need to be registered for VAT.

Frank is a basic rate taxpayer while Nora is a higher rate taxpayer. For tax years in which this applies, tax planning could include ensuring that Frank is paid income to use up this allowance, if income is available from the business. However, for personal reasons, spouses may not wish their individual financial circumstances to be dictated too closely by tax planning. This will depend on the individuals' own preferences.

In the UK, IR35 seeks to counter tax avoidance by what are called 'personal service companies'. IR35 seeks to prevent workers from setting up limited companies via which they would work as employees to take advantage of a more favourable remuneration structure. A business could be caught by these rules if the end client exercises a degree of control over the work.

Section E

7. Any lifetime transfer made seven years before death or earlier will usually be exempt from IHT. The exception to this is the chargeable lifetime transfer (CLT), the most important example here being a transfer into a discretionary trust.

    All gifts between husband and wife or between partners in a civil partnership are exempt from IHT, whether made during the donor's life or on death. If the transferee spouse/civil partner is not domiciled in the UK, the exemption is limited to £325,000 (2014/15) in total on a cumulative basis.

    Whether made during the donor's life or on death, transfers or gifts are exempt if:

    ▓ Made to a charity recognised by HMRC

    ▓ Made as a gift to important national institutions

    ▓ Transfers (to a non-profit body that will usually be expected to provide public access) of land and buildings which, in the opinion of the Treasury, are of outstanding scenic, historic or other interest

    Certain types of property are exempt from IHT, as follows.

    ▓ Property situated outside the UK and owned by a person not domiciled in the UK.

- Property held in trust situated outside the UK, unless the settlor was domiciled in the UK when the trust was created.

- A reversionary interest in settled property situated within the UK, unless the interest was acquired for money or money's worth. When the life interest in an 'interest in possession' trust dies, the capital value of the trust is included as part of their chargeable estate. The reversionary interest only receives the net value of the trust assets after inheritance tax is paid. This rule avoids double inheritance tax on the capital value of the trust.

Habitual lifetime transfers, made out of income and such that the donor's lifestyle will not be affected by the gift, are exempt from IHT. (An example would be a parent making regular premium payments into a life policy on behalf of his or her children.)

Gifts made during the donor's lifetime (but not on death) not exceeding £250 per recipient per fiscal year are exempt from IHT.

Gifts made during an individual's lifetime (but not on death) in consideration of marriage are exempt from IHT. Gifts by a parent of the bride or groom are exempt up to £5,000. Gifts by a grandparent, great grandparent or even more remote ancestor are exempt up to £2,500. Gifts by anyone else are exempt up to £1,000.

Over and above all the other exemptions, any gifts made by an individual during their lifetime (but not on death) are exempt from IHT up to £3,000 per fiscal year.

8. A chargeable disposal occurs in the following cases, unless the disposal is exempt.

- Sales and gifts of assets or parts of assets
- Receipts of capital sums following the surrender of rights to assets
- The loss or destruction of assets
- Appropriation of assets as trading stock

The chargeable disposal occurs on the date of the contract (where there is one, whether written or oral), or the date of a conditional contract becoming unconditional. This may differ from the date of transfer of the asset. When a capital sum is received on a surrender of rights or the loss or destruction of an asset, the disposal takes place on the day the sum is received.

For tax planning purposes, an individual may wish to accelerate a gain into an earlier tax year to obtain earlier loss relief or to delay a gain until a later tax year when an unused annual exemption may be available.

All forms of property, wherever in the world they are situated, are chargeable assets unless they are specifically designated as exempt. The following are exempt assets.

- National Savings & Investments (NS&I) Certificates and Premium Bonds
- Foreign currency for private use
- Decorations awarded for bravery (unless purchased)
- Gilt-edged securities and qualifying corporate bonds
- Tangible wasting assets with a remaining life of under 50 years, including private cars
- Debts (except debts on a security)
- Investments held in individual savings accounts (ISAs)

Transfers of assets on death are exempt disposals.

There are also exemptions for enterprise investment scheme (EIS) shares and venture capital trust (VCT) shares.

9. **Residence and domicile**

From 6 April 2013, a new statutory **residence test** was established, and the concept of 'ordinary' residence was abolished for tax purposes.

If an individual satisfies any of the following automatic overseas tests, then he is non-resident.

Automatic overseas tests

(a) Was resident in the UK for one or more of the three previous tax years and spends fewer than 16 days in the UK in the current tax year

(b) Was not resident in the UK for any of the previous three tax years and spends fewer than 46 days in the UK in the current tax year

(c) Leaves the UK to carry out full-time work overseas

(d) Dies in the current tax year, subject to conditions which include spending fewer than 46 days in the UK.

If the individual does not satisfy any of the automatic overseas tests, the individual will be automatically UK-resident if he meets any of the following automatic UK tests.

Automatic UK tests

(a) He spends 183 days or more (ie more than six months) in the UK during the tax year

(b) There is a period of more than 90 days, part of which falls within the tax year, when he has a home in the UK and no home overseas (disregarding any home at which he is present for fewer than 30 days in the tax year)

(c) He dies in the current year, subject to conditions which include having been UK-resident in the previous three tax years

(d) He meets a full-time UK work test, as set out in the taxation rules.

If the individual meets none of the automatic overseas tests and none of the automatic UK tests, he must look at the 'sufficient ties' test, which compares the number of days spent in the UK against the number of 'connection factors' that apply, such as whether he has a UK-resident family, or accommodation in the UK.

A person is **domiciled** in the country in which he has his permanent home. A person may be resident in more than one country, but he can be domiciled in only one country at a time.

Where the individual was born determines his or her domicile of origin. A person retains this domicile until he acquires a different domicile of dependency (if, while he is under 16, his father's domicile changes) or domicile of choice if he permanently settles in another country.

A resident and domiciled individual is taxed on his general earnings on a receipts basis.

A non-resident is taxed on his general earnings in respect of UK duties on the receipts basis but there is no UK income tax on foreign earnings (those in respect of non-UK duties).

A UK resident who is not UK domiciled may claim the remittance basis for a particular tax year, so that he is only liable to UK income tax on overseas income to the extent that it is brought (remitted) to the UK. Such an individual is liable to the remittance basis charge if he claims the remittance basis for a tax year, subject to the following residence rule.

■ If the individual has been UK-resident for at least seven of the nine tax years preceding that tax year, the remittance basis charge payable is £30,000 annually.

■ If the individual has been UK-resident for at least 12 of the 14 tax years preceding that tax year, the remittance basis charge payable is £50,000 annually.

Resident 'non-doms' who have been resident in the UK for less than seven years can still elect for the remittance basis of tax, but there is no annual charge.

December 2010 Examination Answers

Part 1 – Portfolio Construction Theory

Section A

1. (a) **C** Longer-dated bonds are more exposed to movements in yield. Bonds with lower coupon have more value tied up in their terminal value.

    (b) **B** Preferred shares carry a fixed dividend, not a growing dividend.

    (c) **C** Bonds with higher duration will be the most convex. In general, the higher the coupon rate, the lower the convexity of a bond.

    (d) **B** A European option can only be exercised at its expiry date. The higher the exercise price, the lower is the value of an option to buy it.

    (e) **C** Bondholders hoping for a payout are likely to want the company to conserve cash and reduce risk. Equity holders have a low prospect of receiving a payout from assets of the company, and so have little if anything left to lose: they could gain however from the company taking on risk.

    (f) **A** Beta is the covariance of the investment relative to the market, divided by the variance of the market.

    (g) **B** The expected yield will be lower than the promised yield, because the expected yield factors in the probability of default.

    (h) **C** A factor portfolio comprises stocks with different risk exposure to different economic factors, eg interest rates, inflation. Stocks are selected such that the portfolio is strongly affected by one factor (a beta close to 1) but weakly affected by other factors (a beta nearer to 0).

    (i) An index portfolio may be constructed using the following techniques.

    - Stratified sampling, which involves constructing the portfolio based on a sample of securities from the total population comprising the index.

    - Factor matching, which means using securities selected on the basis of a number of factors or risk indices.

    - Co-mingling, which refers to the use of co-mingled collective funds –this may be especially suitable for clients with relatively small portfolios and may provide an acceptable compromise between the transaction costs of complete indexation and the tracking error of stratified sampling.

    (j) g = Annual dividend growth rate

    $g = (3.50/1.20)^{1/10} - 1 = 0.1130$, ie 11.3%

    (k) The profits that a company does not pay out in dividends are retained.

    Retention rate = 1 – [Payout ratio] = 1 – 0.63 = 0.37, ie 37%

    (l) (i) Formula for portfolio risk:

    $$\sigma_{a+b} = \sqrt{p_a{}^2\sigma_a{}^2 + p_b{}^2\sigma_b{}^2 + 2p_a p_b Cov_{ab}}$$

    where:

    $cov_{ab} = \sigma_a \sigma_b cor_{ab}$

    Portfolio variance = $(0.6^2 \times 0.04) + (0.4^2 \times 0.09) + 2 \times 0.6 \times 0.4 \times [0.3 \times \sqrt{0.04} \times \sqrt{0.09}]$

Portfolio variance = 0.0144 + 0.0144 + 0.00864 = 0.03744

(ii) Portfolio standard deviation = $\sqrt{0.03744}$ = 0.1935, ie 19.35%

(m) (i) The standard deviation of quarterly returns is given in the question as 0.05998.

When annualising a standard deviation, take the square root of the number of observations per year – in this case, four, because the returns are quarterly.

Annualised standard deviation = 0.05998 × $\sqrt{4}$ = 0.12, ie 12.0%

(ii) The annualised return requires de-compounding by the number of years – in this case, 2.75 years.

Annualised return = $(110/100)^{1/2.75} - 1$ = 0.0353, ie 3.53%

(iii) **Annualised performance numbers**

Merit: They standardise performance numbers over long periods and so indicate what an investor can expect to achieve over a longer time period.

Drawback: They have the effect of smoothing performance and not reflecting the fluctuations. This may lead a client to invest not fully understanding the implications of the variability of returns likely to be experienced. Risk along the way may be too high for the client's risk tolerance.

(iv) **Real v. nominal performance numbers on overseas market**

For:

■ The protection and growth of real wealth and purchasing power is a cornerstone of wealth management. Real numbers provide clients with this information.

■ They improve understanding of performance delivered by the wealth manager.

■ They show the actual performance of the underlying securities. Grossing up the inflation component can flatter the return obtained for the risk taken, and therefore present an inaccurate picture of asset returns and risk relative to the Security Market Line. Real numbers show the risk attached to producing real returns. If the investor seeks inflation exposure, there may have been safer ways of achieving this – for example, via cash instruments in the same market offering a compensating higher interest rate.

■ Real performance is relevant because exchange rates tend not to adjust (as the Fisher effect predicts) over anything other than the long term.

Against:

■ Risks associated with currency, interest rate and inflation are part of international investing. The active manager's return should include all active decisions.

■ The inflation rate that matters is the investor's domestic inflation rate. The selection of an overseas inflation rate is arbitrary because it is not the inflation rate that the client is trying to protect his/her purchasing power against.

■ If the exchange rate is simultaneously adjusting, as the Fisher effect predicts, then adjusting for inflation in local currency terms and then converting to the investor's domestic currency is double counting.

■ Real performance numbers can be hard to interpret, and clients may be confused.

(n)   Using the Capital Asset Pricing Model to calculate the required return for Stock A and Stock B:

Required return for Stock A = 2% + 1.9 × (6% − 2%) = 9.6%.

As the expected return for Stock A is 11.4%, Stock A is underpriced according to CAPM.

Required return for Stock B = 2% + 0.8 × (6% − 2%) = 5.2%.

As the expected return for Stock B is 5.2%, Stock B is correctly priced according to CAPM.

In the chart below, the expected/required return is plotted on the y-axis, against beta on the x-axis.

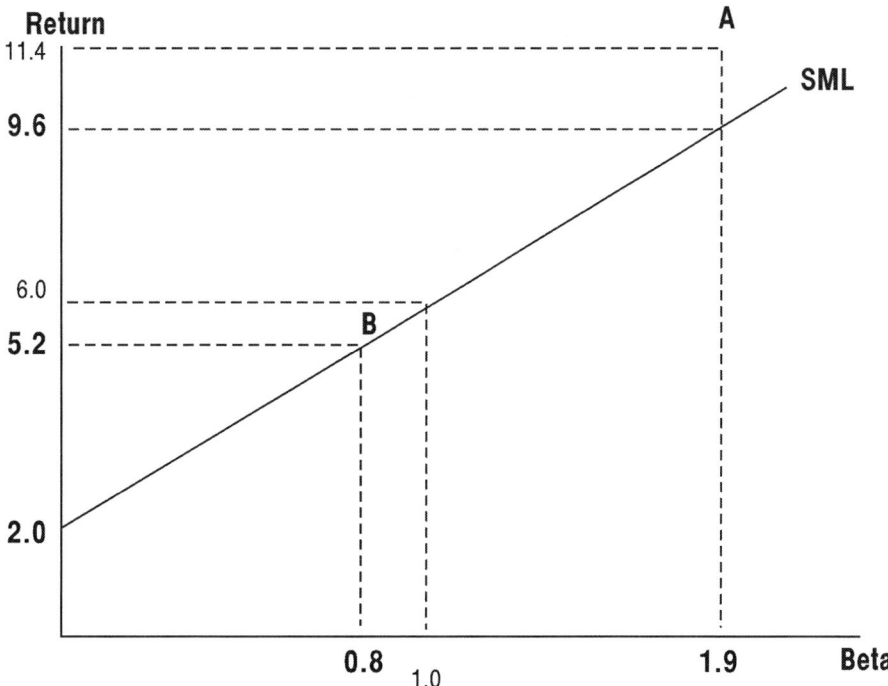

(o)   (i)   Conversion value for US$100 nominal is: 25 × 3.80 = US$95.00

The bond is trading at US$120, and so the premium is currently US$120.00 − US$95.00 = US$25.00.

The premium as a percentage of the conversion value is therefore:

25/95 = 26.3%

(ii)   The convertible bond enables the holder to exploit the upside potential of equity while retaining the safety of a bond.

Investors can be expected to pay a premium for instruments that offer equity growth potential but remove equity downside risk. The convertible bond in this question essentially has an attached call option.

The premium suggests that investors value the option highly. A higher premium, other things being equal, indicates that:

■   The option to convert has a long time to run ie there is higher potential for growth in the share price.

■   The underlying stock is expected to perform strongly.

■   The underlying stock is intrinsically valuable due to low probability of default and high credit rating.

Section B

2.   Human capital is the stock of competences and attributes enabling a person to use their labour to produce economic value. Human capital is a more 'equity-like' asset if its price fluctuates more with the economic cycle, as equities do. Human capital is more 'bond-like' if its price fluctuates less cyclically and if the tendency is for workers' pay and employment to vary less with changing economic fortunes of business enterprises.

   Reasons why human capital may be more equity-like than historically presumed are based on these changing dynamics within the modern workplace:

   ■   Workers have more company shares and share options than used to be the case.

   ■   A 'bonus culture' is quite common for some levels of staff in some industries.

   ■   Public listed employers have directors who are performance-remunerated and so are motivated to 'right-size' the firm's resources to the economic cycle, including staff.

   ■   Increasing use of contract, temporary and part-time employment arrangements makes people's employment and income more closely tied to the fortunes of companies and the economic cycle.

   ■   Workers have acquiesced to new and more flexible employer practices by permitting the rise of defined contribution pensions. This means that many people now start their earnings career expecting to change employer frequently, which permits employers also to adopt greater flexibility.

   If the hypothesis of more equity-like human capital is accepted, then inter-temporal portfolio theory indicates that workers should diversify away from equity-like job risk. At its heart, diversification means human capital and financial capital doing different things.

   At the start of a person's earnings career, human capital is relatively high and financial capital is typically low. This implies a relatively low exposure to equity investments when young. The usual diversifying asset class to select is fixed income.

   A person starting out with a low equity allocation would then increase this allocation as financial capital grows and human capital declines. Moving forward in years, at a certain age lifestyling of asset allocation would start.

   Lifestyling involves reducing the variability of returns in the financial portfolio. This usually means reducing the allocation to equities. The combined effects are a distinct 'hump' shape to the lifetime allocation of equities.

   Of course, clients exhibit a variety of different human capital characteristics, which is when the interaction of wealth manager and client starts to get interesting. Understanding clients and their employment becomes more important.

Section C

3   (a)   Forward contracts are 'tailored' contracts, customised in terms of size and delivery dates. Futures contracts are standardised contracts in terms of size and delivery dates.

   Forward contracts are private or 'over-the-counter' contracts between two parties, and so arranging them may involve search costs. They are an obligation, and so are difficult to reverse. Futures contracts are standardised contracts between a customer and a clearing house, and are often traded on an exchange. These characteristics makes futures contracts more liquid, and usually more suitable for portfolio investors.

   The profit or loss on a forward contract is realised on the delivery date. The price agreed is paid usually upon physical delivery. Profits and losses on futures contracts are realised immediately, as they are marked to market.

For forward contracts, margins are set once, on the day of the initial transaction. For futures contracts, margins must be maintained to reflect price movements.

(b)   If a mining company has sold production forward, it has reduced exposure to the spot market. It may have done so to hedge exposure to fluctuations in commodity prices.

Forward sales and hedges may mean the shares of the company are a poor proxy for the spot market. If the company has hedged unwisely, it may now be locked into an unfavourable future commitment.

If a wealth manager is optimistic about the spot market and a future price trend in a commodity, he or she will wish to hold a stock that it is a good proxy for the spot market. However, the wrong stock will perform relatively poorly, and so returns to the less informed manager may be poor.

4.   The yield curve demonstrates the relationship between bond yields and their maturities and is very closely linked to the term structure of interest rates. The yield curve is normally expected to slope upwards.

Several explanations have been postulated to explain the shape of the yield curve, ranging from the theoretical pure expectations model to the more pragmatic segmentation theory.

The basic combination of alternative theories explaining the shape of yield curves propose that it is driven by:

■   The liquidity premium and preferred habitat models
■   Market expectation of future interest rates

Liquidity preference theory states that if an investor's money is invested in longer term (and therefore riskier) stocks, then they will require a greater return or risk premium. Short-term liquid stock carries a lower risk and therefore requires a lower return. Longer maturity results in higher risk which, in turn, results in higher returns or yields. As regards causality, this theory assumes that spot rates are established by the market from which forward rates and yields may be derived. This risk premium gives rise to the normal upward sloping yield curve.

Pure expectations theory takes us back to the linkage between spot and forward rates. This theory argues that the yield curve is a reflection of spot rates and that spot rates in turn are a reflection of the market's expectation of forward rates. The yield is the weighted average of spot rates, and spot rates equate to the geometric mean of forward rates.

As regards causality, this theory assumes that forward rates are established by the market from which spot rates, and hence yields, are derived.

While the yield curve will undoubtedly reflect risk/return effects, it will also reflect expectations and other influences. It can be argued that the short term is dominated by expectations of future rates, whereas the medium term and long term may be more influenced by expectations of inflation and the liquidity premium, both overlaid by the effects of supply and demand.

The pure expectations theory of the yield curve suggests that the only real driver to yields and spot rates is the market expectation of future interest rates. Therefore, if the market's expectation of future interest rates is flat, the yield curve, the spot curve and the forward curve would all be flat horizontal lines, corresponding to the current rate.

However, if the other theories are correct, it may be that even if the market's expectation of interest rates were that there would be no change, then the yield curve might have an upward slope as a result of the liquidity premium.

Wherever the yield curve is upward sloping, the spot rate will lie above it and the forward rate will lie above that. This would tend to insert an upward bias into forward rates.

5.   Value investing involves identifying efficient firms whose shares are inexpensive and undervalued. Such stocks are attractive for their safety margin compared with intrinsic value. Evidence from long-run returns suggests that value stocks have enhanced expected returns. Value stocks have a relatively high book-to-price ratio and therefore usually lower beta, which should make them less risky. This should make value investing appealing to most types of investor. Low beta should mean low returns, so higher returns represent an anomaly that disconfirms the efficient market hypothesis. The strategy of the value investor is generally to wait for the market to correct, which can take a long time.

Growth investing involves identifying securities with great and often rapid growth prospects, often at an early stage of development. This tends to involve a focus on small and medium capitalisation firms where there is less analyst following and where the science behind the firm may only be patchily reported. It also means investing in large companies where there is an expectation that the market has underestimated the firm's growth prospects. Growth strategies include emerging markets, recovery shares, internet and technology stocks, smaller companies and special situations. Growth stocks generally have a lower book-to-price ratio and therefore usually higher beta, which should make them more risky. This might make growth investing appealing to fewer types of investor.

Momentum investing is a system of buying stocks or other securities that have had high returns over the past three to 12 months, and selling those that have had poor returns over the same period. The theory is that stocks price movements exhibit 'momentum' in their trends. This tendency should not be easy to exploit in a relatively efficient market.

Two hypotheses used to explain the effect in terms of an efficient market are as follows.

(1)   That momentum investors bear significant risk for assuming this strategy and so higher returns are compensation with higher risk taken

(2)   That momentum investors are exploiting behavioural shortcomings in other investors, such as investor herding and investor over- or under-reaction. Momentum is the fourth factor found in explaining long-run returns, in addition to beta, small capitalisation and value, according to Carhart's extension of the three-factor Fama-French model.

Part 2 – Taxation and Trusts

Section D

6.   To: James

Re: Tax matters

Date: 10 December 2014

(a)   **Possible sale of house**

A gain on disposal of a property that is not the taxpayer's principal private residence(PPR) – for example, a buy-to-let property, is liable to capital gains tax (at 18% basic rate or at 28% higher rate). The base cost will be the cost of acquisition plus subsequent improvement expenditure that has not been allowed for tax. You would be able to set your total gains for the year against your annual CGT exempt allowance (£11,000 for 2014/15). You may wish to consider the tax year in which to sell, for CGT planning purposes.

If a property is the investor's PPR, the sale of the property will be exempt from capital gains tax. A married couple or a civil partnership can only have one PPR. If you have more than one residence, you can nominate which one is to be treated as your PPR within two years of acquiring the second property.

(b)   **Possible sale of CRH shares**

You have made a chargeable gain of £1,250 less selling costs on these shares, at the price stated. Shares may fluctuate greatly in value, so the eventual gain (or loss) on disposal, which will be based on the arm's-length disposal proceeds, may be quite different from this figure. Costs may be set against the gain, although these are likely to be small for stock transactions.

You are considering a disposal or part-disposal of these shares. On a part-disposal, a proportionate part of the original cost will be set against the proceeds to calculate the chargeable gain.

You would be able to set your total gains for the year against your annual CGT exempt allowance. You may wish to consider the tax year in which to sell shares for CGT planning purposes, so as to best make use of the annual allowance or a year in which you are only a basic rate taxpayer, if applicable.

(c)   **Rent from Spain summer house**

You are a UK resident and are accordingly taxed on your worldwide income.

Profits from rent – whether from residential or commercial property – are treated as follows for tax purposes.

- Profit will be taxed at the taxpayer's marginal rate.
- Each year's profit is taxed in that tax year.
- Mortgage interest and certain other expenses relating to the property being let can count as a deductible expense to set against the letting income.

You will be able to set tax levied by Spain against the tax on the rental income from the house.

Broadly, a person is domiciled in the country in which he has his permanent home, and domicile is distinct from nationality and residence. If you are a non-domiciled UK resident, you may claim the remittance basis so that your income will only suffer UK tax when it is remitted to the UK. In that case, the significant penalty of the remittance basis charge of £30,000 annually would be payable if, as a non-domiciled individual, you have been resident in the UK for at least seven of the nine tax years preceding the year in question. If an individual has been UK-resident for at least 12 of the 14 tax years preceding that tax year, the remittance basis charge payable is £50,000 annually. It would be necessary to consider your tax circumstances overall.

(d)   **Your company salary and the company's corporation tax**

Against the salary from your company, you will be able to set the personal allowance of £10,000 (2014/15). The remainder will be liable to basic rate (20%) income tax.

Assuming that all of the company's expenses of £50,000 are allowable for tax purposes, the company would appear to have taxable profits of £30,000.

Depreciation charged by a company in its financial accounts is not allowable expenditure for tax purposes, since the company determines the depreciation rates. However, the company is permitted to make a deduction in place of depreciation, which is referred to as capital allowances. This is essentially another name for depreciation, but calculated by reference to tax legislation.

Corporation tax is calculated as a percentage of the taxable profits of a company. For a company such as yours, with taxable profits of £300,000 or less in their chargeable accounting period, the small companies' rate of 20% (Financial Year 2014) is payable.

(e)   **Rights issue and bonus shares**

The key difference between a bonus issue and a rights issue for capital gains tax purposes is that, with a rights issue, the new shares are paid for and this results in an adjustment to the original cost. Bonus shares are issued without any consideration being paid and the original cost for capital gains tax purposes is unchanged.

If, as the shareholder, you do not take up your rights but sell them to a third party without paying the company for the rights shares, the proceeds are treated as a capital distribution and will be dealt with either under the part-disposal rules or, if not more than the higher of £3,000 and 5% of the value of the shareholding giving rise to the disposal, as a reduction of original cost.

Section E

7.   **Larry: Income Tax Computation 2014/15**

	Non-savings income £	Savings income £	Total £
Income from employment	85,000		
Non-dividend savings income		5,000	
Net income	85,000	5,000	90,000
Less personal allowance	(10,000)		(10,000)
Taxable income	75,000	5,000	80,000

	£	£
Income tax on non-savings income		
£31,865 × 20%		6,373
£43,135 × 40%		17,254
Tax on savings income		
£5,000 × 40%		2,000
Income tax liability		25,627

Larry may have suffered withholding tax on his non-dividend income. Subject to any tax treaty between the UK and the jurisdiction levying the withholding tax, Larry may be able to claim a credit for the amount of the withholding tax suffered.

8. **Bare trust**

A trust may be a bare (or 'simple') trust, where there is a sole beneficiary. In such a trust, the trustee has no discretion over payment of income or capital to the beneficiary, who has an immediate and absolute right to both capital and income. The beneficiary of the trust can instruct the trustee how to manage the trust property, and has the right to take actual possession of the trust property at any time.

Income arising in a bare trust is assessed on the beneficiaries of the trust. The trustees are not required to file a self-assessment return or deduct tax at source.Where the settlor of the trust is the parent of a minor unmarried beneficiary, the trust income is assessed on the settlor under the anti-avoidance rules.

Interest in possession trust

An interest in possession trust arises where a beneficiary, known as an 'income beneficiary' or a 'life interest', has a legal right to the income or other benefit derived from the trust property as it arises. For example, the life interest may have the right to occupy a house during his or her lifetime, or an income beneficiary the right to receive income from the trust property for a specified period or until death. On the death of the life interest/income beneficiary, the assets of the trust will be held for the benefit of the second class of beneficiary, known as the remainderman or the reversionary interest. A trustee of an interest in possession trust has the duty to safeguard the interests of both classes of beneficiary.

Interest in possession trusts enables individuals to benefit from the property while protecting them from their own improvident actions, since they are unable to spend the capital value of the trust. In addition, they will keep the trust property protected from the life interest's creditors, should the life interest become bankrupt.

Income is taxed in the first instance on the trustees. The trustees do not have a personal allowance, nor is the trust income split into different bands of income as it is for an individual. Instead all trust income is taxed at the basic rate of tax applicable to the type of income.

Discretionary trust

A trust may be a discretionary trust where the trustees exercise their discretion as to which beneficiaries will be entitled to receive income or capital from the trust. The exact rights of each beneficiary are not determined in advance. This can be of use in family situations. First of all, it may enable the settlor to control the conduct of the beneficiaries by the trustee's use of discretionary powers. Second, it keeps the trust flexible. For example, the settlor can constitute a discretionary trust for the benefit of a class of people, such as his grandchildren. If a new grandchild is born after the trust is set up, the grandchild will automatically rank as a beneficiary.

Income used to pay trustees' expenses is taxed at the basic rate of tax, ie 10% where such expenses are paid out of dividend income, 20% when paid out of savings income or non-savings income. The amount of income so used is the amount of the expenses, grossed-up at 10% or 20% as appropriate. Dividend income is used to cover such expenses before savings income and then non-savings income is used.

Once expenses are deducted, discretionary trusts then have a standard, or basic rate, band of £1,000 (2014/15). The first £1,000 of taxable income is taxed at the basic rates, ie at 10% (dividends), 20% (savings and non-savings income). As for individuals, the basic rate band is applied first to non-savings income, then savings income and finally dividends. Many smaller trusts will have no further tax to pay and will not need to file a tax return.

Where a settlor has made more than one settlement, the £1,000 is divided by the number of settlements made by the same settlor, with a minimum amount of £200 for each trust.

Any remaining income is taxed at one of two special trust tax rates. These are 45% (on non-dividend income) and 37.5% (on dividend income) (2014/15) – known as the 'trust rate' and the 'dividend trust rate' respectively.

9. Quoted shares are valued at the lower of:
    - The quoted bid price plus one quarter of the difference between the bid and offer prices, and
    - The average of the lowest and highest recorded bargains on the day

Prices are taken from the Stock Exchange Daily Official List (SEDOL).Where the share is being quoted ex-dividend, the net amount of the next dividend should be added to the value.

Where quoted investments are sold by an executor at a loss in the twelve-month period after death, the loss on sale is deducted from the value of the investments before inheritance tax is charged. This prevents there being a loss due to the forced sale of shares to meet inheritance tax liabilities.

The following conditions must be met.

- The seller of the shares must be the person liable to pay tax on them.
- The investments must be listed.
- The sale must take place within 12 months of death.

The value of the chargeable estate is reduced by the loss on sale, which is calculated as the difference between the sale proceeds (or market value of the shares, if significantly higher) and the value of the shares in the estate. This may then result in a repayment of inheritance tax.

Where part of the proceeds is reinvested in other investments within two months of the last relevant sale in the twelve-month period, the relief is restricted by the following fraction.

Restriction = Loss × [Purchase price of new investments]/[Gross proceeds from investments sold]

Valuations in unquoted securities are more difficult to decide, as there is no active market in the shares.

Under the self-assessment procedures, taxpayers are responsible for either calculating the appropriate amount of tax due or, in the case of individuals, for providing the appropriate figures to enable HMRC to calculate it on their behalf. If a valuation is not provided on the correct basis, a taxpayer's tax return may be challenged by HMRC.

The correct basis of valuation for tax purposes is the 'market value' as defined in S160 Inheritance Tax Act 1984, that is: 'The price which the property might reasonably be expected to fetch if sold in the open market at that time, but that price shall not be assumed to be reduced on the grounds that the whole property is to be placed on the market at one and the same time.'

Appropriate valuation methods the taxpayer may use include earnings, assets, dividend yield or an industry-specific valuation method. The taxpayer should consider the company's performance and financial status as shown by, say, three years' accounts up to the valuation date, any information normally available to shareholders, the size of the shareholding and shareholders' rights, the company's dividend policy, yields and price earnings ratios of comparable companies or sectors and the commercial and economic background at the valuation date.

There may be ongoing negotiations with HMRC's Shares and Assets Valuation (SAV) in order to establish an accepted valuation.

June 2010 Examination Answers

Part 1 – Portfolio Construction Theory

Section A

Examiner's comment

Section A of the paper assesses candidates' broad knowledge of the syllabus. This included testing candidates' familiarity and comfort with financial instruments, portfolio construction, portfolio risk, diversification, principles of investment and investment premiums.

There were 16 parts to question 1. The mean, median and modal mark was 25.7, 26.5 and 29.5 respectively out of 40, with a standard deviation of 5.1. The maximum mark was 32 and the minimum 10.

(a), (b), (c), (d), (e) and (f) were multiple choice questions worth one mark each. The correct answer to each was a), a), b), a), c), b). Many candidates obtained 5 out of 6. A majority of candidates failed to answer (c) correctly. The correct answer is that there are two sources of risk within a single factor model; systematic risk, and everything else which is idiosyncratic.

1.   (a)   **A**   All investors will hold a combination of a broadly based market index and the risk-free asset.

     (b)   **A**   Modern portfolio theory does not assume that portfolios are perfectly negatively correlated.

     (c)   **B**   The single factor model (CAPM) assumes that each security contains:

         ■   Systematic risk

         ■   Unsystematic risk

     (d)   **A**   International CAPM assumes that the risk-free rate is the investor's domestic risk-free rate and the market portfolio is a market capitalisation weighted portfolio of all worldwide risky securities.

     (e)   **C**   The slope of the characteristic line gives the stock beta, the intercept gives the stock alpha.

     (f)   **B**   An investment objective of 7% pa return is an absolute return objective, a relative return objective would relate the target return to, say, a risk metric.

     (g)   **Arbitrage pricing theory**

         Examiner's comment. A common mistake was for candidates to add the risk-free rate to each of the three factors.

         Under APT the expected return is given by:

         $r = r_f + b_1F_1 + b_2F_2 + b_3F_3$

         where:

         b_1, b_2, b_3 are the relevant factor sensitivities

         F_1, F_2, F_3 are the relevant factor risk premia

         giving:

         $r = 3\% + 1 \times 10\% + 2 \times 7\% + 0 \times 6.0\% = 27.0\%$.

(h)   **Cross rates**

1 / 0.7775 = US$ 1.286 / £1

1.286 / 1.8325 = US$ 0.702 / C$1

The US$/C$ spot cross exchange rate is 0.702.

(i)   **Beta**

$$\beta = \frac{\text{Covariance}_{im}}{\text{Variance of the market}} = \frac{0.005}{0.05^2} = 2.0$$

(j)   **Total risk**

$$\sigma_i^2 = \sigma_s^2 + \sigma_u^2 = 17^2 + 8^2 = 353$$

$$\sigma_i = 18.788\%$$

Examiner's comment. This question tested candidates' understanding of portfolio risk. The answer required transforming standard deviations into variances, and variances back into a standard deviation.

(k)   **Stock selection**

A is underpriced by 8% and B underpriced by 5%, so on the face of it there is a greater gain to be had by investing in A rather than in B. An investor may, however, choose to invest in B for the following reasons.

- Security B is a better fit to his current portfolio based on its correlation, providing a greater correlation benefit.

- The investor may be quite undiversified and Security A may have excessive unsystematic risk.

- The beta of Security A may be considered either too high or low for the risk objective of the portfolio. Security B may have a more suitable beta.

- The market liquidity of Security A may be low, increasing transaction costs and ability to rapidly sell at quoted prices.

- Ethical reasons.

- The investor could be targeting yield or growth and Security A may not be appropriate.

- The investor may be running a tracker fund and Security A may not be part of the index followed.

- Security A may have less information availability and therefore greater uncertainty and potential for negative surprise.

Examiner's comment. This question tested candidates' critical appraisal skills around portfolio construction. The question asked why an investor may rationally select a security for portfolio inclusion that had a lower expected return than another security.

(l)   **CAPM appraisal**

Examiner's comment. The question was well answered by candidates, with many scoring full marks. Some candidates confused the required return and expected return. Their calculations were correct but their interpretation of the answer they had calculated was not. These candidates suggested incorrectly that Stock A was undervalued and Stock B overvalued.

The required return from a security based on its systematic risk can be determined through CAPM using:

$$r = r_f + \beta(r_m - r_f)$$

We can then compare the expected return and the required return, and three possibilities arise.

- ▨ Expected return > Required return ⇒ Security is undervalued
- ▨ Expected return = Required return ⇒ Security is fairly valued
- ▨ Expected return < Required return ⇒ Security is overvalued

Security A

Required return = $3 + 1.7(7 - 3) = 9.8\%$

Expected return = 9%

Conclusion: For a diversified investor, Security A is overvalued based on its systematic risk.

Security B

Required return = $3 + 0.9(7 - 3) = 6.6\%$

Expected return = 8%

Conclusion: For a diversified investor, Security B is undervalued based on its systematic risk.

(m) **Superior voting rights**

Examiner's comment. This question was not well answered by candidates. There are two main reasons, corporate control and corporate governance. No candidates identified corporate control even though empirical research suggests that this is the key explanatory variable. Some candidates had no comprehension of dual class stock, and interpreted the question as meaning preference shares and ordinary shares, which it clearly does not.

Corporate control

Shares with greater voting rights are more valuable in a takeover bid as most bidders target control. The price premium reflects the joint probability that a takeover offer will be made and that the bid price of voting shares will be higher than those with fewer voting rights.

Corporate governance

Holders of voting shares have the ability to influence the corporate governance agenda, as well as ensure a line of accountability from corporate managers, through the board of directors, to owners of the firm. This occurs as holders of voting shares appoint directors who provide leadership and make strategic decisions. Dissatisfaction with corporate performance or governance may be registered by voting against re-election of one or more directors or for the appointment of alternative candidates.

Holders of voting shares usually also have the opportunity to vote for appropriate director remuneration, audit, Articles of Association, Charter and Bylaws, as well as certain corporate actions. The value of governance is involvement in the stewardship of portfolio held firms and the ability to influence the firm's trajectory and its value.

(n) **Diversification**

Examiner's comment. For this question on portfolio risk, every candidate provided a stock workbook answer that did not critically appraise the empirical research or make mention of whether their answer holds in practice. A more skilled answer would mention how recent empirical research finds that the co-movement of world financial markets has increased over time, with this reaching a peak at times of high perceived risk. The story of portfolio diversification is therefore not so simple. Increased correlations make real, ex-post, diversification harder to achieve. Unsystematic risk is harder to remove when low positive, zero, or negative correlations are in practice difficult to find. No candidates tried to explain why institutional portfolios most often hold 70 lines of stock or more, a persistent anomaly to the story above.

Empirical studies have shown that total risk falls asymptotically towards systematic risk and that unsystematic risk is almost completely eliminated once a portfolio contains around 15 and 30 securities. These studies have shown that, in the UK, the portfolio risk is around 34.5% of the risk of the average stock held.

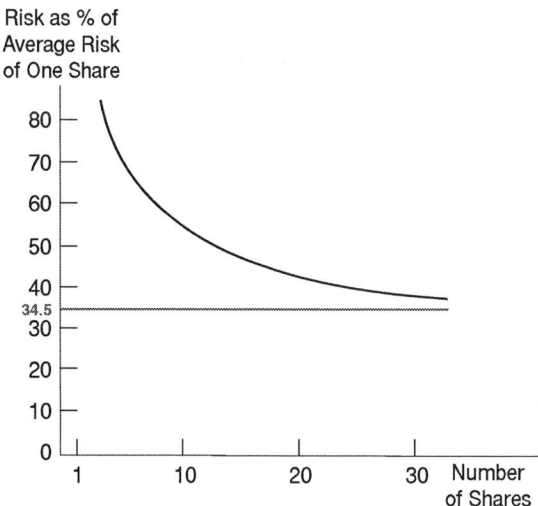

One consequence of this observation is that holding more than 30 securities simply raises transactions costs for little extra risk reduction benefit. An argument could, therefore, be put forward that a portfolio should hold no more than 30 securities. However in a very large portfolio this would not be practical as it may result in the outright ownership of 30 businesses. For practical reasons, therefore, larger portfolios must hold more.

A practical limitation of this observation is that the studies were undertaken in fairly normal and benign market circumstances, however in more extreme circumstances security correlations tend to increase, moving towards one. In a stock market crash securities tend to be highly positively correlated, all falling together. With higher correlations more securities are needed to effectively diversify and some more recent studies have suggested that a minimum of 100 securities should be held.

(o)   **Global systematic risk**

Examiner's comment. The question was not at all well answered by candidates. Stock answers were given that did not bear close correspondence to the question. This may stem from an outlook which is orientated to the home market. Examples of global systematic risk were given that included inflation, the interest rate, the exchange rate, and government stance. Several of these factors exhibit marked idiosyncratic variation which is, to a degree, diversifiable. Examples of risk factors that affect all securities together, regardless of jurisdiction, would be factor inputs such as oil, water and other essentials commodities for which there are few or no substitutes. Event-specific common factors also make good examples eg millennium bug.

Global systematic risk factors are factors that affect risky securities world-wide. Such factors would include:

* Global economic condition and the impacts of any financial contagion, such as the effects of the credit crunch.

* Global interest rates, as expressed in the investors domestic currency.

■ Global inflation rates, influenced by world-wide commodity prices that themselves may be highly affected by weather conditions (especially for foodstuffs) and the occurrence of natural disasters.

(p)   **Portfolio theory risk formula**

The general formula for combining risks is:

$$\sigma_{a+b}^{2} = p_a^2\sigma_a^2 + p_b^2\sigma_b^2 + 2p_a\,p_b\sigma_a\sigma_b Cor_{ab}$$

That may alternatively be expressed as:

$$\sigma_{a+b}^{2} = p_a^2\sigma_a^2 + p_b^2\sigma_b^2 + 2p_a\,p_b Cov_{ab}$$

Or:

$$\sigma_{a+b} = \sqrt{p_a^2\sigma_a^2 + p_b^2\sigma_b^2 + 2p_a p_b Cov_{ab}}$$

Answer: This is formula (i).

Where the correlation coefficient is +1, this formula reduces to formula (iii) – the risk of the portfolio is the weighted average risk.

Where the correlation coefficient is zero, this formula reduces to formula (iv).

Section B

Examiner's comment. Section B of the paper tested candidates' application of findings from behavioural finance for the improvement of wealth management for clients.

The question was not especially well answered, with a mean mark of 7.4 out of 20 and a median and modal mark of 8.0. The standard deviation was 2.8. The maximum mark was 15 and the minimum 0. Low marks were given for answers that were not structured around providing a response relevant to the question.

Some candidates gave answers on how behavioural finance contributes to an explanation of asset returns and asset pricing. This was a wasted effort. The question asked how the contribution of findings from behavioural finance may assist the design of wealth management products and services for the improvement of client outcomes. The focus is on improvement of outcomes for clients. Below are a few examples that could have been used and that have gained popularity recently.

2.   **Behavioural finance**

Behavioural finance finds that individuals exhibit over-confidence. This means that individual investors tend to focus on the upside of, say, medium risk, and not the downside. As a result, individual investors tend to interpret medium investment risk as meaning a fairly low chance of loss, more similar to low risk. This suggests a focus on up-front education and the risk/reward trade-off, with careful framing and drawing on insight and evidence, including possibly that from the medical profession and other countries which have developed techniques for making risk 'feel real'.

Limited time and cognitive capacity mean people have problems inferring relevant facts when striking decisions even when they may have all the relevant information. Behavioural finance refers to this as bounded rationality. Bounded rationality means that wide choice and complex investment menus lead to choice overload. Outcomes include procrastination, reduced satisfaction, less participation. This finding suggests that the wealth manager should limit the propositions forwarded to clients. This should include a small number of carefully thought through, properly differentiated, offerings. Doing so makes it easier for individuals to select a suitable investment or buy-in to a particular plan.

Behavioural finance finds widespread evidence of loss aversion. Individuals are more concerned with losing value than acquiring gains. Loss aversion with loss avoidance behaviour is a potential problem because it may presage a drop in contributions or opting out of investment altogether. What individuals think and do as they evidence an interim loss of various kinds is important. The relationship between attitude to loss and time is not linear: an enduring loss is more important than an otherwise identical one-off loss. 3 year 'tipping point' is found to apply in which investors may stop investing after a run of bad performance. This lends itself to loss aversion strategies such as dynamic asset allocation and constant proportion portfolio insurance (CPPI). This also suggests that a wealth manager could focus on communication strategies in order to help mitigate loss avoidance behaviour.

In the early years, the conventional approach is for relatively high risk investment. Yet behavioural finance finds a tendency to value a good more after it is incorporated into the status quo – an endowment effect. This means that a successful trial period based on regular contributions or a lump sum with smooth and steady gains may contribute to a saving habit and continuation. The endowment effect suggests a low risk start. It is not worth a potentially bumpy start before the investment has gained psychological value. A high risk start may lead to a poor experience and to withdrawing from regular saving or investment which is not in the individual's long-term interest.

Behavioural finance finds inertia, or myopia. Once people have made decisions, they tend to leave them unchanged. There is also regret aversion. This means that people regret a poor decision more than they take satisfaction from a good decision. As a result, individuals tend to hold on to securities too long. Myopia coupled with regret bias means people are unlikely to change asset allocation to manage risk close to retirement or toward the end of the investment planning horizon. Behavioural finance suggests lifestyling of investment should be automatically performed as clients near retirement or draw close to meeting a fixed liability. Lifestyling means giving-up some potential gains in order to more robustly protect against loss.

Section C

3.   (a)   **Asset allocation**

Empirically, a high risk allocation with very few assets makes almost no difference to end-period returns. The client's regular savings are likely to constitute a high proportion of her total financial wealth, and it would be unusual to recommend all of a person's financial wealth is subject to high risk. Furthermore, it is not unreasonable to assume that the client's human capital is more equity-like than bond-like (low incomes have greater correlation to the business cycle). In order to diversify away from equity-like human capital, portfolio theory suggests low risk financial assets. Finally, refer to the answer in Question 2 concerning developing a psychological attachment to a saving habit. A high risk start may lead to a large drop in value that causes the client to stop saving altogether.

Increase risk as the size of assets starts to grow beyond some threshold, perhaps years three to ten. Then start to move the portfolio into lower risk assets that are a suitable match for the asset that is intended to be purchased, be that nominal or real.

It is reasonable to assume that the price of the physical asset will grow with inflation and so, at a minimum, an inflation-plus return is likely to be appropriate, although we do not have information to confirm this.

(b)   **Income level and risk capacity**

Examiner's comment. Not one candidate mentioned State benefits, although this should be obvious from a reading of the client circumstances.

Low income places a person at or near the level of State benefits. This provides a floor to downside risk, or a guarantee, and potentially limitless upside, the complex area of means testing aside. People on low income with low financial wealth are close to the value of the guarantee and this can, quite rationally, lead to a high risk tolerance in spite of low capacity for risk taking when their total wealth is considered. This option-like characteristic can explain high risk tolerance. There is little to lose from investment risk taking. People with greater financial wealth have more to lose in absolute terms for they are further away from the guaranteed floor of State benefits. Not one candidate mentioned State benefits, although this should be obvious from a reading of the client circumstances.

4.   **Market distinctions**

Market A: Standard deviation (SD) not high. SD underestimates risk because of statistically significant skewness and kurtosis. Kurtosis implies that for much of the time the market moves very little, much less than predicted by a normal distribution. There is greater severity of large negative returns than predicted by a normal distribution. This negative skewness is evidenced by the mean being to the left of the median.

Market B: SD relatively high. SD underestimates risk because of statistically significant skewness and kurtosis. Negative skewness is highly significant. Skewness implies the number of large negative returns is more frequent and the severity of negative returns larger than predicted by a normal distribution. Negative skewness is evidenced in the mean being markedly to the left of the median. There is platykurtosis, meaning the distribution of returns is less centred on the mean than predicted by a normal distribution. This market moves in both directions away from the mean more than predicted by a normal distribution, hence the higher standard deviation.

Market B likely to be more risky than market A as evidenced in the SD, kurtosis and skewness. The mean and median of market B is larger, as would be expected by a trade-off between risk and return. Greater mean return comes at much greater risk. Market B is more volatile and less predictable than market A, based on a normal distribution.

Examiner's comment. There was a mean, median and modal mark of 2.3, 2.5 and 1.5 respectively. The maximum mark was 4.0 and the minimum 0.5.

5.   (a)   **Loss aversion strategy**

Loss and risk are different. This is a consistent finding from behavioural finance. Many individuals suggest they have medium investment risk tolerance but are highly loss averse. As a result, the investment strategy is highly understandable. The strategy is not contradictory.

There are concerns about the choice of benchmark that is a yardstick for the selling strategy. There are doubts concerning the selection and suitability of selling 25% of equities in response to an 8% drop. There are concerns about the lack of information on the mechanics of moving out of cash and re-entering the market. From the viewpoint of market timing, there are concerns about a low equity weight at what might be the inflexion point of the market. This is especially so given that some of the best return days can be clustered around the worst return days. From the viewpoint of liquidity, there are concerns about selling into falling markets and realising prices that may exacerbate the loss.

However, from the viewpoint of loss aversion, this strategy remains quite sensible. An appropriate operational focus for a wealth manager is to work through the logic and trajectory of the strategy with the client.

(b)   **Effectiveness in a financial crisis**

Without doubt the loss aversion strategy is not elegant, but it would have been highly effective at stopping the severity of loss given the more than 40% fall in equity markets of late. For a drop of 32% or more in equity markets her loss is capped at 20%. For every per cent drop in excess of 32% she will encounter no more than 20% loss. The drop in value on the equity portion of her portfolio would have been half that of the drop in the value of the overall market in the recent financial crisis.

(c) **Alternatives**

Guarantees can be expensive, in the order of 300bps. Hold equities and buy put options, hold cash and buy call options, or hold equities and sell futures. However, derivative strategies tend to be short-dated and would need to be continuously rolled over, at financial cost, even though the event they are designed to protect may only occur one in every five or ten years. Risk sharing products exist but these also reduce upside, so do not fit so well with the high risk appetite.

Part 2 – Taxation and Trusts

Section D

Examiner's comment

This sitting's Taxation paper was answered by 49 students (with one candidate returning an empty exam booklet). Overall, the standard of the exam scripts showed a marked improvement on recent years but standards still varied considerably.

The Case Study, Question 6, continues to cause weaker students problems because of the need to have prepared most of the course and have a reasonable understanding of the bigger advice picture. Better prepared students handled it easily and produced some really good answers. Two things should be remembered: first, the question calls for candidates to give advice and secondly, three lines of advice rarely score as many marks as 30 lines. In other words, it is important when answering the question to focus your responses on the questions being asked and to deliver more than simply the minimum. Recall that it is a 20 mark question out of the available 30 marks in total, so it is deserving of at least two third of your time in the examination room.

There was one small quibble with a number of candidates answers to the Case Study – while these candidates correctly identified that the person concerned was a UK-domiciled and resident person, many went on to suggest that keeping the income 'offshore' was a good way of avoiding tax. It might be a good way of 'evading' tax but such avoidance schemes do not work! Candidates lost easy marks as a result.

6. (a) **Share disposal and CGT**

CGT is payable on the chargeable disposal of a chargeable asset by a chargeable person, however since the gain has been made overseas the tax treatment will depend on his residence status. A chargeable person is a person who is resident in the UK. Non-residents are exempt from CGT.

The rules on residence for tax purposes are complex and were changed on 6 April 2013.

Each day on which Albert is in the UK at midnight is counted as a day of presence in the UK. For 2014/15, if Albert remains in the UK from his return date of 31 December, he will have been in the UK for 96 days in this tax year.

Albert therefore does not meet the 'automatic UK test' for residence of being in the UK for 183 days (six months) or more in the tax year.

However, Albert could be regarded as UK-resident for tax purposes in 2014/15 if he meets one of the other 'automatic UK tests', such as if:

(i) There is a period of more than 90 days, part of which falls within the tax year, when he has a home in the UK and no home overseas (disregarding any home at which he is present for fewer than 30 days in the tax year), or

(ii) He meets a full-time UK work test, as set out in the taxation rules

If he does not meet any of these conditions, Albert could be considered resident under the 'sufficient ties' test, which compares the number of days spent in the UK against the number of 'connection factors' that apply, such as whether he has a UK-resident family, or accommodation in the UK.

The size of the gain is as follows.

	£
Proceeds	3,000
Cost	(1,800)
Chargeable gain	1,200

(b) **Principal private residence**

Albert purchased a house over nine years ago, but has been renting it to some work colleagues for the last seven years while he has been in Dubai. We presume from how this question has been phrased that the property was his principal private residence before he went abroad, although this should be confirmed.

While there may be a lack of information as to whether Albert will be considered resident for UK tax purposes, there appears little doubt that he is UK-domiciled. He is a UK citizen and so the UK is probably either his domicile of origin or domicile of choice. For income tax and capital gains tax purposes, whether or not someone is domiciled in the UK is generally relevant only if they have foreign income and/or gains during a tax year. Broadly, individuals who are resident and domiciled in the UK pay UK tax on their worldwide income and gains as they arise.

Under normal principal private residence rules, any gain is wholly exempt where the owner has occupied the whole of the residence throughout the period of ownership. Where personal occupation has been for only part of the period of ownership, only a proportion of the gain will be exempt. Specifically:

$$\text{Exempt gain} = \text{Total gain} \times \frac{\text{Period of occupation}}{\text{Total period of ownership}}$$

In addition, the last 36 months of ownership are exempt in all cases if at some time the residence has been the taxpayer's main residence, hence we have the following.

Period	Status	Exempt Months	Total Months
December 2005 to December 2007	Owner occupied	25	25
January 2008 to January 2012	Let		49
February 2012 to January 2015	Deemed owner occupied	36	36
Total period of ownership		61	110

Chargeable gain

Hence, the chargeable gain can be calculated as follows.

	£
Proceeds	340,000
Cost	(200,000)
Total gain	140,000
Exempt gain $\left(140,000 \times \dfrac{61}{110}\right)$	(77,636)
Chargeable gain	62,364

(c) **Rental income from Dubai**

From April 2015, Albert will be considered both resident and domiciled in the UK and will therefore be taxable on his worldwide income as it arises.

In particular, he will be taxed on:

▪ Any rental income received from his Dubai property

▪ Any interest earned on his overseas bank accounts

As a consequence, his rental income from his Dubai flat will be treated as foreign property income and will be subject to the same tax rules as for UK property income. The remittance basis does not apply to Albert, since he is both resident and domiciled in the UK.

In addition, any interest earned must be declared on his UK tax returns though any tax withheld at source by the Luxembourg tax authorities will be eligible for double tax relief against his UK tax liability. This applies irrespective of whether or not the cash is drawn from the account and remitted to the UK. Hence, Albert will not be able to roll it up offshore.

The treatment of these items up to April 2015 will depend on Albert's residence status. If he is non-resident for tax purposes, they will be exempt; if he is resident, the income will be taxable.

(d) **Earnings and interest**

Once more, the tax treatment of Alert's interest income will depend on his deemed tax status for the 2014/15 year.

If Albert is considered non-resident, then the overseas interest would be tax-exempt, although the UK interest would be fully taxable, as would the UK earnings. If he is deemed to be resident, then the sources of income will be taxed.

Albert's interest income on his UK bank account will be paid net of basic rate tax, whereas interest earned on the Dubai bank account would be received gross. In both events, Albert will be liable to higher rate tax on the gross amounts and will need to pay the extra 20% on the UK account and the full 40% on the Dubai account.

In addition, given his earned income, Albert's personal allowance will be tapered. Assuming the interest figures given are gross and the income is fully taxable, his taxable income will be as follows.

	£
Earnings	100,000
Interest	9,000
Total income	109,000
Personal allowance (W)	(4,940)
Taxable income	104,060

Hence Albert's personal allowance will be:

Personal allowance = £10,000 − (½ × [£109,000 − £100,000]) = £5,500

(e) **Inheritance tax**

Inheritance tax (IHT) is a tax on gifts or transfers of value made by a UK-domiciled individual.

Gifts and transfers are liable to IHT. However, there are a number of specific exemptions that may apply.

As lifetime transfers to individuals, these gifts (net of exemptions) will be PETs.

Gift to Mary

	£
Gift made January 2015	10,000
Less:	
Marriage exemption*	(1,000)
Annual exemption (2014/15)	(3,000)
Annual exemption (2013/14)**	(3,000)
Value of gift (a PET)	3,000

* Mary is Albert's niece: hence, he is neither a parent (where the exemption is £5,000) nor a remoter ancestor (where the exemption is £2,500).

**Assuming Albert has not made any gifts in previous years, then he will have the annual exemption for 2013/14 available for use this year.

Gift to Malcolm

	£
Gift (a PET)*	5,000

*The annual exemptions are applied chronologically and have already been used against the gift to Mary. The small gift allowance can only be used against gifts with a total value of £250 or less.

Gift to charity

His transfers to charities established in the UK are wholly exempt from IHT and so will not give rise to any tax liability and will not be treated as a PET.

Section E

7. Gain on disposal

The disposal of part of a chargeable asset is a chargeable event for CGT purposes. The chargeable gain (or allowable loss) is computed by deducting only a fraction of the original cost of the whole asset. The fraction is:

$$\frac{A}{A+B} = \frac{\text{value of the part disposed of}}{\text{value of the part disposed of} + \text{market value of the remainder}}$$

The balance of the cost is used when the rest of the asset is sold.

Hence, the chargeable gain on this disposal is as follows.

	£
Disposal proceeds	90,000
Less: cost (*Working*)	(47,647)
Chargeable gain	42,353
Less: Annual allowance (2014/15)	(11,000)
Chargeable gain	£31,353

Working

The cost of the four chairs being sold is: $\dfrac{A}{A+B} \times \text{cost} = \dfrac{90,000}{90,000+80,000} \times £90,000 = £47,647$

8. Relief for post-death sales (post mortem relief)

Where personal representatives sell listed shares, authorised unit trust units or shares in an open-ended investment company (OEIC) at a loss within twelve months of the date of death, they may make a claim to reduce the value of the free estate.

To calculate the relief, all sales within the period (whether at a gain or a loss) should be netted and relief can be claimed for any net loss. In calculating the net loss, any disposal costs are disregarded.

Asset	Probate value £	Sale value £	Relief claim £
M plc	130,000	100,000	30,000
P plc	35,000	25,000	10,000
			40,000

Hence:

Revised probate value = £400,000 – £40,000 = £360,000

9. (a) **Bare trust**

A bare trust is one where there is a sole beneficiary who has an immediate and absolute right to both the trust capital and the income received by the trust from that capital, the trustee having no discretion over payment to the beneficiary.

(b) **Interest in possession trust**

An interest in possession trust is one where the beneficiary of a trust has an immediate and automatic right to the income from the trust as it arises. The trustee must pass all of income received, less trustees' expenses, to the beneficiary. The beneficiary who is entitled to the trust income is known as the life tenant or as having a life interest. The beneficiary who is entitled to the trust capital is known as the remainderman or capital beneficiary.

(c) **Discretionary trust**

In a discretionary trust, the trustees are the legal owners of any assets or property of the trust and are responsible for running the trust for the benefit of the beneficiaries. The trustees have discretion about how to use the income received by the trust. They may also have discretion about how to distribute the trust's capital and in many such trusts the trustees may choose to accumulate income (see accumulation trusts below).

(d) **Accumulation and maintenance trust**

An accumulation and maintenance (A&M) trust was a special type of discretionary trust which could be created for children up to the age of 25, and which had favourable IHT treatment. It has not been possible to create an A&M trust on or after 22 March 2006.

With an A&M trust, the trustees can accumulate the income within the trust. They will often do this for young beneficiaries until they become legally entitled to the trust property or the income arising from this property. Income that has been accumulated becomes part of the capital of the trust.

(e) **Charitable trust**

A charity is a body of persons or a trust that is established for charitable purposes only. The phrase 'charitable purposes' covers:

- The relief of poverty
- The advancement of education
- The advancement of religion
- Certain, though not all, purposes beneficial to the community

A charity is exempt from income tax on any income generated where that income is to be applied for charitable purposes.

Charitable trusts are those set up for charitable purposes. Such trusts enable the settlor to give some degree of individuality to a gift, specifying how it may be used and, as charities, are free from tax.

December 2009 Examination Answers

Part 1 – Portfolio Construction Theory

Section A

1.   (a)   **C**   Total returns are a combination of income and capital gains.

      (b)   **B**   An asset that cannot easily be sold quickly at a reasonable price is 'illiquid'. During the financial crisis of the late 2000s, mortgage-backed securities became illiquid when the market for them effectively seized up, and there were no ready buyers.

      (c)   **B**   Risk premiums concern the systematic return for holding types of securities and are not calculated from the return of an individual security.

      (d)   The investor's desired return is the amount of return the investor wants to achieve based on his or her expectations of what is possible.

           The required return can be:

           (i)   The amount of return the investor needs to achieve in order to invest, as can be derived using the Capital Asset Pricing Model, and/or

           (ii)   The amount of return needed to meet a liability where this is the objective of long-term investment planning.

      (e)   Required return for Stock A = $4\% + 1.5 \times (10\% - 4\%) = 13\%$. The expected return for Stock A is 12%. This means that Stock A is overvalued.

           Required return for Stock B = $4\% + 1.0 \times (10\% - 4\%) = 10\%$. The expected return for Stock B is 11%. This means that Stock B is undervalued.

      (f)   The expected UK pound sterling return will be equal to the local currency Yen return (the Yen interest rate) plus any currency appreciation (depreciation).

           The Yen will appreciate by 3% because the inflation differential favours the Japanese Yen and the real rate is assumed to be constant.

           In order to maintain the same real exchange rate, the UK pound sterling will depreciate by the inflation differential.

           The UK pound sterling return on the Japanese bond is therefore the 2% Japanese interest rate plus 3% Yen appreciation, which is 5%.

      (g)   E(R) = Expected return

           $E(R) = 0.6 \times ((0.04 + (1.2 \times 0.03)) + 0.4 \times (0.04 + 0.01 + 0.005)$

               = 4.56% (expected equity return) + 2.2% (expected bond return)

               = **6.76%**

      (h)   Private equity funds may be invested in various types of enterprise, such as business start-ups, management buyouts and firms in financial distress. Once these investments have distributable profits, income can be generated.

           Real estate generates income through rent paid by occupiers.

           It can be anticipated that infrastructure projects such as roads, ports and power stations can generate an income ◆ through distributable profits on contracts, or through recurring tolls, fares or other revenue where the project is structured to provide the holder with this income.

Commodities stand apart from the other asset classes mentioned because there is not a natural return-generating process to back a buy and hold strategy for commodities. Commodities are not a productive asset class. An ingot of gold does not pay a dividend: it simply stays in a vault, although it may be sold for jewelry or industrial uses.

There is accordingly no intrinsic basis for the valuation of commodities other than supply and demand.

Perhaps more than any other asset class, speculation is a key driver of the returns (prices) obtained for commodities. For soft commodities, which are mostly foodstuffs, supply factors such as good or bad harvests affect commodity prices significantly.

Without a durable and repeatable underlying return generating process, the existence of a risk premium to commodities is questionable.

There may be some minor systematic elements to nominal (as opposed to real) returns on commodities in that commodities tend to be priced in US dollars and can be a hedge against inflation.

(i) The question was well answered by candidates, with many scoring full marks.

The market beta cannot be a number other than unity (1) because beta is the slope of the regression line between the market and itself. The regression, or correlation, of a variable with itself is 1.

(j) Payout ratio = D/Earnings

According to the dividend growth model:

Price = $D_1 \times 1/(r_e - g)$

Price/Earnings (P/E) ratio = Payout ratio/(Required rate of return − Expected growth rate of dividends)

ie P/E = Payout ratio/$(r_e - g)$

= 0.65/(0.13 − 0.08) = **13**

(k) Beta = (Standard deviation for stock/Standard deviation of market) × Correlation coefficient

Beta = (0.30/0.16) × 0.7 = **1.313**

(l) Assume that the par value of the bond is £1,000.

Price = $Par/(1 + YTM)^n = 1000/1.07^{20}$ = £258.42

Par = £1,000

YTM = yield to maturity

n = number of years to maturity

(m) Assume the par value of the bond is £1,000. The calculation can be performed in two ways.

1. Current yield = Coupon/Bond price per £1.

8% = Coupon/(£1,250/£1,000)

Therefore:

Coupon = 8% × 1.25 = 10%, or £100 (ie 10% of £1,000 par)

2. Coupon ÷ £1,250 = Current yield = 0.08.

Therefore, Coupon = £100.00

(n)   Investment vehicles that can use leverage:

■   UCITS III (Undertakings for Collective Investments in Transferable Securities) allows UCITS funds to borrow up to 10% of their net asset value, but only on a temporary basis

■   Investment trusts

■   QISs (Qualified Investor Schemes) are permitted to borrow up to 100% of their net asset value

■   Unregulated vehicles, eg hedge funds

■   Private equity funds and real estate funds may have also borrow funds to provide leverage

Merits. Leverage can support returns in rising markets where returns exceed the cost of borrowing. The Capital Asset Pricing Model shows that gearing increases both risk and expected return. However, even in rising markets, gearing based on variable interest rates is subject to interest rate risk.

Drawbacks. Leverage can increase losses in falling markets. This can be compounded because the cost of borrowing still has to be met and illiquidity in falling markets can make it difficult to expedite selling and can thus compound losses.

Section B

2.   **Examiner's comment**. A major mistake was to assume that the objective was best met through a very high equity weighting. A majority of candidates decided that it is better to seek high returns regardless of risk, even if this meant overshooting the objective by pursuing maximum return. There is no mandate for this approach and it is does not fit well with the remit of the question. Candidates who suggested aggressive allocations without regard to risk obtained low marks. The danger with such an approach is that it puts at risk a large proportion of the value of the accumulated pension saving, and this is potentially extremely damaging.

Virtually all candidates had at least 60% allocation to equities and a majority had close to 80%. Every candidate had a UK equity weighting exceeding the total of the international equity weight. In some cases the UK equity weight was four times the international equity weight. The aim of the scheme is to achieve the return objective at minimum risk. It is most unlikely that this will be best achieved through a relatively undiversified equity portfolio. Candidates did not offer a convincing explanation for the proposed major departures from world equity weights that they were suggesting. It should be noted that a DC pension has no liabilities to match that might conceivably justify some additional weight to the UK. An alternative portfolio construction that was not mentioned by candidates would be to ignore long-only listed equities entirely and to opt for a high proportion of fixed income combined with a significant proportion allocated to highly active mandates and alternatives.

The objective of the default fund is to support the payment of a pension. Pension contributions accumulate and invest, an annuity is (most often) purchased, and this provides a principal form of retirement benefit to individuals and households. The scheme is a DC scheme, so members bear the investment risk. The requirement of paying pensions in retirement and of members bearing investment risk immediately suggests that safety of investment is paramount – major or catastrophic loss would mean that there would be little or no pension from this source, at a significant detriment to members' future quality of life. A prudent and justifiable approach is therefore to seek to attain the return objective with the least investment risk possible (ie seeking a specific investment return with minimum variance). The return objective is not especially demanding, suggesting a balanced portfolio that would not require a high weighting to equity risk.

An aggressive allocation with a high equity allocation is not appropriate because it involves a risk of underperforming relative to the return objective, which the portfolio should be designed to achieve with minimum risk.

An appropriate allocation of assets might be as follows.

- Equities 40%

    - *Passive funds:*
      USA 10%
      Asia excl. Japan 10%
      Japan 5%
      European 5%
      Pacific Rim 5%
      UK 5%

- Fixed interest securities 40%

    - Conventional bonds 20%
    - Inflation linked gilts 20%

- Activist funds 10%

- Real Estate Investment Trusts 5%

- Money market funds 5%

The fund is constructed on the basis that equities are the chosen inflation plus asset. The long-term equity risk premium is about 3%, so a 40% allocation to equities should deliver close to 1.5% above a risk free rate and about 2% above CPI.

If 40% is in equities, this will mean that a similar weight can be made in bonds. This will limit downside risk as well as bring protection. Inflation linked bonds are used to get close to CPI because they link to the RPI. The bond portfolio can also contain conventional bonds to hedge against possible periods of deflation as well as to provide returns.

With passive management of equities in the main developed markets, charges can be kept low. The extra basis points available due to passive management can be spent on active strategies that offer the potential for high alpha. This allows small allocations to active mandates and alternative asset classes, for example activist focus funds, private equity, hedge funds and even guaranteed return products. An allocation of 5% is included for REITs to add diversification into the property sector.

Section C

3. (a) There is no knowledge of the client's circumstances, tolerances, constraints, tax position, liquidity needs or needs for income and growth. The maturing of the bonds may be intentional, with the cash flow organised to meet an upcoming liability. Alternatively, the client may be highly risk averse. Without knowledge of the client, some kind of guaranteed short-term investment such as an interest-bearing deposit, a money market fund or short-term Treasuries appears to be the most appropriate choice.

   There is no basis and therefore no remit to do anything else.

   (b) In normal circumstances, the appropriate course of action is to meet the client and to develop an understanding of their circumstances, tolerances, constraints, tax position, liquidity needs and needs for income and growth. This will lead to setting an investment objective and a risk constraint with the client. A strategic asset allocation is then developed that is the most appropriate fit for the objective and constraint. A key skill of the wealth manager is to decide the investment approach necessary to best achieve this.

4. **Examiner's comment**. At Masters level, it seems entirely reasonable to expect candidates to be cognisant of major points in economic history and to be able to mix these with an up-to-date knowledge of investment. Candidates could also have noted that overall portfolio diversification depends on the covariances of all portfolio-held securities with each other and not just bivariate correlations to US equities.

    (a) The values are bounded by +1 and −1 because the correlation coefficient is a measure of the linear dependence between two variables. The maximum linear dependence is perfectly linearity, or 1. The maximum value is also 1 because the correlation coefficient between two variables is the covariance of the two variables divided by the product of their standard deviations.

    (b) The following observations can be made.

    ■ Japanese equities have historically provided good diversification when mixed with US equities in normal market conditions.

    ■ All the correlations are positive in sign, suggesting that diversification remains partial.

    ■ The correlations were relatively high in 1971–1975 and then again in 1996-2000. Both periods were subject to major world shocks, first the oil price shock and then the stock market falling from a historically high valuation as the value of technology stocks collapsed. At times of crisis it appears that correlations increase. This means that the benefits of diversification reduce during periods of global market stress.

    ■ The periods 1971–1975 and 1996–2000 aside, there is a gradual increase in correlations, from a low base, between major investable equity markets and the US equity market. This suggests that the benefits of diversification within major equity markets is gradually reducing.

5. **Examiner's comment**. This question did not ask for a description of active versus passive management. It concerned investing indirectly via funds versus investing directly in individual securities.

    BPP note. The answer below provides more detail than would be required to achieve the relatively low allocation of five marks for this question.

    (a) **Advantages of funds**

    ■ Investors can achieve diversification relatively cheaply.

    ■ There is a lower cost of trading, because the investment cost is shared with others.

    ■ The investor can share in specialist pooled vehicles that allow access to certain desirable risk exposures.

    ■ Investors can have a share in pools that contain other similar-minded asset owners with similar investment goals, eg activist funds, index tracking funds, socially responsible investment funds.

    ■ Some funds may be exempt or use instruments that do not incur stamp duty.

    ■ Some funds can be switched without triggering capital gains tax whereas direct holdings would be liable. Tax is paid only on eventual disposal.

    ■ Dividends paid within the fund may not be taxable unless paid out to unit/share/policy holders.

    ■ Some fund vehicles do not have to pay Value Added Tax (VAT) on fund management charges.

Disadvantages of funds

- Funds are not bespoke or tailored.

- Funds add at least one further layer of fees/charges.

- There can be a lack of transparency of unit pricing methodology, commission sharing arrangements, time of day when valuations are struck, revenues and risks around stock lending and whether class action settlements are taken-up.

- There may be principal-agent problems concerning poor investment decisions, mismanagement and even fraud.

- Pooled funds experience net cash inflow or outflow which a wealth manager invested into it has no control of. If such flows affect the cash holdings of the pooled fund then beta will fluctuate as the percentage of cash held by the fund fluctuates. If money flows into pooled funds when expected stock returns are high (ie at or near their low inflexion point), and if managers take some time to allocate new money according to their usual investment styles then the funds will have large cash holdings at times. Large cash holdings imply low betas at a time when expected returns are high. The effects of new money flows on a fund's beta will depend on the magnitudes of the flows, the size of the asset holdings, and the speed with which new money is invested. Research shows a strong correlation between net cash flows and concurrent stock market returns, suggesting a connection between cash flows to funds and expected returns.

(b)   Investment suitability criteria when selecting actively managed funds will include the following.

- Quantitative assessment such as the Sortino ratio, Sharpe ratio, Treynor measure, Jensen's alpha, Appraisal ratio and Information ratio.

- Consistency, stability and durability of return generation and risk management.

- Qualitative measures, including financial strength of fund, seasoning, and assets under management.

- Investment philosophy, investment style, costs, charges, how active, quality of cash management.

- Regulatory history, tax and current regulation, including regulatory protection of the fund.

(c)   Aspects to be mindful of in the construction of the portfolio when using funds include the following.

- The funds when combined should do something other than obtain a beta of 1. A fund of funds can easily tend towards a beta of 1 because it is an overall average.

- It is essential that the funds, when combined, must actually diversify. Real ex-post-diversification needs to be achieved and not ex-ante diversification. Ensuring that differing funds are actually uncorrelated in practice requires analysis of good data on prior performance as well as knowledge of the stability of the investment approach and process. Of particular importance are the covariance and the marginal contribution to overall portfolio risk.

- If the funds own some similar securities, it is important that the risk and return of the funds remain significantly different from one another.

Part 2 – Taxation and Trusts

Section D

6. **MEMORANDUM**

Date: 3 April 2015
To: Charles
From: Adviser
Subject: Tax advice

I outline here my advice relating to the transactions you are considering, as well as some general tax advice relating to your proposed departure from the UK.

(a) **Sale of house**

If the house is your principal private residence (PPR), there will be no tax to pay on the expected capital gain of £70,000. You can only have one PPR. If you have more than one residence, one can be nominated as your PPR, but this would need to have been done within two years of acquiring the second house.

If the house is not your PPR, the gain will be chargeable to capital gains tax at the appropriate tax rate, but the annual exemption (£11,000 for 2014/15) can be set against your net capital gains. The rate at which the capital gains will be taxed depends upon your tax position for 2014/15. That part of the gain (if any) falling within the unutilised basic rate band will be taxed at 18% and the rest at 28%.

(b) **Sale of 2,000 Marks & Spencer plc**

This proposed sale represents 2,000 (40%) of your original holding of 5,000 shares, which you bought when their value was £30,000.

Thus, the base cost for CGT purposes of the shares sold is £30,000 × 40% = £12,000 and, if disposal proceeds are £8,000, there is a loss for CGT purposes of £4,000. This loss can be set against capital gains on other disposals.

(c) **Sale of four cars**

Private cars are exempt from Capital Gains Tax, and so these disposals will have no CGT consequences.

(d) **Sale of stamp collection**

The information I have been given tells me that you have just purchased the 'Flowers' stamps, on 1 April 2015, for £7,000, and that the remainder of the collection was built up over time. The whole collection was valued at £20,000 on 1 April 2015. The non-Flowers part of the collection was valued separately at £15,000 on 1 April 2015. If the whole collection were sold, there would be a gain of £13,000 (£20,000 – £7,000), *less* earlier acquisition costs.

The stamps are treated as chattels for CGT purposes. You only need to include in your Tax Return any gain on the disposal of a chattel where the disposal proceeds were more than £6,000. Disposal of the stamp collection could be split between years (and between you and your spouse, if applicable) to reduce capital gains tax. However, it may be that you wish or need to sell the whole collection at one time.

Minimising the chargeable gain on disposal of the whole collection would require identifying earlier acquisition costs, which I do not currently have information about.

(e)   **Tax planning advice**

The following tax planning points may help you to reduce or manage better your tax liabilities.

■   If you have a spouse, then part of the stamp collection could be transferred to your spouse before the disposal. (Transfers between spouses are exempt from CGT.)

■   The objective of transferring assets to the spouse before disposal would be to make use of her annual CGT exemption.

■   You have indicated that you plan to live outside the UK for a few years. The following points are relevant.

■   Individuals are liable to CGT on the disposal of assets situated anywhere in the world if, for any part of the tax year in which the disposal occurs, they are resident in the UK.

■   If a gain made on the disposal of an overseas asset suffers overseas taxation, relief will be available in the UK against any CGT on the same disposal.

■   Normally a disposal of assets situated in the UK is not a chargeable event if the vendor is not resident in the UK at the time of disposal.

■   Temporary non-residents, such as you plan to become, may be taxable on gains realised while they are abroad if:

   –   They are outside the UK for less than five years between the years of departure and return

   –   They were UK-resident for the four out of the seven years immediately preceding the year of departure

■   Net gains realised in the year of departure are taxed in that year. Subsequent gains/ losses are chargeable/allowable in the year of return as if they were gains/losses of that year.

Section E

7.   **Relevance of terms**

(a)   **Residence**

From 6 April 2013, a new statutory residence test was established, and the concept of 'ordinary' residence was abolished for tax purposes.

If an individual satisfies any of the following automatic overseas tests, then he is non-resident.

Automatic overseas tests:

(i)   Was resident in the UK for one or more of the three previous tax years and spends fewer than 16 days in the UK in the current tax year

(ii)   Was not resident in the UK for any of the previous three tax years and spends fewer than 46 days in the UK in the current tax year

(iii)   Leaves the UK to carry out full-time work overseas, or

(iv)   Dies in the current tax year, subject to conditions which include spending fewer than 46 days in the UK

If the individual does not satisfy any of the automatic overseas tests, the individual will be automatically UK-resident if he meets any of the following automatic UK tests.

Automatic UK tests:

(i)   He spends 183 days or more (ie more than six months) in the UK during the tax year

(ii)   There is a period of more than 90 days, part of which falls within the tax year, when he has a home in the UK and no home overseas (disregarding any home at which he is present for fewer than 30 days in the tax year)

(iii)   He dies in the current year, subject to conditions which include having been UK-resident in the previous three tax years, or

(iv)   He meets a full-time UK work test, as set out in the taxation rules

If the individual meets none of the automatic overseas tests and none of the automatic UK tests, he must look at the 'sufficient ties' test, which compares the number of days spent in the UK against the number of 'connection factors' that apply, such as whether he has a UK-resident family, or accommodation in the UK.

(b)   **Domicile**. A person is domiciled in the country in which he has his permanent home. Domicile is distinct from nationality or residence. A person may be resident in more than one country, but he can be domiciled in only one country at a time.

A person acquires a domicile of origin at birth, which is normally the domicile of his father. To acquire a domicile of choice a person must settle in another country with the clear intention of making his permanent home there. Long residence in another country is not in itself enough to prove domicile of choice.

Being resident but non-domiciled in the UK allows someone to claim to be taxed on overseas investment income on a remittance basis. Someone who claims the remittance basis for a tax year and who has been UK-resident for at least seven of the nine tax years preceding that tax year is liable to pay the remittance basis charge of £30,000 annually. If the individual has been UK-resident for at least 12 of the 14 tax years preceding that tax year, the remittance basis charge payable is £50,000 annually.

(c)   **Fiscal year**. The tax year, or fiscal year, or year of assessment runs from 6 April to 5 April. For example, the tax year 2014/15 runs from 6 April 2014 to 5 April 2015.

(d)   **Exempt income**. Income that is exempt from income tax does not need to be included in the tax computation and this includes, for example:

■   Scholarship income
■   Betting and gaming winnings
■   Income on investments in an Individual Savings Accounts

8.   The CGT computations are as follows.

	Mike £	Michele £
Capital gains	10,250	7,500
Capital losses	4,750	(9,000)
Net capital gains/(losses)	5,500	(1,500)
Annual exemption*	(5,500)	-
Chargeable amount	-	-
Losses carried forward	-	1,500

*This is restricted to amount of the actual capital gain made, up to the maximum annual exemption £11,000 for 2014/15

9. **Uses of offshore funds**

The term 'offshore fund' refers to funds run outside the UK, usually in low tax areas. These include the Channel Islands, the Isle of Man, the Cayman Islands, Hong Kong and Bermuda. In recent years, Luxembourg and Dublin have also become 'tax havens' within the EU.

Offshore pooled investments may be useful for those who require a wider choice of funds than is available onshore.

- Offshore funds may be attractive to investors who wish to use currency funds or hedge funds.

- Some investors may find offshore funds attractive for tax reasons:

    - There may be income and capital gains tax advantages for UK expatriates who are non-UK resident and for non-UK domiciled UK residents. For non-UK domiciled persons, there may be inheritance tax advantages.

    - For most taxpayers however, any tax benefit of offshore funds is limited to a possible deferral of tax payments resulting from income being paid gross.

Offshore funds: UK taxation

In general terms, there will be no tax paid by an offshore fund. However, there may be withholding tax which may not be reclaimable by the fund. In addition, a fund may be subject to a small amount of local tax.

The taxation of the individual investor will depend on the status of the fund.

- The relevance of reporting fund status for UK investors is that gains realised on disposals of investments in reporting funds will in most circumstances be subject to tax on chargeable gains.

- Gains realised on disposals of investments in non-reporting funds ('offshore income gains' or OIGs) will be subject to less favourable treatment as they will generally be charged to tax on income on gains as they arise.

- Those not resident in the UK will pay no UK income tax or capital gains tax on an offshore holding but they may be subject to tax charges in their new place of residence

June 2009 Examination Answers

Part 1 – Portfolio Construction Theory

Section A

1. (a)   The correct answer is D.

    (b)   The correct answer is D.

    (c)   The correct answer is D.

    (d)   Coupon reinvestment risk arises because the yield to maturity computation assumes:

    (i)   That all coupon flows can be reinvested

    (ii)   That all coupons will be reinvested at the promised yield to maturity

    Reinvestment will in practice occur at interest rates that prevail when coupons are paid, and these are subject to uncertainty. It is not possible to predict what rates will be available in the market at the times when coupons are paid. Therefore, reinvestment risk will be present in this case. The risk will be higher if the yield to maturity is high relative to the capital value of the bond, since more money must then be reinvested over the life of the bond.

    (e)   **Examiner's comment**. Answers were of a very variable standard. The key to a good mark lay in setting out clearly the motivations for the answer provided. A common mistake was for candidates to state that the risk premium referred to any type of return earned above a risk-free rate for any security.

    The risk premium is a compensation for exposure to market risk. This is expected to be linked to a structural phenomenon that is repeatable. Currency does not fit well with this description. It is not an asset class. Assets held in various foreign currencies are no more likely to yield a higher return because they happen to be priced in a different base currency.

    Holding a diversified mix of foreign currencies for a period of time is not expected to consistently earn a return. Currencies are volatile and do impact on security returns but in normal conditions this is expected to reflect inflation and interest differentials rather than a premium attached to the actual currency. Based on this reasoning, there is unlikely to be a risk premium to holding foreign currency. This can help to explain why many investors hedge foreign currency exposure.

    (f)   The cash flows derived from a bond may include coupons and a redemption value. The cash flows derived may be weighted according to an appropriate discount factor, to reflect the differing risks of cash flows received at different times.

    The duration of a bond represents a weighted average period of time to the receipt of the benefits of a bond. The weightings used are the present values of the cash flow benefits.

    In the case of a zero coupon bond, the only cash flow occurs on redemption. Therefore, arriving at the duration becomes simple: the duration of a zero coupon bond maturing in five years time is five years.

    (g)   **Examiner's comment**. Good answers took the position of a long-term investor. The key to a good mark lay in setting out clearly the motivations for the choice given in the answer.

    Inflation is a major concern to a long term investor. Economic history shows that returns on conventional government bonds can be significantly eroded by inflation.

    Commodities are a volatile asset class.

The returns and yields on property can be volatile, and this can be compounded by problems of illiquidity.

This leaves ten-year inflation-linked government bonds as the lowest risk asset class. These will protect against inflation risk. However, there remains the risk of deflation, so even inflation linked UK government bonds are not risk free to a long term investor.

(h)   If the exchange rate for US dollars in Australia is 0.7927 then the equivalent quote in the United States for Australian dollars is 1/0.7927.

Therefore, the quote in the United States for Australian dollars is 1.26.

In practice, there will be a spread between quotes to buy or sell a particular currency, representing income for market makers.

(i)   Some fund managers invested large amounts of client capital in the shares of listed companies in the financial sector with only a partial understanding of their risk exposures and the way that globalisation has increased the interconnectedness of these risk exposures with the real economy. There was a focus on the quantity of profits rather than on how profits were being made and how repeatable this was. This was made worse because in many cases institutional investors are themselves banks.

Section E of the 2008 Combined Code on Corporate Governance (which became the UK Corporate Governance Code) proposes that institutional shareholders should enter into a dialogue with companies based on the mutual understanding of objectives. This is designed to help ensure the directors discharge their duties in a manner that benefits shareholders. In order to be effective, this process requires a sufficient number of major shareholders to take a long-term view and to engage constructively with the companies in which they invest through dialogue and the use of their voting and other rights.

In other instances fund managers failed to address concerns with either the executive or the non-executive directors (NEDs) of financial companies. NEDs are a cornerstone of the corporate governance process because they are the principal governance agents on the board for shareholders. They represent the interests of shareholders. Effective running of the board requires the NEDs to understand the viewpoint of the body of shareholders. Section D of the Code proposes that the chairman ensure that the views of shareholders are communicated to the board as a whole, and in particular the NEDs, so that the latter can develop a balanced understanding of the issues and concerns of major shareholders.

(j)   **Examiner's comment.** This question meant more than simply highlighting that share prices were volatile.

Equity finance is the permanent risk capital of a company which is designed to shoulder all idiosyncratic risk. As such, a holder of shares in a company is a 'residual claimant'.

A residual claimant is in a riskier position than holders of other financial instruments of the company, such as bonds, for the following reasons.

(i)   Dividends are paid to shareholders only after the company has paid bondholders, preference shareholders, and decided the level of profits to hold-back and reinvest itself. Nobody can be sure what dividend, if any, a company will pay. It depends what profit the company has made and how confident the company is about the future. When a company anticipates tough times ahead, prudent financial management will normally lead it to at very least consider cutting the dividend.

(ii)   Equity holders have a low priority over a company's operating assets in the event of bankruptcy. The common shareholders receive a payout only after all creditors have first been paid. If there is nothing left the share price falls to zero and shareholders will lose their entire investment.

(k) Let Stock A be represented by 'a'.

The market is represented by 'M'.

Beta = Covariance of the investment and the market / Variance of market

Beta = $cov_{a,m} / var_m = \sigma_a \sigma_m Cor_{a,m} / var_m = 0.45 \times 0.16 \times 0.4 / 0.16^2 = 0.0288 / 0.0256 = 1.125$

(l) Investing in the shares of companies means that an investor can gain exposure to the economic growth of a country. Corporations pay salaries to households and individuals, as well as provide tax revenues that fund government expenditure and pay salaries of government workers. Increases in factor prices can be passed on in selling prices so that company earnings should increase. Due to this participation in economic growth, equities are known as growth assets.

Second, firms reinvest their earnings rather than make full payout to equity holders. This means that a major proportion of returns stand to come from capital appreciation rather than income payments as firms use profits to grow the business further.

(m) Two explanations can be given of the significance of earnings.

Firstly, as a company grows, more is paid in salaries. This growth should enable the value of shares also to grow. For this reason, shares in companies can be seen as matching salary-related liabilities and goals set by pension schemes. Accordingly, the value of equities are said to be linked to earnings.

Secondly, in theory, the values of equities are based on the present value of future earnings. The higher are expected earnings or earnings-generating capacity, the higher is the market value of equities. Within this cash-flow meaning of earnings, the value of equities is said to be linked to earnings.

(n) **Examiner's comment**. A common mistake was for candidates to add the risk-free rate to each of the three factors, thereby calculating a return in excess of 14%.

Expected return = 2% + (1.5% × 1.0) + (3.5% × 2.0) + (6.0% × 0.0) = 10.5%

(o) **Examiner's comment**. A common mistake was for candidates not to compound the after-tax returns.

The expected after-tax return is calculated as follows.

$100 \times [1 + 0.07 (1 - 0.25)]^{10} = £166.81$

Section B

2. **Portfolios and risk**

(a) The following diagram illustrates the expected return and risk for possible combinations of two risky investments A and B (ie, different proportions of funds invested in each), assuming three different degrees of correlation.

If we have all of our funds invested in B, we will receive all of its returns (r_b) and face all of its risk (σ_b). As we start to invest in A, we will start to move along the appropriate line towards A. How far along that line we are depends on what proportion of our funds are invested in A. Ultimately, when we are 100% invested in A, we will be at A, ie receive just A's return r_a and face just A's risk σ_a.

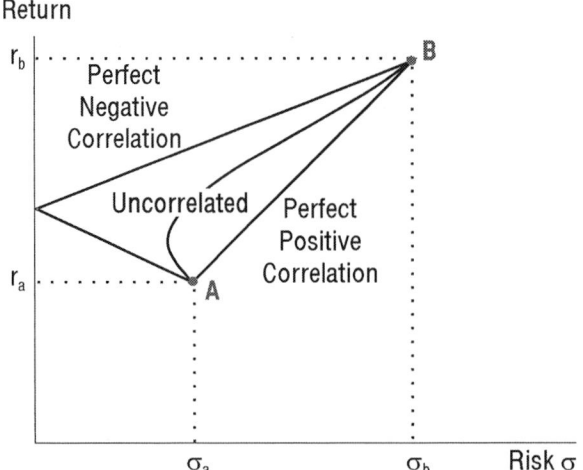

With perfect positive correlation (1.0), the resultant risk and return are the weighted average of the two investments risks and returns, and there is no benefit from diversification.

When the investments are perfectly negatively correlated (−1.0), it is possible to find appropriate proportions such that risk is completely diversified away.

When there is zero correlation between the investments, the particular choice of portfolio (ie the split of funds between the two investments) can be derived from indifference curves, depending on the level of risk aversion of the investor.

(b) With more than two investments, the number of different portfolios multiplies, introducing various combinations of investments as well as differing proportions invested in each. The calculations of combined risks and returns of multiple-investment portfolios becomes more time-consuming, but the underlying principle of diversification remains.

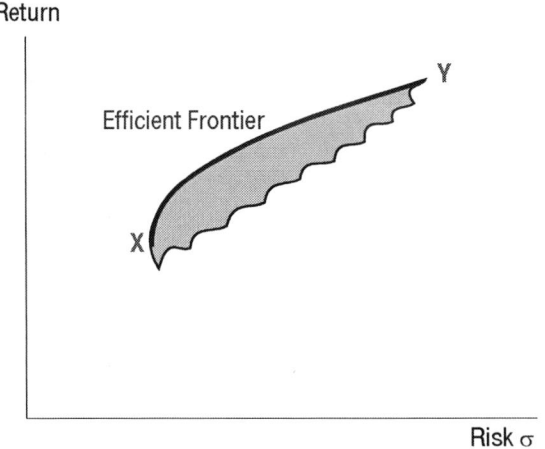

The diagram shown plots risk and return for portfolios constructed from all the possible available risky securities. The shaded area is the opportunity set showing the risk-return of the various possible portfolios that could be constructed.

Even without indifference curves, we can rule out all portfolios except those falling on the upper edge of the area between points X (the minimum risk portfolio) and Y (the maximum return portfolio) in the diagram. This line is known as the efficient frontier because it dominates all other possible portfolios.

(c) In the absence of a risk-free stock, each investor selects the best portfolio from the efficient frontier based on his own personal indifference curves. If we now include the possibility of borrowing or lending at the risk-free rate, then any point falling on a straight line through r_f and any point on or beneath the efficient frontier is now a potential portfolio.

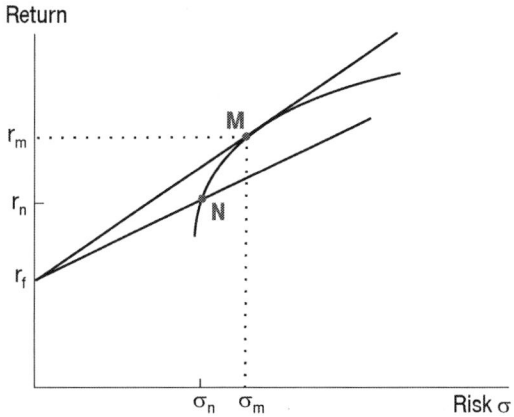

Looking at just two alternatives, N and M, on the efficient frontier, which would an investor choose? Regardless of the investor's attitude to risk, and therefore regardless of indifference curves, portfolios constructed from a combination of r_f and M provide a higher return for the same level of risk as those constructed from a combination of r_f and N and therefore must represent the optimal set of opportunities. The line through M gives the greatest return at any level of risk. Hence all diversified investors would choose to invest somewhere along this line, known as the Capital Market Line.

The exact proportions in which any one investor would choose to invest could be determined by reference to his indifference curves. However, all would choose some combination of r_f and M.

Security returns are normally expressed in nominal terms and so the risk-free rate should be expressed in the same way. The appropriate specification for the risk-free rate is one that matches the holding period of the risky assets.

(d)   The efficient frontier is constructed as shown in (b) above. It lies at the edge of the opportunity set of portfolios that can be constructed from available risky securities. The frontier comprises those portfolios on the edge of the opportunity set, for which risk is minimised for a particular level of return.

(e)   The portfolios on the efficient frontier are fully diversified. Diversifiable risk has been removed. As a result, the risk and return obtained will be similar to that of the market. This suggests that the major focus of the efficient frontier as well as the securities market line is beta. An investor should not be prepared to pay active fees for beta performance. Only passive (index) fees should be paid. A separate fee may need to be paid to obtain advice about the appropriate long-term strategic asset allocation that is on (or close to) the efficient frontier. Active fees only need to be paid if the investor wants to go further and attempt to generate an alpha.

Section C

3.   (a)   **Examiner's comment.** A common mistake was to try to use an asset pricing model for the calculation.

The forecast return is calculated as follows.

(Terminal price + Dividends – Start price)/Start price

For Stock A:

Expected return = (31 + 2 – 25)/25 = 32%

(b)   Beta = $cov_{b,m}$ / Market portfolio variance

So:

$cov_{b,m}$ = Beta × Market portfolio variance (ie square of standard deviation)

= $1.2 \times 0.4^2 = 0.192$

where b is stock B and m is the market.

(c)   The securities market line can be used to examine relative valuation by comparing the forecast return (FR) and required return (RR).

FR = (Terminal price + Dividends − Start price)/Start price = (10.8 + 0 − 10)/10 = 8%

RR = Risk-free rate + Beta × (Return on market − Risk-free rate) = 4 + 0.5 (12 − 4) = 8%

Since FR = RR, stock C is correctly priced.

4.   (a)   The idea of a premium for illiquidity in bonds is controversial because there are often well developed secondary markets. Due to this, an investor does not have to hold a bond to maturity. However, corporate bonds are often not as liquid as government bonds. As a result of this potential inability to readily realise a corporate bond at quoted prices, a premium may exist.

Corporate bonds are also subject to greater credit risk than government bonds. Credit risk is the risk of a de-rating or uprating in the credit worthiness of an issuer to reflect the probability of default. Since credit risk cannot be eliminated by diversification, an investor is expected to require a risk premium.

(b)   Both the probability that the firm cannot repay par value to its various claimants as well as market capitalisation should be related to expectations for corporate earnings, cash flow and profitability.

Most of the time, the market value of a firm is a long way from the par value of its liabilities. When the market value is a long way above par value equity, risk and credit risk may have a low correlation. When the cushion of market capitalisation shrinks close to the par value of liabilities, equity risk and credit risk naturally have more in common. Correlation may then increase.

For example, if investors forecast difficult and risky times ahead for the firm, so the prospect that the firm's ability to repay creditors in full is more doubtful and this can be expected to lead to a closer relationship between equity risk and credit risk. Some firms with consistently lower valuations than others also have closer correlation between their equity and credit risk.

(c)   An investor who has sought diversification by holding both bonds and equities is likely to sell bond B. Holding bond B has significantly greater exposure to equity-like risk which the investor is trying to diversify through investing in bonds. All other risk factors are highly similar.

5.   (a)   Preferred stock can be valued by dividing the annual dividend by the required rate of return. The shares need to yield 7%. With the preference share, a perpetuity the value of the annual dividend (£1) is capitalised at the required rate of return (7%).

Present value of dividend / Required return = 1.0 / 0.07 = £14.29

(b)   The shares need to yield 10%.

The value of the annual dividend (90p) is capitalised at the required rate of return (10%).

Price = 0.9 / 0.1 = £9.00.

(c)   Preference shares pay a fixed dividend, albeit a fixed amount of an original nominal value. The dividend may be paid even if the company is making a loss. If no dividend is paid, the dividend due is accrued and the cumulative dividend is then paid before ordinary shares.

Thus, preference shares are higher ranking in dividend payments than ordinary shares.

Secondly, preference shares have less participation in increasing dividends than ordinary shares but are higher ranking in a winding-up. This means that preference shares are less volatile and more protected.

Thirdly, there is the possibility of some capital gain if the perceived credit quality of the issuer firm improves.

Part 2 – Taxation and Trusts

Section D

6.   **Examiner's comment**. 40% of the scripts scored ten marks or above out of the 20 marks available. Some skipped answering part (a) of the question, throwing away 25% of the 20 marks available. Working out the basic difference between a company and a sole trader should not have caused so much trouble.

   (a)   When starting in business, Tommy's first decision is whether to trade as a company (with the individual as a director taxable on earnings) or as an unincorporated business, either as a sole trader or a partnership.

   A sole trader or a partner is liable for business debts to the full extent of his personal assets. A limited company's shareholder's liability is limited to any amount unpaid on his shares.

   A company might obtain equity finance through venture capital institutions and can borrow by giving a floating charge over its assets as security whereas a sole trader or partnership cannot do this.

   A business may be seen as more reputable or creditworthy if conducted through the medium of a company, but there are compliance costs (eg annual returns and audit).

   The effects of marginal tax rates and national insurance are also relevant.

   In choosing a business medium, Tommy should also bear in mind that a sole trader will be denied enhanced state benefits that are available to an employee who pays Class 1 national insurance contributions. Self-employed persons do not build an entitlement to the State Second Pension.

   The restrictions on deducting expenses against earnings may make self-employment rather more attractive than employment as a company director.

   Generally, a business held by a company will bear tax earlier than a business held by a sole trader or partnership.

   (b)   A trader's profits whether retained or withdrawn are taxed at a marginal rate of 40% on taxable income of £31,865 to £150,000 and at a marginal rate of 45% on taxable income over £150,000 (2014/15). Class 2 and Class 4 national insurance contributions are also payable.

   A controlling director/shareholder can decide whether profits are to be paid out as remuneration or dividends, or retained in the company.

   Where remuneration is paid, the total national insurance liability is greater for a company than for the proprietor of an unincorporated business.

   Companies have no equivalent of the opening year rules that apply for income tax purposes. For a sole trader or partnership, profits earned when basis periods overlap are taxed twice. Relief is available for such overlap profits but that may not take place for many years.

   Losses in the first four years of an unincorporated business can be used to obtain tax repayments (using early trade losses relief). With corporation tax, a company's losses are not available to reduce shareholders' taxable income.

   The business may need to register for Value Added Tax purposes, depending on its level of turnover.

Tommy should consider what could happen if things go wrong with his business. In running down an unincorporated business, the proprietor may be able to cover any balancing charges with loss relief. Taking a business out of a company (disincorporation), or winding up a corporate trade altogether is more complex and involves both tax and legal issues.

(c)   Inheritance tax (IHT) is only a consideration where Tommy's business or company is to be passed on to the next generation. An outright sale of the business to a third party does not constitute a transfer of value for IHT purposes.

When a taxpayer wants to pass on a business, a major question exists as to whether to gift the assets now or wait until death.

If the assets are given during lifetime, there may never be an IHT liability, either because the PET does not become chargeable or because the gift is covered by business property relief provided the transferee still owns it (or other relevant business property) at the time of the transferor's death.

A lifetime gift will be subject to capital gains tax (CGT) at some point, either on transfer or on sale of the assets by the transferee assuming a gift relief claim is made. However, a transfer of assets on death receives a free uplift in the CGT base cost to current market value and any business property is passed on with the benefit of 100% BPR.   If the business is hit by recession, the gain may be fairly low in any case.

Some other tax pitfalls exist which can be avoided provided they are identified and acted upon. The main areas to consider include the following.

(i)   Holding assets, such as business premises, outside the company or partnership restricts BPR to a rate of only 50%. This reduces to nil if the shares or partnership interest are disposed of before the business premises.

(ii)   Where a lifetime gift is made, it is important that the property remains 'business property' for the next seven years and that the transferee retains ownership of it (or owns alternative business property) to prevent a charge to IHT on a sudden death.

(iii)   If there are buy and sell arrangements included in the Articles of Association or partnership or shareholder agreements, BPR may be denied.

(iv)   It will be important to ensure that a gift does not fall foul of reservation of benefit rules.

(d)   One difference between companies and individuals is that companies do not benefit from an exemption from tax on the first £11,000 of total gains (2014/15).

Chargeable gains for an individual are taxed at a rate of 18% to the extent they fall within the utilised basic rate band. The remaining gain will be taxed at 28%. By contrast, companies' gains are charged at normal corporation tax rates (for FY 2014: 21% main rate, 20% small companies' rate).

The principal disadvantage of incorporation is the double charge to tax arising when a company sells a chargeable asset. Firstly, the company may pay corporation tax on the chargeable gain. Secondly, the shareholders may be taxed when they attempt to realise those proceeds, either in the form of dividends or, when the shares are sold, incurring a further charge on capital gains.

If there are no tax advantages in the company owning an asset, the asset should be held outside the company, perhaps being leased to the company. The lessor may receive rent without restricting IHT business asset relief. However, rent received will restrict entrepreneurs' relief for CGT.

Section E

7. **Examiner's comment**. The question was generally well answered with over half the candidates scoring three or more marks out of the five available.

    (a)   The main purpose of the Trustee Act 2000 was to widen the investment powers and powers of delegation for trusts that do not specifically have wide investment powers. Trustees and their advisers must follow the Act unless the trust deed overrules the Act.

    (b)   **Major changes**

      ▪   Wider investment powers
      ▪   The power to delegate
      ▪   A statutory duty of skill and care applying to trustees
      ▪   Trustee remuneration permitted when acting in a professional capacity
      ▪   Authority for trustees to insure trust property

    (c)   **Special duties of trustees**

      ▪   To be aware of the need for diversification and suitability of trust investments
      ▪   To obtain and consider 'proper advice' when making or reviewing investments
      ▪   To keep investments under review

    (d)   The Act allows trustees to delegate to agents any of their functions, including their powers of investment, meaning that trustees can employ discretionary fund managers and delegate many other decision-making functions. There are exceptions to the power of delegation in respect of the distribution of trust assets, appointment of trustees and whether fees should be allocated out of income or capital.

      The Act gives to trustees the power to insure in full any property that is subject to the trust against risk of loss or damage due to any event as if the property were their own. The premiums may be paid out of income or capital funds of the trust.

    (e)   The Act imposes a statutory duty of skill and care, which applies when trustees carry out certain functions such as exercising their powers of investment, employing agents, using nominees and custodians and insuring trust properties. This is a subjective test that takes into account the knowledge, experience and professional status of the trustee, with higher standards generally being expected of investment professionals than of lay persons.

8. **Examiner's comment**. Around half the candidates attempted this question. Most struggled to score the five marks available, with less than half scoring three or more marks.

	£
Lifetime tax payable	
On first £325,000 (assuming nil rate band applicable on 30 March 2008 is the same as current nil rate band)	–
On next £175,000 at 20%	35,000
Additional tax payable on death	
On first £325,000	–
On next £175,000 at 40%	70,000
	70,000
Less: Taper relief (5–6 years: 60% × £70,000)	(42,000)
	28,000
Less: Lifetime tax already paid	(35,000)
Additional tax due	Nil

No tax is payable nor repayable.

9. **Examiner's comment**. Almost all candidates managed to score three or more marks. Answers were sometimes very brief, perhaps too brief to give a proper explanation of each term which carried one mark each.

(a) With holdover relief (gift relief), if an individual gives away a qualifying asset, the transferor and the transferee can jointly elect, or where a trust is the transferee, the transferor alone can elect, by the 31 January which is nearly six years after the end of the tax year of the transfer, that the transferor's gain be reduced, potentially to nil. The transferee is deemed to acquire the asset for market value at the date of transfer less the transferor's deferred gain.

(b) A gain on sale of an individual's or married couple's / civil partnership's main or only home is exempt from capital gains tax. A married couple / civil partnership can only have one principal private residence. Where a person has more than one residence, they can nominate which one is to be treated as their principal private residence within two years of acquiring the second house.

(c) Gifts of qualifying assets or parts of assets are exempt from CGT. Qualifying assets comprise business assets and transfers subject to an immediate inheritance tax charge. Gift relief (holdover relief) is available on both outright gifts and sales at an under-value of business assets. If a disposal involves actual consideration rather than being an outright gift but is still not a bargain made at arm's length, the proceeds are deemed to be the market value of the asset and any excess of actual consideration over allowable cost is chargeable immediately and only the balance of the gain is deferred. The amount chargeable immediately is limited to the full gain.

(d) An individual may defer a gain arising on the disposal of any type of asset if he invests in qualifying EIS shares. The 'frozen', or deferred, gain will usually become chargeable when the shares are disposed of, subject to a further claim for the relief being made.

The amount of the gain that can be deferred is the lower of:

(i) The amount subscribed by the investor for his shares, which has not previously been matched under this relief, and

(ii) The amount specified by the investor in the claim, which can take into account the availability of losses and the annual exemption

(e) CGT taper relief has been withdrawn, and has not applied to gains made since 6 April 2008. (When it applied, taper relief could reduce the amount of the gain chargeable to CGT. The amount of relief available depended on whether the asset was classed as a business or non-business asset and also on the length of time an asset has been held after 1998.)

December 2008 Examination Answers

Part 1 – Portfolio Construction Theory

Section A

1. (a) **Examiner's comment.** A common mistake was for candidates to state that securities need to be negatively correlated. In practice this is very rarely found for liquid instruments.

    The relationship between portfolio risk and the number of portfolio constituents (lines of held stock) is typically non-linear.

    Risk falls rapidly as the number of stocks held increases above 1, with the fall-off in risk reducing as greater numbers of stocks are added. There comes a point where holding more securities brings about only marginal reductions in risk. This point comes approximately between 20 and 25 securities.

    By investing across global markets, an investor can remove the risks that are specific to individual markets, countries and industries and achieve a lower level of risk per unit of return than if investing in a single market. A globally invested portfolio is exposed only to the worldwide level of systematic risk, eg energy and climate, that influence the world in general and that cannot be further diversified away. Systematic risk is itself relative, with the level of systematic risk for a country being higher than that of the world. Diversification allows the portfolio not to be tied to the economic performance of any one country.

    Diversification can reduce or eliminate unsystematic risk, but there remains a floor to the level of risk, and this is represented by systematic risk.

    (b) **Examiner's comment.** A common mistake was for candidates to include per cent based costs such as stamp duty.

    The positive relationship implies that portfolio costs will rise as the number of securities in the portfolio increases, and this may be for the following reasons. [Only three need to be cited.]

    ■ Greater information acquisition costs, as a portfolio extends to smaller capitalisation securities, overseas, and to different themes and sectors

    ■ An element of fixed costs in trading commissions

    ■ More trade processing, corporate actions, and cash management in the back office

    ■ Greater custody costs associated with some overseas jurisdictions

    (c) The correct formula for the risk of the portfolio is (i).

    $$\sigma_{a+b} = \sqrt{p_a{}^2 \sigma_a{}^2 + p_b{}^2 \sigma_b{}^2 + 2p_a p_b Cov_{ab}}$$

    The correlation between the two securities is 0.27. In this case, there is imperfect positive correlation between the two securities, and the portfolio risk formula reflects the weighted covariance between the two assets.

    (d) **Examiner's comment.** Common mistakes included drawing a straight line between points A and B, a curve that bowed out from the Y axis rather than toward it, and a frontier that was higher and to the left of points A and B.

The efficient frontier is sketched in the following diagram.

Efficient Frontier

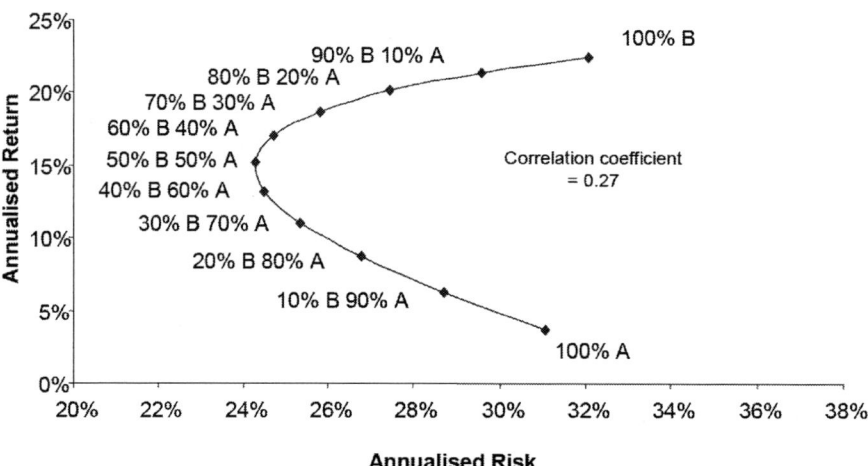

The shape of the efficient frontier can be explained as follows.

■ The correlation is relatively low at 0.27, and so significant diversification gains are expected. The frontier will not be a straight line between points A and B but will bow toward the Y-axis, as shown.

■ Diversification gains are limited however because the direction of the correlation is positive rather than negative. The frontier will not intersect the Y-axis (if drawn to intersect the X-axis at a risk level of zero), as would occur if the investments had perfect negative correlation.

■ As the frontier moves closer to 100% A or 100% B, risk dramatically increases per unit of return as diversification stops having an effect. This has the effect of making the 90/10 and 80/20 combinations more spread out.

(e) The capital market line is shown as the dotted line on the diagram below.

Efficient Frontier

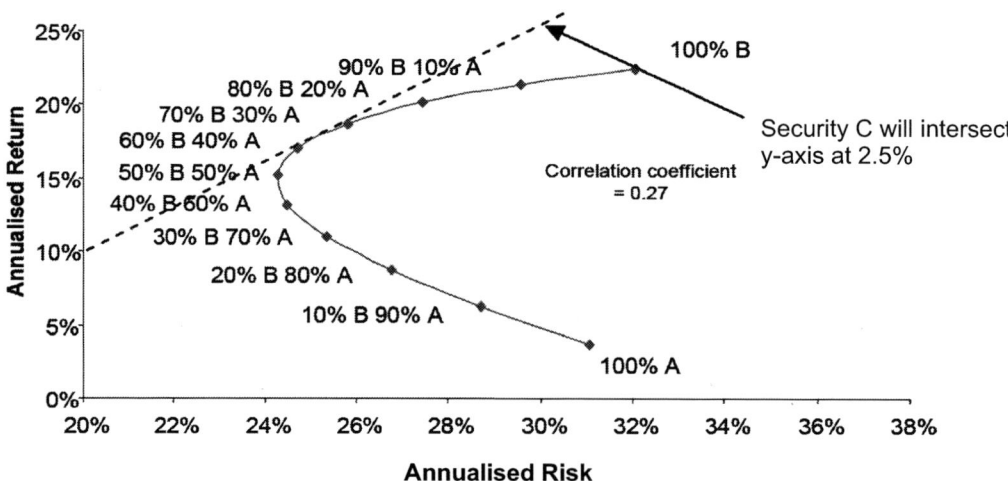

The capital market line (CML) will intersect the Y-axis (which cuts the X-axis at X = 0: not shown in the chart in the question) at 2.5% (ie at point Y = 2.5%, X = 0). The CML will also be tangential to the efficient frontier.

■ Risk-averse investors will locate on the CML closer to the Y-axis.

- More risk-tolerant investors will locate on the CML close to where it meets the efficient frontier.

- Higher risk-seeking investors will locate on the CML to the right of this area. We would not expect investors, in theory at least, to locate inside and to the right of the CML.

(f) $Cov_{ab} = \sigma_a\sigma_bCor_{ab} = 0.31 \times 0.32 \times 0.27 = 0.026784$

(g)   Reasons why the investor might select a portfolio away from the efficient frontier:

- Securities regulation and prudent person laws may limit exposures to overseas assets, foreign currency exposures and derivatives.

- According to portfolio theory, individuals or households should seek appropriate diversification of their total portfolio. Within a total portfolio approach, holdings of financial assets are only one input. An efficient total portfolio is formed by an individual or household combining all financial, physical and human capital assets, and giving consideration to expected future income and liabilities over the particular planning horizon. Physical and human capital assets are not as divisible as financial assets, and so financial assets may more easily be allocated so that total portfolio risk is minimised for a set of expected liabilities. This may require a skew to the holdings of financial assets so that, at the level of the individual investor, a financial portfolio is not of itself fully diversified.

- The investor may be overweight in domestic securities because of a home investment bias.

- An investor may prefer a particular portfolio tilt that does not reside on the efficient frontier, eg desire for income rather than growth, or he or may have faith-based or ethical-based investment requirements.

- The investor may feel safer with a portfolio based on a peer group benchmark that limits exposures in order to be in line with what like investors are doing or general market practice and advice.

- Diversification may prove to be too costly for a small investor.

- The investor may have areas of ignorance.

(h)   The regulation, which deals with disclosure, is a statutory requirement. The disclosure requirement does not remove the requirement that trustees make decisions that are in members' best financial interests. The regulation cannot be construed as a requirement on trustees to invest in a socially responsible way. The disclosure takes place within the Statement of Investment Principles. More detailed instructions are most often reflected in individual investment manager contracts. Peter needs to consider what is in members' best interests. One part of this is considering the scheme's position on responsible investment and disclosing the investment stance that is being taken.

(i)   The corporate governance arrangements of institutional shareholders in portfolio firms involves a patchwork of industry-based regulation, and a mix of political encouragement, threat and pressure, all of which are voluntary.

The role of institutional shareholders in the corporate governance process is largely concerned with the degree of influence which should be exerted over companies in order to advance their clients' financial interests, normally through engagement and the exercising of voting rights. In order to encourage this, the ISC principles (now incorporated in the UK Corporate Governance Code) request that fund managers:

- Have a policy on monitoring and intervention
- Monitor performance and establish regular dialogue with portfolio firms

- Intervene where necessary
- Evaluate the impact of engagement
- Report to clients

(j)   The voting recommendation is voluntary. There are very few barriers to voting shares held in UK-domiciled listed companies. Shares held in overseas domiciled listed companies do sometimes have a number of impediments.

Reasons for stock not being practicable to vote

- The time and costs involved in the voting of some overseas shares and potential problems due to registration difficulties, differential voting rights, rights of minority shareholders, share blocking and verification of the delivery of the votes

- Voting information being received by the fund manager too late to make an informed voting decision prior to the AGM

- Stock being on loan

- Where client consent is needed and the client is out of reach

- Where a holding is too small to be worth researching how to vote

(k)   The prototypical intermediated investment setting involves shareowner principals delegating the investment management of their financial savings to institutional fund manager agents who then act as temporary principals to corporate manager agents of portfolio firms.

(The Combined Code on Corporate Governance has now become the UK Corporate Governance Code.)

According to agency theory, imperfect monitoring, imperfect contracts and different objective functions from those of principals will lead fund managers agents, if left alone, to act in their own rather than the clients' best interest.

Compliance departments, investment management mandates, short-term contracts, alignment of fees, and regular client reporting are all mechanisms used to reduce the agency problem. In addition, the Corporate Governance Code and the ISC principles attempt to reduce potential fund manager myopia by ensuring that institutional shareholders act as owners on behalf of final investors in their interactions with corporate manager agents.

Institutional Pension scheme Investment As a Three Tier Principal Agent Relationship

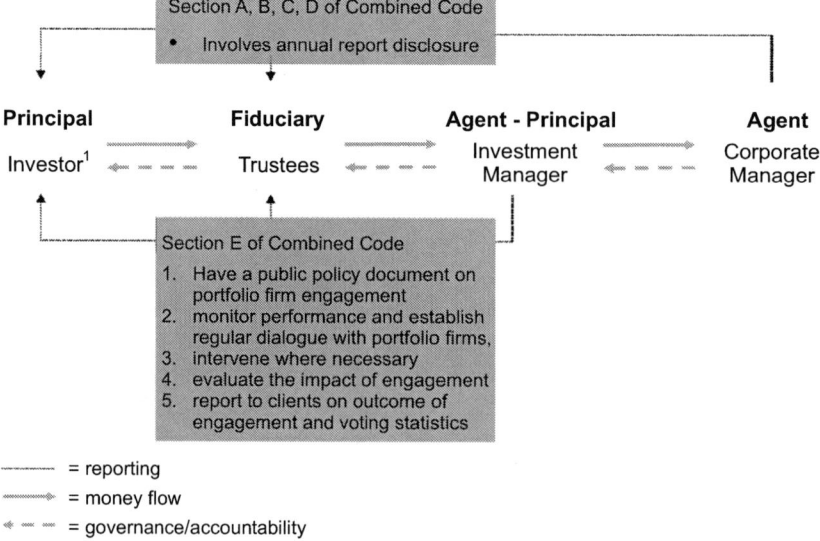

----------- = reporting

-----------▷ = money flow

◁ --- --- = governance/accountability

[1]Collective investment scheme unit holder/sherholder, life insurance policyholder, pension scheme member, charity, church, foundation

Section B

2.   The efficient markets hypothesis (EMH) broadly states that, at any time, share prices are fairly valued on the basis of all existing information. A market is said to be 'efficient' if prices reflect, in an unbiased way, all relevant information available to market participants at the time. If the efficient markets view is correct, then capital values guide scarce resources toward the right firms – an appropriate outcome in terms of welfare economics. Furthermore, if securities are priced efficiently, their prices reflect forecasts of expected benefits from future cash flows capitalised at appropriate discount rates, ie: all expected rates of return are consistent with their perceived risk.

The EMH is based on the following assumptions.

■   A large number of profit maximising participants who analyse and value securities independently of one another.

■   New information regarding securities arrives to the market randomly. New information must, by definition, be unpredictable and random otherwise it would not be new information.

■   Profit maximising investors adjust security prices rapidly to reflect the effect of new information.

■   Dealing costs are not too high, the relevant information is available to a sufficient number of investors, and no individual participants are of sufficient wealth that they can in any sense dominate the market.

If securities are priced efficiently, their prices reflect forecasts of expected benefits from future cash flows capitalised at appropriate discount rates. Of course, individuals can disagree, and it is this disagreement which results in transactions. The aggregation and resolution of expectations in the transaction process produces an unbiased valuation in an efficient market.

Broadly speaking, the evidence suggests that efficient markets can be divided into three forms that are classified according to the degree to which information may be reflected in share prices and the availability of that information. When originally postulated, the three forms of the strong version were named the weak, semi-strong, and strong forms, but these were subsequently reclassified by Fama's 'weaker' version of the EMH in the 1990s into returns predictability, events study, and private information, the names coming from the tests used to assess the efficiency level.

The weak form of the EMH states that all information that can be discovered from past price movements has already been incorporated into the current share price. This implies that it should not be possible to predict future price movements from past price movements, or to produce superior returns on the basis of past information, since any such information available from past prices has already been taken account of in the current price.

The concept of returns predictability asks: can an investment pattern of returns be predicted from historical patterns? If the answer to this question is 'No', then the market has at least this level of efficiency.

The semi-strong form of the EMH states that current share prices not only reflect the information referred to in the weak form, but also incorporate any information that has been published about a company (all publicly available information). For example, release of preliminary figures by the company constitutes new information and the share price will move to reflect this.

The semi-strong form allows for directors and other insiders of the business to have a superior level of knowledge and hence, to have an advantage when dealing in shares. When insiders deal (illegally) on the basis of their knowledge of price sensitive information, their very actions may cause the price to move.

With the semi-strong form of the EMH, it can be appropriate for directors to make decisions about share issues and repurchases, for example, on the basis that they have superior information.

Events studies observations in major markets have shown that prices do respond to the release of new information and, traditionally, many people have suggested that share markets tend to exhibit this level of efficiency. The evidence appears to support this level of market efficiency in most major markets.

The strong form of the EMH is based on the premise that share prices fully reflect all information, whether publicly or privately. It would be impossible for even the most corrupt investor to find out anything which the share price did not already reflect.

All forms of active investment management based on fundamental analysis can be associated with weak form market efficiency.

Active growth investing [(a)(i)] seeks to identify firms that are more likely to grow cash flows and profits in the future. The growth investor can exploit even information in the public domain, under conditions of weak form or semi-strong form efficiency, for example if a stock is poorly researched by the market.

Value based investing seeking out informational efficiencies [(a)(ii)] seeks to identify underpricing of stocks as a result of information being inadequately processed by other investors. This is consistent with investment success in weak form-efficient markets.

A value-based investment style based on corporate inefficiency [(a)(iii)] is compatible with a strong-form efficient market, as well as weaker informational efficiency. The EMH is concerned the information reflected in share prices rather than with underlying corporate inefficiencies. For example, a value investor may identify that a company's cost base is higher than its competitors and that this has depressed its share price. The investor may buy into the stock, anticipating that at some point, management will change or the existing management will address the problem and reduce the costs.

Small capitalisation securities [(a)(iv)] are often not closely followed by market participants, and are less well covered in the media. This can make them particularly susceptible to an actively managed investment approach. This approach may be successful with weak or semi-strong form informational efficiency.

An actively managed portfolio of large capitalisation securities [(a)(v)] is not best suited within semi-strong or strong form efficient markets, and will be associated with weak form efficiency. Large cap stocks are more closely followed by market participants and, as a result, there are fewer pricing anomalies for active management to exploit. Since it is more difficult to outperform on large cap indices, one would expect to observe significant passive management of large cap portfolios, as indeed occurs.

Passive or index-based management [(b)] is appropriate for strong-form efficient markets. If markets have strong-form efficiency, an active fund manager cannot make better than average returns except by luck. Passive management can achieve results that are as good, at less cost.

In reality, different forms of the EMH may hold at the same time in different markets. Due to this, different investment styles may be used contemporaneously but applied to different security subsets – as evidenced in the core-satellite approach to investment, which may involve an indexed core fund together with an actively managed peripheral fund.

Section C

3   (a)   Based on the investor's assumptions, the Yen will appreciate by 3% because the inflation differential favours the Japanese Yen and the real rate is assumed to be constant. In order to maintain the same real exchange rate, UK pound sterling will depreciate by the inflation differential. In reality, a different outcome is likely.

(b)   The local currency Yen return on the Japanese bond is the 2% interest rate.

(c)   The UK pound sterling return on the Japanese bond is equal to the Yen interest rate plus the currency appreciation. This equals 2% Japanese interest rate + 3% Yen appreciation. Hence, the UK pound sterling return is 5%, assuming that the Yen appreciates as the investor predicts.

4.   (a)

Asset Allocation for Sheila Timsbury-Higgins			
Years to retirement	Equities	Bonds	Cash
10	100%	0%	0%
8	80%	15%	5%
6	60%	30%	10%
4	40%	45%	15%
2	20%	60%	20%
0	0%	75%	25%

(b)   The approach known as 'lifestyling' is based on investing in relatively high risk areas only while the individual is young, and the remaining period before benefits are drawn is long. As retirement approaches, the fund is gradually moved across to more secure areas to consolidate those gains.

In the case of this client, we propose a progressive reduction in equities to 0% at retirement, with progressive increases in bonds and cash holdings, resulting in 75% weighting for bonds and 25% for cash at retirement.

The lifestyle approach recognises people's wish on approaching retirement to consolidate gains already made from investment through their working life, and reduce the risk of those gains being eroded by last minute, possibly short term, downward movements in value.

UK pension legislation requires that an individual uses the value accumulated in a defined contribution pension plan to purchase a life annuity by 75 years of age, with the option to take up to 25% of the value of the fund in cash at retirement. Since the 25% cash lump sum is tax-free, it is widely expected that individuals will take it. The remaining 75% of the pension value is then used to purchase an annuity. This legislation explains why most lifestyle funds start to switch from growth assets, such as equities, close to retirement, to a final pre-retirement allocation of 75% bonds and 25% cash. The cash can protect the portion of the fund likely to be taken as a lump sum, while the bonds hedge the interest rate risk in the annuity price: if long-term interest rates fall before the client's retirement, annuity prices will rise, but there will have been a corresponding increase in bond prices.

5.   (a)   Beta = Covariance / Variance = $0.25 / 0.3^2$ = 2.78

(b)   Systematic and unsystematic risks are combined by adding variances and then taking the square root to obtain the standard deviation.

$$\sigma_i^2 = \sigma_s^2 + \sigma_u^2$$

Systematic risk

Standard deviation = σ_s = 0.19

Variance = σ_s^2 = 0.19^2 = 0.0361

Unsystematic risk

Standard deviation = σ_u = 0.06

Variance = σ_u^2 = 0.06^2 = 0.0036

$$\sigma_i^2 = \sigma_s^2 + \sigma_u^2 = 0.0361 + 0.0036 = 0.0397$$

Standard deviation (total risk, expressed in standard deviation terms) $= \sigma_i = \sqrt{0.0397} = 0.1992 = 19.92\%$

(c) Standard deviation is a good measure of dispersion, or variability, where data are normally distributed about the mean.

As noted in the question, the sample return distributions of securities and market indices often exhibit leptokurtosis – there is both a greater concentration of observations around the mean than a normal distribution and a greater concentration of observations in the extremes of the distribution. Put differently, relative to a normal distribution, securities and market indices tend to have a great many ordinary event days. Periodically these are punctuated by a greater number of extreme event days than would be expected.

The distribution of security and market index returns tends also to be negatively skewed. Put differently, the extreme event days tend to be negative. The normal distribution under-estimates the probability of both of these occurrences and therefore mis-estimates the risk to which investors are actually exposed.

Part 2 – Taxation and Trusts

Section D

6. (a) The maximum double taxation relief will be the tax deducted in the foreign country, up to the amount of the UK tax payable.

Gerry: Income tax computation for 2014/15

Taxable income	Non-savings income
	£
UK earnings	50,000
Overseas earnings – gross (£10,000 + £2,200)	12,200
Net income	62,200
Less personal allowance	(10,000)
Taxable income	52,200

Tax		£
Non-savings income		
£31,865 × 20%		6,373
£20,335 × 40%		8,134
		14,507
Less double taxation relief		
Germany income (lesser of £5,000 and UK tax £4,000)	4,000	
Austria income (lesser of £200 and UK tax £880)	200	
		(4,200)
UK tax liability		10,307

(b) Self-assessment is a system intended to reduce the costs of administering the tax system and to rationalise payment dates.

You have the choice of either filling in the details on the tax return and leaving HMRC to calculate any tax due, or calculating the tax himself. The return must be submitted by 30 September after the end of the fiscal year, if you intend HMRC to calculate the tax due. Alternatively, if you calculate your own tax liability, you can submit the form by 31 January. For those taxpayers submitting a return by 31 October, further tax due is collected through PAYE. For others, any payment is due by 31 January.

Late submission of returns incurs an automatic £100 penalty, which may be increased by £60 for each day late.

Payments on account apply usually to the self-employed, such as you, and those who pay less than 80% of last year's income tax at source.

The basic principle is that you will need to make two equal payments on account of your tax liability for the year on 31 January in the fiscal year and 31 July in the following year. The payments on account will be based on your total income tax liability of the previous year. In addition, there will be a final 'sweep-up' payment on 31 January of the following year, based on the self-assessment total. This final payment will consist of all tax due from you, including income tax, capital gains tax.

There is an onus on you to keep sufficient records to prepare your tax return, if required to do so or requested by HMRC to do so. These must be kept for at least 22 months after the end of the relevant fiscal year.

POA dates for the fiscal year 2014/15 are summarised as follows.

- ▧ 31 January 2015: First payment on account, based on 2013/14 tax liability
- ▧ 31 July 2015: Second payment on account, based on 2013/14 tax liability
- ▧ 31 October 2015: Submission of tax return, if requiring HMRC calculation
- ▧ 31 January 2016: Submission of tax return, if the taxpayer is providing tax calculation

(c) **Exempt lifetime transfers.** Any gifts made by an individual during their lifetime to another individual (such as from you to either of your sisters) or certain trusts (but not discretionary trusts) will usually be exempt from IHT, unless they are made in the last seven years of the individual's life, when they will be chargeable for inheritance tax. A lifetime gift is therefore potentially exempt from IHT at the date of the gift. If the donor survives seven years thereafter, it becomes exempt. This rule prevents tax avoidance by giving away all one's property immediately prior to death.

The first £325,000 of gifts in the seven-year period will not be chargeable for inheritance tax, since they will fall within the exempt band, at 2014/15 rates. This means, however, that the estate at death would be fully chargeable, since lifetime transfers would have already used up the exempt band.

Any IHT due as a result of such a gift will usually be payable by the recipient of the gift. The amount of tax due will vary depending on how long the donor survived after making the gift. If the donor died within three years of making the gift then IHT will be due at the full 40% rate. If the donor died within three to seven years of the gift being made, then the rate of IHT falls. The inheritance tax rate payable is reduced by a percentage, depending on how long before death the transfer was made, as follows.

Exempt lifetime transfers. In your case, you may wish to consider how gifts made to either of your sisters falls under the IHT rules.

Gifts made during the donor's lifetime (but not on death) not exceeding £250 per recipient per fiscal year are exempt from IHT. Any number of donees will qualify for this exemption in any one fiscal year (for example, ten gifts of £200 each in the fiscal year would all qualify for this exemption if made to different individuals). However, if gifts made to one individual in the fiscal year exceed £250, none of the gifts to that individual will qualify for this exemption.

Other examples of exempt transfers include certain gifts made during an individual's lifetime in consideration of marriage.

Over and above all the other exemptions, any gifts made by an individual during their lifetime (but not on death) are exempt from IHT up to £3,000 per fiscal year. The annual exemption is available for carry forward for one year.

(d) Inheritance tax exemptions and reliefs.

- ▧ Nil rate band: £325,000, on death

- ▧ Potentially Exempt Transfers

- ▧ Excluded property (eg, property outside the UK)

- ▧ Reversionary interest in settled UK property, unless the interest was acquired for money or money's worth

- ▧ Gifts to spouses or civil partners (which may be relevant for the future)

- Gifts to recognised charities, certain political parties and important national institutions, and for the public benefit

- Small gifts (£250 per recipient per fiscal year)

- Normal expenditure out of income

- In addition, annual gifts exemption of up to £3,000 per fiscal year

- Business property relief, agricultural property relief and woodlands relief

(e) The following IHT planning points should be borne in mind.

(i) You should make a will. If you die intestate, your estate will be distributed according to set rules laid down in law, in the Administration of Estates Act.

(ii) The IHT exemption of £325,000 (2014/15) is available on your death.

(iii) If you wish to give away assets in your lifetime, they will not be chargeable to IHT if you survive for seven years, and there are reductions for gifts made at least three years before death. However, it is not permitted to make 'gifts' to other individuals while still retaining a beneficial interest in the assets given away: this is called a 'gift with reservation'.

(iv) You may wish to consider the use of a trust to hold the farm or other assets. However, the capital value of the assets is brought into the value of your estate if you hold a life interest in the income from the trust.

(v) Agricultural property relief should be borne in mind, for the future. This can provide 100% IHT relief, where the donor has vacant possession. To be eligible as a donor, you must normally have occupied the property for the previous two years and have owned it for at least seven years.

(vi) If you give 10% or more of your net estate to charity, the IHT rate is reduced to 36%.

Section E

7. **James: Income tax computation 2014/15**

	Non-savings income £	Savings income £	Dividend income £	Total £
Income from employment	20,000			
Interest income		7,000		
UK dividends			33,000	
Total income	20,000	7,000	33,000	
Less personal allowance	(10,000)			
Taxable income	10,000	7,000	33,000	50,000

	£	£
Income tax on non savings income		
£10,000 × 20%		2,000
Tax on savings income		
£7,000 × 20%		1,400
Tax on dividend income		
£14,865 × 10%		1,486
£18,135 × 32.5%		5,894
Tax liability		10,780

8. **Share pool**

	No. of shares	Cost £
November 1990 acquisition	2,500	25,000
April 1992 rights issue (1 for 5)	500	4,000
	3,000	29,000
May 2013 sale	(2,000)	(19,333)
c/f	1,000	9,667

	£
Proceeds	30,000
Less cost	(19,333)
Gain	10,677

9. **Residence and domicile**

From 6 April 2013, a new statutory residence test was established, and the concept of 'ordinary' residence was abolished for tax purposes.

If an individual satisfies any of the following automatic overseas tests, then he is non-resident.

Automatic overseas tests

(a)   Was resident in the UK for one or more of the three previous tax years and spends fewer than 16 days in the UK in the current tax year

(b)   Was not resident in the UK for any of the previous three tax years and spends fewer than 46 days in the UK in the current tax year

(c)   Leaves the UK to carry out full-time work overseas

(d)   Dies in the current tax year, subject to conditions which include spending fewer than 46 days in the UK

If the individual does not satisfy any of the automatic overseas tests, the individual will be automatically UK-resident if he meets any of the following automatic UK tests.

Automatic UK tests

(a)   He spends 183 days or more (ie more than six months) in the UK during the tax year

(b)   There is a period of more than 90 days, part of which falls within the tax year, when he has a home in the UK and no home overseas (disregarding any home at which he is present for fewer than 30 days in the tax year)

(c)   He dies in the current year, subject to conditions which include having been UK-resident in the previous three tax years

(d)   He meets a full-time UK work test, as set out in the taxation rules

If the individual meets none of the automatic overseas tests and none of the automatic UK tests, he must look at the 'sufficient ties' test, which compares the number of days spent in the UK against the number of 'connection factors' that apply, such as whether he has a UK-resident family, or accommodation in the UK.

A person is **domiciled** in the country in which he has his permanent home. A person may be resident in more than one country, but he can be domiciled in only one country at a time.

Where he was born determines the individual's domicile of origin. A person retains this domicile until he acquires a different domicile of dependency (if, while he is under 16, his father's domicile changes) or domicile of choice if he permanently settles in another country.

A resident and domiciled individual is taxed on his general earnings on a receipts basis.

A non-resident is taxed on his general earnings in respect of UK duties on the receipts basis but there is no UK income tax on foreign earnings (those in respect of non-UK duties).

A UK resident who is not UK domiciled may claim the remittance basis for a particular tax year, so that he is only liable to UK income tax on overseas income to the extent that it is brought (remitted) to the UK. Such an individual is liable to the remittance basis charge if he claims the remittance basis for a tax year, subject to the following residence rule.

- If the individual has been UK-resident for at least seven of the nine tax years preceding that tax year, the remittance basis charge payable is £30,000 annually.

- If the individual has been UK-resident for at least 12 of the 14 tax years preceding that tax year, the remittance basis charge payable is £50,000 annually.

Resident 'non-doms' who have been resident in the UK for less than seven years can still elect for the remittance basis of tax, but there is no annual charge.

June 2008 Examination Answers

Part 1 – Portfolio Construction Theory

Section A

1. **Examiner's comment**. The ten parts to Question 1 were generally either answered very well or very poorly.

    (a) The calculation of the 36-month portfolio return was well performed by virtually all candidates, and the vast majority scored full marks for part (a).

    Correct answers were set out along the following lines.

Weight	Return	Product of weight × Return
0.7	15.30%	10.71%
0.2	21.20%	4.24%
0.1	11.10%	1.11%
		Total = 16.06%

    (b) **Examiner's comment**. Candidates showed very weak understanding of the calculation required to compute an annualised standard deviation. 27 out of 28 students obtained 0 marks on this question. The question was in fact very straightforward. The monthly standard deviation of returns was provided in the question. Candidates were simply asked to calculate the annualised figure from the monthly figure given. The most straightforward way to compute an annualised standard deviation is to multiply by the square root of the return periodicity, eg weekly, monthly, quarterly. In this instance the return observations were monthly, requiring students to multiply by the square root of 12, or 3.46.

	Monthly standard deviation of returns	Multiplied by square root (12)
Active portfolio	3.90%	13.51%
Passive portfolio	3.65%	12.64%
Benchmark	3.60%	12.47%

    An alternative derivation is to square the standard deviation to obtain the variance, multiply the variance by the number of observations in an annual period – in this case 12 – and then square root the annualised variance to obtain the annualised standard deviation.

    (c) **Examiner's comment**. A large majority of candidates showed that they did not understand how to calculate an annualised return from a 36 month compound return. The 36-month return performance was provided in the question. Candidates were required to calculate the annualised return from the 36-monthly figure given. Many students obtained 0 marks and two students had the formula right but the answer wrong and received a mark. 9 out of 28 students who answered correctly obtained full marks. The question requires that the 36 month return be decompounded.

    The standard formula for an annualised holding period return is:

    $(1 + \text{holding period return})^{(1/N)} - 1$

    where N = number of years

In this question, N = 3

Answers could be set out along the following lines.

	36 month return performance	$(1 + \text{return})^{(1/3)} - 1$
Active portfolio	16.06%	5.09%
Passive portfolio	17.10%	5.40%
Benchmark	17.40%	5.49%

(d) **Examiner's comment**. The question was very well answered by all candidates, with a mean mark of 3.5 out of 4. Candidates obtaining good marks described growth investing, why and when it is used, and measures employed to identify growth stocks.

Growth investing and thematic investing often coincide. Thematic investing can be likened to a derivative of growth investing in that it often involves companies poised to benefit and grow from changes in a set of underlying conditions, be they economic, regulatory, legal and/or business.

(e) **Examiner's comment**. The question was also answered very well, with a mean mark of 3.2 out of 4. For the first part of the question good answers described value investing, why and when it is used, and measures employed to identify value stocks. For the second part of the question, good answers emphasised that value investing based on informational inefficiency at root involves some kind of informational advantage.

In order that an individual investor can know more than the market (absent inside information) this normally requires the market to be informationally inefficient. Value investing based on economic inefficiency is a different prospect altogether for it is entirely consistent with an informationally efficient market. This strategy involves buying shares in firms that are operationally inefficient, whose prices may very well be efficient, and engaging to remove these inefficiencies by bringing about changes in corporate governance, policy and strategy that improve fundamental economic performance and reduce agency problems.

(f) **Examiner's comment**. Answers were of a very variable standard. Candidates scoring full marks mentioned a good number of the following points.

■ An unconstrained optimisation will usually take no account of transaction costs, liquidity, investability, availability of financial instruments, tax, government restrictions, market value and currency risk.

■ An unconstrained optimisation may calculate using past performance data whereas the portfolio allocation may be based on expected performance data.

■ The portfolio will usually take account of client mandate restrictions such as security and market limits, lower expected macroeconomic risk of developed markets, lower currency risk and a peer group home bias that may be difficult to ignore.

(g) **Examiner's comment**. A large majority of candidates showed that they did not understand how to calculate the proportion of an active portfolio's company specific risk. Candidates needed to first of all figure out that the question concerns a diversified investment setting. This is readily discernible from the question which concerns an EAFE benchmark. In a diversified setting, the benchmark has a beta of 1, ie all risk is market risk. Second, candidates needed to figure out how to use a correlation coefficient.

The question provided the correlation coefficient for the monthly returns of the active portfolio and the monthly returns for the benchmark.

The square of the correlation, R^2, represents the proportion linked to market risk.

For the active fund, $R^2 = 0.82^2 = 67.24\%$

Hence, the stock-specific risk can be calculated as: $1 - 0.6724 = 32.76\%$

(h) **Examiner's comment**. The question was generally very well answered by candidates, with the mean, median and modal mark of 5.4, 6.0 and 7.0 respectively. The question required candidates to describe three indexation techniques.

A number of indexation techniques could be drawn on to answer this question, including; full replication (duplication), stratified sampling, factor matching, co-mingling and a cash portfolio that is 'equitised' using derivatives. Candidates did draw on these, and needed only to provide an adequate description of each for full marks.

(i) **Examiner's comment**. Almost all candidates demonstrated a basic understanding of the concept of tracking error. But only very few candidates were able to demonstrate the critical reasoning needed to propose why a large pension scheme might become concerned as tracking error on a passive index fund moves away from zero.

Good answers brought in topics relevant to pension schemes. One answer is that the pension scheme, if a defined benefit type, may have set the investment benchmarks so as to meet expected liabilities and pension payments as they come due. A non-zero tracking error suggests under-performance relative to the benchmark and introduces shortfall and payment risk. A second answer is that many pension schemes employ a core-satellite approach.

Passive portfolio management is often employed as a 'core', with the aim of doing no more than delivering the market beta, with active portfolio management employed as a 'satellite' to deliver alpha. A non-zero tracking error may imply that the passive portfolio is not efficiently delivering the market beta, and by definition delivering some other type of risk, and therefore not doing its job. This may not fit well with portfolios run by other managers hired by the pension scheme and introduce unanticipated and costly scheme wide risks.

(j) **Examiner's comment**. The question was generally well answered, but a number of candidates chose to omit the question. Tracking error has a number of explanations. Good answers noted that the benchmark has no costs and (if total return) assumes immediate and full reinvestment of income.

Good answers also listed a number of reasons for tracking error, including some of the following.

- Local market prices, currency conversions and rates not being the same for the portfolio and benchmark

- Dividends paid net of tax for the portfolio and gross of tax for the index

- Reinvestment of dividends is on pay date for portfolio but on ex-dividend date for index

- Cash flows may be too small to invest

- Some cash always held by portfolio but index always has zero cash

- Lot sizes

- Index rebalancing, constituent changes and index calculation rules

- Survivorship bias of index

- Transaction costs, including stamp duty, bid-offer spread, broker commission, trade clearing, settlement and custody costs, fund accounting, depositary

- Type of index replication strategy of the portfolio

Section B

2.   **Examiner's comment**. This question was generally not well answered, with a maximum mark of 19 out of 20, a minimum of 2 and a mean and median mark of 10. One key reason for a low mark was a poorly structured answer. Most candidates were aware of the various alternative asset classes, but, on the whole, could provide little beyond a long general description of each asset class, when what was required was a demonstration that candidates could appraise the investment effect of including alternative asset classes within a conventionally invested portfolio. A number of candidates incorrectly equated risk with diversification.

   (a)   **Expected return:** alternative asset classes are expected to be more risky than conventional asset classes due to a mix of underlying characteristics, fewer pricing points, lower liquidity, uncertain distributions and indivisibility. Given a trade-off between risk and required return alternative asset classes should have a higher expected return. There are exceptions, for instance yields on infrastructure funds may be more certain than a near all-equity fund, but in the overall sense the premise of adding alternative asset classes is greater expected return, as argued in the 2001 Myners Review on Institutional investment.

   (b)   **Diversification:** whilst individually risky, when judged in the context of a portfolio alternative asset classes may not be risky, and this can contribute greater return per unit of risk ie alpha yielding at the portfolio level. Diversification is so powerful that an unconstrained portfolio optimisation will often allocate much greater weight to alternative asset classes than fund managers would consider practicable. Diversification will vary by type of asset. Private equity may offer far less diversification since unlisted firms are often exposed to the economic cycle in the same way as listed firms are. Commodities are variously linked to the economic cycle, and therefore their diversification potential. For hedge funds, potential diversification can be traced to the particular strategy. Infrastructure funds, depending on the underlying project, are often characterised by permanent and relatively stable income and thus provide significant diversification.

   (c)   **Risk:** different from diversification, alternative asset classes vary in their exposure to inflation risk, leverage, short selling, failure rates, capital distribution, perishability, manager selection risk, adverse selection, moral hazard and agency risk.

   (d)   **Liquidity:** alternative asset classes vary as to their liquidity, and are often less liquid than conventional asset classes. A number of students proposed that liquidity was overcome once an alternative asset vehicle was listed on an exchange. This is not entirely correct. Underlying assets may have fewer pricing points and only infrequently mark to market. An investor may then have to trade on stale or incorrectly estimated prices. Volumes can often be small, so the desire to buy and sell may significantly move prices against trading positions. Minimum notice and investing periods hinder exit following upturns and downturns in the market. Even with minimum notice periods, significant demand from investors to sell at the same time can often not be met from liquidity or more ready realisable holdings and may require forced selling of physical underlying assets at distressed prices.

   (e)   **Divisibility:** alternative asset classes can be lumpy and indivisible, and therefore lead to large lot sizes. For small and medium size investors this can prevent small exposures to the assets, and make any exposure gained a risk in terms of the overall portfolio allocation to this asset.

   (f)   **Transaction costs:** alternative asset classes encompass a number of transaction costs including, but not limited to, high legal costs for private equity transactions, high search costs for Infrastructure funds (there are few of them and those that there are may not be suitable), storage costs for commodities, front and back end fees for hedge funds and within fund costs and charges.

Section C

3.   **Examiner's comment**. There were no incorrect answers to this question but there was significant variability in the quantity and quality of answers. Overall the question was not especially well answered, with a maximum mark of 3.5 out of 5 and a mean and median of 2.5. Low marks were awarded to candidates who demonstrated only a limited knowledge of the investment planning process. Higher marks corresponded to candidates whose answer reflected a well-defined focus and a good working knowledge of the core material. A very strong answer would have included the following elements.

Establish client circumstances

- Life cycle concerns: young/old
- Married/single/children
- Wealth
- Human capital
- Financial commitments/liabilities

Establish client constraints

- Tax position
- Ethical preferences
- Need for liquidity
- Time horizon
- Regulatory/legal

Establish client return objectives

- Capital preservation
- Capital appreciation
- Income
- Total return

Establish client risk tolerance

- Conventional methods

- Note that investors require compensation for risk: asset pricing theories and the capital market line

From the above:

- Create an investment policy statement
- Set the investment strategy
- Form capital market expectations
- Create the strategic asset allocation for the benchmark.

Establish investment management

- Method of investment management
- Investment mandate and constraints

4.   **Examiner's comment**. A majority of the candidates who answered this question demonstrated a good grasp of the Capital Asset Pricing Model. Answers were generally of a very good standard, with a mean mark of 4.0 out of 5 and a median and maximum of 5 out of 5.

A small minority of candidates gave an incorrect answer. A further small minority of candidates gave the correct calculation but an incorrect analysis of the answer. This candidate cohort suggested that stock A was undervalued when in fact it was overvalued, and that stock B was overvalued when in fact it was undervalued.

Candidates in this group seemed to confuse that the investor estimates a return (ie what he or she will receive) (12% and 11% for Stock A and Stock B respectively) and that the CAPM gives the required return that an investor needs to compensate for the systematic risk taken (the CAPM calculated return) (13% and 10% for Stock A and Stock B respectively).

Answers

The required return for Stock A = 4% + 1.5 × (10% − 4%) = 13%.

Stock A is overvalued for its estimated return is 12%, ie it lies below the Security Market Line

The required return for Stock B = 4% + 1.0 × (10% − 4%) = 10%.

Stock B is undervalued for its estimated return is 11%, ie it lies above the Security Market Line

5. **Examiner's comment**. Few candidates answered this question, but those that did tended to do so very well, demonstrating excellent applied critical reasoning. The mean mark was 3.8 out of 5, median 4.0 and mode 5.

   (a) The principal risks to a holder of gilt-edged and corporate bonds were well understood, with a small minority of candidates providing excellent answers.

   Good answers will have included inflation risk, interest rate risk, reinvestment risk, investment grade risk, default risk and sector spread risk.

   (b) The principal risks to a holder of shares and bonds in the same company in which the interest rate risk of the bonds has been fully hedged was also well understood, with once again a small minority of candidates providing excellent answers.

   Good answers will have noted some similarity of risk exposures, and discussed inflation risk, cash flow risk (dividends are discretionary and capital appreciation is sensitive to cash flow), and default risk (bondholder ranks higher in company payouts).

Part 2 – Taxation and Trusts

Section D

6.   **Examiner's comment.** The question had 20 marks available evenly split among five sections covering a different aspect of the syllabus. The case study was used to illustrate a typical situation that could be faced in practice. If candidates can advise a client well under examination circumstances, then they should be able to do so in real life. Equally, if candidates find it difficult to deal with a case study in an examination, it is usually clear that they are not ready to advise clients even at an overview level.

20% of this year's candidates were unable to answer one element of the case study. 30% of candidates scored a very low mark or zero on one element of the case study. Approximately two thirds of the candidates scored very highly on this question with scores of 15 or above with more than 14% of candidates scoring the full 20 marks.

(a)   Capital gains are taxed at 18% to the extent they fall within the unutilised basic rate band and the rest is taxed at 28%.

John has 10,000 shares in Marks and Spencer plc. Gains can be set off against his £11,000 annual CGT exemption (2014/15), in the year of disposal.

Disposals are matched with acquisitions in the following sequence.

   ▪   On the same day
   ▪   In the next 30 days
   ▪   In the share pool

All of the shares are past purchases and so only the share pool is relevant. All the shares were acquired after 31 March 1982 and so all are added to the pool at cost.

The share pool is constructed as follows.

	No. of shares	Cost £
17.1.88 Acquisition	5,000	4,250
22.2.91 Acquisition	3,000	3,540
14.10.95 Acquisition	1,000	2,120
26.9.03 Acquisition	1,000	4,220
	10,000	14,130
Disposal tranche	(2,000)	(2,826)
c/f	8,000	11,304

Each tranche of 2,000 shares disposed of will have a base cost of £2,826, assuming that no further shares are purchased.

(b)   John's assets are worth around £4.2 million.

Inheritance tax (IHT) will be chargeable at 40% on the total value of John's chargeable estate on death that exceeds £325,000 (2014/15). A reduced rate of 36% will apply if 10% or more of the net estate is given to charity.

If John makes any lifetime transfers and survives seven years after giving them, the transfers will be free of IHT. However, note that John cannot give away the family home (eg to his children) and continue to live in it, and gain any tax advantage. The gift will be treated as a 'gift with reservation'.

Potentially exempt transfers that are made within seven years of death are allocated a form of taper relief after three years.

Gifts between husband and wife are always exempt from IHT, for a spouse who is domiciled in the UK.

If John has made gifts to charity, the gifts will be exempt from IHT.

There is a small gifts exemption covering £250 per recipient, and an additional annual exemption for gifts up to £3,000 per fiscal year.

(c) We are concerned here only with income tax savings.

John should be able to take a tax-free lump sum (normally 25%) from his pension fund, on taking benefits.

John could use Venture Capital Trusts to save income tax on dividends, but only if he wishes to invest in risky ventures.

If Mary is not a taxpayer or is not a higher rate taxpayer, then transferring assets and the attached income to her could reduce the overall tax liability.

John could make full use of his ISA allowance of £15,000 (2014/15 'New ISA' maximum, applying from 1 July 2014), to shelter dividends from higher or additional rate tax. ISAs are also free from capital gains tax.

(d) How can a suitable trust be established?

A discretionary trust may be set up by will. The discretionary trust allows the transferee flexibility about who is to benefit from the trust and to what extent. This can be useful if there are beneficiaries of differing ages and whose financial circumstances may differ.

Although gifts to trusts during lifetime can lead to an IHT charge (a CLT), there can be tax benefits from setting up trusts during the settlor's lifetime.

If a discretionary trust is used, the settlor can preserve the maximum flexibility in the class of beneficiaries and how income and capital should be dealt with.

If the settlor is included as a beneficiary of the trust the gift will be treated as a gift with reservation.

What are the long-term tax advantages of a trust?

The rate of inheritance tax on principal charges and exit charges within a discretionary trust set up by will depend on the settlor's cumulative transfers in the seven years before his death and the value of the trust property.

There is a chargeable lifetime transfer (CLT) when a discretionary trust is set up. The trust suffers the IHT principal charge once every ten years and the exit charge when property leaves the trust.

With regard to lifetime trusts, as long as the cumulative total of CLTs in any seven year period does not exceed the nil rate band, there will be no lifetime IHT to pay on creation of the trust. The trust will be subject to IHT at 0% on the ten year anniversary and later advances, unless the value of the trust property grows faster than the nil rate band.

(e) **Examiner's comment**. This part involved an international element and capital gains tax. A number of candidates failed to spot the possibility of Spanish tax on the sale of the Spanish cottage and the interaction between double tax relief. Other candidates spotted the double taxation problem but did not understand how the double taxation relief system operated. Generally though, candidates made a good attempt at answering this question and the majority of candidates achieved the top mark.

Gains on sale of the Spanish cottage will be liable to capital gains tax at the appropriate rate. If the cottage was bought before 31 March 1982, the base cost will be the 31 March 1982 value. Otherwise, the gain will be the proceeds less the actual cost.

Where an asset is bought and/or sold in overseas currency, it must be translated into sterling using the rate applicable at the time of purchase or sale. The gain or loss is always calculated based on sterling figures.

Double taxation relief (DTR) is available to offset any double taxation suffered on assets disposed of abroad.

Section E

7. **Examiner's comment**. This question involved the calculation of a UK person's tax liability with an international element which involved double tax relief. Most candidates spotted the problem and managed to calculate Mr T's tax liability correctly. Those that laid the answer out nicely were rewarded and answers with slight mistakes were only penalised slightly.

Mr T	£	£
Income from profession		50,000
Overseas income (10,000 + 17,500)		27,500
		77,500
Less: Personal allowance		(10,000)
Taxable income		67,500
Tax on first £31,865 @ 20%		6,373
Tax on balance £35,635 @ 40%		14,254
		20,627
Less: Overseas tax relief		
First source: overseas tax paid	3,000	
UK tax liability (£10,000 × 40%)	4,000	
Relief limited to overseas tax paid:		(3,000)
Second source: overseas tax paid	4,500	
UK tax liability (£17,500 × 40%)	7,000	
Relief limited to overseas tax paid:		(4,500)
Tax liability		13,127

8. This question involved the calculation of a gain/loss on the sale of an asset. The question is simpler to answer for 2014/15 than for the tax year when it was originally set, since some old rules (regarding taper relief and indexation) no longer apply. Therefore, such a question would not be allocated as many as five marks now.

	£
Disposal proceeds	92,000
Cost	(38,000)
Gain	54,000

9. **Examiner's comment**. This question involved calculating of the revised probate value of the shares. The key point to remember was that the commission and dealing costs were not deductible.

	£	£
Total initial probate value		500,000
Relief		
Total proceeds of shares sold (£27,000 + £49,000)	76,000	
Total probate value of shares sold (£60,000 + £38,000)	(98,000)	
		(22,000)
Revised probate value		478,000

Notes

(a) The total sales in the period are aggregated, regardless of whether they give profits or losses.

(b) Dealing costs are not included in the calculation.

INLEIDING

DIE ANGLO-BOEREOORLOG was 'n bloedige botsing van ideale en visies. Aan die een kant het die Boere-gemeenskap van die Zuid-Afrikaansche Republiek (Transvaal) en die Republiek van de Oranje-Vrijstaat die ideaal gekoester om hulle gebiede as selfstandige state te behou, en aan die ander kant was daar die visie van die Britse imperialiste soos lord Chamberlain, Cecil John Rhodes en dr. L.S. Jameson om die hele gebied van Kaap tot Kaïro onder die beheer van die Britse kroon te plaas. Vanselfsprekend was die Engelse se oë ook begerig op die Transvaalse goudmyne gerig om hulle kapitalisme te stimuleer en die koloniale aspirasies te bekostig. Dit was 'n stand van sake wat onvermydelik tot oorlog moes lei. So het dit ook gebeur. Vanaf Oktober 1899 het enkele tienduisende Boere hulle gebied probeer verdedig nadat die twee republieke se ultimatum aan die Engelse koloniale re-gering in die Kaap verwerp is.

Die Britte was daarvan oortuig dat dit net 'n skermutseling van 'n paar maande sou wees, maar tot hulle groot verbasing het dit hulle nege maande geneem voordat hulle Pretoria kon beset en daarna nog twee jaar voordat hulle die Boeremagte kon oortuig om die guerrillastryd te staak en die Vrede van Vereeniging op 31 Mei 1902 te onderteken. Die oorlog was op daardie tydstip die bloedigste, die langste en die duurste sedert die een wat Engeland teen Napoleon gevoer het. Die Engelse het amper tweemaal soveel manskappe op die slagveld verloor as die Boere, maar duisende van laasgenoemdes se vroue en kinders het in die Engelse konsentrasiekampe gesterf en 'n groot aantal van hulle plase was totaal verwoes as gevolg van Kitchener se taktiek van verskroeide aarde.

'n Opvallende kenmerk van hierdie oorlog was dat dit in Europa en Amerika baie simpatie vir die Boere en hulle saak opgewek het en, tweedens, dat daar 'n geweldige hoeveelheid gedigte, verhale en romans in die buiteland aan die oorlog in 'n hele reeks tale gewy is. Die verontwaardiging oor die Engelse aggressie, hulle moordlus en materialisme is motiewe wat in al die tekste gedurig beklemtoon is. Daar teenoor word die moed van die Boere geplaas, die geregtigheid van hulle stryd en hulle wetlike drang na vryheid. Selfs in Engeland was daar heelwat mense wat gevoel het dat die Britse regering van die tyd 'n groot fout maak. Hulle is egter deur die meerderheid van die bevolking as onpatrioties uitgeskel.

In Nederland en Vlaandere was daar ook 'n besonder sterk anti-Engelse gesindheid as gevolg van die "Boeren-oorlog". Vanaf die Eerste Vryheidsoorlog (1880–1881) het baie Nederlanders en Vlaminge weer bewus geraak van die stamverwantskap wat daar tussen hulle en die Afrikaners bestaan het. Die feit dat die Boere die Engelse op Majuba verneder het, het baie tot die verbeelding gespreek. Nederland het in dié stadium skynbaar 'n groot behoefte aan heldhaftigheid gehad en aan iets wat hulle nasionale trots weer kon opwek. Die Vlaminge het die Boeresimpatie gedeel. In die konteks van die Vlaamse Beweging was hulle volop in die stryd teen verfransing gewikkel. Die Boere se dapperheid en hulle stryd vir selfstandigheid het hulle dus geïnspireer in hulle verset teen die Franstalige oorheersing in België. Des te meer nog in 1899 toe die Anglo-Boereoorlog losbars in Natal. Berigte oor die vordering van die stryd en oor spesifieke veldslae is telegrafies oorgesein en in besonderhede in die meeste Europese koerante gerapporteer.

Dit was nie net joernaliste wat oor die oorlog geskryf het nie. Ook bekende Nederlandse digters soos Willem Kloos, Albert Verwey en P.C. Boutens en 'n groot aantal geleentheidsdigters het hulle penne opgeneem om die ongeregtigheid van die oorlog aan te kla en die lof te sing van die Boere wat dit waag om die kolossale mag van die Britse "empire" aan te pak. Selfs die liedjiesangers op markpleine en in die strate het die Boerehelde en hulle leiers geprys.

Die bewondering vir die moed van die ver stamverwante was grensloos. Dit was ook duidelik in die feeste, manifestasies en optogte ter ere van besoekende Boeregeneraals of van president Kruger en sy gevolg toe hulle in Desember 1900 in Europa aangekom het.

Vanselfsprekend was dit nie net in die buiteland dat dié vernietigende oorlog die onderwerp van poësie was nie. Hier in Suid-Afrika is daar sowel aan die kant van die Boere as die Engelse oorlogspoësie* geskryf. Eintlik was die oorlog 'n besonder groot stimulus tot die skryf van Afrikaanse poësie. Ons dink hier veral aan digters van die Tweede Beweging soos Jan F.E. Celliers, Totius, C. Louis Leipoldt en Eugène Marais, wat in mindere of meerdere mate die oorlog self meegemaak het, in kontras met die Nederlandse digters wat natuurlik op afstand geskryf het en so hulle verontwaardiging geuit het. Celliers het ook 'n dagboek oor sy oorlogservaringe gehou wat later gepubliseer is, maar dit is in Nederlands en nie in Afrikaans nie geskryf. Die Nederlands wat in daardie stadium nog steeds vir geskrewe dokumente in Suid-Afrika gebruik is, was taalkundig nie altyd van die beste gehalte nie omdat dit lankal nie meer 'n gesproke taal was nie. Dit was dikwels 'n mengsel van Nederlands en Afrikaans, 'n soort tussentaal. Ook enkele minder bekende Suid-Afrikaanse digters soos P.J. Perold, eweas F.W. Reitz, oud-president van die Oranje-Vrystaat, en dominee A. Moorrees het hulle poësie in Nederlands geskryf, of in die mengsel van Nederlands en Afrikaans. Dit is ook die geval in die poësie van heelwat anonieme volksdigters.

Hierdie bundel wil nie net 'n bloemlesing van bekende Afrikaanse en Nederlandse digters se poësie oor die Anglo-

---

* Sien M. van Wyk Smith, *Drummer Hodge. The poetry of the Anglo-Boer War (1899–1902)*. Pretoria: Protea Book House, 1999. Vir 'n bloemlesing uit die Afrikaans en Nederlandse poësie, prosa en dagboektekste oor die Anglo-Boere-oorlog, sien E. Jansen en W. Jonckheere, *Boer en Brit: Afrikaanse en Nederlandse tekste uit en om die Anglo-Boereoorlog*. Pretoria: Protea Boekhuis, 1999.

Boereoorlog wees nie. Daar word ook aandag gevra vir die werk
van Afrikaanse en Nederlandse geleentheidsdigters wat almal
ewe sterk oor die oorlog gevoel het as die digters wat dit dalk
estetieser of met 'n groter woordkrag en taalvermoë kon uitdruk.
Ons wil 'n vollediger prentjie van dié oorlog gee soos dit in dig-
vorm in die twee verwante tale gestalte gekry het. Om dié rede
sluit ons ook 'n aantal gedigte van onbekende digters in wat
nooit gedruk is nie of in klein, tans vergete tydskriffies wat in Sint
Helena of Ceylon se krygsgevangenekampe gepubliseer is. Hulle
word nog in museums of instellings soos die Nasionale Afrikaanse
Letterkundige Museum en Navorsingsentrum (NALN), die
Oorlogsmuseum in Bloemfontein en enkele ander argiewe
bewaar. Dié lang vergete stemme moet ook weer 'n slag
gehoor word, veral omdat dit die mins geskoolde van al die
digters was. Dit was meestal eenvoudige mense wat die
swaarkry en lyding persoonlik ervaar het. Hulle was
regstreeks betrokke in die oorlogsgeweld en het uit die hart
geskryf. Hierdie soort spontane poësie wat soveel opgekropte
gevoelens tot uitdrukking bring, vorm 'n onmisbare deel van
'n bloemlesing soos hierdie een.

Die gedigte is hier so gerangskik dat hulle rofweg die
verloop van die oorlog probeer volg vanaf die begin in die
lente van 1899 tot die einde van die ellende in Mei 1902.
Ook die dood van president Paul Kruger in Switserland in
1904 word betrek en die aankoms van die ou leier se lyk in
die Kaap wat A. Moorrees diep ontroer het en hom tot die
skryf van 'n roulied geïnspireer het. Die bloemlesing eindig
met 'n gedig wat die Vrystaatse oud-president en digter, F.W.
Reitz, op die dag van Christiaan de Wet se begrafnis op 8
Februarie 1922 geskryf het. In die gedig ry generaal De Wet
en sy aghonderd man nog 'n laaste keer oor die veld. Die
oorlog was in die stadium al amper twintig jaar verby.

Die titel van die bundel is gebaseer op die derde strofe
van Totius se gedig "Vergewe en vergeet" wat soos volg
lui:"Jy het mos, doringstruikie, / my ander dag gekrap; / en

daarom het my wiele / jou kroontjie plat getrap." Dié woorde word deur 'n ossewa tot die doringstruikie gerig, simbool van die Boerenasie, wat platgetrap was maar wat, volgens die digter, sy kroontjie weer sou oprig.

Ondanks die subtitel van hierdie bloemlesing is drie Engelse gedigte ook opgeneem. Twee is anoniem en het in 'n blaadjie van 'n krygsgevangenekamp op Ceylon verskyn. Die derde kom uit 'n nooit gepubliseerde bundel van Joubert Reitz, seun van die digter en oud-president van die Oranje-Vrijstaat, F.W. Reitz. Omdat die tekste duidelik deur Boere geskryf is, het ek besluit om hulle by die versameling te voeg.

Tot slot nog 'n besondere woordjie van dank aan die Oorlogsmuseum van die Boererepublieke te Bloemfontein en in die besonder Elria Wessels en Leandré Hanekom wat gehelp het met die bymekaarmaak van ongepubliseerde oorlogs-gedigte. Ek is ewe veel dank verskuldig aan Ena van der Walt van die Nasionale Afrikaanse Letterkundige Museum en Navorsingsentrum te Bloemfontein wat ook bepaalde tekste gevind het wat ek nêrens anders kon kry nie. Sonder hul hulp sou ek hierdie bloemlesing nooit voltooi het nie.

Die platgetrapte kroontjie

J.E. Banck

Een lied voor Transvaal*

Wij vrije mannen van Transvaal
Zijn fier op eigen volk en taal,
Het strijden is ons daaglijksch werk.
Het maakt ons vaardig, moedig, sterk,
Den koning van het dierenrijk,
In menig opzicht zeer gelijk,
Die zich verweert met klauw en tand,
Wanneer zijn erf wordt aangerand.

De storm steekt op, de lucht betrekt,
De Tafelberg is reeds gedekt,
Het woelig feestgelag begint,
Waarbij de kloekste geest verwint;
Wij zweren trouw aan Afrika,
De krijgsleus blijft *Constantia,*
Zoo koppig als de Kaapsche wijn,
Kan slechts een volk van boeren zijn!

De steenbok, de giraf en struis
Ontvluchten voor het krijgsgedruis,
Verspreiden in de wildernis
Beweging en ontsteltenis.
Te wapen Kaapland en Natal,
Oranje-Vrijstaat bovenal,
Gij allen, die uw oorsprong eert,
Gezamenlijk den Brit gekeerd!

---

* 's-Gravenhage: Koninklijke Nederlandsche Boekhandel M.M. Couvée, z.j.

Als een geboren ruitervolk,
Verschijnen wij, gelijk een wolk,
Of vliegen als een damp uiteen
En jagen met den stormwind heen!
Met ons geloof, als krijgsbanier,
Met God voor oogen, als vizier,
Den Staten-Bijbel, als patroon,
Wacht in den hemel ons het loon.

Gewapend met de trouwe buks,
Bestijgen wij de bergen fluks,
Verschuilen ons in kloof en spleet
En houden ons ten strijd gereed;
De kogel mist zijn doelwit niet,
Zoodra ons oog het wild bespiedt,
Wanneer het schot wordt losgebrand,
Bijt ook een roodrok in het zand.

Het woest en onherbergzaam oord,
Gevloekt tooneel van twist en moord,
Werd omgetooverd in een hof,
Die ieder door zijn aanblik trof;
Veroverd met ons zweet en bloed
Op zwart gespuis en wild gebroed,
Door heldenmoed en noeste vlijt
Tot wettig eigendom gewijd.

De vrijheid blijft het hoogste goed,
Bezegeld met ons offerbloed;
De vrijheid blijft de grootste schat,
Dien ons gezegend land bevat,
Meer dan het goud, de diamant,
Ons toegestrooid met volle hand,
Dan alle schatten saam vergâard,
Ons meer nog dan het leven waard!

Wij bukken voor geen overmacht,
Want onverzwakt blijft onze kracht,
Wij volgen dan het oude spoor
En trekken altijd verder door
En altijd dieper landwaarts in,
Het oude lied, – een nieuw begin, –
Wij stichten ons gemeenebest
Te midden van het leeuwennest!

Wij zijn gedoemd in de woestijn
Een zwervend herdersvolk te zijn,
Dat overal zijn tenten spant
En opgaat naar het heilig land.
De republiek welvarend, vrij,
Geen vreemde dwang of heerschappij,
Een onafhanklijk volksbestaan,
Of ons Transvaal moet ondergaan!

D.F. Malherbe

Oorlog*

In die Noorde daar ver, waar die spore
      van die trekker se wawiel nog staan,
is 'n woelende wereld gebore,
      waar die trekker die pad het gebaan.
Naar die Noord waar die grasvelde wuiwe,
      waar die trekker se wieg het gestaan,
waar die Vaalstroom vreedsaam voortskuiwe,
      jaag die hongerende mensdom aan.
Eeuw van goud en geniete
      van hogere strewe ontdaan,
waarin edele drome wegvliete
      en in geldsug is ondergegaan!
En die goud word die appel van twiste,
      rijk gelaagd in die rande se skoot –
'n jonkvrou so skoon maar vol liste,
      aan haar vrijers ellende en dood!
Trotse mag waar rijke en trone
      en grote nasies voor vlug,
die Draak wat jaloers hierdie Skone
      bewaak is nog jong maar gedug!
"Op kommando," so klink o'er die velde
      die woord wat die lugte deurwiel;
van die ploeg in die sa'el vlieg die helde
      deur die geest van die vaadre besiel,
bereid om alles te gewe
      ver die land met trane besproei –
heilig grond waar die trekker sijn lewe
      het geoffer, sijn bloed het gevloei.

---

* *Karroo Blommetjies. Afrikaanse gedigte.* Kaapstad: Van de Sandt de Villiers Drukpers Maatschappij Beperkt, 1909, pp. 39–40.

P.J. Perold

Het uitbreken van den oorlog*

Twist begon; de stormen nadren;
    Goud, meer goud zoo klonk het voort;
Zie de arenden vergadren
    Om het aas uit ieder oord.

Uit de dicht bevolkte landen;
    Uit Europa's laagste klas,
Spoelden heen naar deze stranden
    Wat reeds daar bedorven was.

Slaven stroomden met hun heeren;
    Krethi Plethi naar Transvaal,
Werken niet, maar speculeeren,
    Was hun doel hier altemaal.

Slaven werden hier heloten,
    Maar in ketenen van goud
Heeft hen ook dien ruil verdroten;
    Milner schreef tot hun behoud!

Ook de Diamanten Koning
    Hielp tot troost van het gemoed,
Sprak van verven bij zijn woning
    Maar hij verfd' de kaart met bloed!

Elk Kapitalist ging samen
    Van Euroop en van Transvaal:
"Teekent voor ons geld uw namen,
    Slaven gij, van 't Kapitaal".

---

* *De weduwe of tafereelen uit den Engelschen oorlog 1899–1902.* Kaapstad:
Hollandsch-Afrikaansche Uitgevers Maatschappij, 1903 pp. 9–11.

Ook wou men Majuba wreken;
  Jemieson's mislukte tocht,
't Goud lokt aan; al hoort men spreken,
  Dat men dat, noch landen zocht!

Samen werkten alle machten;
  Vijanden gansch zonder tal,
Die voorwendsels slechts bedachten
  Elk gemunt op uwen val.

Schikken ja, maar met bedrieging
  Met het wapen in de hand;
Geeft toe, dan volgt 't hem zoo eigen,
  Grooter eisch aan zijnen kant.

Oorlogswolken pakken samen,
  Aan den hemel van den staat,
Wie nog vrede wil beramen
  Vindt het is, helaas! te laat.

"Afrikaanders, Mannen, Broeders,
  Op, beschermt uw dierbaar erf".
Roepen helden, smeeken moeders;
  "Of gij overwint of sterft!"

Jan F. E. Celliers

Vryheidslied*
(By die Uittog)

Vrome vaa'dre fier en groot!**
Deur vervolging, ramp en nood,
was hul leuse, tot die dood:
    Vryheid, Vryheid!

Erf'nis van hul moed en trou
is die grond waar ons op bou,
juigend tot die hemelblou:
    Vryheid, Vryheid!

Ere wie die dood mag lei
om te rus aan hulle sy –
met die sterwenswoord te skei:
    Vryheid, Vryheid!

Op dan broers, en druk hul spoor!
Voorwaarts, broers, die vierkleur voor!
Laat die veld ons krygsroep hoor:
    Vryheid, Vryheid!

Woes geweld mag hoogty hou,
kettings mag ons lede knou
maar die leuse bly ons trou:
    Vryheid, Vryheid!

Jukke mag vir slawe wees:
manneharte ken geen vrees,
duld geen boei vir lyf of gees:
    Vryheid, Vryheid!

---

* *Die vlakte en ander gedigte.* Kaapstad: Tafelberg-Uitgewers, 1974, pp. 38–39.
** Die Voortrekkers.

Totius

Trekkerswee (fragment)*

Is 't oorlog? … In oom Koos se huis
woel almal net om klaar te kry.
Daar word geslag weer en gebak,
en buite voor die agterdeur
trek reeds die seuns die bokwa reg
om op te pak.

Die harte voel nie lekker nie,
die woorde het angstig-min geword –
soos steeds by donker voorbesef,
by die vergeefse angsgevraag
van hoe en waar
die ontwaakte lewenslot sal tref.

Lughartig praat 'n enkele seun
hoe hy die Engelsman sal skiet,
maar moeder maan: My kind, my kind!
Die seun wyk willig vir die woord,
want, ja, daar was 'n kleinigheid
wat hy nog aan sy saal wou bind!

Dis amper klaar … Daar kom hul aan,
die burgers van die omtrek, want
oom Koos die is nog veldkornet …
Straks staan hul, teuel in die arm
en met geboë hoof,
want een gaan voor in smeekgebed.

---

* Deel 2: 13 en 14. *Versamelde gedigte.* Kaapstad: Tafelberg-Uitgewers, 1988,
  pp. 169–171.

Die vrouens staan effens opsy,
met arrems oor mekaar gevou,
nou dat hul taak is afgedaan.
Nou kan hul eers hul smart besef,
en enkle droog met voorskoot-punt
al die eerste oorlogstraan.

Dan skuif en skok, met gang en draf,
die burgers op hul perde weg –
dit lyk somaar 'n mengelklomp!
Maar tussen hulle flikker-blits
geweldig in die lenteson
die blinkgemaakte mauser-tromp!

Oom Gert wat hom meer tuis voel by
dié ruiterskaar – hy het oom Koos
sy krygsmansdiens al aangebied –
die luister hoe die jongspan in
hul oorlogsblydskap sing
die klanke van 'n oorlogslied:

Kom, burgers, trek die perde reg:
nou vrou en kind goeien-dag geseg!
Jongkêrels, los die nôi se hand;
en seuns, verlaat jul moeders, want
daar gaan 'n strydroep deur die land!
Gryp nou die teuels bymekaar –
die vierkleur is weer in gevaar!

Die regterhand gryp die visier,
die bors oorkruis 'n bandelier;
die spore in die sonskyn blink,
stiebeuels teen mekaar weerklink,
die ketel aan die saal rinkink.
Kom, burgers, hou nou bymekaar –
die vierkleur is weer in gevaar!

Laat aan die trippelaar sy pas,
maar hou die vuurge hingste vas.
Die agterstes moet ingalop
tot binne-in die ruiter-trop –
die ponie en die bossie-kop.
Kom, burgers, ry so bymekaar –
die vierkleur is weer in gevaar!

Trek burgers, almal nou geteld,
al voort maar deur die wye veld,
en of jul al omlaag verdwyn
of op die heuwels weer verskyn –
wys altyd weer die slingerlyn.
Kom, burgers, trek so bymekaar –
die vierkleur is weer in gevaar!

Jaag, burgers, jaag oor rant en rots
wanneer jul teen die vyand bots.
Ruk in, spring af en pos gevat
aan die onwrikbre ryperd-blad
Mik fyn, kyk waar die stoffie spat!
Staan, burgers, staan dan bymekaar –
die vierkleur is weer in gevaar!

En moet jul val, val dan met eer,
met die oog die vyand toegekeer;
val op die grense, man en perd,
die oue vierkleur is dit werd,
en die eerkroon wink al uit die vert.
Val burgers, val dan bymekaar –
die vierkleur is weer in gevaar!

Digter onbekend

Oorlogskans (fragment)*

't Morgenrood! 't Morgenrood!
Spelt my alligt een vroege dood;
Als de krygs trompetten klinken
Zal de Stryd my wreed verminken,
My en menig kameraad.

Onverwacht! Onverwacht!
Word myn levensloop volbracht –
Gisteren noch te paard gestegen,
Straks op 't Slachveld neergezegen,
Morgen reeds in 't koele graf.

---

* Aangehaal deur M. van Wyk Smith in *Drummer Hodge. The poetry of the Anglo-Boer War*. Pretoria: Protea Book House, 1999, p. 205. Hierdie lied is 'n vertaling van die Duitse skrywer Wilhelm Hauff (1802–1877) se *Reiters Morgensang*. Die teks is ongetwyfeld verwant aan "Môrerood" wat aangehaal word in P.W. Grobbelaar, *Kommandeer! Kommandeer! Volksang uit die Anglo-Boereoorlog*, Pretoria: J.P. van der Walt, 1999, p. 65. Grobbelaar se optekening uit die volksmond, wat hy beskikbaar gestel het, lui soos volg:

Morgenrood
Wilhelm Hauff
(vertaal uit die Duits)

Morgenrood, morgenrood,
Wenkt gy my ten vroegen dood.
Straks zal de trompet weerklinken,
En ik stervend nedersinke
Ik en menig kameraad.

Onverwachts, onverwachts
Houdt de dood ons in zyn macht.
Gisteren fier in zaal gestegen,
Heden dood ter neer gezegen,
Morgen reeds in 't koele graf.

Als een bloem, als een bloem
Is des mensen kracht en roem.
Als twee rode, frisse rozen
Ziet men uwe wangen blozen,
Maar de rozen welken ras.

Daarom stil, daarom stil
Voeg ik naar 's Heeren Wil.
Van myn post wil ik niet wyken,
En moet heden ik bezwyken,
Ik sterf den braven ruiterdood.

Digter onbekend

Oorlog lied*

1

Liefste hoort nu naart myn lied
het kost my veel en zwaar verdriet
het is tog waar ik gaan nu weg
om voor ons land en volk te veg

2

Ik was tog altoos trouw geweest
u bemin met myn hart en geest
maar nu moet ik op het oorlog gaan
en u voor altoos hier laat staan

3

Liefste gedink tog aan myn woord
dat gy van my al heeft gehoord
maar nu op het punt om te vertrek
daar na die ou comando plek

4

Liefste gedink tog ook aan my
zoo veel maal zit ik aan u zy
ik is getrouw dat zal ik bly
totdat die dood ons twee zal schei

5

Door vuur en haal kruit en loot
moet ik strij tot den dood
en is het dan ook myn [lot]
beveel ik u in de hand van God

---

* Manuskrip PD 21 80/4, NALN, Bloemfontein.

6

Ach breek de tyd van scheiding aan
de bazuin die klink ons moet nu gaan
om daar voor ons land te gaan veg
totdat ik in myn grafje legt

7

Vaarwel vrienden vaarwel allen
gedink aan my als ik vallen
want voor den vyand kruit en loot
moet ik stryden tot den dood

8

[…]* myn dierbaarste
[ik] kint u als myn eennigste
[vaar]wel vaar wel nog duizen keer
[u s]iet my zeker nimmer meer.

---

* Die aanvang van alle strofereëls in hierdie strofe ontbreek in die oorspronklike manuskrip.

Frederik van Eeden

De Geboorte eener Natie*

Verspreide Boeren ploegen 't wijde land
weiden hun kudden, vestend naar God's Recht
hun hard bestaan op de twee zuilen hecht
van Vrijdom en het zware werk der hand.

Op Handel en op Woeker tronend legt
een machtig Rijk welhaast heel d' aard in band,
noemt zich beschaving's Kamper en Gezant
en droomt all' volken aan zijn troon geknecht.

Het steekt den nooit verzaadden muil naar voren
zich blindlings aan den gouden buit vergapend
en slaat 't klein volk met krijg in dommen trots,

zoo sloeg Hephaistos eens het hoofd eens Gods,
en als Athene, weerbaar en gewapend,
werd het groot Afrikaander volk geboren.

October 1899

---

* *Van de passielooze lelie,* Amsterdam: Versluys, tweede druk, 1908, p. 52.

D. F. Malherbe*

Agter klippe en krans
verskuil en verskans
lê hul stil –
die ko'els deur die lug
in vliegende vlug
sissend gesaai
en verspil.
Brekende bomme
voor, agter, alomme
skiet skerwe.
"Burgers, ons lot
onder blitse se spot
– vloektafereel –
is o'erwinning geheel
of sterwe!"
En altijd deur onder
die donder,
verdowend gedreun …
In stormende swaai,
in driftige drang,
in woedende gang
o'er die vlak –
jagend gerij
van ruiters gesprei
wat steiger
en sak!
Spiegelend spel
van skitterend staal,
weerglimmend geglans
van dansende straal!

* *Karroo Blommetjies. Afrikaanse gedigte.* Kaapstad: Van de Sandt de Villiers
Drukpers Maatschappij Beperkt, 1909, pp. 40–41.

Wolke van rook
waar vure in woed,
wemelend gewoel
immer sterker gevoed!
En altijd deur onder
die donder,
verdowend gedreun,
wat mense en diere
verag
in hul kermend gesteun ...

Nicolaas Beets

De Boeren*

Zult gij een ijdle wereld leeren
    Wat Godsbetrouwen zegt,
Gij strijders in de kracht des Heeren
    Voor vrijheid, erf en recht;
Klein volk van ploegers, herders, jagers,
    Gelasterd en veracht
Door uw hooghartige belagers,
    Gerust op overmacht?

Gij, in hun oog nog half barbaren,
    Alleen verdelging waard,
Maar Heldenkroost van Martelaren,
    Niet van hun bloed ontaard,
Gij predikt Koningen en Volken,
    Hoe groot en machtig: Hij,
Die zetelt boven lucht en wolken,
    Is machtiger dan gij.

De God dier psalmen en kronijken,
    Daar onze ziel bij leeft,
Zal nooit doen wanklen of bezwijken
    Die Hem zijn eere geeft.
"Op wagens, paarden, en op helden
    "Zij onze vijand stout,
"Maar wij, wij zullen de eer vermelden
    "Van Hem die ons behoudt!"

---

* *Gedichten*. Vierde deel, zesde druk. Leiden: Sijthoff, p. 237.

Behoud hen, Heer der legermachten,
      Sta Godlijk aan hun zij,
Verhoog hen, die Uw heil verwachten,
      Verplet hun weerpartij!
Laat nog de stervende eeuw ervaren,
      Dat waar Ge in glans verschijnt,
't Boos opzet van geweldenaren
      Als rook en damp verdwijnt.

1899
4 November.

Albert Verwey

Aan den schrijver van "Een eeuw van onrecht"*

Gelukge die aan d'ingang van een eeuw
Voor groote daden staat en klaar en boud
Uw taak – de taak van heel uw volk – ontvouwt,
Vol van de grootheid waar ik steeds om schreeuw.

Een volk trok uit, schiep de woestijn tot tuin:
De vreemd groef goud uit schaarsbeploegde kloof;
Nu zijn voor recht, voor reê, goudgeergen doof …
Stel rij aan rij 't scherp schot op rotsge kruin!

Sterv' de adel van 't Caucasisch ras: hun dood –
Om 't bloem-doorgroeide puin speel 't Bantu-kind,
Vragend wat bloeit zo rood, wat klaagt die wind? –
Blijk' helden-daad die 't lievend leven sloot.

Hijn vrijheid leefde en sterv' met hen. Heil, heil!
Vrijheid geen woord maar volk, dat waagde – èn won? –
O, won! *Gij* weet: zuid-afrikaanse zon
Schijnt schoonst hadt ge ééns voor haar uw leven veil!

---

* *Dagen en daden.* In: *Verzamelde gedichten,* p. 166. *Een eeuw van onrecht* (Dordrecht, 1899) was 'n boekie of 'n pamflet van J.C. Smuts uitgegee onder die naam van F.W. Reitz waarin die outeur(s) dit duidelik maak waarom die Tweede Vryheidsoorlog onvermydelik was. Dié apologie het in 1900 in 'n paar Europese tale verskyn.

Albert Verwey

De Toegela*

Hun strijd op de bergen
Wonnen de helden:
Heel de rivier langs
Lagen ze in kuilen
En achter steenen,
Stonden in schansen,
Stormden en schoten, –
En daar granaatschroot
Rondom hen barstte,
En gele dampen
De lucht verpestten,
Daar klip en bergen
Dreunden: 't kanonvuur
Van weerszijds rolde, –
Stonden de helden,
Stormden en schoten,
Of knielden in kuilen
En achter stenen:
Heel de rivier langs
Op alle bergen
Wonnen de helden
Hun strijd.

---

* *Verzamelde gedichten.* Tweede deel. Amsterdam: Versluys, 1912, pp. 177–179.

Als de lijn van die bergen
In avondhemel,
Als het bed dier rivier
Gegroeid in de kloof, –
Staat in de verbeelding
Van alle volken
De strijd van die helden
Voor altijd.

Als blinkende sterren de toppen kronend
Der Drakensbergen, –
Als sterren van 't zuiden in 't veelomstreden
Toegelawater weerkaatst, –
Zoo blijven op hoogten
Van geest en in laagten
Van troeble gedachten
Blinken uw namen:
Colenso!
Spioenkop!
Als hoopvolle lichten
In menslijken nacht.
En wanneer in uw vaalte,
Westerse velden,
De helden vielen,
En alle gedachten
In 't donker duiz'len, –
Zeggen wij zacht
Die gewijde namen:
Spioenkop!
Colenso!
En denken: een volk, gedoemd tot sterven,
Zou zulke daden
Niet doen.

Digter onbekend

Spion Kop, January 24th 1900*
In memory of the men who fell at Spion Kop

You know we Boers stormed Spion Kop,
    't Was an eventful day;
And as we neared its bloody top
    We heard our General say:
"Schiet kèrels, schiet! the foe is there!
    And every rugged rock
Gave back the murderous rifle fire,
    Which from our Mausers broke.

The foe fought well, but nought on earth
    Could stand that fatal fire,
And despite drill and discipline
    We forced them to retire.
And even as we scaled the height
    We heard our General cry:
"Schiet, kèrels, schiet! en sta niet stil,
    We either win or die!"

---

* *Diyatalawa Dum-Dum*, vol. 1, nr. 1, 10 September 1900. Die *Diyatalawa Dum-Dum* was 'n kamptydskriffie wat met die hand in Engels en Nederlands geskryf en uitgegee is.

And 'midst that hail and shot and shell
 Which fell on every side
And seemed as if the gates of Hell
 Had been thrown open wide
Blood splashed to rocks and soaked the ground;
 And every step we took,
The shells which fell from all around
 The very ground they shook.
Yet, now and then, 'twixt shot and shell
 We heard our General cry:
"Schiet, kèrels, schiet! en sta niet stil,
 We either win or die!"

Ch. D. te Deventer

Gebed voor de Boeren*

Gij, die in den Hemel woont
En uw hulp den Boeren toont,
Die nu wagen goed en leven,
Om den vijand te doen beven,
Die vertredet uwe eer;
Wilt eens hooren, lieve Heer!

Gevet den Transvaalschen held,
Die getogen is te veld –
En, voorzien van kloeke mannen,
Heeft zijn tenten uitgespannen
In Natal – naar zijn begeer;
Wil ons hooren, lieve Heer!

Geeft hem wijsheid ende kracht,
Dek hem met uw trouwe wacht,
Laat getroost zijn ruiters draven,
Laat gerust zijn knechten graven,
Geef hem gunstig wind en weer;
Wil ons hooren, lieve Heer!

Wees gestadig aan zijn zij,
Als hij op de batterij
Spelet met zijn grove ballen;
Laat de muren voor hem vallen.
De rondeelen storten neer;
Wil ons hooren, lieve Heer!

---

* Gepubliseer in *De Zwolsche Courant* (datum onbekend). Die teks is geïnspireer deur 'n gedig wat die sewentiende eeuse digter Jacob Revius in 1629 geskryf het tydens die beleg van 's-Hertogenbosch deur Frederik Hendrik, die stadhouder van Holland.

Neem den vijand zijnen moed,
Neemt hem wijsheid ende spoed,
Neem hem koren ende haver,
Neem hem krijger ende graver.
Neem hem harnas en geweer;
Wil ons hooren, lieve Heer!

Komt Brittanje voor den dag
Om hun heir te bieden slag,
Of om Ladysmith t' ontzetten,
Uwe adem moet hem pletten.
En wegblazen als een veer;
Wil ons hooren, lieve Heer!

Zendt hij hem in haren nood
Wijn of voeder, kruit of lood,
Datet blijven onderwegen,
Latet van ons zijn gekregen;
Smijt zijn wapenen omveer;
Wil ons hooren, lieve Heer!

Rhodes laat van zijnen schat
Niet ontvangen dit noch dat!
Geef dat hij na lange hopen,
In zijn eigen nest gekropen
Zuigt zijn pooten als een beer;
Wil ons hooren, lieve Heer!

d'Uitkomst van den krijg beschaam,
Chamberlain en Rhodes saam,
Vrijheid zij de beide Staten
Als onwrikbaar goed gelaten.
Dat zij vrij zijn als weleer,
Wil ons hooren, lieve Heer!

Gij zijt die de krijgers vuurt,
Gij zijt die de machten stuurt,
Gij kondt wonderlijk behouwen,
Op uw gunste wij vertrouwen,
Niet op ruiter ofte speer;
Wil ons hooren, lieve Heer!

Geeft hun Mafeking in handen,
Moge Kimberley verbranden,
Ladysmith zij hun ten buit,
Buller in zijn loop gestuit.
Ijdel zij John Bull's beramen
't Vast Europa hoopt dit, Amen.

C. Louis Leipoldt

Vandag*

Wat van die nag, o wagter op die wagplek?
Wat van die nag wat hom sterloos oor ons strek?

Nie deur die knal van bomme en kartetse;
Nie deur die suis van koeëls, die blits van sabels;
Nie deur die rook van huise, ru in vlam;
Nie deur die wilde war'lende rumoer
Van krygsgedrang en woeste oorlogswoede;
Nie deur die haat van vrind teen vrind as vyand;
Nie deur die wrok wat wanhoop wins sal gee;
Nie deur die onreg wat vir reg beken word;
Nie deur die mag waar rede voor verpand word;
Nie deur die skimp wat smart tot smaad verander;
Nie deur die druk van dwang en dwing'landy;
Nie deur die hardgegesperde band van griewe;
Nie deur die skand' van skaars-betaalde skuld
Word volke en nasies opgebou tot sterkte
En lewenskrag en louter selfbestaan,
Of uitgedoof die glinsterglim wat gloei
Diep in die volk se siel, en wat sal vlam
Met voller glorie ná die worstelstryd.

Vermom deur haat, jaloersheid en verdriet,
Staan volk teen volk, geduldig lydend, vas
In al wat dierlik in die mensheid woel –
Elk mislik in homselwe as die nag
Met skemerstreling tot oorpeinsing lok
En elk sy dag oordink en in sy hart
Vergifnis vir sy eie val moet vra.

---

* *Versamelde gedigte.* Kaapstad: Tafelberg-Uitgewers, 1980, pp. 143–144.

Leer dat die louter liefde vir jou land
Die groter liefde vir jou medemens
Nie uit- maar insluit; dat die paradys
Nie meer op die manier van Mohamed
Alleen bevolk word deur soldate-dood;
Leer dat die band wat volk aan volk moet heg,
Nie meer verbreek mag worde deur 'n hand
Wat nie almagtig is nie; dat die see,
Die lug hierbo, die aarde waar ons trap,
Vry vir elk mensekind moet wees en bly –
Nie afgebaken soos 'n agterwerf
Vir een of ander wat die sterkste is.
Leer dit en lewe na jou leer, en ly
Totdat jou wêreld ook dieselfde les
Geleer het, en wat mens is, mensheid ken.

Jacoba Maria Steenkamp

by belmons heuvel*

geschreiwe in 1902

by belmons heuvel die eerste dag
toen de vrystaters te rugge slaan werd
door de britsemag
kniel daar een jongeling schoon en teer
de trots van zynen moeder neer
toen zyn vader aan hem zeg
bleif by uwe moeder en houw myn afaere reg
was zyn andwoord god zy haar behoeder
maar ik gaat aan u zyde veg
voor myn land en voor haar reg
zal ik staan en zal ik veg
dood of lewe dag of nag
zal ik veg voor vrystaats vlag

Daar op belmons heuwel
lag dertig man gesneuwel
en ook de jongeling vol moed
lag daar de worstel in zyn bloed
zyn vader o die smart
zag het bloed stroom uit zyn kinderhard
nooid werd een droever schouspel
hier bevind
dan de vader by zyn stervend kind
zyn vader bleef hem by
tot hy als oorlogspressenier werd weg gely

---

* Manuskrip 6727/1, Oorlogsmuseum van die Boererepublieke, Bloemfontein.

gy jongeling merk waardig
is belmons graf u louwerkransch wel waardig
ook dat u gedagtenis
nooid uit ons land word uit gewis
die jongeheld vrees voor geen nood
slegs veertien jaar en hy is dood

Willem Kloos

Zuid-Afrika*

Ging nu voor 't laatst de zon van Holland tanen,
    Die, hoog en stout, in 't verre Zuiden stond,
    Omdat ons ras gerechten strijd aanbond
Met 't huurlings-rot der diplomaten-vanen?

Is dan de stem des bloeds een ijdel wanen,
    En draait het leven even rustig rond?
    O, ligt voor eeuwig, met gesloten mond,
Der Vrijheid lijf gesmoord in bloed en tranen?

Ja, nu de Dietsche zaak daar ginds als dol spant,
    Blijven wij rustig treuren over 't lijkje,
        Dat, Holland's kind, fier viel voor Holland's eer!

Ja, wij, de zonen van ons zwaar, oud Holland,
    Wij, die hier zitten in ons kalm-log Rijkje,
        Zien 't aan, en zeggen: " 't Spijt ons wáárlijk zeer"!

20 Maart 1900.

---

* *Verzen*. Amsterdam: Versluys, 1913, p. 309.

Eugène van Oye

Aan Engeland[*]

"Zoo is de snoodste daad dus van onze eeuw geschied ...
En 't Volk, dat haar beging, verzinkt van schaamte niet
in zijn modderpoel van eerloosheid en schande!
Neen, – 't Is er trotsch op! en de bloedbevlekte handen,
met goud gevuld, het steekt ze in dronken, driesten spot,
verbijsterd en verbeest, omhoog, ten reinen God
des Rechts! – "Ei! recht? Ik heb het in mijn handen hier – en
almachtig is 't: het goud!" –
                     De roovers zegevieren. –
"Ja, 'k weet het wel dat ik een dief, een schurk ben, maar
ik heb de macht, dus 't recht een schurk te zijn, nietwaar?"
Genoeg. De wereld walgt ... O tijden in verwachting,
komt, – schopt dat vuige Volk in de eeuwige verachting!"

---

[*] *Transvaal*, jg. 1, nr. 33, 17 Junie 1900, p. 1 soos opgeneem in: A. Smits. *Betrekkingen tussen Vlaanderen en Zuid-Afrika.* Brugge: Wiek Op, 1943, p. 146.

Eugène van Oye

Aan de Vorsten*

"En gij, gij ook, gij kroon- en scepterdragers, ridderen
van Eer en Recht, – komt hier!
                              Lakeien der aanbidderen
van 't gulden kalf, ginds pleegt het goud een Volkenmoord!
De ziel der Menschheid gruwt en schreeuwt ten hemel …
                                        Hoort! –
Gij hoort niet … Spreekt! – Gij zwijgt …
                              Maar eens zal Iemand spreken,
die, niet om goud te koop, Gerechtigheid moet wreken:
O Wraakgodinne der Geschiedenis, verrijs!
Uw gloeiend ijzer op die knechtenhoofden! Wijs
me heel dien narrenboel van femelende laffen
ten schandpaal!
            Vorsten! zoo moet uw verraad u straffen
en zal 't. Ge kunt nu gaan … Uw vonnis is geveld.
Wascht u de handen nu.
                  Wanneer het Judasgeld? …

Oostende, 30-5-1900.

---

* In: A. Smits. *Betrekkingen tussen Vlaanderen en Zuid-Afrika*. Brugge: Wiek Op, 1943, pp. 146–147. Oorgeneem uit *Transvaal*, jr. 1, nr. 33, 17 Junie 1900.

Digter onbekend

Bij het vertrek der Belgische Ambulancie te Antwerpen*

Zij togen naar het oorlogsveld
    Ons brave, dappre landgenooten,
En iedereen kwam toegesneld
    Om eerbiedvol het hoofd te ontblooten.

Hun oog ontschoot de helle vlam
    Der vastberadenheid! Zij togen
Ter hulpe van den broederstam …
    En tranen welden ons naar de oogen!

Verbeelding zag hen reeds aan 't werk:
    Gewonden helpen en verplegen,
Door heilge naastenliefde sterk
    Te midden van den kogelregen.

Wij drukten hen ontroerd de hand:
    "Brengt onzen wensch den Boerenhelden!
Keert allen ook naar 't vaderland
    Om ons hun zegepraal te melden!"

---

* *Boerenalmanak 1902*. Antwerpen: Van Tasselt, 1902, p. 16.

Jan F. E. Celliers

Die Stryd*

Droef en lank was die nag,
grys en guur breek die dag –
　　ver ruis die reën …
In gebede geskaar,
in die reën bymekaar,
smeek ons af in gevaar,
　　Vader, U seën!

Stil, soos skimme wat kom,
sluip die vyande om –
　　nader en nader …
Daar's 'n blits! Daar's 'n knal!
Hoor die slae dreunend val!
"Voorwaarts één, voorwaarts al!" –
　　Lei ons, Al-Vader!

Vaarlands grond drink die bloed,
nog vol vryheid se gloed –
　　warm uit die wonde;
menig sterwende sug
dra 'n groet deur die lug
bo die wapen-gerug –
　　ver in die ronde.

---

* *Die vlakte en ander gedigte.* Kaapstad: Tafelberg-Uitgewers, 1974, pp. 40–41.

O, die lippe wat bleek
om 'n waterdronk smeek –
　　wonde wat brande!
Ongehoord, ongeag,
menig kermende klag
waar die woelende slag
　　dreun oor die rande.

In die dood, liewe God,
lei U hand nog ons lot
　　soos in die lewe.
Mog U wil dit begeer,
aan U voete, o Heer,
lê ons die lewe weer neer,
　　eenmaal gegewe.

En in eensame nag
staat die sterre se wag –
　　stil en van verre –
oor die helde se skaar
tot hul ruste vergaar,
onbelas, onbeswaar –
　　veilig gebêre.

F.W. Reitz

Majuba "uitgewist"*

Majuba is nu uitgewis
Gered is Eng'lands glorie!
Ja! als men van niets anders wis
Dan was 't 'n mooie storie.

Wat baat het om *één* slag te win
En tienmaal klop te krijgen
Zoo'n zegepraal beteekent min
Zij moesten 't liefst verzwijgen.

Weet niemand waar *Colenso* staat?
Zal 'k *Maârsfontein* nie roeme?
Mag ik van *Modderspruit* nie praat?
Spionkop zelfs nie noeme?

En *Stormberg* ook en *Tweefontein*
Tweebosch en *Bakenlaagte*?
Zoo menig slagveld, groot en klein,
Waarvan wij hen verjaagde.–

Te *Paardeberg*, met tien teên één
Daar heeft de Brit "gewonnen"
Maar weet niet ieder 't was alleen
Door hulp van zijn kanonnen?

---

* *Oorlogs en andere gedichten.* Potchefstroom: Het Westen, 1910, pp. 62–63.

Cronjé heeft met vierduizend man
Lord Kitchener doen beseffen
Wat of de Boer verrichten kan
Bij een wanhopig treffen.

Zo bij den Brit Majuba-dag
Als "uitgewist" mag gelden
Kan zonder schroom onz' nageslach'
Ook *Paardeberg* vermelden.

Willem Kloos

Generaal Joubert* †

Gelukkig heeft de dood Uwe oogen nog geloken,
    Vóór dien verfoeibren stond dat Gij zoudt moeten zien
Uw stoeren legertros, door 't Britsch geschut gebroken,
    Half liggen op de vlakte en half wanhopig vliên

O, hadt Gij 't ooit beleefd, hoe ware uw bloed gaan koken,
    Hoe haddet Gij gehoond den gelddorst van die liên,
Hoe hadde Uw strenge mond het sterke woord gesproken:
    "Zoolang Ik leef, o, God! zal nooit de schand geschiên,

"Dat de eerlooze Engelschman ons forsche land komt steken
    In 't hart-zelf en zijn hand aan onze hoofdstad slaat,
Want twintigvoud wij steeds op 't Britsch geboefte wreken
    Den fieren krijgsmansdood van elken Boer-soldaat,
En hoeveel burgers ook op 't slagveld reeds bezweken
    Het sterkt ons slechts in kracht van dapperheid en haat!"

29 Maart 1900.

---

* *Verzen* (deel 3), Amsterdam: Versluys, 1913, p. 310.

Totius

Mei 1900*

Toe het ek hierdie pad gegaan,
'n swerwer oor die oseaan,
'n vlugteling uit my vaderland,
en in my hart 'n plek wat brand.

Die grense agter my was dig.
En vóór, wie sou die sluier lig?
Die vriend wat help was ver van my,
gebrek en donkerheid – naby!

Maar God was besig – deur my leed
verdof het ek dit nie geweet –
om uit my lewe in vreemd'lingskap
– die ruwe rots – 'n beeld te kap.

---

* *Versamelde gedigte*. Kaapstad: Tafelberg-Uitgewers, 1988, p. 430.

Henry E. Dosker

(fragment uit 'n langer gedig)*

'k Zie de strijdbanieren wapp'ren. –
    Englands' roode leeuwenvlag,
En de vierkleur der Transvalers –
    boven 't woeden van den slag.
Wie zal 't winnen? Wie zal wijken?
    God des hemels help Transvaal!
Dat de wreede volkendwinger
    toch hun vlag niet nederhaal!

Ziet zij deinzen, weiflen, zwichten
    voor der Boeren moordend vuur.
'k Zie den leeuw al brullend vluchten.
    Albion thans slaat uw uur!
Voorwaarts mannen rept uw handen,
    wreekt de dooden aan uw zij,
Regent kogels, regent bommen
    op het heir der dwinglandij!
't Geldt uw alles, – huis en have,
    't erf waarvoor gij hebt gestreên;
't Geldt uw vrijheid, 't geldt uw volksaard,
    't geldt uw toekomst, uw verleên.
Laat 't verleden u bezielen, –
    Potchefstroom, Pretoria,
Langnekpas, Ingogo's rotsen,
    schimmen van Amajuba!

---

* Manuskrip 532/8 NALN. Fotokopie van 'n knipsel uit 'n nie-genoemde en nie-gedateerde Nederlandse koerant.

Babylon is eens gevallen;
    't Grieksche rijk verkeerde in puin;
Rome is in 't niet verzonken;
    Spanje boog de trotsche kruin!
't Hooge hart zal eenmaal beven.
    Albion uw uur genaakt!
MENE TEKEL staat geschreven,
    waar de hand uw muren raakt.
In het graf, dat gij wilt delven
    voor de vrijheid van Transvaal,
Zinkt uw eigen macht straks neder.
    Want ik hoor der helden taal –
Liever duizend dooden sterven
    voor de vrijheid van het land,
Dan dat ooit de vierkleur zinke,
    neergehaald door Englands hand.

F.W. Reitz

Commandant Danie Theron.*
Gesneuveld op Gatsrand 5 Sept. 1900.

Op den 5den September stierf Danie Theron
Een der dapperste krijgsmannen onder de zon
Zelfs zij, die nooit weenden, die stortten een traan
    Toen zij hoorden dat Danie was heengegaan.

Maar wij droogden die tranen en sprak' slechts één woord
"Wee hem! die onz' Danie Theron heeft vermoord!"
We reden er heen bij nach, en bij dag
    Om de plaats te bereik' waar onz' doode held lag.

Wij vonden zijn graf – en wij zagen hem daar
Ons hoop was verdwenen – helaas het was waar –
Ja! Danie is dood – nooit zien wij hem weêr,
    Maar hij viel als een held op het slagveld van eer.

Wij legden hem weêr in zijn eenzame graf
Wijl elk kameraad zijn getuigenis gaf
Van hoe edel hij was, hoe vriend'lik, hoe trouw,
    Zó woest als een leeuw, zó têer als een vrouw.

De man van onz' keuze, ons Danie is weg
Hij, die ons aanvoerde in menig gevech'
Zal ons nimmermeer leiden – zijn werk is gedaan
    Hij stierf, dat zijn natie mocht blijven bestaan.

---

* *Oorlogs en andere gedichten.* Potchefstroom: Het Westen, 1910, pp. 25–27.

Toen de vijand uittrok ging Danie alleen,
Hij reed te verkennen waar zij wilden heen,
En boven op Gatsrand daar vond hij een wacht
    Van vijf of zes man der vijandlijke macht.

Maar hij, onverschrokken, greep naar zijn geweer,
En schoot dad'lik drie der patrouille daar neer
De anderen vluchtten – zij wisten ook niet
    't Was 'n enkele man – die weêrstand daar biedt.

Nu werd als gewoonlijk kanonvuur gelost,
Maar die eenzame man stond pal op zijn post,
De derde bom trof hem – noodlottige feit
    Ons held had gestreden zijn uiterste strijd.

Als de vijand gewaard' dat niemand meer schoot
Toen reed hij daarheen en vond Danie dood,
Verbaasd om te zien – wat één man had gewaagd,
    Die hun heele patrouille alleen had verjaagd.

Daar ligt hij begraven – maar niet alleen hij
Want de drie die hij doodde, die liggen daarbij;
'n Man zóals Danie, komt zelden maar voor,
    Al zocht men geheel ook de wereld hem door.

Een vijand beslist en gezworen was hij
Van kapitalistische dwingelandij,
Zijn volk had hij lief, en ging met hen mee,
    Door alle gevaren in oorlog en vrêe.

Toen dié schurk Monypenny in zijn vuil Jingo blad,
De vrouwen der Boeren belasterd had
Had hij groote berouw, en dat gauw genoeg
    Toen Theron hem de bril van zijn ogen sloeg.

En ook op het slagveld, heeft Danie getoond,
Dat vaderlandsliefde nog steeds in hem woond'
Wij weten het goed – want ons heeft hij geleid
    Hij was vooraan den spits in iederen strijd.

Hij wist ook zeer goed – dat het Jingose plan
Was ons land aftevatten – als hij het maar kan,
Transvaal houdt zijn naam en gedacht'nis in eer,
    Want dapperder man ziet gij nimmer ook weer.

Rhenosterkop, 10-2-1902.

Digter onbekend

In exile*

Farewell our own dear native Land
Oh, Fare thee well
We leave your shores a mournful band
And rythmic beat of sea on strand
Alone can tell,
The yearning breaking of each heart.
In that dread hour when we must part
Who love thee well
Our misty eyes are strained on every hill
And glade of green
And though they fade we feel the thrill
Of murmering in each rippling rill
Till anguish keen
Will once again a fresh hold take
The dear dead voices of the veld awake
The might have been.

---

* *Diyatalawa Dum-Dum*, vol. 1, nr. 1, 10 September 1900. Die *Diyatalawa Dum-Dum* was 'n kamptydskriffie van die Diyatalawakamp op Ceylon wat met die hand in Engels en Nederlands geskryf en uitgegee is. Die laaste strofe van die gedig is onduidelik.

Van Kerckhoven-Donnez

Groet aan Paul Kruger*

Ik groet U, diep in 't hart bewogen,
O! eed'le grijsaard hoog geacht;
Uw helder hoofd in rouw gebogen,
Glanst als het starlicht, in den nacht
Zoo zwart van 't heiligst rechtverbreken,
Van woest geweld voor winstbejag,
Van euveldaad en schurkenstreken,
Bedreven onder Britsche vlag!

Gij staat daar als een' heil'ge bake
Onwrikbaar in de bloed'ge zee,
Waar and'ren naar veroorv'ring haken,
Vraagt gij slechts vrijheid, rust en vrée.
Gij hebt Uw hart, Uw ziel, Uw sterven
Gewijd aan Volk en Vaderland,
Aan 't land waar zooveel helden sneven
Door rooversbenden overmand.

Gij hebt zoovele vrome borsten
Doorboord met 't moordend staal en lood
Die eigen erf verdeed'gen dorsten
Zien sluim'ren, in den heldendood! …
Gij zaagt uw weeld'rige akkerlanden
Vertrapt, vernield, gedrenkt met bloed! …
In 't zweet gebouwde hoeven branden
Der dapp're boeren trouw en goed! …

---

* In: *Gedenknummer Antwerpen-Transvaal.* Antwerpen, 1902. Die voornaam
van die digter word nie vermeld nie.

Gij zaagt de vrouwen prijsgeven
En kind'ren, grijsaards, ongehoord
Als wilde dieren voortgedreven
Uit hun geliefd geboorte-oord.
Het oord der fiere vrije zonen
Gesloopt, geslecht, door vreemde hand.
Betaald met keizerlijke kronen
Omdat er goud was in Uw land.

En afgesloofd en moé geleden,
Het hart gewond door ramp en wee,
Hebt Gij voor 't dierbaar land gebeden,
Uw blik gewend naar overzee.
Vol hope nog, weemoedig tevens,
Trotseerdet Gij den Oceaan,
(Een bange tocht op 't eind des levens)
Voor vrijheid en voor volksbestaan.

En thans wordt Gij in zegetochten
Door gansch Europa toegejuicht,
(Lijk vorsten nooit genieten mochten)
Omdat Gij voor geen onrecht buigt.
Nu, klinkt het uit millioenen monden:
"Europa! Sluimer langer niet."
"Sta op! voor 't recht zoo snood geschonden"
"Het is uw plicht, het volk gebiedt!"

Dit blijv' Uw hoop na zoveel rampen,
Na zooveel lijden onverdiend,
Waarin uw heldenvolk blijft kampen
Voor 't land door eigen hand ontgind.
Gegroet, O! Kruger hoofd dier dapp'ren,
Eens late God, ten zegepraal,
Voor immer in een vijfkleur wapp'ren:
Oranje-Vrijstaat en Transvaal! …

Antwerpen, Xber 1900.

P.C. Boutens

Aan S.J.P. Kruger*

I

Waar felle schaduw tiert noch zonneschijn,
In Westerland, dat door zijn wolkgeloken
Vensteren 't daglicht kleureloos gebroken
    Voelt schrijnen, artsenij-verdoofde pijn;

    Hier waar moê slaven in hun schemermijn
Geruischloos over 't vreugdloos werk gedoken
Leven en sterven en de onuitgesproken
    Waarheid meêneme' in 't eeuwiglijk-stilzijn, –

Hoe staat hier plotseling de scherpgekante
Toren van uw slagschaduw, Groote Grijze,
Eenig massief in 't neevlig-transparante? …

    Is het dan waar, wat geen gelooven kon,
Dat nog menschschoudren boven wolken rijzen,
    Menschoogen opzien in Gods simple zon?

II

Hoort, tonen zwaar uit klokkenmonde
Klinken zich vol tot woorden samen:
Oude, metaalheldere namen,
Dingen die wij niet meer verstonden;

---

* *Stemmen*. Amsterdam: Van Kampen, 1920, pp. 100–101.

Klankklaar en maatvast saamgebonden
Al de bloedwarme, felle, eenzame
Hartkreten die verdwalen kwamen:
Werelds oud volkslied weêrgevonden …

     Omniet? – De wind heeft ze gehoord
En joelt ze door de winternachten.
     En echo leert ze woord voor woord
Aan klankbodem van stilste schachten.
       Zij gaan voortaan van reê tot reê
       Op golfmuziek van eeuwge zee.

Hubertino

Aan Kruger en zijn Helden (fragment)[*]

Hulde, hulde, driemaal hulde,
Hulde voor het dapperst bloed,
Dat de wereld gansch vervulde
Met de wond'ren van zijn moed!

Eer U, volk, dat men vermomde
Tot barbaren, woest en wild;
Maar dat vorst en volk verstomde
Door den adel van zijn schild.

Eer u, Helden en Heldinnnen,
Groot in waarheid, niet in schijn,
Waar de dochteren leeuwinnen,
Waar de knapen leeuwen zijn!

Eer u, ridderlijke scharen!
O! bij uwer helden roem
Zijn de Kitcheners barbaren,
Die ik slechts met afschuw noem.

Eng'land kan uw faam niet schenden,
Want, op ridderlijk gebied,
Reiken al zijn rakkersbenden
Nog tot aan uw enkels niet!

't Graf uit thans, verwentelde eeuwen,
Met uw glorie, met uw eer;
Legt hier voor dit ras van leeuwen
Al uw roem en luister neer!

---

* Antwerpen: Ernest Sele, 1902, pp. 34–36.

Alles zal uw glorie melden,
Eerafdwingend, edel diet:
Volk van Ridders en van Helden
Tegenover een bandiet!

J. Groneman

Boerenoorlog (fragment)[*]

    Helden van heldenstam,
Sterk door de kracht van 't Geloof,
Sterk door de macht van het Recht,
Sterk door een eerlijken wil,
Die van geen wijken weet
En niet weifelen kàn!
    Zie, wij eeren uw moed,
Wij bewondren uw kracht
En wij lijden mèt u.
Zonen van *onze* vaadren!
    O, ga voort op uw weg,
Recht af op 't heilige doel:
Vrijheid op eigen grond,
Vrijheid na slavernij,
Vrijheid van zeden en taal,
Vrijheid voor vrouw en kind! …
    Ga, zonder aarzelend omzien,
Ga, maar om 't *leven* te winnen,
Ga den *dood* tegemoet.
Ga, en *geloof* aan den zege,
Want uw geloof is uw macht!

(…)

---

[*] 's-Gravenhage: Gebrs. J. & H. van Langenhuysen, 1900, p. 5.

Helden van heldenstam!
Helden van 't Geuzengeslacht!
Levend en stervend voor alles
Wat ook *ons* lief is, voor vrijheid,
Vaderland, taal en geloof.
    Helden van *onzen* stam –
Spreke ook uw naam soms van ander
Bloed, maar aan 't onze verwant –
Broeders! volhardt tot het einde,
Vast verzekerd dat *wij*,
Indiërs, omdat we leven
Ver van 't Vaderland,
Maar door geboorte of afkomst
Hollandsche geuzen als *gij*,
Mèt u leven en hopen,
Mèt u lijden en rouwen,
Maar mèt u jublen en juichen
Telkens als weer een zege
Zeegnend uw worsteling steunt.

(PLECHTICH)

    Mogen *wij*, als ook
Onze beurt eens komt,
En dezelfde vijand
Met een vloot van vlugge
Sterke pantserkruisers,
– Die *u* niet konden schaden –
Java op komt eischen,
Voor *ons* recht, als *gij*
Durven kampen of sterven! …

(Jogjakarta, 20 December 1899)

Albert Verwey

Lof van Botha*

Wat is bewondring die de dooden eert
En van de levenden niet weet? Ik prijs
Het liefst den held zoolang hij leeft. Zijn daad
Blinkt schooner nu dan door een nacht van tijd.

Zoo prijs ik Botha. Bij Colenso won
Den dag hij tegen een tienvoudig heir.
Spioenkop zag hem die ten aanval wees,
De Toegela toen 't allerlaatst hij stond.

Bij Dalmanutha klonk zijn stem. Den dood
Van u o helden zag zijn oog niet droog –
Veertig die vielen daar 't kanonschroot borst –
Talrijker dappren redde 't leven hij.

Vrouw die hij zond, uw Ridder loven wij.
Wij leven in een laffen lagen tijd.
Helden die heerlijk leven loven wij.
Reinige ook ons, o lieve Vrouw, zijn Daad.

---

* *Verzamelde gedichten*. Tweede deel. Amsterdam: Versluys, 1912, pp. 211–212.

F.W. Reitz

De "Lady Roberts"*

Hier staat de "Lady Roberts"**
Hoera! voor Ben Viljoen,
Hoera! voor Generaal Muller.
Want hulle het dit gedoen.

Die Trekboer en Boslanser***
Die kom haar hier beskouw,
Dan zeg hulle "alle wereld!"
Waar krij jul hier die vrouw?

Dan zeg ons "die ou Lady"
Is 'n Nieuwejaars present
Wat Ben Viljoen gestuur het
Aan onze President.

Dan wordt di trekboer wakker
En trek weer met zij goed,
En di arme ou Boslanser
Di krij weer nieuwe moed.

Lord Roberts is al huis toe
Die Veldheer het getrap
Maar d' ou vrouw het hij hier laat blij,
Sij hou van "Mieliepap".

---

* *Oorlogs en andere gedichten*. Potchefstroom: Het Westen, 1910, pp. 2–4. Die
oorspronklike manuskrip 5000/1330 is in die Oorlogsmuseum van die Boererepublieke, Bloemfontein. Oor hierdie gedig en die musikale bewerking daarvan,
sien: P.W. Grobbelaar, *Kommandeer! Kommandeer! Volksang uit die Anglo-
Boereoorlog*, Pretoria: J.P.van der Walt, 1999, p. 119.
** Skeepskanon wat die Engelse gebruik het teen die Boere. Dit is in Desember
1900 deur genl. Ben Viljoen en sy manne onderskep.
*** Mense wat nie aan die stryd deelneem nie.

Van ons arme families
Brant hij di huise af,
Di mans kan hij nie win nie,
Dus moet hij vrouwens straf.

Maar s'n "ou Lady Roberts"
Di lyddiet uit kan stort,
Di stuur hij naar Helvetia
En zet haar in 'n fort.

Daar, dacht hij, is sij veilig
Want die "verditste" Boer
Leg net maar achter klippers
Met zij "verdatste" roer.

Hoera! voor di Boksburgers,
Hoera! voor di Polies,
Hoera! ook voor Johannesburg,
En Kitchener is nou vies.

Eer dat hul weer kon natgooi*
Het Boksburg al "verjaar"**
Eer hij zij broek kon aankrij
Toe was die ding al klaar.

Hul vat sij ammunitie
En sij kannonne af
Vang honderde soldate
En trap ver Tommy kaf.

---

* Natgooi: skiet.
** Verjaar: gewen.

Dis maar "Gorilla" oorlog
Zeg Meester Chamberlain;
Maar als dit lang zoo voortgaat
Dan maal ons Tommy fijn.

Lord Roberts van Kandahar,
Lord Kitchener van Karthoem,
Lord Buller van Colenso
Die wordt só hoog geroem.

Voor wat? Die arme Kaffer
Met schild en assegaai,
Het hulle met Bom-maxim
Zoo prachtig afgemaai.

Maar nou dat hul teên mausers
En witmense moet veg
Leg Kitchener op Pretoria
En die ander twee is weg.

Ja, Roberts van *"Kandaar"*
Is nie Roberts van *"Kanhier"*,
En dat Tommy hier moet blijwe
Is nie enkel voor plesier.

Hij het die land oorwonne
En alles annexeer,
Maar ons dappere Generale
Verslaan hom keer op keer.

Hou vol dan Afrikaners
Di vijand moet hier weg.
Hij mag ons nie overwin nie
Want onze zaak is *reg*.

Tautesberg, Januari 1901

R. Drost

Onze Vader*

Onze Vader in den Hoogen,
Sla toch Uw ontfermende oogen
Op de Boeren in hun jammer.
Help ze Vader in hun strijden,
Die voor hunne Vrijheid lijden.

Als Gij helpt, Almachtig Vader,
Kan geen vijand ze verplettern!
Red de kinderen; troost de vrouwen,
Die op Uwen arm vertrouwen.

God Almachtig, Heer der Heeren,
Wil toch Englands moordlust keeren.
Gij zijt machtig! Gij kunt helpen!
Help de Boeren, die gelooven:
Onze Vader woont daarboven.

---

* *Gedenknummer Antwerpen-Transvaal 1900.*

G.F. Dannhauser

'n Dappere Generaal.*
Ter ere fan De Villebois.

Hiir rys di flag der fryhyd in
    Suid Afrika so skoon
En dapper feg 'n klyne folk
    Fer fryhyds erekroon.

Europa geef di Boere geld
    En medelyde wel,
Dog almal bly fêr uit di fuur,
    En sorg mar fer hul fel.

Mar Villebois staan op en roep
    Tot Frankryk luid en klaar:
o Seuns fan so 'n frye land!
    'n Folk staan in gefaar!

'n Klyne, mar 'n dappre folk
    Feg an di suide kus;
Sal ons hul daar so laat fertrap
    En stil sit hiir gerus?!! …

Mar Eng'land was 'n sterke ryk,
    En Frankryk roer sig niit;
De Villebois alleen ruk fort
    Na Afrika's gebiid.

---

* *Ons Klyntji*, Junie 1903, p. 66. Daar is 'n amper identiese gedig van Charles Kestell (die seun van ds. J.D. Kestell wat tydens die Boereoorlog gesneuwel het) in die Oorlogsmuseum in Bloemfontein. Kestell se teks oor De Villebois is in Nederlands geskryf. Dit is onmoontlik om te sê wie die oorspronklike digter is.

En hy feg dapper fer ons land,
 Hy help ons met syn raad;
Ja, geef syn lewe selfs fer ons –
 Ferwaar, 'n heldedaad.

Jou heldemoed, o Villebois,
 Het ons in stryd ge'eer;
Mar by jou heldegraf gekniil,
 Fereer ons jou feul meer.

Di graf sal immer hiir getuig:
 "Hy stiirf gelyk 'n held!
Fer onse fryhyd en ons folk
 Rus hy hiir in ons feld."

Adama van Scheltema

Het Hollandsch hart vergeet zijn Broeders niet*

Hebt gij 't gehoord, hoe onze broeders lijden,
Het Zonental door Neerland steeds beheerd,
Dat Britsch geweld, sterk door den nood der tijden,
Ons met de Kaap als heeft van 't hart gescheurd?
Maar 't Boerenras boog nooit zijn nek als slaven,
Daar 't eer zijn grond dan d' vrijheidsvaan verliet,
En 't Hollandsch hart, trotsch op de wakk're braven,
Vergeet, verlaat in nood zijn broeders niet.

Gehoond, geplaagd, door haat en list besprongen,
Vervreemdde 't hart der Boeren van hun grond,
Doch weken ze ook, steeds meer terug gedrongen,
Tot waar, naar 't scheen, hun vrijheid ruste vond;
Vergeefs, geen stroom, geen bergpas maakten veilig
De heldenschaar door 's Luipaards oog bespied;
Maar was geen woord van eer den Brit ooit heilig,
Ons Hollandsch hart vergeet zijn broeders niet.

Kan onze macht, geknot in bange dagen,
Door Frankrijks zwaard en Englands vriendschapsschijn,
Geen schild hun biên voor valschheidslist en lagen,
Toch kunnen wij den broedren broeders zijn.
Laat broedertrouw in woord en offer spreken,
Voor vrijheid staan en pleiten daad en lied,
Zoo spreke ons hart der broederen hart ten teeken,
Oud-Nederland vergeet zijn kindren niet.

---

* In: M. Molenaar. *Transvaal gedichten. Een lauwerkrans den Boeren gevlochten.* Sneek: De Boer, 1902, pp. 80–81.

Digter onbekend

Engeland en Transvaal*

Engelsman, jou Volks Verleijer,
Het jij al vergeet ver Dreijer:
Ik zal denk hoe oud ik word,
Aan zijn bloed door jou gestort.

Engelsman, jou regt verdraaijer,
Vrijheidsmoorder, land verraijer.
Wij denken nog aan Slachters Nek,
Met ons broeders bloed bevlekt.

Engelsman, vraagt jou geweten,
Het jij al Natal vergeten,
Tranen en bloed legt daar gestort,
Die nooit weer vergeten word.

Engelsman jou wet vertreder,
Meet jou grond maar altijd breeder,
Wij denken nog aan Davids graf,
De Diamant Veld naam jij af.

Engelsman, jou vrede vrager,
Lage lafhart, witvlag drager,
Denk toch steeds aan Doornkop,
Waar de Boer jul het geklop.

Engelsman, moet toch niet praten,
Van jou dapper soldaten;
Menig slagveld het jul gevlucht,
Waar jullie nou nog om zucht.

---

* Manuskrip 3635/6, Oorlogsmuseum van die Boererepublieke, Bloemfontein.

Engelsman, Tractaat verbreker,
Denk jij niet daar is 'n wreker.
Voor jullie onrecht aan Transvaal
Zal die Heer jul laat betaal.

Engelsman, jou dag zal naken,
Want er leef een God der Wraken.
In den dag van groot gericht,
Kom jou werken aan het licht.

Albert Verwey

De stam van 't volk*

De stam van 't volk doet nu zijn loten beven
Omdat een twijg herplant in vreemde streek
Gewond beweegt: geheimnisvol geleek
Eén leven nog door stam en twijg te streven.

Verwantschap trilt in 't bloed en luide spreek'
Ze in eendre taal en dring' de hand tot geven;
Want krachtloos zijn we en ons is niets gebleven
Van hulp die steunde en macht die niemand week.

De stam van 't volk doet nu zijn blaadren ruisen
En vreugd voor 't minst is 't ritslen all' tezaam.
Te lang in stilt hing elk voor zich alleen.

Eén bloed is 't al, hier kronklend, daar aan 't bruisen,
Eén taal is de onze en de onze eenzelfde naam –
Eén is ons voelen, zij 't ook in geween.

---

* *Dagen en daden.* In: *Verzamelde gedichten*, p. 144.

P. Hauptfleisch

Englands beschaafd oorlogvoeren met Transvaal*

1
Ons volk is in jammer en rouw gedompeld,
Want de vijand verwoest en verplundert ons land,
Zelfs weerlooze vrouwen en hulp'looze kind'ren
Worden schaamt'loos bezoedeld en onteerd door zijn hand.

2
De vijand berooft hen van voedsel en kleeding
Het bed wordt hen onder den lijve ontrukt
Geen bidden, geen pleiten, geen smeekstem mocht baten
Ze gaan voortgejaagd, weenend, mishandeld, bedrukt.

3
Daar ligt er een moeder met een zuigling in de armen,
Die slechts eenige dagen het levenslicht zag
Doch met verdierlijkt gevoel wordt de moeder met zuigling
Door den woestaard verjaagd van het bed waar zij lag.

4
Een zestal van Albions beschaafde soldaten
Grijpt een vluchtende vrouw die van angst sich versteekt
Zij staan om haar henen en beurtlings pleegt ieder
Een Godtergend schanddaad waar 't harte van breekt.

5
De jeugdige maagd met blozende wangen
En engelen onschuld het sieraad der jeugd
Wordt wreed en geducht door den woestaard gegrepen
Haar onschuld vertrapt hij vergaan is haar vreugd.

---

* Manuskrip 5423/73, Oorlogsmuseum van die Boererepublieke, Bloemfontein.
Identiese teks deur ene J.A. Pienaar in die NALN-argief.

6

Met woeste barbaarschheid, die door niets wordt beteugeld,
Volvoert hij zijn duivelsch onzeedlijk geweld.
Verbrandt en verwoest en verplundert de hoeven
En weerlozen worden tot mikpunt geteld.

7

Noch grijsheid, noch onschuld noch zuigling noch moeder
Zijn bevrijd of verschoond van hun ruige geweld
Zulk' gruw'len! O God, hoe lang zult Gij dulden
Gepleegd door een hebzucht naar goud en naar geld.

8

O Albion, weet het wij zweren u wrake!
En die wrok is door u zelf geplant en gekweekt.
Wij zweren u plechtig een loon naar uw werken
En zeegnen eenstemmig de Hand die ons wreekt.

9

Zelfs de Kaffer roept "Schande" en walgt van u daden,
Hij bestempelt uw doen als "barbaarsch" en "gemeen".
Hoe gij ook al toedekt of tracht te verschoonen
Maar schandvlekt op schandvlekt spookt steeds om u heen.

10

De hand die schreef: "Mene en Mene en Tekel",
Schrijft weldra hetzelfde voor uw Jub'lende schaar! ...
Uw hart zal verstommen! O Albion weet het! ...
Gij kunt God niet bespotten! ... Ongestraft niet ... voorwaar!

11

Spot vrij, dat wij biddend op God blijven wachten,
En betuigen en vasthouden dat Hij regeert,
Uw spot zal met sidd'ring te laat u berouwen
Als een worrem die lustig uw wortel verteert!

12
Uw dag is aanstaande om loon te ontvangen,
De God onzer vaad'ren leeft nog en regeert
Hij hoort het geroep van de hulplooze schare
Wier stem gij versmaadt en met snoodheid onteert.

13
Bedrukten, beproefden, gij weed'wen en weezen
Gij broeder die strijdt met een bloedende hart!
Heft het oog naar omhoog! legt uw zaak in Gods handen!
Hij aanschouwdt uw verdrukking, Hij weet wat uw smart.

14
De dag der vergelding komt langzaam, maar zeker;
Uw zaak is rechtvaardig; en eens komt de tijd,
dat gij zult aanbidden Gods wegen en leiding,
en ruste genieten na bloedigen strijd.

Buiskop, 23 Feb. 1901.

Joubert Reitz

What were your thoughts?*

I

Have you ever been surrounded by the enemy at night,
Who, with bayonets and rifles, to your left and to your right,
Hedge you in and drive you closer, pouring in a hail of lead;
Forcing you to make a breastwork of the dying and the dead!
Have you heard the cannons roaring and the rifles' sharp report,
Have you heard the shrapnel's shrieking and the big gun's lazy snort,
Have you ever been in danger such as here you'll surely find:
What were the things you thought of, what ideas were in your mind?

II

Did you think of home and parents, did you think of child or wife,
Did you entertain the notion that you might have lost your life,
Did the thought come up before you that 'tis now you may be sent
To appear before your Maker where all those others went
Who are lying dead around you, to give answer at the court
Of the great Almighty's Justice for the misdeeds that you wrought;
Did you think that if you ever had the chance to start again,
You would leave the broader roadway and go down the narrow lane?

---

* Uit die ongepubliseerde digbundel "WAR en ander gedigte", 1903, pp. 22–23. Manuskrip 355, NALN, Bloemfontein. Joubert Reitz was die seun van president F.W. Reitz wat self gedig het (*Oorlogs en andere gedichten,* 1910). Die ander broers, Hjalmar en Deneys het ook geskryf. Hjalmar publiseer *De dochter van de Handsopper (1903) en* Deneys is die outeur van die beroemde *Commando* (1929).

III

No! I think, if you'll remember all the things you thought of when
You were fighting like a demon, you will find that your thoughts then,
Were not quite so pure and holy as they should be when you stand
As death's door, which might be opened now for you at God's
command.
Oh, No! you were but as a brute and thought but that to slay
Was your especial mission, be the chances what they may,
You had but become a savage wishing to avenge the blood
Of your dead and dying comrades lying down there in the mud!

Joubert Reitz

Skrapnel*

Skrapnel!
Is Hel!
Dit vluit en dreun,
Gekwestes kreun,
Dit raas, dit klap, dit kletter.
Dit gons, dit sis,
D'is raak, d'is mis!
Wat voorkom is verpletter.
Die bomme huil,
Ons hou ons skuil,
D'is hel!
Skrapnel!

Skrapnel
Is hel!
Hij trek verbij
Ons asem vrij;
Maar lang kan dit nie duur,
Want keer op keer
Dan kom hij weer
En bars in vlam en vuur.
En al wat leef,
Die koes en beef.
D'is hel,
Skrapnel.

---

* Uit die ongepubliseerde digbundel "WAR en ander gedigte", 1903, p. 24.
Manuskrip 355, NALN, Bloemfontein. Sien die voetnota by Joubert Reitz se
gedig "What were your thoughts?" (p. 85).

C. Louis Leipoldt

Aan 'n seepkissie*

Hulle het jou in Eng'land gemaak, seepkissie,
    Om hier in ons land as 'n doodkis te dien;
Hulle het op jou letters geverwe, seepkissie,
    En ek het jou selwe as doodkis gesien.

Klein Jannie van ouboetie Saarl, seepkissie,
    Het hier in die kamp met sy sussie gekom –
En jy was bestem, soos jy weet, seepkissie,
    Daar oorkant in Eng'land tot doodkis vir hom!

Klein Jannie van ouboetie Saarl, seepkissie,
    Was fluks en gesond, vir sy jare nog groot;
Maar hier in die kamp, soos jy weet, seepkissie,
    Was hy maar drie weke, en toe … was hy dood!

Onthou jy vir Jannie? Jy weet, seepkissie,
    Hy het in sy speletjies met jou gespeel;
Die son het sy krulkop geskilder, seepkissie,
    So blink as sy strale, as goud so geel.

Op die Vrydagmôre – onthou jy, kissie –
    Het Tannie gesê: "Ag, klein Jannie die hoes!"
En die Vrydagaand, soos jy weet, seepkissie,
    Was Jannie se lewe al half verwoes.

Hulle het jou op Saterdagmiddag, seepkissie,
    Gedra na sy tent as 'n doodkis daar!
Die wit gesiggie – jy weet, seepkissie,
    Die handjies gevou en gekruis oormekaar.

---

* *Versamelde gedigte.* Kaapstad: Tafelberg-Uitgewers, 1980, p. 30.

Hulle het jou in Eng'land gemaak, seepkissie,
    Om hier vir ons kinders as doodkis te dien;
Hulle het vir jou lykies gevinde, seepkissie,
    En ek het jou selwe as doodkis gesien.

Totius

Kindergraffies*
Men zal zijn bloeisel afwerpen. Job 15:33.

My vaderland 'n boomgaard was
    met keur van vrugtebome,
waarin die voorjaar rustig droom
    sy kleur'ge lentedrome.

Die kindertjies die bloesems is
    met ongespeende vruggies,
waardeur die loue asem speel
    van blye lenteluggies.

En nes die bloesems het hul ook,
    met ogies wonderreine,
hier in die wêreld in rondgekyk –
    die baie, liewe kleine.

Helaas, dat hul te gou, te gou
    die wêreld in gekyk het,
en onverwagte rypnag oor
    hul ogies neergestryk het.

En nou val van die moedertak
    die kleur'ge duisendtalle
tussen die swarte sooie in –
    die liewe bloesems alle.

* *Versamelde gedigte*, Kaapstad: Tafelberg-Uitgewers, 1988, pp. 18–19.

My vaderland die boomgaard is,
    die bloesems is die kleine,
wat in die lydensnag te saam
    die ogies sluit, die reine.

Nou lê hul almal, almal daar,
    die bloesems tussen sooie,
en rus die stille, stille rus
    van liewe kleine dooie.

Die bome staan nog vele daar,
    maar almal sonder vruggies,
en wag met stille, stille hoop
    op nuwe lenteluggies.

C. Louis Leipoldt

'n Nuwe liedjie op 'n ou deuntjie*

Siembamba, Siembamba
Mame se kindjie, Siembamba!
Vou jou handjies same
    En sê ame,
Mame se kindjie, Siembamba!   – LOKASIELIEDJIE

Siembamba, Siembamba,
Mame se kindje, Siembamba!
Vou maar jou handjies saam, my kind:
Hoor tog hoe huil die noordewind!
Hier in die kamp is alles stil,
Net maar die wind waai soos hy wil;
Net maar jy self kan kreun en steun:
Niemand sal hoor nie, niemand, seun!
Almal is besig! Oor die land
Drywe 'n wolk van die noordekant –
Swart soos die rook uit die skoorsteen puil,
Swart soos die nag, en nes roet so vuil:
Vou maar jou handjies dig tesame,
Sluit maar jou ogies, en sê ame!

---

* *Versamelde gedigte*. Kaapstad: Tafelberg-Uitgewers, 1980, p. 22.

Siembamba, Siembamba,
Mame se kindjie, Siembamba!
Jy, wat die hoop van ons nasie is;
Jy, wat ons volk so min kan mis;
Jy, wat moet opgroei tot 'n man;
Jy, wat moet plig doen, as jy kan:
Jy, wat geen deel aan die oorlog het;
Jy, wat moet sing uit pure pret –
Jy moet verkwyn in 'n kinderkamp,
Jy moet vir vrede word uitgestamp:
Vou maar jou handjies dig tesame,
Sluit maar jou ogies, en sê ame!

Siembamba, Siembamba,
Mame se kindjie, Siembamba!
Kinkhoes en tering, sonder melk:
Bitter vir jou is die lewenskelk!
Daar is jou plek, by die graffies daar –
Twee in een kissie, 'n bruilofspaar!
Alles vir ons wat die oorlog hou –
Alles vir ons, en niks vir jou:
Jy het van ons jou plig geërwe –
Plig om as kind vir ons land te sterwe!
Al wat jy wen, is dat ons onthou:
Meer was die vryheid as kind of vrou!
Vou maar jou handjies dig tesame,
Sluit maar jou ogies, en sê – ame!

Digter onbekend

Leun sterk*

Kind, dat Ik liefheb, leun op mij <u>leun sterk</u>.
Laat maar 't gewicht der zorgen, die u kwellen, Mij voelen.
Ja, Ek weet uw last, Mijn werk.
Mijn maakzel zijn die smarten, die u kwellen,
Ek telde ze af, en het met eigen hand,
Die naar uw kracht, en naar mijn hulp gewogen;
Toen Mijne hande ze u oplei, uit den Hogen, sprak Ik.
Ik zal als schepper bij u zijn,
Naar mate gij Mij deel geeft in uw pijn, zal <u>Ek</u> niet gij
het wicht uws kruises dragen, en zal Ik u, Mijn kind,
Gelijk Ik heb beloofd, omringen met Mijn gunst.
O leg uw hoofd aan Mijne borst, gij moogt stout moedig vragen
Of zou Mijn kracht, die eeuwig schiep en draagt,
te kort zijn, waar Mijn uitverkoorne klaagt?
Leun sterker steeds, hoe meer gij aan Mijn skoot,
De smart betrouwt van uwe sorg en nood,
Hoe meer u hart nog binnen u zal roemen;
Ik mag leunen op mijn God, en Hem mijn vader noemen.

---

* Manuskrip 5784/16, Oorlogsmuseum van die Boererepublieke, Bloemfontein.

C. Louis Leipoldt

In die konsentrasiekamp*
(Aliwal-Noord, 1901)

O, pazienza, pazienza che tanto sostieni!
(DANTE)

Jou oë is nat met die trane van gister;
    Jou siel is gemartel, deur smarte gepla;
Van vrede en pret was jy vroeër 'n verkwister;
    En nou, wat bly oor van jou rykdomme? Ja,
'n Spreekwoord tot steun – daar's geen trooswoord beslister:
    "Geduld, o geduld, wat so baie kan dra!"

Hier sit jy en koes teen die wind wat daar suie
    Yskoud deur die tentseil, geskeur deur die hael –
Jou enigste skuil in die nag teen die buie;
    Die Junie-lug stort oor die stroom van die Vaal –
Jy hoor net die hoes van jou kind, en die luie
    Gedrup van die reëndruppeltjies oor die paal.

'n Kers, nog maar anderhalf duim voor hy sterwe,
    Brand dof in 'n bottel hier vlak naas jou bed.
('n Kafhuis gee makliker rus: op die gerwe
    Daar lê 'n mens sag, en sy slaap is gered!) –
En hier in die nag laat jou drome jou swerwe
    'n Aaklige rondte met trane besmet.

---

* *Versamelde gedigte.* Kaapstad: Tafelberg-Uitgewers, 1980, pp. 24–25.

Hier struikel die kind wat te vroeg was gebore;
    Hier sterwe die oumens te swak vir die stryd;
Hier kom 'n gekerm en gekreun in jou ore;
    Hier tel jy met angs elke tik van die tyd;
Want elke sekond' van die smart laat sy spore
    Gedruk op jou hart, deur 'n offer gewyd.

En deur elke skeur in die seil kan jy duister
    Die wolke bespeur oor die hemel verbrei;
Geen ster skyn as gids; na geen stem kan jy luister
    (Eentonig die hoes van jou kind aan jou sy!)
Wat sag deur die wind in jou ore kom fluister:
    "Geduld, o geduld, wat so baie kan ly!"

Vergewe? Vergewe? Is dit maklik vergewe?
    Die smarte, die angs het so baie gepla!
Die yster het gloeiend 'n merk vir die eeue
    Gebrand op ons volk; en dié wond is te ná –
Te ná aan ons hart, en te diep in ons lewe –
    "Geduld, o geduld, wat so baie kan dra!"

J.A. Lombard

My Moeder*
(En die Here self sal alle trane van hulle oë afvee)

In die Konsentrasiekamp Bloemfontein

Dis tente, tente, waar jy kyk
In die Konsentrasiekamp,
Wat strek oor wye vlakte heen
In rye, rye lank.
Ons het veilig op ons plaas gewoon
Toe die Kakies ons kom vang,
Die huis afbrand, die vee wegvoer;
Ons kleinspan was só bang.
Hulle laai ons op 'n ossewa
Na Bloemfontein se Kamp,
Waar ellende, dood en honger heers
Vir vrou en kind, 'n ramp.

Ek sien nog hoe ons elke aand
By moedersknie kom staan;
Die handjies vou, gebed opsê
Dan saggies bed toe gaan:
    "Ik ben 'n kindjie klein en teer
    Dat weinig krag bezit,
    Ik wou zo graag gelukkig zyn,
    Maar ach hoe word ik dit?
    Ach lieve Jezus, zie my aan,
    En onderwyst my dan;
    Hoe dat ik van myn zonden vry,
    En zalig worden kan."

---

* Manuskrip 4923/3, Oorlogsmuseum van die Boererepublieke, Bloemfontein.

Ek sien nog hoe sy by die kers
Elke aand 'n stukkie lees;
Dan bid sy hard vir almal saam;
Met God ken sy geen vrees.
    "Behoed ons mans op oorlogsveld,
    Hou oor ons kroos U hand;
    Bring hul, daar ver oorsee weer trug
    Na hulle vaderland.
    Beskerm, O Heer, ons Land en Volk,
    Ons vryheid en ons Vlag;
    Gee stryders wat getrou kan bly;
    Gee moed en lewenskrag."

Ek sien nog hoe sy dikwels gaan
Na die dam ver buite die kamp;
Om daar die wasgoed te gaan was,
'n Haas uitgebluste lamp.
Solank as sy die wasgoed was
Het ons daar rond gespeel;
Tot eendag dat sy nie kon gaan
Die koors was haar te veel.
Die liggaam kon geen weerstand
Bied, deur lyding afgemat;
'n Moeder met 'n kroos van vyf
Wie ken haar liefde en smart?

Ek sien nog hoe hul om haar staan
Bekendes kom haar troos;
Dan draai sy na my broer en sê,
    "Beloof, versorg my kroos.
    Hul vader is daar ver oorsee,
    Kyk jy na hul belang.
    Kom, laat ons nog vir laas saam sing
    Die dierb're ou gesang:
    Sla 't oog, myn ziel! op 't ander leven,
    U toegewezen erfenis
    Waar gy, met heerlikheid omgeven,
    God eeuwig ziet gelijk Hy is."

Ek sien ons in die doode-tent,
Vyf kindertjies so klein;
En tussen ons 'n blom gepluk
Die skoonste in Godstuin.
Loop sag die grond is heilig hier,
Geheilig deur Gods hand.
'n Moeder lê haar offer neer
Vir Volk en Vaderland.
Slaap rustig edele moeder,
Na al u smart en wee;
In die huis van God, u Vader,
Word u trane afgevee.

Jan F. E. Celliers

Die Kampsuster*

Suster Anna, ek voel dis die dood wat kom:
slaat ope die tentdoek, na buitekant om,
dat my oë vry oor die bulte gaan. –
Suster Anna, ek hoor 'n kerkklok slaan.

Ek hoor hoe die kindertjies roep vir my;
van ons klompie moes ek nog die laaste bly.
Kom neem tog my hand, soos jy dikwels doet –
ag, altyd was suster vir ons so goed.

My man hy lê ver langs Toegéla-stroom af,
en niemand weet waar of hy rus in sy graf;
ag, suster, en neem nou die Heer nog vir my,
dan is Pieter allenig nog owergebly.

Ek weet hy bly staan met sy roer in sy hand –
ja, trou tot die dood, vir sy volk en sy land;
en mog dit so wees dat die Heer hom behoed,
so bring hom tog, suster, sy moeder haar groet,

en sê vir hom, selfs op die donkere rand**
het jy vrese nog bewing gevoel aan haar hand;
en dit was haar troos, dat haar Pieter sal hou
aan sy God en sy land, aan sy ere en trou.

---

* *Die Vlakte en ander gedigte*. Kaapstad: Nasionale Pers, 1941, p. 78.
** Die rand van die graf.

Die kindertjies, Breggie en Japie en Faan,
het suster die een ná die ander sien gaan;
en jy sê daar's 'n plekkie vir my nog gebly,
waar moeder kan rus aan klein Fanie se sy.

Die ou huis se murasie staat swart en ontbloot,
waar almal so saam was om moeder haar skoot;
maar ver van die huis en verstrooi deur die land,
rus almal tog saam in die Here se hand.

Oor die velde kruip saggies die awend se grou;
maar, suster, ek sien nog die hemel se blou. –
Daar rol 'n gedreun oor die bulte aan –
suster Anna, ek hoor 'n kerkklok slaan …

Totius

In die kamp*
Als zich hun ziel uitschudt in de schoot hunner moeders.
Klaagl. 2:12.

Kind:
My moeder, my moeder, ek het tog so honger;
Kom gee my tog gou-gou 'n klein stukkie brood!

Moeder:
My kindjie, jou moeder die weet jy het honger,
maar kom eers en rus op moeder se skoot.

Kind:
My moeder, ag, help my, ek kan nie meer loop nie,
ek voel tog so moeg al; my honger is groot.

Moeder:
My kindjie, jou moeder die weet dat jy moeg is,
maar slaap bring versterking op moeder se skoot.

Kind:
Maar, moeder, hoe huil jy en snik so baie?
En waarom is moeder se oë so rood.

Moeder:
My kind, dit is trane wat jy nie verstaan nie;
kom, slaap net 'n bietjie op moeder se skoot.

Kind:
My moeder, ek kan nie, ek het tog so honger,
gee eers aan jou kindjie 'n klein stukkie brood.

* *Versamelde gedigte*, Kaapstad: Tafelberg-Uitgewers, 1988, pp. 15–16.

Moeder:
Nee, kom maar my liefling, rus eers in my arme,
en as jy ontwaak, help die Heer uit die nood.

Kind:
Ek kan nie meer wag nie van honger, my moeder;
maar waarom tog so? Het die Heer ons verstoot?

Moeder:
Nee, liefste, verstoot sal die Vader ons nimmer,
maar hier in die tent is geen krummeltjie brood.

Kind:
Geen brood nie, my moeder, ek kan nie meer hou nie.
Moet ek dan verhonger op moeder se skoot?

Moeder:
Nee, kindlief, die son is al amper weer onder,
en is dit weer awend, dan kry ons weer brood.

*

Haar kindjie slaap in by die soete gedagte:
    as ek weer ontwaak help die Heer uit die nood.
Die moeder ontvang met vermagerde hande
    Haar deeltjie oplaas – maar die kindjie was dood.

Hester Jacoba Strauss

Als de wereld mijn laatste vaarwel heef gehoord*

Als de wereld mijn laatste vaarwel heef gehoord,
    En blyde ik zal gaan naar myn rust,
Als fluisterend men spreken, en zeg zy is dood,
    In den Hemel ik zie van naby,
O! zullen er zyn aan de poorten van goud,
    Die wachten verlangend naar my.
Daar wachten verlangen; verlangend daar wachten
    Die wachten verlangend naar my.

                  H.S. 21-11-1901
                  Bethulie camp

---

* Ongenommerde manuskrip, Oorlogsmuseum van die Boererepublieke, Bloemfontein. Die volgende nota is deur H.J. Strauss op die manuskrip getik: "Hier onder die 'gediggie' van my Moeder in Bethuliekamp die dag nadat haar seuntjie Michiel van Brede Strauss (26 Maart 1899 – 20 November 1901) in die kamp oorlede is."

Een krijgsgevangene

In de gevangenis[*]

Om in gevangnis te verkeer,
Is geen gemaklijk zaak,
En wil jul mij strak nie geloof ,
Zal ik dit duidlijk maak.

Die ergste van die ongemak
Wat ons lij in die Kaap,
Is dat een mensch bij dag of nach
Geen uur kan lekker slaap.

Dit raas en gons die heele dag
En nach door in jou kop;
Zul zing en skree en gaat te keer,
En niemand durf hul stop.

Half acht begin die klaaggezang
Van sentries op de wacht,
Hul zing en skree zoo na makaar
Die heele lieve nacht.

Half een begin de kokken reeds
Hun ketels uit te spoel,
En twee uur is er in het kamp
Alreeds een groot gewoel.

Niet slechts van kokken maar soms ook
Van menig jonge man,
Wiens heupbeen op die harde plank
Toch niet meer houden kan.

---

[*] Verzen uit het gevangenkamp te Groenepunt (deel 4). *De Gids*, 65, 3, 1901,
pp. 93–98.

Om nachten aldus door te breng,
Kan ieder wel verstaan,
Is voor een mensch erg ongezond,
En tast jou leelijk aan.

Soms voel een mensch z'n kop zoo groot
Als heel ons aardbol is,
Jou maag voel naar, jou rug voel lam,
In 't kort jij voel niet frisch.

Jij vraag en krijg van alle kant
Gewillig goede raad,
Maar wat jij ook gebruik of doet,
Daar 's nie wat jou wil baat.

Jij hol nou naar die dokter toe
Om bij hem hulp te zoek;
"Ou Bietje Beter" is zijn naam,
Die vent kan leelijk vloek.

Hij sèh dan net, haal uit jou tong,
En gee jou dan een drank,
Daaruit een emmer vol geschep,
Voor maagpijn, blind en mank.

Aldus gedokterd moet jij gauw
Mijnheers vertrek verlaat,
Al peinzend of die drankie jou
Nou wel zal schaad of baat.

Ons dokter is een mooie man,
Net effentjes vol sproeten,
Ook niet te veel, net van zijn kop
Tot onder aan zijn voeten.

Sproeten is voor mij niet leelijk
Ik zie het zelden raak,
Dit lijk maar net soos plekkies
Door vliegen daar gemaak.

Maar voor ik strak mijn mond verbrand,
Door dokter uit te leg,
Soos dit eigentlijk moet wees,
Zal ik liefs niet meer zeg.

Ik zal jul van gevangenis
En wat er meer voorval,
Maar liever beetje meer vertel,
Als jul nog luistren zal.

Al morgens net om half ach uur
Dit is mos Jiems zijn wet,
Al voel jij nog zoo ziek en naar,
Dan blaas daar een trompet.

Dan moet jij alles maar laat vaar,
Ofschoon dit jou erg kwel,
Er kom een heele zwetterjoel
Van Khaki's om te tel.

De Boeren word dan aangekeer
Soos ganse naar een hok,
Hul slaat jou wrintig niemand o'er,
Ook zelfs niet eens ons kok.

Dan word die Boeren ingespan,
Zoo twaalf twaalf voor 'n tent
En kom 'n Khaki met 'n boek
Ons allen reeds bekend.

Kort bij hem stap die beugelaar,
En ook nog een lakei,
Gekleed in Khaki net en glad,
Met sabel in zijn zij.

Zoo stap zul dan van tent tot tent
Om ieder Boer te tel,
En is die spul dan afgeloop,
Dan is het weer "All's well".

Die Boeren zaai dan uit elkaâr
Naar ieder kant en oord
Een ieder zet zijn bezigheid
Naar hartelus weêr voort.

Om elf uur blaas daar weêr 'n beul,
Als teeken dat hul nou
In bijzijn van ons kommandant
Kom kampinspectie hou.

Ons dokter en die kolonel,
En nog een heele boel
Ziet jij dan net, hier in daar uit,
Die heele kamp deur woel.

Die Boere moet dan retireer
En net die Korporaal
Staat in genoemd capaciteit
Voor z'n tentdeur als 'n paal.

En krij hul soms bij ongeluk
Daar in die rij 'n tent
Die zich daar zonder korporaal,
En gansch alleen bevind,

Dan moet jij zien hoe dapper hul,
Nou met die tent daar veg,
Hul hou zoo wrintig maar nie op
Voor dat hij onder leg.

En het hul dan die slag gewin,
En tent dit geverloor,
Dan is die heele stoeierij met
Die arme tent weêr o'er.

Hul bezoek dan kook en waschplaatsen,
En ook die andere plek,
Dan is inspectie afgeloop,
En stap zul door die hek.

De potte word dan aangebreng,
Daar van die kookplek af,
Een ieder doet dan trouw zijn plicht,
En loop die pot gauw "kaf".

Zoo gaat dit maar die heele week,
Er 's geen verwisseling
En mensch die hou mos in die reel,
Soms van verandering.

Ons staan dan Zondag bij die draad
Om beetje uit te kijk,
Maar 't duur niet lang of ons is zóó kwaad
Dat ons zoomaar kan bezwijk.

Daar's Klierkop, Kortoor, Hottentots,
Gemix met Mosambiek,
Daar's Streepkop, Grikwa, Engelsman,
'N gansche Jingokliek.

Hul skree dan: "Boer, waar is jou pas?
"Wat kijk jij soo ver mij?
"Waar 's nou die groot sjambok van jou?"
En vloek ons soms daarbij.

Dan zwel ons puur van gramschap op,
Want wie kan zooiets staan?
Maar ons moet die Satans maar laat loop
Deur ons nie uit mag gaan.

Maar als hul ons toch een dag weêr,
Mag stel op vrije been,
Dan hoor men in die gansche Kaap,
Geslaan, gekerm, geween.

Dus vrienden staan maar goed jul man,
En hou een rukkie uit:
Ik wil jul nog net een ding sèh,
En dan mijn rijmpie sluit.

Dit is wel zwaar om zooveel smaad
En ongemak te lij,
Maar binnen kort gaan ons na huis,
En zijn dan altoos vrij.

Maar laat ons toch die Jingokliek,
Voor hoon ons aangedaan,
Die dag net gauw eers allen vang,
En vreeslik stukkend slaan.

Dirks*

Die Kok!

I

Die zwaarste werk, wat daar bestaan
Voor die kerels in die tent,
Hul wens dit almaal naar die maan,
Of na die wereld ze end,
Dit is om met die pot te spook,
En voor die twaalf nou kos te kook.

II

Jij krij mos van die Engelschman,
Dit moet jul almaal weet,
Een pot, wat ook voor koffie kan
Moet dien, dit vooral niet te vergeet.
Diezelfde pot word in gekook, gebak en ook gebraai,
Of jij kook jou kleere daarin uit,
Ja, dat die vuilgoed draai.

III

En verder krij ons van die verbrande goed,
Een kommetji vrinde zoo groot als mijn hoed.
Toe ons hul eerst krîj, het ons strîj gehad,
Of ons daaruit moes drink of daarin moes bad.
Hul gê ook bord, lepel, vork en een mes;
Om die spul schoon te maak is regtig een pes.

IV

Die arme kok moet die eerste opstaan;
Hij wil liever slaap, maar dit zal nie gaan.
Hij moet mos nou eerst koffie maak,
Wat die Rooies ons gê en beesagtig sleg smaak.
Partij keers is dit zoo zwart als die nag,
Want jij moet glad nie ieder keer melk verwach.

---

* Die skrywer se voornaam is onbekend. Manuskrip afkomstig uit die National
English Language Museum, Grahamstad.

V

Nou moet die dinner wordt gemaak,
Dit is van alles die zwaarste taak.
Want uit een mager stuk beesvlijs
Moet jij beefsteak bak, wat almal prijs.
Of is die goed weer pure vel,
Moet jij zag vlijs kook, bedenk dit wel.
Want anders krij jij, dit is ver vas,
Van die twaalf nou leelijk op jou bas.

VI

Maar die ergste als jij sop moet kook,
En jij moet in die wind daar spook,
Met die sopgoed uit England hier gestuur,
Al heeltemaal beschimmel, galzig en zuur.
Wat jij een mijl ver kan ruik,
En deur die Khakis zelf nie wordt gebruik.
Dit brand zoomaar an, en als dit gebeur,
Gloo mij die dag, zal jij jou leve betreur.

VII

Nou moet weer die verbrande pot,
Wordt schoongemaakt ... treurige lot.
Die kok wordt nou zoo erg besmeer,
Jij denk hij het gewerk met teer.
Als jij hom hier zoo rond zien loop,
En vrâ: "Wil jij die job verkoop?"
Hij spring van blijdschap uit zijn vel.

VIII

Maar als nou tweemaal in die week,
Hier "Bully Beef" en drôo "Beschuit"
Wordt ingebreng, wordt hul almal bleek,
En wil maar net die tent weer uit.
Die kok, want hij het nie verdien,
Want die heel klomp wil met hom spook,
En schrouw: jij moet: "flikkedelle" maak en pap ook kook.

IX

Jong, en als die zon begin te zink,
Dan moet hul weer kom koffie drink.
En krij hul daarbij een stukkie zuur brood,
Dan hoor jij weer "Kok val jij nou dood."
Gê ver ons een brood, wat gaar is gebak,
En laat staan die rouw goed in die zak.
En partij keers kom een paar laat om te eet,
Dan wil die kok hul amper opvreet.
Want hij moet maar alles geduldig verdrâ,
D' is genoeg om jou sommer die krans af te jâ.

X

Zoo zal jul almal met mij o'ereen moet kom,
Dat die arme kok krij dit maar net hot om.
En jul kan hom dit glad nie verwijt,
Al raak hij nou en dan een verkeerde woord kwijt.

W.H. Boshoff

De Jonge Cronjé*

Hebt gy ooit van den dood van den Jongen Cronjé
In het Groenepunt kamp gehoord?
Die, wyl hy met open Bybel er stond
door een kogel wreed werd doorboord.

Een bedestond bracht hen daar tezaam,
Daar stonden zy nacht na nacht,
Wyl een lampje dat hing aan 't heiningdraad,
Een flikkerend licht hun bracht.

'T Gezang was luid, en lieflyk, en zoet,
Men droomde van geen gevaar,
Toen meteen de wacht riep: "Af van het draad!"
Tot de lustig zingende schaar.

Opeen verneemt men de knal van 't geweer,
Weergalmende aan het strand,
En hy, de beminde, valt neer op den grond,
De Bybel geklemd in de hand.

Hy sterft in den nacht, geen moeder is daar,
Die hem kust of de hand hem drukt,
Doch eer hy sterft, getuigt hy het nog:
"Onschuldig den dood ingerukt."

---

* Manuskrip 4830/5, Oorlogsmuseum van die Boererepublieke, Bloemfontein.
Dié gebeurtenis is in die pro-Boerekoerant *South African News* van 5 Mei
1900 gerapporteer. Volgens M. van Wyk Smith, *Drummer Hodge*, p. 212, was
'n Engelse vertaling van dié gedig as 'n ballade baie gewild in Kaapstad. Hy
gee ook die Engelse weergawe van die eerste strofe van die gedig.

O Jongeling, uw naam staat geschreven omhoog,
In het boek des Levens by God,
En uw Kroon is reeds op uw slapen gedrukt,
Hoe droevig op aard ook uw lot.

Uw Vaderland riep u op tot den stryd,
Getrouw aan uw huis en uw haard,
Getrouwer nog, echter, waart gy aan Hem
Die eens voor u stierf op aard.

Gy luistert thans niet meer naar aardsche muziek,
Gy zoekt thans niet meer naar licht,
Maar zingt thans het lied der verlosten omhoog
In het land waar de duisternis zwicht.

Eens banneling hier, verwinnaar thans daar,
Waar men looft en eeuwiglyk leeft,
Wyl de vrienden kring nog voor "den vyand" bidt
Tot God die de zonde vergeeft.

Steynsburg, 18 November 1902.

Digter onbekend

Die waterkar*

1

Als jy nog rond loop in die kamp
Dan hoor jy net met een
O'magtie daar's die waterkar
En allen hol daar heen.

2

Nou wed ik dat jul graag wil weet
Wat is die water kar,
Een mensch moet hier voorzichtig wees
Maar luister darm mar.

3

Die waterkar die is een ding,
Hoe zal ik jul nou sëh?
Dit is twee wielen in een as
Waar 'n Groote vat op lëh.

4

Die dryver zit daar boven op
Hy ry die vat aba
Ik zou nog seh hoe hy dan lyk
Maar vrees hy zal my jäe

5

Hy ry dan na die dorpsfontein
En maak die vat daar vol
Hy kom dan terug en skree n slag
En dan ziet jy net hol

---

* Manuskrip 1676/9. Oorlogsmuseum van die Boererepublieke, Bloemfontein.

6
Jy ziet die blikke emmers gryp
In aller Grootste haast
Want draai jy net een rukkie nog
Dan kom jy mos ou laast

7
Daars nooiens vrouwens kindertjes
Een heele zwetterjoel
Jy moet jou ziek lach om te zien
Hoe hul o'er water woel

8
Party hou hul net erg astrand
Een ander is weer laf
Jy moet net oppas of hy sny
Jou straal zoo voor jou af

9
Daar staan dan ook een vat fiscaal
Ik weet nie wies die ou
Misschien zal jul hem zelvers ken
Zijn hond ze naam is Blou

10
Hij staan daar voor een vrouwenshulp
En keer die mans soms voor
Maar weinig is hier in het kamp
Wat na die ou wil hoor

11
Want almal het al uit gevind
Die ou zorg eerst voor hom
En is zy emmers strykend vol
Dan kan die vrouwens kom

J.G. Engela

Hulda. Maria. Engela*

H ier heeft de hand der liefde my,
U w kind een plaats gegeven.
L aat dat u ten bewyse zy,
D at ik nu van den dood eens vry
A ltoos by Hem zal leven.

M yn' lieve Moeder treur niet meer,
A anbid Zyn groote magt,
R ust aan Zyn boezem lief en teer,
I n Hem is leven troost en kracht,
A ch! gy behoeft niets meer.

E n Broeder, Zusters, hoort ook gy
N aar Zyne lief'drik stem.
G od gaf ook eens Zyn bloed voor u,
E n roept u door myn' dood tot Hem.
L aat Jezus in u hartjies woon,
A an Kanaan's kust krygt gy een Kroon.

Diyatalawa, Ceylon,
Oktober, 1901.

---

* Manuskrip, NALN, Bloemfontein.

Eugène N. Marais

Winternag*

O koud is die windjie
    en skraal.
En blink in die dof-lig
    en kaal,
so wyd as die Heer se genade,
lê die velde in sterlig en skade.
    En hoog in die rande,
    versprei in die brande,
is die grassaad aan roere
    soos winkende hande.

O treurig die wysie
    op die ooswind se maat,
soos die lied van 'n meisie
in haar liefde verlaat.
In elk' grashalm se vou
    blink 'n druppel van dou,
en vinnig verbleek dit
    tot ryp in die kou!

---

* *Versamelde gedigte*, Pretoria: J.L. Van Schaik, 1955, p. 9.

F.W. Reitz

De Wet's Krismis-Box*
25 Dec. 1901.

In Harrismit wijk, bij Elands-rivier,
Daar wou di soldate hul Krismis vier
Maar Hoofd-Commandant, Oom Christian de Wet,
Het die mooie spulletjie daar kom belet.

Hij trek hulle bij in die oggend vroeg,
– In een half uur tijd toe had hul genoeg –
Want toe leg hul daar verstrooid op die grond
Al meer dan 'n honderd gedood en gewond.

Twee honderd die vang hij en "schut hulle uit",
En maak bovendien nog 'n taamlike buit
Van dertig wa'ens met klere en kos,
En 500 paerden die krij hij ook los.

En buiten dit alles nog 'n drietal kanonne
Het hij in diezelfde slag ook gewonne,
Maar die Tommies het hij verlof gegeef
Die Basuto's te zé dat De Wet nog leef!

Ook meer dan 'n honderd kiste patrone
Die vat hij saam, om net te tone,
Dat hij ach dit nie voor heel orthodox
Tevrede te wees met *één* Krismis-box.

---

* *Oorlogs en andere gedichten*. Potchefstroom: Het Westen, 1910, pp. 23–24.
Hierdie gedig verwys na die slag van Groenkop (ook Krismiskop of Surprise
Hill genoem).

Die Engelsman hou mos al te grag
Van persentjies te geê op daar die dag
En De Wet het getoon hij er nix têen had
Om zelfs van 'n vijand geskenke te vat.

Net één week tevore, toen werd daar verhaal
Dat De Wet met 'n honderd man vlug en ronddwaal
Maar nou dat hij hulle het "opgetel"
Nou moet hul dit weer glad andersom stel.

Nou lui dit weer: "Hij viel hulle an
"Met 'n groot overmag van twaalf honderd man"
"Want had hij dit tog met minder gewaâ
"Dan kreeg hij daar ongetwijfeld ook slaâ!

Die Spreekwoord zeg – maar mij lijk dit zó
Of die Engelse volk dit nie wil glo –
Dat "Al loop di leugen ook nog zoo snel
"Di waarheid die achterhaal hom wel."–

Febr. '02.

Digter onbekend

Krisjan de Wet*

Wi noem jy wel 'n flinke fent? – De Wet.
By Boer en Engelsman bekend? – De Wet.
Wi het Jan Boel** so faak ferras,
Syn tryn en manne angetas?
Dis Kristian de Wet; dis Kristian de Wet.

Wi is di held fan Koringspruit? – De Wet.
Wi won daarby 'n grote buit? – De Wet.
Wi is nou daar en dan weer hiir?
Wi fliig fan Sand- na Vaalrifiir?
Dis Kristian de Wet; dis Kristian de Wet.

Wi is die dappre Generaal? – De Wet.
Wat d' Engelsman ontneem syn maal? – De Wet.
Ferskyn, ferdwyn ter goeder uur
En Roberts maak di lewe suur?
Dis Kristian de Wet; dis Kristian de Wet.

Wi breek gedurig spore op? – De Wet.
En slaat di fyand op di kop? – De Wet.
Wi is die skrik fan d' Engelsman,
Wat Kitchener ni fange kan?
Dis Kristian de Wet; dis Kristian de Wet.

---

* *Ons Klyntji*, Januarie 1904, p. 14. Die volgende nota is aan die gedig toegevoeg:
"Geagte 'Ons Klyntji' en medeleser. – Ek was oek 'n krygsgefangene te Ceylon
en di liid is gedig deur een fan di krygsgefangene te Ragama kamp, Ceylon, 'n
paar maande foor di frede gesluit is. Ontfang almal myn beste groete,
J.J. Beukes, Burgersdorp." P.W. Grobbelaar (1999: 120) skryf 'n soortgelyke
lied toe aan die bekende Danie Theron.
** Jan Boel staan vir John Bull, die bynaam van die Engelsman.

Wi is di Vrystaat uitgestap? – De Wet.
An twé di Generaals ontsnap? – De Wet.
Wi is fereend met De la Rey?
Wi maak di Boere frinde bly?
Dis Kristian de Wet; dis Kristian de Wet.

Wi stort di Boere moed weer in? – De Wet.
Wi toon di ware fryhydssin? – De Wet.
Wi maak dat alles reg sal kom
Tot hyl fan d'Afrikanerdom?
Dis Kristian de Wet; dis Kristian de Wet.

Digter onbekend

Die Hensopper*

Dis 'n uitlandse woord en 'n uitlandse daad,
En die ware betekenis is eintlik verraad.
Al wat daarop rym, is net maar opstopper,
En dis wat hy verdien, die gemene hensopper.

---

* Getikte manuskrip 1664/13, Oorlogsmuseum van die Boererepublieke, Bloemfontein.

F.J. Straus

Oertel wil gaan "handsop"*

(Op 'n sekere aand sit 'n jongetji met 'n mysi en gesels, en uit 'n grap seg hy fer haar dat hy wil gaan "handsop". Di mysi dog hy meen dit en fertel dit an haar pa, wat hom dadelik arresteer en na di Landdros toe stuur, wat hom egter weer fry spreek. Syn naam was Oertel en di mysi hare Kali. Dit is gebeur in Mariko kort voor di frede.)

"Gou, Kali, breng di rime en maak fer Oertel fas!
Want Oertel wil gaan 'handsop': hy moet nou in di kas!"
Hul fat syn ammunisi en syn geweer toen af.
En stuur die arme Oertel toen dorp toe op 'n draf,
Foorwaar, di arme Oertel, hy was hoog in di nood!
Foorwaar, di arme Kali, sy dog dit kos syn dood!
Hy loop toen deur di huis,
Tot agter di Kombuis.
Toen word hy so ferwoed,
Dat hy toen somar groet.
Hy klim syn perd toen op
En trek op 'n gelop.
Hy kom by di kantoor
En dog hy moes ferloor.
Mar wat, di dapper Oertel is daarom net 'n mot,
Al is hy in di pekel, jul moet hom ni meer spot.
Mar wat, di arme Oertel kom net weer lekker los.
Toen seg hy: "Alla, sussi, dit kon myn lewe kos."
Di kerels wat gaan fry
Ry Kali nou ferby.
Hul is fer Kali bang.
Sy sal hul oek lat fang.

Distr. Bloemhof
15 Aug. 1902.

---

* *Ons Klyntji*, Junie 1904, p. 93.

Cronjé

Op een Verrader*

Verrader monster, vloek der aarde,
Vernederd schepsel der natuur;
Gods wraak die uw tot heden spaarde
Verdelg uw eens deur de helse vuur.
Neen, Hy doet uw slechts bezeffen
Hoe verachtlik uwe daden zyn
Geen blikzemstraal kan sneller treffen,
Geen donder meer verschriklik zyn.
Dan zal uw ziel zich krimpend wringen,
Gevoelen wat haar waarde was.
Op de jongste dag die eens zal dagen
Zal men lezen op uw graf:
"Hier legt de vloek van vriend en maagd
Wat Vaderland de doodsteek gaf."

---

* Manuskrip 6289/3, Oorlogsmuseum van die Boererepublieke, Bloemfontein.
Onderaan die teks staan die volgende in dieselfde handskrif: "Geskryf deur
ene Cronjé wat op die slagveld gebly het tot die laaste en toe moes oorgee
a.g.v. "joiners". Sy vrou en kinders is almal dood in die kamp en sy plaashuis
afgebrand. Na die oorlog bly hy by sy suster Tant Catharina Grobbelaar van
Luiperdspruit, Trompsburg. Daar kon hy nie tot rus kom en loop gedurig op en
af totdat hy met die vers tevoorskyn kom. Toe roep hy vir Nettie van Vrede (15
jr) wat ook by haar tante (dieselfde Tant Catharina) inwoon, en Oubaas
Grobbelaar (6 jr) en leer hulle die vers en vra hulle om dit nooit te vergeet.
Tant Nettie (nou Botha) is vanjaar 85 en ken dit nog soos die dag toe sy dit
geleer het."

Martinus L. Lotter

Bermudas Lied*

Hier zit ik aan Bermudas strand,
    Met een verbrijzeld hart,
Verbannen uit mijn Vaderland.
    O Heer! wat bitter smart.

Mijn Geest zweeft oor de Oceaan;
    Mij hart bezwijkt van pijn,
Want daar zie ik ellende aan,
    Van die mij dierbaar zijn.

Verwoest vertreden is het land,
    Dat mij een schuilplaats bood.
De wonings is als afgebrand.
    O Heer! wat bitter nood.

Waar zijn die van morgens vroeg,
    Tot in des avonds laat,
De akkers scheurden met de ploeg.
    Of zwoegen in de grond?

Ach velen hunner zijn geveld,
    Door vijands vreeslik lood,
Ja menig trouw dappere held,
    Vond in de strijd de dood.

---

* *Uit de Oorlog. Gedichten over Gevechten in Grikwaland West, enz., en Namen van Gevangenen te Tokai.* Paarl: Paarl Drukpers Maatschappij Beperkt, 1913, pp. 30–32.

En menig een verloor de moed,
  En zocht daar elders heil,
Vertrad zijn eigen broeders bloed:
  O snoodheid zonder peil!

En velen zijn in hunne hand,
  Hier drukt hetzelfde lot,
Verbannen uit hun dierbaar land,
  Verscheurd van vriend en maagd.

Waar zijn de moeders die haar kroost,
  Verzorgden dag en nacht,
Wier blik de kloeke vader troost,
  Als zij hem tegen lacht?

De moeders zijn zeer zwaar gestraf,
  Gevoerd in hunne kamp;
En anderen zijn in het graf,
  Bevrijd van leed en ramp.

Die kampen, ach! hoe zwaar voor hen,
  Die daar in moeten zijn,
Hun smart en lijden kan geen pen
  Beschrijven, zonder pijn.

Ja moeder; ik versta uw smart
  God geve kracht en troost,
Uw echtgenoot gescheurd van 't hart
  En och! waar is uw kroost?

Uw kleinen vragen u met smart;
  Wanneer komt vader thuis?
Die vraag doorboort uw moeders hart,
  Verzwaart uw bitter kruis.

Hoe menig traan werd dan geschreid;
    Hoe menig zucht geslaakt;
Door smart de boezem oopgerijt,
    Als d'Avondstond genaakt.

Ach, hoe eenzaam zit zij hier neer,
    In 't onherbergzaam oord.
Versterk hen, geef hun kracht, O Heer!
    Versterk hun door uw woord.

Mijn vrouw mijn kind vergaat van smart,
    De ellende drukt mij neer.
Zij zijn wreed ontscheurd van mijn hart,
    Ach ik bemin hen teer.

Zie, hoe de groot overmacht,
    Die zwak' vrouwen verteert
O Heer, geef toch de zwakken kracht,
    Vertroost hen in hun leed,

Des vaders erfnis, dierbaar land,
    De prijs des helden bloed,
Is gans verwoest door vijands hand,
    Vertreden met de voet.

Ik zie der groten over macht.
    Ontbloot uw arm, O Heer!
Schenk aan de zwakken moed en kracht,
    En werp ons vijand neer!

O Heer wij denken aan ons schuld;
    Wij hebben zwaar misdaan,
Maar Vader heb met ons geduld
    En neem ons offers aan.

Verlos ons uit des vijands hand,
    Uw groote Naam ter eer.
Ach! breng ons weder naar ons land,
    Getrouwe Hemel Heer.

Mijn bede stijg tot u O, Heer!
    Die in de Hemel zijt,
Verlos ons van die vreeslik lot,
    Van deze bange strijd.

Verdrijf d'overmacht door uw kracht,
    Geef ons ons erfdeel weer,
Opdat het laatste nageslacht
    Uw almacht roem' O Heer.

Eliza Laurillard

Steeds nog!*

Steeds nog duurt de menschenslachting
En de rechtsverkrachting voort.
En ontboeide hellemachten
Blazen dreiging nog en moord.

Heil'ge toorn doorgloeit de volken.
't Hart, in opstand, brandt en bruist.
De aad'ren zwellen, 't bloed wordt kokend.
't Oog schiet vuur, de hand wordt vuist.

Maar gij, *grootste en hoogste machten*!
Blijft gij roerloos? Gij alleen?
Snijdt niet wat de volken voelen
Ook door uwe harten heen?

't Moet wel – Maar, als gij niets *doen* kunt,
Spreekt dan toch, spreekt toch een woord!
Voor den vrede hadt ge een lofspraak,
Hebt een vonnis voor den moord.

Voor den moord, zoo laag, zoo gruwzaam,
Als die heden de aarde ontzet.
Die verwensching *hier* doet rijzen.
Daar een schreiend smeekgebed.

Spreekt toch, als de vuile wraakzucht
Tegen *vrouw* en *kind* zich keert,
Waar de *man* niet is te treffen,
Die voor land en recht zich weert.

---

* In: D. Wouters. *Na veertig jaar: Documents humains*. Nijmegen: Moorman, 1940, p. 90.

Spreekt toch, als de laffe boosheid
Vrouw en kind tot borstweer maakt,
Wijl haar anders 't heldenwapen
Van den man en vader raakt. –

Vreest gij, dat gewapend spreken
Heel den wereldvrede breekt,
Nu dan, spreekt dan ongewapend,
Maar, – in naam des Heeren! – *spreekt!*

't Zwijgen van uw forsche stemmen
Doet miljoenen harten pijn, –
Daad zal reeds uw *spreken* wezen,
Reeds *die* daad uwe eere zijn.

Willem Zuidema

Een lied voor Zuid-Afrika*
(Wijze: *Dat 's Heeren zegen op u daal.*)

Welk is het volk, dat onverslapt
De dwinglandij in gruizlen trapt?
Dat nooit zal bukken, hoe 't ook ga?
Dat is ùw volk, Zuid-Afrika!

Wie is de man, in eenvoud groot,
Die allen listen weêrstand bood,
De Zwijger van zijn volk weldra?
Dat is ùw hoofd, Zuid-Afrika!

Welk is het beste recht op aard
En 't best verweerd door 't burgerzwaard?
Dat zegeviert, wie tegensta?
Dat is ùw recht, Zuid-Afrika!

Welke is de strijd met kleine kracht,
Waarin der wereld grootste macht
Nu wijken moet met schande en schâ?
Dat is ùw strijd, Zuid-Afrika!

Wie is het, die de krachten schenkt,
Waarin de zwakheid dat volbrengt
Door 't rotsgeloof in Zijn genâ?
Dat is ùw God, Zuid-Afrika!

---

* *Voor Zuid-Afrika. Rijm en onrijm.* Amsterdam: Hollandsche Stoomdrukkerij
& Uitgevers Maatschappij, 1901.

Martinus L. Lotter

Gedicht op Tokai*

Tokai is zo een snaakse plek,
    Zo als er ooit bestond;
Men loopt er soms als ene gek,
    Gedurig in het rond.

Dan weder als een malkop schaap,
    Dat rondloop op 'n neder;
Ook somtijds als een stomme aap,
    Dat springen heen 'n weder.

Recht in 't midden een hoge brug,
    Een wacht loop er op rond,
Die letten moest naar elk gerug,
    Des nacht weer op de grond.

Wij hadden er een vel viool,
    Hij speelde rechte vals,
Zijn neus geleek een klein pistool,
    Hij liet ons daagliks wals.

Ook was hij nors als ene beer
    Die elk een wil verscheur;
Hij diende Jan met groot onneur;**
    En steld' ons soms teleur.

---

* *Gedichten over Gevechten in Grikwaland West, enz., en Namen van Gevangenen te Tokai.* Paarl: Paarl Drukpers Maatschappij Beperkt, 1913, pp. 34–36. Tokai was die naam van 'n tronk.
** onneur: honneur (Frans): eer.

Hij joeg ons somwijl naar het bad,
 Al rillen w' van koude,
Geef niets om al kost 't wat,
 Zo lang hij zijn ambt behoude.

Maar zijne loopbaan was niet lang,
 Waarmee hij speelde;
Want hij leed hierna aan zijn wang,
 Dokters kon niet heelde.

Hij moest Tokai maar toen verlaat,
 En ging toen naar de Kaap
Ja spoedig moest zijn sterfuur slaat
 En is dan zo ontslaap.

In 't begin was ons toegestaan,
 Van buiten in t' krijgen,
Waar voor wij onze geld liet gaan,
 Als dadels 'n ook druiven.

Ook was ons eerst de gunst verleen,
 Bede op te zende
Met luide lofzang 'n gebeen
 Ons tot de Heer t' wende.

Maar hoor daar riep heer Jan ons op,
 In 't midden van de dag,
En zeg dat hij ons bidden stop,
 En lofzang in de nach.

Het was voor ons een zware taak,
 D' Godsdiens op te geven
De mens kan tot iets groots geraak;
 D' Heer geeft kracht in 't leven.

Weer schielik op een ander keer,
    Riep hij ons daadlik op,
Van buiten krijg gij ook niets meer,
    Ja zelf de vruchten word gestop.

Maar een voorwaarde stel ik u,
    Als gij uzelf wil voed',
Dan geef ik u het voorrech nu,
    Leef slechts dan op uw goed.

Zo gingen velen er voor in,
    Zich zelven t' verzorgen,
Maar anderen weer 'n wijzer zin.
    'n At het pap van d' morgen.

Het voedsel dat men eten moet,
    Is aardig om te zeg;
Rijszoep is voor een kranke goed
    Voor een gezonde sleg.

Want bonen soep den ene dag,
    Met wortelen 'n rapen,
Geyste vlees overzee gebracht,
    Liet ons dikwijls gapen.

Het is niet al wat er in is,
    Patats, pampoen, nog meer,
Kool, uien is zo zeer gewist.
    Maar 't doet de buiken zeer.

Soms is de soep zo dik als pap,
    Niet aangenaam de reuk,
Een ieder moet dan voorwaarts stap,
    En moet geen woord dan spreek.

Totius

Die balling*
Bij de zee is bekommernis, men kan er niet rusten. Jer. 49:29

Wanneer die skeemring, droef en vaal,
oor St. Helena neer kom daal,

en golf by golf, nou uitgewoed,
vermoeid hul neerstort aan sy voet –

dan staan hy op die strand, die man
so swaar beproef, so ver verban;

dan leef weer op die droewe klag,
in helder brief-skrif hom gebrag;

in seegedruis en awendwind
hoor hy die klaaglied van sy kind:

"Ag, liewe vader, oor die see,
hoor tog die woorde van my wee;

"want, vader, ver van ons vervreem,
die dood het sussie meegeneem;

"hier is haar laaste woorde nog;
o Bring my na my vader tog!"

En aan sy voet slaan slag op slag
die golf as weerklank op die klag.

---

* *Versamelde gedigte.* Kaapstad: Tafelberg-Uitgewers, 1988, pp. 24–26.

"En verder, vader, hoor my nood:
My lief klein broertjie is ook dood."

Die golfslag in die rotskuil stuit
met dowwe toon en klaaggeluid.

"En dit skryf ek nog wenend neer:
My liewe moeder is nie meer.

"Solank sy nog in lewe was,
het trou haar hand ons opgepas."

Die golwe staan op ry aan ry
en klaag nou saam uit medely.

"Ag, kon ek op die windjie tree,
dan loop ek, vader, oor die see!

"Ag, kon ek net die vloed oorspan,
dan kom ek, vader, wreed verban!"

En aan sy voet die afgrond grom:
Geen voet wat oor my diepte kom!

"Ek kan nie, vader! Sug met my
dat my die dood ook mag bevry."

*

Hy hoor 'n lisp'ling – sê die wind:
Sy't ook gesterwe, daardie kind?

'n Droef gedreun rys uit die see,
en droewer klink sy laaste bee:

"Ag, maak 'n end, maak gou 'n end
aan al my weedom en ellend."

*

Die skeemring daal dan telkens neer;
maar hy staan op die strand nie meer.

J.D. Cilliers

St. Helena (fragment)*

St. Helena! hoeveel jammer
    En ellende zaagt gij niet,
Sinds wij hier als bannelingen,
Op uw bodem overgingen,
    Hoeveel hartzeer en verdriet.

Hoeveel, hoeveel bittre tranen,
    Zijn niet hier alreeds gestort;
Hoeveel lijden niet geleden,
Hoeveel zielestrijd gestreden,
    Menig leven niet verkort!

Want vanaf uw dorre bodem,
    St. Helena, roept het bloed,
Zoo koelbloedig hier vergoten,
Van hen, alhier doodgeschoten,
    Wrake over 't snood gebroed.

Ach, hoe vele medeburgers
    Leiden hier het leven af,
Voor hun kroost van zooveel waarde
Rusten ze hier in rotsig aarde
    In het kille, stille graf.

---

* In Nienaber, P.J.: *Boere op St. Helena*. Kaapstad: Nasionale Boekhandel, 1950, pp. 229–230.

Om van hier nooit weer te keeren
    Naar hun zoo geliefd tehuis;
Gun hun dan hier stil te rusten,
St. Helena, op uw kusten,
    En bedek hen met uw gruis.

O, bewaar hen, St. Helena,
    Eenmaal als het God behaagt,
Worden allen, jongen, ouden,
Die we hier aan u toevertrouwden,
    Uit uw schoot teruggevraagd.

Houdt het vast in uw geheugen,
    St. Helena, weet voor goed,
Dat gij eenmaal na dit heden,
Als getuige op zult treden,
    En naar recht getuigen moet.

Van wat hier is voorgevallen,
    't Zij bedekt of onbedekt;
Eenmaal wordt het al ontsloten,
Spreekt 't onschuldig bloed vergoten,
    Dat uw bodem heeft bevlekt.

Doch zij rusten, en misgunnen
    Wij hun toch die ruste niet;
Want hun strijd is hier volstreden,
En bedenkt dat hier beneden,
    Niets toch bij geval geschiedt.

Laten wij die hand slechts kussen,
    Die hier dikwijls zwaar kastijdt;
Wees geduldig, wil niet vreezen,
Hij, die slaat, zal ook genezen,
    Wonden heelen op Zijn tijd.

Daarom slechts op Hem vertrouwen,
    Al schijnt ook Gods weg verkeerd;
Nimmer zal Hij ons vergeten,
't Zij genoeg voor ons te weten:
    Een getrouwe God regeert.

Deadwood-kamp met al uw tenten,
    Hutten, huizen, als ze hier staan;
Met uw doorndraad, met uw palen,
Steeds zult ge ons voor de oogen dwalen,
    Nimmer uit 't geheugen gaan.

Levenslang zal 't in ons blijven,
    De herin'ring aan elk' stap
Hier gedaan, ja, nooit vergeten
Al die maanden, hier gesleten,
    In ons Krijgsgevangenschap.

Lief en leed, hier ondervonden,
    Zuur en zoet, alhier gesmaakt,
Doe ons stil zijn, doe ons buigen,
En wij zullen eens getuigen
    "God heeft alles welgemaakt."

J.F. Schumann

Smarte en grieve[*]

In deze kamp
    Word menig ramp
Gevoel, gezien vernome; –
    Die een lijk droef
Een tweede stroef,
    Nog een geplaag met droome.

Een het een maag
    Wat hem veel plaag
Deur overdaad (of schaarste?)
    Een het een puis –
Wit is *zijn* kruis,
    Hij dink hij het die zwaarste.

Een het een been,
    En als dit rêen
Loop hij tien maal manker;
    Een het een voet
Wat pijn aandoet,
    Hij zegt dit vreet zoos kanker.

Een het een rug
    Wat hom laat zug,
Gevrete trek en krom gaan;
    Een het een kop,
Met 'n zeer daarop
    Dat hij van pijn soms stom staan.

---

[*] *De Krijgsgevangene*, nommer 3, 22 Juni 1901, p. 2. *De Krijgsgevangene* was 'n blaadjie wat deur en vir die krygsgevangenes in die Deadwood-kamp (naby Jamestown) op die eiland Sint Helena uitgegee is. Die redakteur was ene H. Everitt.

Die een die ziet
  Tot zijn verdriet
Gezichte, visioene,
  Nog een die zeg,
"Dit is nie reg,
  "Ik het geen kouse, schoene."

Een het een tand
  Wat pijn en brand,
En hom laat taal gebruike
  Zoo vreeslik, dat
Heel Blikjes stad
  Naar vuur en zwavel reuke!

Nou moet ik stop, –
  Mijn gare is op
Ook wil ik eers gaan "dinner";
  Ik word ook wel
Gegrief, gekwel –
  Maar wat! dit is nou minder.

C. Louis Leipoldt

Droom en doen*

"Scheepers lê begrawe in Graaff-Reinet se sand!"
    Kêrel, droom jy nog van gisternag?
Vol aanlokkende kleure is die blomtuin van ons land;
    Voller nog die toekoms wat ons wag.
Weg is tent en wasbank van die konsentrasiekamp;
    Weg die skrik van Martjie Louws gesag;
Weg die las van smarte wat so aaklig op ons harte
Swaar gedruk het in die wrede, ellendig' oorlogsdag.

"Scheepers lê begrawe in Graaff-Reinet se sand!"
    Kêrel, droom jy nog van gisternag?
Hoor hoe raas die stampers bo-op die Witwatersrand,
    Net soos branders van die see so sag;
Oor die hoë dakke, oor die wye veld,
    Op die koel wind in die middernag,
Vreugdevol, tevrede met die werk en plig van hede,
Sing hul sag 'n welkom vir ons beter, nuwer dag.

"Scheepers lê begrawe in Graaff-Reinet se sand!"
    Kêrel, droom jy nog van gisternag?
Waar die veld verskroei is deur die woeste najaarsbrand,
    Kan jy weeld'rig' weiland-gras verwag:
Siele wat gefolter is deur pyn en skimp en smart,
    Word gelouter deur hul eie krag.
Wil jy vyand lewe, nooit vergeet en nooit vergewe,
Bitter bly alleen staan as ons groet 'n beter dag?

---

* *Versamelde gedigte.* Kaapstad: Tafelberg-Uitgewers, 1988, pp. 140–141.

"Scheepers lê begrawe in Graaff-Reinet se sand!"
    Kêrel, droom jy nog van gisternag?
Speur jy nog geen dagskyn in die ooste oor ons land,
    Goue lig wat helder teen ons lag?
Dra jy nog jou droefnis, wat die duister duisendmaal
    Donkerder sal maak as middernag?
Sit jy nog te temer in eergisteraand se skemer?
Ons het reeds geworstel met die taak van nou vandag.

"Scheepers lê begrawe in Graaff-Reinet se sand!"
    Kêrel, droom jy nog van gisternag?
Plaas jou liefde en ywer, alles wat jy het, as pand
    Vir die luister-toekoms wat ons wag.
Hy's die grootste patriot wat al die mensdom min,
    Wat vergifnis bo vergelding ag;
Wat kan ly en lewe, bloed versoen, en haat vergewe,
Altyd yw'rig werksaam vir 'n beter, nuwer dag.

Broeder, toe die Noodlot ons gelei het tot die rand
    Waar vertwyf'ling niks sien as die nag;
Suster, toe die doodswolk donker oor ons vaderland
    Oorgetrek het met die Dood se mag,
Was jou siel so stukkend dat dit nie meer siel kon wees,
    Nie meer lig kon uitstraal uit sy krag,
Nie meer mens kon heet nie wat die Liefde nooit vergeet nie,
Sterker en gelouter vir 'n beter, nuwer dag?

"Scheepers lê begrawe in Graaff-Reinet se sand!"
    Kêrel, laat hom rus tot opstaan-dag!
Wat herin'ring vashou van die smarte van ons land
    Staan vir ewig as weergelding wag.
Elke smaad en onreg op die aarde word vergeld!
    Joue nie die plig daarvoor en mag;
Joue nie die oordeel – was dit nadeel, vrind, of voordeel?
Joue net te arbei vir 'n nuwer, beter dag.

P.C. Boutens

Manibus Gideon Jacobus Scheepers*
† 18 Jan. 1902

Vloek dien die dorsten met veil huurlingslood
Schenden uw borsts geheimnis, blank sterk-broos
Heilge van leven; die in lauwe hoos
Spilden den godgegisten wijn uit rood-
Tintelende urn, uw hart, dat steeds zich bood
Open in open strijd, bloedene roos, –
Gij donkre Lacher dien de jonkheid koos
Tot blij voorrijder naar den schoonen dood! …

Stil, – 'k weet: uw moorders hebben u benijd
De schaamte van uw opperste eenzaamheid,
Verheerlijkt plots als zon aan avondkim,
Toen opgezaêld en rijreê om uw schim
De eerwacht van stille bleeke jongren sloot
Ter blijde inkomst in glorierijken dood.

---

* *Stemmen.* Amsterdam: Van Kampen, 1920, p. 102.

D.J. Opperman

Gebed om die gebeente[*]

Heer, waar U noordewind die droë dissel rol
en oor die skurwe brakland jaag van Afrika,
maar eindelik teen 'n doringdraad met pluksels wol
vaswaai terwyl die kraaie en die aasvoëls kla,
laat my ook ná die swerf oor vlaktes heen nou rus
en glo my kind is dood, al hoor ek die berigte
om my krys: "Ek het hom as matroos hier aan die kus …"
"Ek: as stoker op 'n trein …" "Ek: in vaal-geel ligte
van 'n steenkooldorp se kroeg nog nou die dag gesien …"
Glo omgekoop! Of hy sou skielik blink gesteentes
smokkel … blink gesteentes! Selfs dan … Nee, miskien
lê hy tog êrens dood; maar, Heer, dan die gebeente,
wys my, gee my die drag gebeente van my skoot
dat ek nie opgejaag deur hierdie land bly swerf
en soek, maar eindelik rus en weet hy het deur lood
onder twee mudsak ongebluste kalk gesterf.

Snags het ek soms gelê en vrees daar sou iets boos
oor hierdie kind nog kom, want in Middelburg se kerk
staan duidelik in die doopregister sy geboorte
nie na die stand van sy gesternte aangemerk.
En, soos wanneer jy tussen vinger en die duim
die wit son rol en skitter in 'n diamant,
sou hy deur Vrystaat en Transvaal se leiblou ruim
uit spieëls ons stryd laat blits en straal van rant tot rant.
Maar hy móés sterf: die Dood self het hom eers gejag
deur kou riviere van die Kaap, dwarsoor Anysberg
tot in die buitekamer op 'n plaas, waar hy een nag
in koue sweet moes lê en aan borswater sterf …

* *Versamelde poësie*. Kaapstad: Tafelberg/Human & Rousseau, 1987, pp. 178–179.

toe 'n tweede jagter hom van tent na trein, van trein
na tent met doringdraad en bajonet bewaak
en met gemete sorg van arts en medisyne
vir 'n tweede dood, o Heer, stadig gesond kon maak.

En ná die skynverhoor het hulle hom vertel …
voor Graaff-Reinet se sel. O Graaff-Reinet se sel!
Hy was gewone kryger, Heer, en geen rebel.
O Graaff-Reinet se sel … Eségiël! Eségiël!
Vergeef my die gelykenis, Heer: ek weet 'n hond
as hy versadig is, verag die been en murg
maar bêre dit agter 'n bossie in die grond
– behoedsaam, en snuffel met die tweede honger terug:
Teen middernag het op bevel 'n vyf soldate
die kalkwit bondel beendre in die kalkwit doek
met grawe en lanterns in verskeie gate
onder die roosmaryn langs die rivier gaan soek
en herbegrawe … toe u die storm word, Heer; ek weet
U en die vyand het dié nag in die vallei
deur geel geflikker in slagreëns mekaar gemeet
oor wie uiteindelik my kind se lyk sou kry.

Hy moes drie dode sterf, maar hy wat drie maal sterf
die sterf nie meer; hy word nou elke dag gesien
as 'n matroos, of stoker op 'n steenkoolwerf,
in myn of tronk, in sirkustent of 'n kantien –
hy leef in hierdie land nou ewig en altyd!
Maar soveel beendre lê onder die roosmaryn …
Seën, Here, ál die bleek gebeente van die stryd –
ek ken as moeder ná 'n halwe eeu van pyn:
een land vol skedels en gebeente, een groot graf
waaroor U noordewind die droë dissel waai
en spruit en krans vul met die afloskrete van
die aasvoëls, van die wildehonde en die kraai

– dat ons as een groot nasie in dié gramadoelas
met elke stukkie sinkplaat en met elke wiel,
en wit en bruin en swart foelie agter skoon glas
ewig U sonlig vang en na mekaar toe spieël.

Mauritz

Weet, zij bidt*

Iedren avond als de schaduwen
Vallen op ons vaderland,
Zie 'k een moeder in de stilte
Neêrgebogen voor Gods hand;
Op haar knieën en in tranen,
Flauw beschenen door een lamp,
Is zij biddend voor haar liefling,
Ver in Diyatal'wa Kamp.

Zeer geregeld zie ik dan ook
Ied'ren avond, 's morgens weer,
Daar een kleine zacht en teeder,
Ook in 't stof gebogen neêr;
Tranen vloeien uit haar oogjes,
Zuchtend is dat hartje klein,
Zij ook bidt: "God zegen' vader
Daar op Diyatal'wa's plein."

Bid maar voort, houd aan O moeder?
Weet de Heere hoort uw klacht:
Smeekgebeden keer' nooit ledig
Die vertrouw'lijk op Hem wacht.
Leef ook rustig voort, gij kleine!
God bestraal' u met Zijn zon,
Eng'len luist'ren waar gij 'n stilte
Bidt voor vader op Ceylon.

---

* *De Strever,* 6, 25 Januari 1902, p. 32. *De Strever* was die "orgaan der C.S.V. onder die krijgsgevangenen". Dit was 'n weekblaadjie wat elke Saterdag netjies gedruk in die Diyatalawa-kamp (hut 36) op Ceylon verskyn het. Dit het 12 sent gekos (later verlaag tot 10 sent "om zoodoende belangstellenden beter in staat te stellen inteekenaars te worden.").

Eugène N. Marais

Die oorwinnaars*
(By die kindergraffies uit die Konsentrasiekamp van Nylstroom.)

OORWINNAARS vir ons volk,
bly u vir al wat beste in ons is 'n ewig' tolk;
nooit weer sal vyands voet u stof so diep vertrap en smoor
dat ons u langer nie kan sien – en hoor.
Nie onse Helde, wat die magtig' leër
op glansryk' velde kon weerstaan en keer;
nie onse Seuns, wat aan die galg en teen die muur
die diepe liefde vir hul eie moes verduur;
nie onse Moeders, wat met bloeiend' hart en seer,
in swart Gethsemané die ware smart moes leer;
nie onse Generaals, vereer met krans en riddersnoer;
– was waardig vir ons volk die hoge stryd te voer en te oorwin.
       Nie ons, met vuile hand en hart ontrou was waardig om
                           die vaandel hoog te hou.
Maar u, o bleke spokies, in U kermend', klagend' wee,
staan voor ons ewiglik beskermend – uit die lang verlee.

---

* *Versamelde gedigte*. Pretoria: J.L. van Schaik, 1955, p. 26.

Digter onbekend

Vergaderde Bloemen*

Zuid Afrika's leliën, bloempjes zoo rein,
Zeer vroeg afgenomen, nog teeder en klein
Van hier uit een wereld vol kommer en klacht,
Zijn zij naar God's lusthof slechts overgebracht,
Vergaard daar in velden behoorlijk en schoon,
Alwaar zij thans juichende zijn om Gods troon;
O zalige vreugde, die elk nu daar smaakt!
Ja! hemelsche vrede, gelukkig, volmaakt!

Nu waarom dan treurig en nedergedrukt?
Ja waarom o, ouder, uw hart zoo gebukt?
Vertrouw toch den Vader, wees vroolijk, wees blij:
Uw liefling is veilig, de strijd is voorbij;
Uw lam dat gij mindet, dat lief kleine pand
Is nu bij een kudde in 't hemelsche land;
Dus gun hem dan toch nu die zalige rust,
Te zijn bij hun Heiland, te zijn bij hun God.

O weet het, die kleine in dat heerlijk land,
Is wachtend voor moeder op Afrika's strand;
Dat bloempje nu bloeiend bij deez' schoone bron
Die wacht ook voor vader hier ver op Ceylon.
Diamantjes klaar schitt'rend in 't Hemelsche kroon
Gelukkig voor altijd, verhoogd bij Gods Zoon,
Bij Eng'len daarboven in vreugde geschaard
Zuid-Afrika's leliën, de schoonste van d'aard.

> Gedrukt bij "De Strevers Drukkerij"
> "Diijatalawa kamp" ver op Ceijlon. 15. Feb.1902

---

* Manuskrip 5052/1, Oorlogsmuseum van die Boererepublieke, Bloemfontein.

Digter onbekend

Waarom trouw Jul ni*

Kom oompiis en tanniis,
    Oek neefi en nig:
Om eenkeer te trouwe
    Is almal se plig.
Di's oorlog, di's waar,
    En di hinder en pla;
Maar trouwlus di leef nog,
    Di las moet ons dra.
Eers kon ons ni trouw ni –
    Di leeraars, O, wee!
Wat bantjis moes vas maak,
    Di is o'er di see;
Maar President wus mos,
    Di goeie ou man,
'N mens is 'n mens, en
    moet trouw as jij kan.
Hij'd meelij met oukiis
    Wat maatjiis wil he,
"Ons kan en ons wil nog,"
    Het hul' hom gese;
Hij moes toe voorsiining
    In di saki maak –
Want trouwlus bij mense
    Kan jij mos nie staak.

---

* *Di Skoorsteenki*, Lapiiskraal, deel 1, nommer 1, 22 My 1902, p. 1. *Di Skoor-steenki* is tydens die oorlog te velde gedruk deur die Vrystaatse Staatsdrukkery wat destyds onder 'n holkrans gestaan het op die plaas Snymanshoek van mnr. Theodoris Serfontein in die distrik Fouriesburg, die laaste hoofstad van die Oranje-Vrystaat tydens die oorlog. Omdat vrede kort na die verskyning van die eerste uitgawe verklaar is, het daar net een nommer van hierdie tydskriffie verskyn.

Ons het toe mos gelees
    Sij nuwe bevel: –
"In elke distrik wort
    'N Os aangestel;"
Ek meen ni 'n bees ni,
    Fan di soort wat trek,
Nee maar 'n "Anderos,"
    Ek is mos ni gek.
Hul sal nou bevoeg wees
    Om bantjiis te leg,
En paartjiis, di trouw wil,
    Aan èèn te kan heg.
So draai nou maar los en
    Trouw as julle kan,
In onse distrik is
    Neef Janni di man.*

---

* In die kolom wat op die gedig "Waarom trouw Jul ni" volg, staan 'n stukkie wat waarskynlik van dieselfde skrywer afkomstig is en wat die moeite werd is om hier aan te haal, al was dit maar om die term "Ander os" te verklaar:

Gebeurtenisse fan di distrik.

Op di 29ste April het die Anderos fer oom Dawid en tant Hanni in di eg ferbind, maar 'n mens sal nooit sê dat dit di selfde kerel is wat di grappiis fan Hans Breitman verkoop het ni. Hij het 'n manel aan gehat wat so op sij hakskeene fat, en 'n wit boorki, en hij het so plegtig di ferpligtings fer di twee oues afgelees, dat partij mense hom nou Ds Landros noem, maar ons word fertel hij het 'n paar seur lemoene voor di tijd geeet, en sij bakkiis in di plooi gesit, en kon fer geen geld st-r-o-o-p sê ni.

Net twee dage daarna sit hij weer so 'n sedige gesig op en koppel fer ou Karel Boyce en nig Betti an makaar. Di stomme bruid en bruidegom het 'n uur lank moes wag met hulle kiskleere voor dat di anderOS opdraai, di het weer te laat geslaap. Na dat di artikels afgelees was en di bruid aan die agter ent fan di pen vas gehou het om haar naam te teeken, begin di mense hulle met miiligruis te gooi, so dat ou Charli se manel wit was.

Daar fandaan het almaal na Majoorskraal gegaan, en toe het die folkiis koren gesnij, en kapatertji het sij swarte kop gebuig tot die son ondergegaan het.

Digter onbekend

Troost voor bedroefde ouders*

Weent, lieve ouders, niet al te zeer,
Niet lang na dezen ziet gij mij weer;
Ik heb het beter dan gij vermoedt,
Zoo zoet, zoo zalig, zoo eind'loos goed.
Gij bergt mijn lichaam bedroefd in d'aard,
Maar ziet, mijn ziel zweeft hemelwaarts.
En 'k werp in 't zwerven wel bly te moe,
U nog van boven een kusje toe.
God drooge troostend uw' tranen af,
Och, zoek uw liefling toch niet in 't graf.
Ik leef en dartel in 't Vaderhuis.
Ver boven kerkhof en 's werelds kruis.
Ik blijf u wachten in de heerlikheid,
Komt, lieve ouders, uw plaats is bereid.
Weent, lieve ouders, niet al te zeer,
Eens zien we elkander voor eeuwig weer.

---

* *De Strever,* 15 Maart 1902, p. 68.

Mauritz

Ver van hier*

O mijn vriend! denk t'rug aan tijden,
Blijde tijden van voorheen,
Toen slechts vreugde, nimmer lijden,
Altijd zacht uw pad bescheen,
Aan die tijden, nu verstreken,
Onherroepbaar en niet meer,
Aan die jaren, maanden, weken,
Die gij zien zult hier niet weer.

Denk ook nu aan al die vrienden,
Zie! zij zijn ook hier niet meer,
Aan die ouders en die kind'ren,
O zoo dierbaar en zoo teêr;
Zij ook zijn verstrooid op stranden,
Velen zelfs niet meer op aard,
Ja! zij zijn verreisd naar landen,
Ver van huis en ver van haard.

O die dierb'ren en die tijden,
Weg van d' aard en hier niet meer,
Roep' u hard toe door dit lijden:
"Haast u, eer gij valt ter neêr;"
Jaren snellen, dagen vliegen,
Alles is van korten duur,
Al het heden wordt verleden,
Aanstonds komt het scheidingsuur.

Diyatalawa-Kamp
　　Maart 1902.

---

* *De Strever*, 15 Maart 1902, p. 70.

Eugène N. Marais

1902*
(Op die eiland Chiloaan aan die monding van die Sabie;
net vóór die tyding van Vereeniging se vrede.)

GOD van ons Vaders, as U wil bestaan,
dat ons as Staat en Nasie moet vergaan, –
    besoedeld deur verraad, ontrou
    aan alles deur ons Vaders opgebou
    (die ideale vir ons opgegaar
    deur worst'ling van 'n halwe duisend jaar!);
    bedwelmd deur elke lawwe vrees,
    onwaardig langer nog 'n volk te wees;
    ons diepste liefde steeds gesmoor
    om vreemdeling en vyand na te spoor;
    en vuile hande, rooi bevlek,
    met bloed van broer en vriend bedek; –
God van ons Vaders, bly U wil bestaan,
leer ons genadiglik die dood blymoedig in te gaan.

---

* *Versamelde gedigte.* Pretoria: J.L. van Schaik, 1955, p. 27.

Jan. F.E. Celliers

Die weg van eer*

Wat is die weg van eer?
    Om trou te bly
    aan dwing'landy?
Aan afgedwonge woord en daad –
aan wanhoops nood-traktaat?**
Is dit die weg van eer –
     niks meer?
    Om woord te hou
    aan wie ontrou
en woord-verkragting en verraad
nie meer beskou as sondedaad?

Dit is die weg van eer:
    Om, net soos eertyds, trou te wees
    aan vaarlandsbloed, aan vaarlandsgees,
     aan vryheids-ideaal!
Geen woord verpand is bindend woord
as oormagsdwang en onskuldsmoord
    die woord vir ons bepaal.

---

* *Jopie Fourie en ander Nuwe Gedigte*. Kaapstad: De Nationale Pers, 1920, p. 34.
** Traktaat van Vereeniging.

F.W. Reitz

Vaarwel aan die Vierkleur*
(Vereeniging 31 Mei 1902).

Niet langer mag de vierkleur wapperen,
    Met tranen gaven wij haar af.
Zij is met onze dode dapperen
    Verdwenen in een eervol graf.

Gelukkiger zijn zij die vielen,
    Toen nog die vlag werd opgebeurd,
Dan wij die met bedroefde zielen
    Haar zagen in het stof gesleurd.

Voor haar is daar geen blijde morgen,
    Wij scheiden van haar voor altijd
In 't hart der Natie opgeborgen,
    En aan 't verleden toegewijd.

Gewijd aan die haar dapper droegen
    Den trotsen vijand te weerstaan
Wier slappe armen haar omsloegen
    Toen zij den dood zijn ingegaan.

Laat 't nageslacht hen nooit vergeten,
    Zolang het menschdom duren zal,
Tot zelfs de hemelen zijn versleten
    En d'Aarde wankelt tot haar val.

---

* *Oorlogs en andere gedichten.* Potchefstroom: Het Westen, 1910, p. 69.

C. Louis Leipoldt

Vrede-aand*

Dis vrede, man; die oorlog is verby!
Hoor jy die mense skreeu, die strate vol?
Sien jy die hele wêreld is op hol?
Kom, hier's 'n bottel soetwyn; laat ons drink!
Ons het ons nasie in die see gesink;
Ons het geen land meer nie; dis klaar met Kees!
Dis vrede nou! Kom skreeu – of is jy hees
Van lag? Nou, lag maar, want die storie's uit:
Ons nasie's weg, ons kan daarna maar fluit!
Drink, drink jou glas! Die son skyn deur die wyn –
Is dit te soet, of smaak dit soos asyn?
Nou ja, dan kom hier by die venster staan
En skou met my al die gedoente aan.
Daar waai die vlag, daar word hoerê geskree:
Die aandeelmark rys weer, en ons daarmee!
Wat is ons land teenoor die aandeelmark?
Wat 'n kanarievoël teenoor 'n vark?
'n Lelieblom teenoor 'n stronk tabak?
Ons nasie, wat so wild was, is nou mak
En kan getrein word soos 'n jong bob'jaan,
Wat, as hy steeks is, jy weer goed kan slaan.
Hoerê! hoerê! Skreeu saam met my:
Dis vrede nou; die oorlog is verby!

Dis vrede, man; die oorlog is verby!
Hoor jy daar agter hoe die mense huil?
Hoor jy 'n sug, 'n klag? – Dis maar 'n uil –
Die voëls is oral rond, selfs in die stad,

---

* *Versamelde gedigte.* Kaapstad: Tafelberg-Uitgewers: 1980, pp. 35–38.

En oral skreeu hul, oral om ons pad:
Hul weet ons was ook uile. Ons hou saam
'n Bondskongres hier, net soos dit betaam;
Passeer mooi resolusies; maak geraas
En groot lawaai; en trek dan soos 'n haas
Wat bang is vir die roer, weer in die hol
En sit daar van die bewerasies vol!
Nou is die storie uit: die leë glas
Staan droog, wat vroeër so vol met water was;
Die put wat helder water eens kon gee,
Is vol met trane, souter as die see –
So brak as ooit 'n pan in die woestyn
Waarop die son aldae helder skyn –
En bitter net soos gal, want in die put
Het ons ou volk sy trane afgeskud:
En ons moet daarvan drink, die jare deur,
Al sal die smaak ons hart en siel verskeur.
        Nee, boetie, nee, kom skreeu hoerê met my:
        Dis vrede nou; die oorlog is verby!

        Dis vrede, man; die oorlog is verby!
Sien jy die strate vol? Ek sien 'n ramp,
'n Kerkhof by 'n konsentrasiekamp
Met duisend graffies, elk waarvan bewaar
'n Skat, wat alles was wat God aan haar
Gegewe het om eenmaal aan ons land,
In tyd van nood, toe te vertrou as pand!
Sy was die sterkste van ons almal – sy
Wat met gebed en hoop kon samestry!
Sy het die swaarste deel van onse lot
Gedra, gehelp, getroos, gesteun deur God;
En as jy daaraan dink, dan moet jy glo –
Al twyfel jy – daar is tog Iemand bo
Wat so 'n vrou tot yster maak en staal,
Met soveel troos haar steun en hoop betaal;
Maar dan weer dink jy aan haar smart en aan

Die graffies wat daar op die kerkhof staan,
En voel weer twyfel, want 'n mens is swak!
Waarom het Hy die boom gesnoei, die tak
So afgekap tot aan die stam? Waarom
Het Hy haar lot so skeef gemaak en krom?
  Nee, boetie, drink met my; skreeu saam met my:
  Dis vrede nou; die oorlog is verby!

  Dis vrede nou; die oorlog is verby!
Hoor jy die mense skreeu hoerê! Ek hoor
'n Dof gekerm en steune in my oor.
Vêr oor die vlakte dryf die wolke neer;
Daar slaan die blits, daar dreun die donderweer.
Die hael, elk korrel soos 'n kersiepit,
Maak die Karoo-veld net soos marmer wit
En dek die kaal graf van ons laaste kind;
En deur die haelbui huil die noordewind.
Hoog was ons hoop, hoe laag ook was ons hart!
Ons land is duur: die prys – verdriet en smart!
En meer as ons, het sy haar deel gegee,
Haar siel ontroof van liefde, om daarmee
Ons borg te staan; sy het vir ons gedra
Die skuld van gister en die dag daarna;
Op rots het sy gebou, en nie op sand –
Heldin en vrou! – die beste wat ons land
Nog voortgebring het! Skreeu hoerê vir haar
As moet jy skreeu – maar liewers, man, bedaar
En skink weer met my in 'n glas vol wyn:
Dit sal nie ditmaal suur smaak soos asyn,
  Maar heuningsoet soos suiker – en met my
  Drink op haar naam; die oorlog is verby!

  Dis vrede nou; die oorlog is verby!
Dis vrede, ja! Wat sal ons nou begaan?
Sal ons die vrou daar binne weer laat staan
Om kos te kook, te braai, te stoof, te smoor?

Nie meer haar steun verlang nie? nie meer hoor
Haar stem wat in die onweer helder klink?
Sal ons haar siel laat roes? Dié het geblink
Tot aan die kruis-ster toe die donker nag
Rondom ons was en niemand van ons dag
Verwag het nie; toe het haar lig gestaan
As lei-ster vir ons, ligter as die maan,
En soos 'n son geskyn – toe was dit nood!
Dis vrede, maar dié siel is nog nie dood:
Dit lewe nog om ons te lei en maak
Die swaar, swaar vrede plig; die harde taak
Wat voor ons lê, die lewe wat ons wag,
Ons donker pad, so helder as die dag.
Waak oor dié stem! Let op dié siel! Behou
Die beste wat ons nasie het – die vrou!
Gooi neer die glas; die stukkies skop opsy:
Daaruit sal ons geen ander heildronk drink
     As dié aan haar! Maar roep, man, tot dit klink:
     Dis vrede nou; die oorlog is verby!

Jozef J. Kuhn

De Afrikaansche Vrouwen (fragment)*

De historie, o wakkre vrouwen,
Zal aan het wordend nageslacht
Uw moed, uw daden klaar ontvouwen
En tolken van der zwakken kracht.
Met trotschheid zal het nakroost staren,
Door al de wentelende jaren,
Op uwe trouw en heldenmoed.
Het is zoo veel – ook bloedt mijn harte
Als 'k denk aan uw onpeilbre smarte –
Ik weet niet waar 'k beginnen moet!

Zal 'k van de koene huisvrouw melden
Van een beroemde generaal? –
Hoe of de vijanden ontstelden,
Toen, nadat zij haar menigmaal
Beleedigd hadden, zij vernamen
En toen toch tot bezinning kwamen
Wiens teedre gemalin zij was? –
Hoe zij verkoos bij haar vriendinnen
Te blijven, met hen 't slechte bleef beminnen,
Insteê van alles eerste klas? –

---

* Manuskrip, NALN, Bloemfontein.

Zal 'k die koloniale meisjes malen,
Die, met de "vierkleur" in de hand,
De Boeren kusten een'ge malen, –
Schoon daarom in den tronk geland? –
Het feit, in spijt van meerdre rampen,
Geschied in de Natalsche kampen,
U schetsen hier in hellen gloed? –
Hoe zij de "vierkleur" daar ontplooiden,
De "khakies" moedig van zich gooiden
En overwonnen door hun moed? –

Maar neen! – het zal niet noodig wezen
Om 't al te noemen, één voor één.
De nazaat toch zal eenmaal lezen
Der moeders vreeselijk verleên.
Hoe jaagt bij 't tokklen van de snaren
Mijn borst, daar tot die vrouwenscharen
Mijn dierbre moeder ook behoort! –
Men moog' Europa's schoonen roemen,
Hun wijsheid en hun deugden noemen,
Hun schoonheid, die den man bekoort. –

Van trotsch voel ik mijn boezem zwellen,
Omdat 'k een Afrikaner ben.
Hoewel daar banden zijn, die knellen,
Om daden van een deel van hen,
Toch blijven wij hen immer eeren,
En zullen wij hun moed waardeeren,
Zoolang in 't onbekend verschiet
De naam van Afrikâan zal klinken,
En d'Afrikaansche ster zal blinken, –
Of gloort de ster der hope niet? –

Voert, winden op uw vlugge wieken
Mijn lied tot aan het ruwste strand! –
Vertelt daar van het eerlang krieken
Des vrijheidsmorgens van ons land! –
Vereeuwigt voorts in marm'ren zuilen
Het machtig, hartverscheurend huilen
Van moeders in den "Worstelstrijd", –
Opdat men eens dat feest moog' vieren
Wen deze spreuk de vaan zal sieren:
"Leve ons onafhankelijkheid!!!"

St. Helena
Aug. 1902

F.W. Reitz

Io Victis!*
(Heil de Overwonnenen).

Ik zing het lied der veroverden, die gevallen zijn in den slag,
Het lied der gewonden, verslagen, verpletterd door Overmag
Niet het juichend lied des Oôrwinnaars, door de lof der
                                         Natien beloond,
Niet hem die voor dappere daden met lauweren werd bekroond,
Maar het lied van den nedrige zwakke die met hart van kommer
                                         vol
Verliezend, doch dapper speelde zijn stille wanhopige rol.
Wiens hope in assche vergaan is, wiens jeugd heeft geen bloemen
                                         geplukt
Uit wiens handen de prijs die hij zocht, des avonds werd
                                         weggerukt
De dood maakt' een eind aan zijn streven – zijn *Geloof* behield
                                         hij alleen
Hij ging met zijn doelwit verloren, onbemerkt, onbejammerd
                                         daarheen.

Wijl de stem van het menschdom tezamen roept hoera! voor
                                         den strijder die won
Wijl trompetten-geschal hem begroette, en omhoog in de
                                         lucht en de zon
De blijde banieren daar wuiven, en de menigte ademloos snelt
Om den held die bekroond is te volgen – sta ik op het treurige
                                         veld
Waar liggen de mannen die vielen verslaan en gewond – en ik zet
Mijn hand op het voorhoofd des lijders – en ik doe een stille
                                         gebed

---

* *Oorlogs en andere gedichten*. Potchefstroom: Het Westen, 1910, pp. 67–68.

Druk de machtlooze handen en fluister: *Hij alleen is het die*
                                              overwint
Die den goeden strijd heeft gestreden – en den duivel die in hem
                                              is bindt
Die niet van zijn plicht weggelokt werd – door het aas dat die
                                              wereld aanbood
Bereid voor de waarheid te strijden, te lijden, ja zelfs tot den dood.

Wie waren d'oôrwinnaars? Historie! ontrol uwe bladen en zeg
Waren zij het die 't menschdom vereerde, en wierp na een tijdje
                                              weer weg?
Was het Nero of die hij vermoordde? en wie zijn in hoger tel
Die driehonderd dapp're Spartanen – of de Perzen en Xerxes wel?
Van Socrates en zijne Rechters wie houdt men het meeste in eer?
En aanbidden wij Pontius Pilatus – of Jezus Christus den Heer?

Jan F.E. Celliers

Dis Al*

Dis die blond,
dis die blou:
dis die veld,
dis die lug;
en 'n voël draai bowe in eensame vlug –
dis al.

Dis 'n balling gekom
oor die oseaan,
dis 'n graf in die gras,
dis 'n vallende traan –
dis al.

---

* *Die Vlakte en ander gedigte.* Kaapstad: Nasionale Pers, 1941, p. 97.

C. Louis Leipoldt

Die ou blikkie*

Wat is die ding wat jy daar hou?
Wat droom jy oor 'n blikkie, vrou? –
    'n Armsalige ou blikkie?
Wat is die ding tog nou vir jou?

"Ek wil hom skoonmaak dat hy blink
Soos silwer in die sonskyn: dink,
    Die armsalige ou blikkie –
Daaruit het Gert en Griet gedrink.

"Ek wil hom met die grond hier vul,
Hier, waar die suring bloei so gul,
    Die armsalige ou blikkie:
Miskien kan ek my droefnis kul.

"Ek wil daarin 'n plantjie plant
Wat groei aan Griet haar graf se kant:
    Die armsalige ou blikkie
Was vasgeklem in Griet haar hand.

"As ek so in die sonskyn sit,
So blou die hemel bo, so wit
    Die armsalige ou blikkie,
Dan droom ek weer oor dat en dit:

"Ons konsentrasiekamp is daar;
Die oorlog word ek weer gewaar –
    Ag, armsalige ou blikkie,
Waarom het God ons nie gespaar?

---

* *Versamelde gedigte.* Kaapstad: Tafelberg, 1980, p. 38–40.

"Ja, Gert en Griet was heel my hart!
Die plaas is afgebrand en swart –
    En jy, armsalige ou blikkie,
Herinner my nog aan my smart.

"Ons kan die plaas weer opbou – ja,
Jan het al geld te leen gevra;
    Maar, armsalige ou blikkie,
Kan Gert en Griet my ooit weer pla?

Daar is die konsentrasiekamp,
Daar in ons aaklige oorlogsdamp,
    Ag, armsalige ou blikkie,
Dáár is hul lewe uitgestamp!"

Vergeet wat jy gely het, vrou:
Ons is weer vrede-vrinde nou!
    Die armsalige ou blikkie –
Wat is dié ding tog nog vir jou?

"Dit laat my dink aan Gert en Griet:
Al is dit 'n gebroke riet,
    Die armsalige ou blikkie
Is anker teen my sielsverdriet.

"Die plantjie wat hierin sal groei,
Sal elke jaar opnuut weer bloei,
    Ag, armsalige ou blikkie,
Al is my trane opgeskroei;

"Want ek het nog 'n traan gespaar,
Nog 'n paar sugte opgegaar,
    Om, armsalige ou blikkie,
Jou plantjie veilig te bewaar.

"As ek vanaand my kers uitblaas,
Dan werp die maan 'n silwer waas
   Oor jou, armsalige ou blikkie,
En oor ons afgebrande plaas.

"Ek luister; en dit skyn vir my
Klein Gert is weer aan my sy,
   By jou, armsalige ou blikkie.
Om weer 'n slukkie melk te kry;

En Grietjie staan daar by die deur –
Ja, kyk, haar voorskoot is verskeur!
   Ag, armsalige ou blikkie,
Hoe kan ek eensaam wees en treur?

"Die dood het albei weggehaal;
Ons plaas is afgebrand en vaal;
   En, armsalige ou blikkie,
My hart is amper net so kaal.

"Solank jy op die vensterbank
Hier by my staan, so rein en blank
   Kan ek, armsalige ou blikkie,
Nog stil wees en vir God nog dank

"Dat Hy, toe daardie oorlogsramp
My kinders altwee in die kamp,
   Ag, armsalige ou blikkie,
Verstik het my sy oorlogsdamp,

"Nog in my hart die hoop kon gee
Dat ek bedaard was in my wee –
   Ag, armsalige ou blikkie,
Te dink ek sien hul weer, altwee!

"Met jou het Griet en Gert gespeel,
En ek het nog in jou 'n deel;
    Ag, armsalige ou blikkie,
Laat ek my maar nog iets verbeel!

"Verbeelding – dit is alles nou
Wat ek nog het: laat my dit hou!
    Ag, armsalige ou blikkie,
Jy is my anker teen die rou!"

Totius

Hulle kom nie weer*

Hy kom die aand weer op sy plaas,
 sy kragte ingeboet;
en struikel by die kraalmuur neer
 nog met sy laaste voet;
want eind'lik het die dag gekom,
 die lankverwagte tyd,
dat hy sy erfgrond mag betree
 na droef-verlore stryd.

Sy matte blik dwaal orals rond,
 na alle kante heen,
en in die woestheid voel hy hom
 so troosteloos alleen.
Sy plaas het wild en leeg geword,
 maar dit kwel hom nie, nee:
daar skryn nou deur sy strydershart
 'n ander, erger wee.
"My erfgrond, sug hy, is daar nog,
 en ek het weergekeer:
maar net my vrou en kind bly weg,
 e n h u l l e k o m n i e w e e r."

---

* *Versamelde gedigte.* Kaapstad: Tafelberg-Uitgewers, 1988, pp. 26–28.

Die slaap oorval hom tot die dag
　　die oosterkim oorswem;
en vinkeslag die wek hom op
　　met egte vinkeklem:
dis of die môreglanse straal
　　met nuwe krag en kleur
net om hom uit sy droefenis
　　en matheid op te beur.
Sy veldjas werp hy van hom af
　　om dankend neer te kniel
voor Hom wat nuwe lewenslus
　　laat oprys in sy siel. –

Maar nee, daarbinne bly maar nog
　　die skerpe prikkel brand;
dit word deur môresonneskyn
　　net dieper ingeplant!
"Die voëls, sug hy, is daar nog;
　　die dag het weergekeer;
maar net my vrou en kind bly weg,
　　e n h u l l e k o m n i e w e e r."

Daar is nou soveel werk te doen:
　　sy huis is afgebrand
en hier en daar al ingeval;
　　die muurwerk, uitgetand,
verhef hom skril omhoog en klaag
　　dit by die hemel aan –
die lydensvolheid, onverdiend,
　　oor alles heengegaan. –
Die gras en distels in sy huis
　　die ruim hy gou-gou weg,
om voor die aand hom kan oorval
　　sy platjie neer te leg. –

Maar hoe daarbinne reggemaak
    waar die oue prikkel brand?
"Die platjie, sug hy, lê weer reg,
    die mure hou nog stand
en in my oue skoorsteen het
die koffie-rokie weergekeer;
maar net my vrou en kind bly weg,
    e n h u l l e k o m n i e w e e r."

Sy vrugteboord is uitgebrand,
    of woedend neergekap,
Maar nuwe lote 't gou gespruit
    uit die oue wortelsap.
En op sy land waar klitse staan,
    in bitsheid saamgekoek,
waar mensevoet nou tevergeefs
    'n veil'ge voetpad soek, –
daar strooi sy vlugge boerehand,
    na vlugge suiw'ringsdaad,
in vore vars weer opgeploeg,
    die blanke mieliesaad. –

Dit lyk weer na die oue plaas
    en na die oue tyd,
maar net die diepe boesemkwaal
    het nog nie weggeslyt.
"My lande, sug hy, lê daar nog,
    dis alles soos weleer;
maar net my vrou en kind bly weg,
    e n h u l l e k o m n i e w e e r."

Sy krale was eers doods en leeg
en dig begroei met kweek;
maar van sy veetjies het ou Klaas
klein klompies weggesteek.
Nou dat hy in sy wegkruipplek
weer van sy basie hoor,
kom hy ook al met vlugge voet
die laaste randjie oor.
Die stryder gaan hom tegemoet
met vreugde en roem die trou
van Klaas – hy't uit die "leeuemuil"
sy veetjies weggehou. –

Die kraalmuur word weer opgerig
en die oue jong help mee;
maar, ag, nou skryn daar binnekant
eers reg die oue wee.
"My herder, sug hy, het gekom,
my vee het weergekeer;
maar net my vrou en kind bly weg,
en hulle kom nie weer."

C. Louis Leipoldt

Oom Gert vertel*

Ja, neef, wat kan ek, oumens, jou vertel?
Jy wil die storie van ons sterfte hoor?
Nou goed!
       Dis nooit te laat om daarvan nog
Te leer en van gebruik te maak – veral
Vir julle, jongling-mense. Hou maar vas
Aan wat ons het, en staan orent, en neem
Jul aandeel aan ons nasie!
            Maar jy kom
By die verkeerde man; daar's baie ander
Wat jou die storie goed agtermekaar,
En met 'n les daarby, en meer begrip
Van al die politiek ook, kan vertel
As ek: ek weet maar uit my eie siel
En kan maar grawe uit my eie hart,
En dit is baie oud en amper dood –
My hart, meen ek; en waarlik, as jy self
Soveel reeds deurgemaak, soveel gely,
Soveel geworstel, en soveel gesien het
Van wat jy liewers nooit gesien het nie,
Dan was jou hart ook nie meer sonder kraak.
Maar kom – wat kan ek nou vir jou vertel?
'n Lang geskied'nis is dit! – treurig ook,
Want daar gaan snikke en trane deur, ou neef!
Wil jy dit aanhoor? Goed!
              Maar sit, man, sit!
Ek kan jou nie vertel as jy bly staan nie.
Sit daar. (En, Gerrie, gee hom wat te drink!
En Pa kan ook 'n slukkie koffie sluk.)

---

* *Versamelde gedigte.* Kaapstad: Tafelberg-Uitgewers, 1980, pp. 5–11.

Nou ja, jy weet, neef, toe ons mense hier
Almal beteuterd deur die oorlog was,
Het kakies op kommando hier ons dorp
Beset en Martjie Louw geproklameer.
Ou Smith, die magistraat – hy is 'n man
Vir wie ek eerbied voel, al is hy Engels:
Hy was tog altyd nog 'n jentelman,
En het met onse mense akkordeer;
Maar hulle het hom soetjies afgesit
En na Oos-Londen toe gestuur, omdat
Hy nie na hulle pype vlot wou dans,
En in sy plaas 'n kol'nel aangestel;
Sy naam – nou Gerrie, wat was ook sy naam?
Jones? Nee, kind, dit was maar sy offisier –
Jy weet, dié aap met strepies op sy mou.
Ek het dit! Wilson was die vent se naam –
'n Dik, vet kêrel, met 'n grysgeel snor,
En lang slagtande, en rooi in die gesig;
Die mense sê hy suip; maar ek het nooit
Hom dronk gesien en wil ook nou nie meer
Agter sy rug die man beskinder nie,
Al was hy ook 'n deugniet – dit maak niks!
Hy het ons onderdruk; sy hand was hard:
Geen lig mag in die kamers brand; geen mens
Mag buite op die straat gaan ná agtuur;
Orals het hy op ons spioen en selfs
Ons huise deurgesnuffel om te sien
Of ons miskien nie wapens het of kruit,
Patrone, doppies of so iets; hy dag
Ons het 'n heel boel kos byeengegaar
Om vir die Boerkommando's af te gee.
Ja, neef, sy hand was hard! (Hartlam, gee weer
Die suikerpot! Twee klontjies is te min:
Jy weet, Pa drink sy koffie soet.)
                               En ons
Was deur die war daarmee, half uit ons vel;

En niemand van ons mense het geweet
Wat môre of oormôre vir ons wag.
Die dorp was vol gebrom, net soos 'n deeg
Waardeur 'n mens die suurdeeg goed geknee het –
Jy weet hoe rys die ding; nou net so ook
Met onse mense! Maar wat kon ons maak?
Die jongmense veral was baie steeks –
Ons kon hulle byna nie in toom meer hou nie –
En twee van hul het sito omgespring.
(Hartlam, neef Klaas se koppie is weer leeg.)

Een aand kom Bennie Bêrends na my toe,
En met hom Johnnie Hendriks, Saarl se seun.
Hul het die straat so stil'tjies oorgespring
Die skildwag het hul nooit nie eens bespeur nie –
Anders het ek en Saarl daarvan moet hoor
En op die koop 'n boete nog betaal!
Ou Saarl was altyd maats met my gewees;
Maar hy het in dieselfde maand gesterwe
Van kanker in die maag – die Heer se hand!
So het hy nie dié dag oorleef nie. Maar
Ek gaan te vinnig met die saak vooruit.
Hier op my stoel het ek gesit; en daar
Waar jy nou sit, het Bennie ook gesit.
En Johnnie vlak naas hom. Ek sien hom nog –
'n Opgeskote kêreltjie; nog nie
Heel droog agter die ore was hy toe,
Nogal astrant en snip'rig met sy mond,
Dié jaar nog aangeneem. (Gerrie, my kind,
Haal tog die album!) – Hier is sy portret,
En hier is Bennie syne; daar's die reël
Wat sy oorlede ma geskrywe het,
Die dag ná … ná sy dood. Jy kan dit lees:
My bril die pas nie mooi, en in die rook
Kan ek so goed nie sien nie. Lees maar voor!
"Barend Gerhardus Barends," – reg! en nou?

"Geboren op den zesden Mei," – ja reg!
"Ge …" – maak die boek maar toe: ek weet dit al!
(Hartlam, kon neem dit weg! Wat staan jy daar
Beteuterd soos 'n kat? Kom, skink weer in!
Ons het mos melk genoeg en suiker ook,
En Martjie Louw is nou nie in die dorp!)
Ja, Bennie was 'n egte witmenskind –
My peetseun –, en, ofskoon ek self dit sê,
'n Regte mooi soort vroumens-kêreltjie,
So paal-orent en met 'n kaal gesig:
'n Skeermes het hy glo nog nie gebruik nie.
(Hartlam, gaan kyk of Leentjie al die hout
In die kombuis gebring het.)
                                     Ja, ou neef,
Hy het na Gerrie hier gevry, en ek
Was ook nie teen die saak, want Bennie was
'n Uitgeknipte jongetjie vir haar.
Jy sien sy is nog nie goed oor die bult nie;
Maar ons moet almal oor die drumpel klim,
Al is dit ook so swaar ons hart moet breek!
En hartlam sal ook met ons Liewen-Heer
Se seën daaroor stap en haar smart vergeet,
Al gaan dit moeilik – maar dit moet tog gaan!
Maar as ons oor hom praat, dan pas dit tog
Dat ons haar eers die kamer uit sal stuur.
Nou goed! Waar was ek?
                                     Ja, dié aand, toe hul
By my kom raad vra. Bennie had 'n plan:
Hy wou met Johnnie weg na Witkransspruit –
Dáár, so het hul verneem, was Smuts gelaer
Met sy kommando.
                             Ek was amper flou
Om dit te hoor. Ek het vir hul vermaan –
Maar nee!
                     Ag, neef, 'n jongmens is tog steeks!
En Ben was altyd koppig: selfs as kind

Het hy daar baie keer om sla gekry!
En hul was vasbeslote om te gaan.
Ek het twee perde toe by my gehad –
Die kakies het dit nog nie afgeneem –
Ek weet nie waarom nie, maar ek kan sweer
My skuld was dit nie dat die diere nog
Daar in die tuin gestaan het; maar hul het!
Nonnie – my vrou en Gerrie haar ma – sy het
Dieselfde jaar gesterwe in Goudini
Aan hartkwaal, want die oorlog het haar ook
Gebreek in siel en liggaam – Nonnie ook
Het meegewaarsku, maar dit was vergeefs!
"Ons kan dit nie hier uithou nie, oom Gert:
'n Mens moet tog iets vir sy nasie doen."
"Doen? Doen? Iets doen! Ag, wat kan julle doen?
Wat kan ons algar doen?"
　　　　　　　　　Maar tevergeefs.
Nonnie het toe my knapsak volgeprop
Met biltong en beskuit; en ek het self
Die saalsakkies met hardgekookte eiers
En ander padkos volgelaai – want hy
Was tog my peetseun, en dan Johnnie ook
Neef Saarl se seun – en Saarl en ek was maats!
So kan geen mens my dit tog kwalik neem,
Al was ek ook 'n Britse onderdaan:
Kan ek my eie vlees en been sien ly
As ek nog kos het? Nee, neef, ek hou vas –
En my gewete het my nooit gekwel nie!
So, kort en goed, die twee is weg; en hoor,
Dié môre was die heel gespuis om my!
Die kol'nel, soos 'n brommer, gons en gons
En vloek en maak lawaai – maar ek staan pal.
Ek kon mos nie gehelp het dat die perde
Nog in die tuin gestaan het, en ek sê
Dat dit sy skuld was, en nie myne nie;
Maar van die biltong en beskuit en eiers

Het ek hom toe maar liewers niks gesê nie.

Hoe ons die maande deurgelewe het?
Neef, vra my nie! Dié tyd is soos 'n wolk
Wat oor ons hang, en nie net oor ons dorp nie,
Maar oor ons land, die hele nasie oor!

Op een dag kom die nuus … (Wag, hier's sy weer. –
Ag, hartlam, ja die hoenders van die stoep!
Kyk daardie haan; hy krap die blomme uit!)
Nou, een dag kom die nuus – ja, wat 'n skrik!
Johnnie en Ben was albei vas gevang
En in die tronk gestop. 'n Krygsgerig –
Jy weet die res! En daarop weer 'n slag:
Die vonnis was – hul altwee word gehang!
Ons Liewen-Heertjie weet dit was 'n slag!
Ons het ons bes gedoen, maar tevergeefs;
Die vuilgoed skreeu om wraak – en hul moet hang!
Dié môre kom die hoofkonstabel sê:
"Die kol'nel stuur sy komplimente!" – God,
Sy komplimente! – hoor! het jy verstaan?
Verstaan jy, neef? – sy komplimente!
                                        Nee!
Bedaar, bedaar, my hart, al kraak jy ook:
Ons moet die drumpel oor, al breek ons dood!
En: "Asseblief, wil ek op môre kom
En sien hoedat rebelle getrakteer word,
Anders …" Die hoofkonstabel was 'n man;
Hy het hom nie op sy gemak gevoel
Toe hy die boodskap aan my oor kom bring nie;
En ook die kakies, moet ek sê, was goed –
Maar hul moes tog hul plig doen; ek was bly
Dat hul dit nie astrant gedoen het nie.
Die hoofkonstabel – Nichols was sy naam;

Hy't later in die Vrystaat lood geëet
En dit nie goed verteer nie – sê vir my
Die anders het ook so 'n bevel gekry,
En daar sou meer van ons die … nou, jy weet! –
Daar in die tronk aanskou. Hy waarsku my
Ek moet maar kom, al gaan dit bo my keel.

Dié nag het ek en Nonnie nie geslaap.

Ja, ek onthou nog goed: Die dag was koel –
'n Mens vergeet mos so 'n dag nie gou nie!
Met net 'n bietjie oostewind, half koud,
Want Nonnie het daar sinkings van gekry –
Sy het aan sinkings veel gely en kon
Nooit koue goed verdra nie. Soos ek sê,
Die dag was koel; en daarom was my jas
Dig toegeknoop – jy weet, ek hou daarvan
My onderbaadjie te laat spog; vir wat
Dra 'n mens 'n onderbaadjie as geen mens
Dit sien nie? – Maar die weer was regtig fris,
En daarom was my baadjie toegeknoop.
En by die draai, daar onder by die meul,
Het ek die anders almal vroeg ontmoet,
Want, soos ek sê, ons algar was geroep.
Die predikant was daar, en Albert Louw –
Jy ken tog Skeeloog-Louw, neef Klaas? Nou ja! –
En Michiel Nel, en Gys van Zyl, en Piet –
Maar Piet sal jy jou nie herinner nie,
Want hy was voor jou tyd; hy was 'n vent
So sterk soos Simson – arrie, hy was sterk!
En net so steeks as 'n skerpioen was hy!
Maar koddig, neef, en ook 'n grappiesmaker
Selfs as die wolke donker was, en dof
Die donder deur die wolke dreun. Nou ja,
Ons algar het ons foute, en ek wil
Dit nie vir Piet Spanspek so kwalik neem

Dat hy nog altyddeur wou grappies maak
Toe al ons anders mislik was en naar.
"Die wind skeer glad, neef Gert," het hy gesê;
"Jy moet vir Ben jou oorjas leen: miskien
Kry hy swaar weer daar boontoe!" En hy lag!
Maar ek was bly die predikant was daar:
Eerwaarde het hom op die plek berispe
En mooi die kop gewas.
                              "Is dit 'n tyd
Vir pret, meneer Van Ryn?" het hy gevra.
"Foei, foei! Hoe kan u so iets waag vandag
As ons harte vol is, en ons oë
Nog donker-dof met trane vir ons land?"
(Hartlam, jaag tog die hoenders uit! Hul maak
Die werf so vuil; ons kan ons selwers help.)
Maar Piet Spanspek was weer nie op sy mond
Geval nie, en hy het ook voortgegaan
Met grappies maak, ofskoon ons niks van hom
Gehoor het en ook nie geluister het nie.
Ek dink hy was so mislik as ek self
Maar wou nie dat dit opgemerk sou word nie.

Ons het die voorplein van die tronk betree,
En dit was vol met kakies. By die poort
Het hul ons twee-twee toe laat binnekom.
Daar in die agterplaas, daar staan die galg,
En naas hom Ben en Johnnie, hand aan hand,
Want hul was nie geketting; en ons het
Verlof gekry om met hul te gaan praat.
Maar net vyf minute.
                              Ek was stom,
Geheel verbouereerd en sonder tong;
Maar Bennie het my by die hand gevat:
"Oom Gert, dis kant en klaar! Goeiendag, oom Gert!
Sê vir tant Nonnie en vir Gerrie – nee,
Sê liewers niks, want hulle sal verstaan."

En Johnnie, met 'n glimlag om sy mond,
Het ook my hand geskud: "Dag, oom," sê hy.
"Nee, oompie, moenie grens nie!" – Soos ek sê,
Was Johnnie altyd half astrant gewees,
En snip'rig ook. – "Nee, oompie, moenie grens!
Ons het ons plig gedoen, en nou's dit uit."

Toe het hul met die predikant gepraat;
En ek, as naaste bloedverwant van Ben,
Het met hom na die galg gegaan en daar ...
Nee, neef, dis maar die rook! Ek word al oud,
En jou tabak is alte sterk vir my.
Ek self rook swak tabak: jy weet dit maak
My oë nie so seer nie.
                    Waar was ek?
Ja, toe het ons hul almal hand gegee.
Geeneen van ons kon praat nie; Piet was stom
En net so naar as ek; en een van ons –
Ek weet nie wie nie – het ook hard gesnik.

Die kakies het oor Bennie se gesig
'n Sakdoek of 'n kopdoekie of iets
Net soos 'n mus wil trek, maar Bennie vra –
En nog op Engels ook: hy kon dit praat –
Of hulle hom nie sonder dit kon hang nie.
Die kol'nel knik; en toe ...
                    Nee, neef, laat staan!
Wat vat jy weer my hand? Laat bly my hand!
Vervlaks, hoe kan ek nou vir jou vertel
As jy my somaar afbring van my rym?
Blaas net jou rook uit na die ander kant:
My oë is te oud vir jou tabak!
(En, hartlam, haal vir Pa 'n sakdoek.)
                    Nou,
Daar is nie meer nie. Ons het tuisgekom,

En in die kamer hier het ons gekniel;
'n Korte bidstond het die predikant
Gehou vir ons – en daarna was dit uit.

Dié aand nog het neef Piet en Skeeloog-Louw
Die dorp uit na die naaste plaas getrek
en hulle by ons mense aangesluit.
(Hartlam, gee weer vir Pa die suikerpot,
En skink dan nog 'n koppie vir neef Klaas!)

A.D. Keet

'n Roepstem*

Vertel mij van die Oorlog, moeder,
    En van mij boetie, lang al dood;
Vertel ook van die Kampe, moeder,
    En lig mij op uw warrem skoot.

Ag moeder, had ek ook 'n sussie,
    'n Sussie nou al lang al dood?
En waar tog is haar kleine graffie –
    Ik lê so lekker op uw skoot.

---

* *Gedigte*. Amsterdam: Swets & Zeitlinger, 1925, p. 69.

A.D. Keet

Suid-Afrika se helde*
Aan die nagedagtenis van Gen. BEYERS

Wijer en altijd wijer
Wil ik die tyding beier
   Van Afrika se helde,
Gebonde deur die koorde,
Van mannetaal se woorde
   Aan onse vrije velde.

Dis manne van hul woorde,
Van soete taal-akkoorde,
   Op plegtig uur gegewe
Dis manne van hul woorde
Wat nie in alle oorde,
   Op elke tijdstip lewe.

Wijer en altijd wijer,
Wil ik die name beier
   Van onse grote helde,
   Oor Afrika se velde
Wil ik die tyding beier,
Wijer en altyd wijer.

---

* *Gedigte*. Amsterdam: Swets & Zeitlinger, vierde uitgawe, 1925, p. 73.

Digter onbekend

Gedenk*

1

Nog tril ons hart van duldelose smarte,
Nog groei geen grassie op die heilige plek,
Waar grond en klip die bleek gebeente dek.

2

Nog klink die weegeklag aan ons voete,
Die roep om hulp uit honger dood en dwang,
En nog hou die angs ons krimpend hart gevang,
Het bange vraag "Sal ons hul weer ontmoet?"

3

Nog gril die wereld en die nasies bewe,
By die verhaal van al die wrede leed,
En reeds is daar wat roep ons moet vergewe,
Dis al verby, – nou kom 'n nuwe lewe.

4

Hoe kan ons? Nooit kan ons die swaar vergeet nie,
Die kale graftes roep "onthou, onthou"
Gedenk die lyding van jou kind en vrou,
Wat God alleen, geen sterflik mens kan meet nie.

---

* Manuskrip 4192/4, Oorlogsmuseum van die Boererepublieke, Bloemfontein.

Totius

Vergewe en vergeet*
Dat gij niet vergeet de dingen die uwe oogen gezien hebben. Deut. 4:9.

Daar het 'n doringboompie
vlak by die pad gestaan,
waar lange ossespanne
met sware vragte gaan.

En eendag kom daarlanges
'n ossewa verby,
wat met sy sware wiele
dwars-oor die boompie ry.

"Jy het mos, doringstruikie,
my ander dag gekrap;
en daarom het my wiele
jou kroontjie plat getrap."

Die ossewa verdwyn weer
agter 'n heuweltop,
en langsaam buig die boompie
sy stammetjie weer op.

Sy skoonheid was geskonde;
sy bassies was geskeur;
op een plek was die stammetjie
so amper middeldeur.

* *Versamelde gedigte*, Kaapstad: Tafelberg-Uitgewers, 1988, p. 22–23.

Maar tog het daardie boompie
weer stadig reggekom,
want oor sy wonde druppel
die salf van eie gom.

Ook het die loop van jare
die wonde weggewis –
net een plek bly 'n teken
wat onuitwisbaar is.

Die wonde word gesond weer
as jare kom en gaan,
maar daardie merk word groter
en groei maar aldeur aan.

Jan F.E. Celliers

In Ballingskap*
(Clarens – 13 Julie 1904)**

Die awendsonne kus die vlak van die meer;
    die golfie slaat
     'n droewe maat;
die moeë krysman buig sy hoof terneer.

Op sneeuveld kwyn die laaste sonnestraal;
    in kloof en dal
    sluip die awend al;
en landsman liggie roep ten awendmaal;

en om die lamp sit vrou en kinders aan,***
    om eie haard
    en dis geskaard –
en in die ou krygsman oë wel 'n traan.

"Verby, die dae en stille awendstond
    "toe ook vir my
    "met welkom bly
"my huisie het gewag, op vaarlands grond."

En in sy oë lê die verre lig
    wat berge boor,
    en seë oor
herinn'rings weg na Suiderkuste rig:

---

* *Die vlakte en ander gedigte.* Kaapstad: Tafelberg-Uitgewers, 1974, pp. 3–4
(Voetnotas van die digter).
** In die nag van 13 op 14 Julie is Paul Kruger in Clarens in Switserland
oorlede. Die skrywer was toe ook daar.
*** 'n Switserse huisgesin word hier bedoel.

Hy's in die saal, sy roer is in sy hand,
    sy jonge bloed
    vol durf en gloed,
sy oë oor die onbekende land.*

Die veld lê wyd; hy volg die leeu se spoor:
    sy veilig lood
    dra wisse dood;
die oolfants ver trompetter's in sy oor.

Die wagvuur brand; die jakhals huil van ver;
    die roer slaap by
    die jagters sy –
en bo sy hoof die wye sterre-heir.

Die slagveld dreun, hy voer die ruiterskaar
    met wys beleid
    in strawwe stryd;
hy hoor die krygsroep van die swart barbaar.

Hy's in die Raad, hy lê met vaste hand,
    met klem van taal
    en wil as staal
die grondslag heg van Suider-vaderland.

Verby, verby … Die sneeuveld bo vervaal;
    maar hoog omhoog
    ontwaar sy oog
op blanke top 'n verre sonnestraal!**

Die duister grou op gryse berggevaart.
    "Volbrag, volbrag!
    "Wees welkom, nag." –
Sy sieners-oë glimlag hemelwaart.

---

* Paul Kruger as Voortrekker word hier bedoel.
** Aandson op die sneeu: Alpeglorie.

A. Moorrees

Bij de aankomst van het lijk van Paul Kruger*

Uw troon, omringd van dichte wolken,
    Is op gerechtigheid gegrond;
De glans van vorsten en van volken
    Verwelkt voor d'adem van Uw mond.
Gij wandelt door de woeste golven,
    Daar waar geen oog Uw gang bespiedt;
Uw voetspoor, in het schuim bedolven,
    Ontdekt de mensch van gist'ren niet!

Wij zwijgen, waar we niet doorgronden,
    En bukken ons voor Uw bestel,
Al bloedt het hart uit diepe wonden,
    Al blaakt de vuurgloed nog zoo fel;
't Geloof kan 't mistgordijn doorboren
    En baadt zich in der heem'len glans,
Ofschoon het oog geen ster ziet gloren
    Aan den bewolkten hemeltrans.

Gij hebt Uw knecht door diepe wat'ren
    En door het gloeiend vuur doen gaan;
Maar ter verbazing van zijn hat'ren,
    Kon vlam noch watergloed hem schaân.
Al moest zijn zon ter kimme zinken,
    Omfloerst in neev'len van den dood,
Zij zal met nieuwen luister blinken
    Bij 't licht van 's hemels morgenrood.

---

* *Zevenjaartjes. Gedichten.* Pretoria/Amsterdam: De Bussy, 1918, pp. 73–76.

Des avonds klonk het droevig zuchten,
    Het angstig kermen en geween:
De morgen zag de schaduw vluchten
    Voor 't licht dat aan de kim verscheen.
Toen leide d'afgestreden lijder
    Voor immer 't somber rouwkleed neer
Op 't woord: "Wees welkom, trouwe strijder,
    Ga in de vreugd van uwen Heer!"

O, God! heb dank; door Uw vermogen
    Hebt Gij Uw grijzen knecht geschraagd,
Al heeft de last zijn rug gebogen,
    Al werd het uur der rust vertraagd.
Het licht, door Uwe hand ontstoken,
    Bescheen zijn pad door 't donker dal,
Totdat de dag is aangebroken,
    Waarop geen nacht meer volgen zal.

Zuid-Afrika! ontvang uw doode!
    En leg zijn stof, door u beschreid,
Waar, onder d'opgedolven zode,
    Zijn trouwe gâ haar echtvriend beidt.
De bange scheiding is vergeten,
    Met al haar tranen en haar pijn,
Nu zij, zoo wreed vanééngereten,
    Weer in den dood vereenigd zijn.

Ontvang den balling, die na 't zwerven
    Komt rusten in uw moederschoot;
Al moest hij land en maagschap derven,
    Hij vindt ze weder in den dood.
Want naar uw vergelegen kusten
    Ging stervend zijn verlangen uit,
En in uw aarde zal hij rusten,
    Totdat zijn Meester 't graf ontsluit!

Maar in uw harte blijft hij leven
    En in des lands historieblaân,
Waar onuitwischbaar staat geschreven
    't Verhaal van zijn roemruchte daân.
Groot in zijn kracht, waar w'hem aanschouwen
    Als hij met doodsgevaren spot;
Maar grooter nog in zijn vertrouwen,
    Zijn kinderlijk geloof in God!

Jan F. E. Celliers

Blomme*

'n Besoek aan die Konsentrasiekamp-kerkhof by Irene, Maart 1911
(Al die graftes was toegegroei met kosmosblomme.)

Ek kom om 'n kransie van rou te breng,
Op kindergraffies 'n traan te pleng.

Maar kyk, dis 'n fees wat my oog gewaar
van blommetjies, blommetjies aanmekaar,

op ranke stingel oor graffie en steen –
soos graan op die lande, aaneen, aaneen;

soos kindertjies selwe in feesgewaad,
in hupp'lende dans op die windjie se maat;

spierwit hul kleertjies en roserooi –
die sonlig se glans op hul hemelse tooi.

O, moedertjies wat in die verte nog ween
om blompies ontnome, wat God had geleen,

kom kyk, uit elkeen en elk bittere traan
is 'n heldere blompie weer opgestaan.

Dis net of die Vader sê "Vertrou!
"My blomme sal groei oor die kranse van rou,

"Ek gee weer terug wat gegee is aan My:
"waar blomme gesaai is, sal blomme gedy."

---

* *Die Vlakte en ander gedigte.* Kaapstad: Nasionale Pers, 1941, p. 100.

F.W. Reitz

Christiaan de Wet[*]
(na die Duits van Dr. Gadow)

(1)

In die oggend grou
Deur bos en deur sand
Wie ja soos 'n stormwind
Daar oor die land?
En deur drif en rivier
In die skemer ry
Wie roem daardie dappere
Ruiters vir my?
En wat sonder te praat
In die pikdonker nag
Die veld laat weerklink
Met hoefysters-slag?
Dit is die aghonderd
Wat die vyand belet
Die aghonderd ruiters
Van Christiaan de Wet

(2)

Dis die edele stryders
Wat met manlike bors
Vir Vryheid en Reg
Vir hul vaderland dors
Saal op nou! Saal op
Soos die Son ondergaan
En die spoorstawe blink
In die lig van die maan.

---

[*] Manuskrip 2550/98/58, NALN, Bloemfontein. Die gedig is geskryf op die dag van die begrafnis van Christiaan de Wet (8 Febr. 1922).

Daar bars nou die brugge
Die dwarsleërs kraak
Dan vort soos die wind
Eer die Brit kan ontwaak
En sy oë uitvrywe
En blaas sy trompet
"Hier's hy weer. Help ons Kitchener
D'is Christiaan de Wet

(3)

O! eistere Christiaan!
O Ruiter so rat!
In sy eië land ken hy
Ieder bos, ieder pad
Hy ja oor die klippe
Soos 'n bliksemstraal
As hy af op die Brit
Daar rustende, daal
Nou hier en dan daar
Nou vroeg en dan laat
Die moedige man
Wat God nooit verlaat
Mag hy vir sy volk
Die vryheid weer red
O Heer! skenk genade
Aan Christiaan de Wet.

Bloemfontein
8 Febr. 1922   F.W.R.

BRONNELYS

Oorlogsmuseum van die Boererepublieke, Bloemfontein
Manuskripte
    1664/13
    1676/9
    3635/6
    4192/4
    4830/5
    4923/3
    5000/1330
    5052/1
    5423/73
    5784/16
    6289/3
    6727/1
    Ongenommerde manuskripte

Nasionale Afrikaanse Letterkundige Museum en Dokumentasie-sentrum, Bloemfontein
Manuskripte
    355
    532/8
    2550/98/58
    PD 21 80/4

National English Literary Museum, Grahamstad
    Ongenommerde manuskrip

Banck, J.E. *Een lied voor Transvaal.* 's-Gravenhage: Koninklijke Nederlandsche Boekhandel M.M. Couvée, s.j.

Beets, N. *Gedichten.* Vierde deel, zesde druk. Leiden: Sijthoff.

Boerenalmanak 1902. Antwerpen: Van Tasselt, 1902.

Boutens, P. C. *Stemmen.* Amsterdam: Van Kampen, 1920.

Celliers, Jan F.E. *Jopie Fourie En ander Nuwe Gedigte.* Kaapstad: De Nationale Pers, 1920.

Celliers, Jan F.E. *Die Vlakte en ander gedigte.* Kaapstad: Tafelberg, Tweede uitgawe, eerste druk, 1974.

De Krijgsgevangene, 3, 23 Juni 1901.

De Strever, 1–19, 19 December 1901–26 April 1902.

Di Skoorsteenki, Lapiiskraal, deel 1, nommer 1, 22 My 1902.

Diyatalawa Dum-Dum, Diyatalawa Kamp, vol. 1, no. 1, 10 September 1900.

Gedenknummer Antwerpen–Transvaal. Antwerpen, 1902.

Grobbelaar, P. W. *Kommandeer! Kommandeer! Volksang uit die Anglo-Boereoorlog*. Pretoria: J.P. van der Walt, 1999.

Groneman, J. *Boerenoorlog*. 's-Gravenhage: Gebrs. J. & H. van Langenhuysen, 1900.

Hubertino. *Aan Kruger en zijn helden*. Antwerpen: Ernest Sele, 1902.

Jansen, E. en **Jonckheere, W.** *Boer en Brit. Afrikaanse en Nederlandse tekste uit en om die Anglo-Boereoorlog*. Pretoria: Protea Boekhuis, 1999.

Keet, A.D. *Gedigte*. Amsterdam: Swets & Zeitlinger, 1925.

Kloos, W. *Verzen* (deel 3), Amsterdam: Versluys, 1913.

Leipoldt, C. Louis. *Versamelde gedigte*. (Versorg deur J.C. Kannemeyer). Kaapstad: Tafelberg, 1980.

Lotter, M.L. *Uit de Oorlog. Gedichten over Gevechten in Grikwaland West, enz., en Namen van Gevangenen te Tokai*. Paarl: Paarl Drukpers Maatschappij Beperkt, 1913.

Malherbe, D.F. *Karroo Blommetjies. Afrikaanse gedigte*. Kaapstad: Van de Sandt de Villiers Drukpers Maatschappij Beperkt, 1909.

Marais, Eugène N. *Versamelde gedigte*, Pretoria: J.L. Van Schaik, Vyftiende druk, 1955.

Molenaar, M. *Transvaal gedichten. Een lauwerkrans den Boeren gevlochten*. Sneek: De Boer, 1902.

Moorrees, A. *Zevenjaartjes. Gedichten*. Pretoria/Amsterdam: De Bussy, Tweede druk, 1918.

Nienaber, P.J. *Boere op St. Helena. Die oorlogsdagboek van H. de Graaf, verwerk en in Afrikaans oorvertel deur P.J. Nienaber*. Kaapstad: Nasionale Boekhandel Beperk, 1950.

Ons Klyntji, Junie 1903–Junie 1904.

Opperman, D.J. *Versamelde poësie*. Kaapstad: Tafelberg-Uitgewers en Human & Rousseau, 1987.

Perold, P.J. *De weduwe of tafereelen uit den Engelschen oorlog 1899–1902*. Kaapstad: Hollandsch-Afrikaansche Uitgevers Maatschappij, 1903.

Reitz, F. W. *Oorlogs en andere gedichten*. Potchefstroom: Het Westen, 1910 (2de druk, 1911).

Smits, A. *Betrekkingen tussen Vlaanderen en Zuid-Afrika*. Brugge: Wiek Op, 1943.

Totius. *Versamelde gedigte*. Kaapstad: Tafelberg-Uitgewers, 1988.

Van Eeden, F. *Van de passielooze lelie,* Amsterdam: Versluys, tweede druk,1908.

Van Wyk Smith, M. *Drummer Hodge. The Poetry of the Anglo-Boer War (1899–1902)*. Second Edition. Pretoria: Protea Book House, 1999.

Verwey, A. *Verzamelde gedichten*. Tweede deel. Amsterdam: Versluys, 1912.

Wouters, D. *Na veertig jaar: Documents humains*. Nijmegen: Moorman, 1940.

Zuidema, W. *Voor Zuid-Afrika. Rijm en onrijm*. Amsterdam: Hollandsche Stoomdrukkerij & Uitgevers Maatschappij, 1901.